America's Promise

America's Promise

A Concise History of the United States, Volume I

William J. Rorabaugh,
Donald T. Critchlow,
and Paula Baker

ROWMAN & LITTLEFIELD PUBLISHERS, INC.
Lanham • Boulder • New York • Toronto • Oxford

ROWMAN & LITTLEFIELD PUBLISHERS, INC.

Published in the United States of America
by Rowman & Littlefield Publishers, Inc.
A wholly owned subsidiary of The Rowman & Littlefield Publishing Group, Inc.
4501 Forbes Boulevard, Suite 200, Lanham, Maryland 20706
www.rowmanlittlefield.com

PO Box 317
Oxford
OX2 9RU, UK

Distributed by National Book Network

British Library Cataloguing in Publication Information Available

Library of Congress Cataloging-in-Publication Data

Rorabaugh, W. J.
  America's promise : a concise history of the United States / William
J. Rorabaugh, Donald T. Critchlow, and Paula Baker.
    p. cm.
Includes bibliographical references and index.
  ISBN 0-7425-1189-8 (v. 1 : alk. paper) — ISBN 0-7425-1191-X (v. 2 :
alk. paper)
  1. United States—History. I. Critchlow, Donald T., 1948– II. Baker,
Paula C. III. Title.
  E178.R79 2003
  973—dc22

                                2003016131

Printed in the United States of America

♾™ The paper used in this publication meets the minimum requirements of
American National Standard for Information Sciences—Permanence of Paper
for Printed Library Materials, ANSI/NISO Z39.48-1992.

Contents

MAPS

TABLES

Preface

American history consists of such a bewildering array of facts and events that students can easily become overwhelmed and disoriented. A major goal of this book, therefore, has been to *organize* history, that is, to keep students focused on the *ideas* that hold the facts together. We tried to accomplish that goal in several ways.

First, we confined each discussion to the minimum information necessary to understand what happened, why it happened, and why it matters. Second, we begin each major section within each chapter with a preview of the main ideas that will be developed in that section. Third, the section headings and subheadings both highlight main ideas and help carry along the narrative. In addition to providing a conceptual framework, these headings and subheadings offer a practical way to help review for exams.

We sought to integrate the latest scholarship in social, cultural, and political history in this brief textbook. In the process, we tried to capture the rich and often amusing character of the American people. The story of the United States is a tale not only of triumph and tragedy but also of foibles and unexpected consequences. We did not hesitate to bring out that side of the story.

We have also given special attention to the rich literature on the role of ethnic minorities, women, and other groups in shaping American history. In this way we seek to provide a synthetic account of American history that is useful to students, with the expectation that students will seek further details of American history in advanced courses and specialized studies.

We also made room for a glossary at the end of the book. We recognize that terms such as *impressment, free silver,* and *trust* can be confusing. So can the difference between *nationalism* and *nationalization.*

Also at the end of the book is a chronology (timeline) to help students keep track of events. At the end of each chapter is a list of recommended readings. Because we believe that students should read original historical documents whenever possible, we have included primary reading materials in these lists.

Maps have been included in generous numbers for a concise book because we believe that they portray, pinpoint, and illuminate key events.

Among the things we deliberately left out of the book are expensive color illustrations. Sharing students' concerns about high prices of textbooks, we wanted to keep costs, and therefore price, to a minimum. We wanted a book of high quality that every student could afford.

We, the authors, have collaborated on this venture at every point, arguing over nuances and details and debating how best to work often shapeless social and cultural history into a political framework. To satisfy the curious, we confess that Rorabaugh is primarily responsible for chapters 1–15; Baker, for chapters 16–25; and Critchlow, for chapters 26–31.

Acknowledgments

We thank the staff at Rowman & Littlefield who participated in this project, including Jonathan Sisk, Stephen Wrinn, Mary Carpenter, Laura Roberts, and Terry Fischer. We owe special thanks to April Wells-Hayes, the manuscript editor and production editor. We also want to thank Robin Sand for obtaining the photographs and Steve Thomas for the Instructor's Manual and the Web site.

1

A Big Country

OVERVIEW Thousands of years ago, America's first humans arrived from Asia. Hunter-gatherers at first, they eventually spread out across the two continents, developing agriculture and then complex civilizations. Despite advances, they were ill prepared for the arrival in 1492 of the Europeans, who brought sophisticated weapons, horses, and diseases. During the early 1500s the Spanish were able to seize control of the Caribbean islands, Mexico, and South America and to explore much of North America, particularly Florida. At the same time, the French entered North America by way of Canada and made their way south, soon battling Spain for control of Florida, a contest Spain won. Although presenting a challenge to the Spanish presence in the New World, the English came too late to enter into these conflicts; their principal efforts were the search for a Northwest Passage to Asia (which did not exist) and the unsuccessful attempt to establish a colony at Roanoke Island, North Carolina.

PREHISTORY AND THE FIRST AMERICANS

Human beings emerged as a distinct species over millions of years, gradually spread worldwide, and arrived in the Western Hemisphere less than 40,000 years ago. Agriculture developed among the native Americans around 6000 B.C.—about the same time as in the Middle East and Asia—making possible the Western Hemisphere's first complex cultures, the Maya and Aztec civilizations. However, because North America lacked the wealth of useful plants and animals found in Europe and Asia, societies north of Mexico remained less developed.

THE FIRST AMERICANS ARRIVE   About 60,000 years ago, as the last Ice Age began, human beings lived in Africa, Europe, and Asia, but none had yet arrived in the Americas. As the temperature of the earth cooled, more and more of the earth's water became stored in the form of ice at the two poles. The oceans shrank, sea level dropped, and about 40,000 years ago, in a brief period of warming during the Ice Age, a land bridge formed between Asia and North America at the Bering Strait, where Alaska meets Russia today.

A small number of people from Asia, perhaps including as few as four women, crossed this land bridge into North America. Their descendants, who spread across both western continents over thousands of years, were the first Americans. Today, as many as 95 percent of the native peoples in the Western Hemisphere may be descended from this first migration.

The warming trend caused the oceans to rise; the land bridge disappeared, and then the Ice Age returned. About 15,000 years ago ice again became stored at the poles, the oceans fell once more, and the land bridge across the Bering Strait reemerged. More people from Asia, including ancestors of the Eskimo, the Navajo, and the Apache, made their way to the Americas. Some scholars believe that then or earlier a number of migrants may also have come by sea.

HUNTING AND GATHERING IN THE NEW WORLD   We know little about any Americans of this early period except that they were nomads who hunted primarily big game. The Western Hemisphere at that time was home to elephant-like woolly mammoths, big-tusked mastodons, saber-toothed tigers, and gigantic buffalo, as well as bear, moose, elk, and deer. The early peoples supplemented their diet of meat with wild berries, fruits, and nuts gathered from the forests.

Time passed, and the climate in North America warmed. Because of this climate change, or perhaps because the big game had been over-hunted, these large mammals disappeared. Smaller animals were hunted instead, and deer became the most important meat in the diet. The warmer climate also caused the number of edible plants to increase, and they too became more important. The early peoples did not practice agriculture and had no domesticated animals, except for dogs, which they had probably brought from Asia.

Because the Western Hemisphere had been cut off from the rest of the world by oceans for a very long time, its plants and animals developed quite differently. The Americas had no horses, cows, pigs, or sheep to do-

Table 1.1   The Columbian Exchange

From New World to Old World	From Old World to New World
corn, potatoes, sweet potatoes, manioc	horses, cattle, pigs, sheep, goats
coffee, vanilla, tobacco, chocolate	chickens, rats, honeybees
pumpkins, squash, beans, sunflowers	wheat, barley, oats, yams
tomatoes, wild rice, quinine, avocados	sugar cane, onions, lettuce, okra
bell and chili peppers, blueberries	peaches, pears, watermelons
pineapples, pecans, cashews, peanuts	citrus fruit, bananas, olives
petunias, dahlias, marigolds	lilacs, daffodils, tulips, crabgrass, dandelions
syphilis(?)	smallpox, measles, malaria, influenza, amoebic dysentery, diphtheria, chicken pox, typhus, whooping cough, bubonic plague

mesticate. There were no beasts of burden, except llamas in the mountains of South America and large dogs used to pull sleds in parts of North America. Because the early peoples lacked access to the meat protein and the hides of domesticated animals, hunting and fishing remained crucial to survival. For enough wild game to survive to be hunted, however, a low population density was needed; low density in turn prevented the development of complex civilizations. (See Table 1.1).

TURNING TO AGRICULTURE, **6000** B.C.   The Americas did provide important plants, not found in the rest of the world, that could be cultivated. About 8,000 years ago, in the tropics of Central America, native peoples began to plant maize (corn), beans, and squash, and the inhabitants of South America started growing white and sweet potatoes. About the same time, people in the Middle East began to cultivate wheat, and Asians grew rice. Corn was as nutritious as wheat and yielded twice the food value per acre. Unlike rice, which had to be grown in wet paddies, corn could be farmed under widely different conditions.

The early Americans discovered that corn and beans could be planted together; the bean plants climbed up the cornstalks. Corn or beans alone lacked certain nutrients, but the combination provided a balanced diet. Both plants required a long growing season and for centuries were planted only in tropical or near-tropical areas. Gradually, American farmers developed strains of corn and beans that matured more rapidly, and cultivation of these fast-ripening varieties spread throughout North America, reaching the American Southwest in 2500 B.C. and spreading as far north as southern Canada by 500 A.D.

The development of agriculture had a profound effect upon the American peoples. For most, hunting became less important, and wherever soil and climate encouraged crops, the need to maintain vast, unpopulated areas for wild game declined. At the same time, the cultivation of crops made nomadic life impossible, since people had to tend their crops until the harvest.

Unfortunately, corn rapidly depleted the soil; farmers learned to put nutrients back into the soil by burning their fields after each crop. These burned fields also produced an abundance of certain plants, which just happened to provide food for deer. After ten or so years, however, the soil became so poor that the cornfields had to be abandoned. Native peoples then moved on to clear new parts of the forest for fresh fields. In addition, inhabitants seasonally migrated to places that provided different food sources such as fish or fruit.

Thus, the American population did not become as settled as Europe's, where crop rotation was practiced and animal dung was used as fertilizer, or Asia's, where annual flooding replenished the nutrients in the rice fields.

AGRICULTURE PRODUCES MORE COMPLEX CULTURES   A larger, more readily obtained food supply almost certainly led to an increase in population. In areas where agriculture had developed first, such as Central America, the division of labor into specialized tasks produced the highly complex Maya and Aztec civilizations. From around 300 to 900 A.D. the Maya in the area of southern Mexico and Guatemala built cities with pyramidal temples, wrote with word-pictures called hieroglyphs, and knew astronomy.

The later Aztecs, who flourished in central Mexico from 1300 to 1500, built large cities, maintained armies, collected tribute, worked silver, and constructed complex irrigation systems. They also appealed to their gods with bloody human sacrifices.

By 1500 about 25 million people lived in Mexico and Central America. In contrast, the population north of Mexico, where agriculture was less important and relatively new, ranged from one to thirteen million people. Although scholars disagree sharply, recent estimates have tended toward the higher figure.

People in North America depended increasingly on agriculture, but hunting did not entirely disappear. Wild animals, especially deer, continued to be an important part of the diet. Tribal bands were small, and the search for land suitable for new corn fields brought peoples into contact and into conflict. For many, war was an important part of the culture.

Some North American cultures became complex within the limits of their technology. For example, inhabitants of the area that is now Boston trapped fish as early as 2500 B.C. in a complicated weir made up of some 65,000 stakes that covered nearly two acres. Stone tools were common and sometimes elaborate. Arrowheads made by the early Americans are still found frequently in many parts of the United States.

On the other hand, native peoples used copper to only a limited extent, since smelting ore was unknown, and they did not work iron. They made clay pottery, much of it simple and undecorated; however, a few surviving, elaborate pieces from the Ohio River valley suggest that these cultures achieved considerable artistry. Trade was extensive surprisingly early: By 2000 B.C. copper from the Great Lakes was being sent south, and conch shells from the Gulf of Mexico had reached present-day Ontario, Canada.

A fascinating legacy comes from the southeastern woodlands region, which stretches roughly from Kentucky to Georgia, where the inhabitants developed elaborate rituals concerning death. We know nothing about the rites directly, but between about 700 and 1600 A.D. a number of the region's residents constructed enormous ceremonial mounds. Used for the ritualized burial of people and objects, the mounds were often hundreds of feet wide and long. Many of these mounds are still visible, as are similar mounds built in the Ohio River valley under conditions as yet unknown.

NORTH AMERICAN INDIANS IN 1500

Native tribes were small and often fragmented. Gender roles were rigid; religion involved worship of nature or of animals believed to contain spirits; and dexterity working stone, wood, and clay by hand was shown despite limited technology.

Inhabitants survived by different means in different regions. Northeastern tribes depended more upon hunting, while the culture of the southeastern Indians was more complex. Plains tribes lived by hunting buffalo, using bow and arrow and other techniques without horses or guns. Pueblo dwellers in the Southwest farmed the desert, and natives of the Pacific coast harvested shellfish and salmon.

INDIAN CULTURES AT THE MOMENT OF EUROPEAN CONTACT   By 1500 the Indians, as Christopher Columbus misnamed the indigenous peoples, had created complex and sophisticated cultures that Europeans found curious and strange. Although genetically closely related, the different Indian tribes and villages spoke hundreds of languages and thousands of dialects. North of Mexico more than three hundred separate languages were spoken. Social units were governed by complex rules that recognized the primacy of the family-based clan, yet tribes frequently ignored clan loyalty to split into new tribes.

Map 1.1   Location of Native Peoples around 1500

Europeans thought of tribal chiefs as kings, but few chiefs held the absolute power of European monarchs. Although they often inherited their positions, chiefs could be deposed easily. Chiefs generally ruled by following the consensus that emerged from tribal councils. Political discussion and negotiation, both within councils and between tribes, included many rituals, and leaders sealed agreements by passing around and smoking a tobacco-filled peace pipe.

Gender roles were extremely rigid. Men hunted, made war, participated in political councils, and led religious observances. Women planted and harvested corn, prepared food, made clothes, and looked after children. The labor of women produced as much as 90 percent of a tribe's caloric intake.

Kinship was often matrilineal, that is, calculated through female descent, and the relatives of one's mother were more important than those of one's father. In this type of kinship system, a mother's brother might be more important than a father. Although matrilineal kinship honored women, who owned property, including houses, in many tribes they were regarded as inferior. Frequently, women were required to live apart from the community during menstruation.

Premarital sex was common, extramarital sex was accepted, divorce was easy, and yet marriage was a solemn institution. To European eyes, child care had its peculiarities. In a practice common throughout North

America, mothers bound babies to cradle boards so that the babies developed flattened heads, both front and back. Adults indulged children, who enjoyed unusual freedom; young men were expected to endure physical pain inflicted by enemies.

No North American peoples were literate or wove cloth. However, they developed many technological skills. They made digging tools for gardening by using animal skins to bind sharpened stones to wooden sticks. Bows for hunting were light but strong, and arrows were often tipped with sharpened stones.

INDIAN PEOPLES VARY REGIONALLY   Indian cultures showed great regional variation. In the Northeast, with its long winters and short growing season, corn was less important in the diet than game and fish. The Algonquin and Iroquois built snug wooden houses as long as ninety feet. Each long house had a series of rooms and held a number of nuclear families. To protect against enemies, these tribes built their houses inside villages walled with wooden palisades.

In the Southeast, the warmer climate and longer growing season enabled the Creek and Choctaw to plant two corn crops a year. Plentiful food gave rise to denser populations, larger villages, and more powerful chiefs. In this region natives designed housing to let in breezes during the

European artists often portrayed American Indians in fanciful ways, as in this drawing of natives sowing seeds. (Giraudon/Art Resource, NY)

hot summers as well as to protect against winter storms. Families lived one to a dwelling, but villages were usually fenced.

Among the Creek, young men from rival clans played a ball game similar to modern lacrosse, to which it is related. The game involved using a stick with a loop at the end to put a ball through a goal. All the men from two clans played at the same time, with hundreds of players crowding the field. As violent as football, the game had no team strategy. Each warrior-player sought individually to put the ball through the goal. Games sometimes lasted eight hours, and severe injuries, even deaths, occurred. Spectators and players placed many bets, and a clan that lost several matches in a row might disband in humiliation.

In 1500 the plains area, stretching from Texas to the Dakotas and west to the Rocky Mountains, was sparsely populated by Arapaho and Pawnee buffalo hunters. Having neither horses nor guns, they captured buffalo with cunning, for example, by attacks that frightened the animals into self-destructive stampedes. These nomadic Indians lived in teepees, whose buffalo skins and wooden poles could be put up and taken down quickly.

In the dry Southwest the Pueblo tribes, such as the Hopi and Zuñi, built dense villages of adobe houses and grew corn using dry farming techniques, principally mulching to prevent evaporation of water from the soil. The most stationary of all the tribes in North America, they developed elaborate rituals, including rain dances and sun worship, that revolved around the desert landscape. They conducted religious rites in underground ceremonial chambers called *kivas*. One native village, the town of Acoma, New Mexico, was established at or near its present site in 900 A.D. and has been continuously settled since 1075, making it the oldest community in the United States.

Along the Pacific coast from northern California to southern Alaska lived a number of Salish-speaking peoples who lived by salmon fishing. They also harvested shellfish, ate berries and other wild plants, and lived in boxy wooden houses. Their culture provided for redistribution of wealth within the tribe through a ceremony called the potlatch, in which individuals gave away possessions and property. The donors obtained high status for giving; those who received the gifts had to reciprocate or lose face.

EUROPEANS EXPLORE AND EXPLOIT THE AMERICAS

Although the Vikings settled briefly in North America around 1000 A.D., their Vinland colony had been forgotten by the time Christopher Columbus sailed to the West Indies in 1492. Columbus's four voyages touched off a European race for colonial empires in the Americas. The pope tried to divide the New World between Spain and Portugal, but other countries, particularly France and England, ignored the papal decree and sent out their own explorers. The Spanish, however, gained the lead in the early 1500s.

VIKINGS AND OTHERS SAIL BEFORE COLUMBUS   In all probability the first Europeans to visit America were Vikings who sailed across the North Atlantic from Norway in the 900s and 1000s to found colonies in Iceland, Greenland, and Vinland, successively. Most likely led by Leif Eriksson, they maintained a colony in North America at a place they called Vinland, between 1000 and 1010 A.D. Archaeologists have recently located this site in present Newfoundland, opposite Labrador on the shore of eastern Canada.

The Iceland settlement survived, but the Greenland colony died out after about 400 years, and the Vinland settlement was quickly abandoned after encounters with native peoples, whom the Vikings called *Skrelings*.

By the 1400s the early Viking settlement at Vinland had been forgotten, but growing commerce throughout Europe had led to increased exploration in search of trade. It also led to the construction of larger and better ships more likely to withstand the rigors of crossing the Atlantic Ocean. Better rigging enabled ships to sail into as well as before the wind. These ships were small and boxy by today's standards; even in the late 1400s it was unusual for a ship to be more than seventy feet long. Furthermore, vessels tended to maneuver poorly in storms, to be becalmed because their sails could not catch wind, and to be tossed in storms because their anchors were too light.

Despite these disadvantages, other improvements in navigation had taken place. By the 1400s Europeans had good maps and star charts that made it possible to sail confidently outside of sight of land, as well as better knowledge about compasses and astrolabes that aided navigation.

In the 1400s the Portuguese became Europe's premier maritime explorers. They sailed along the African coast, settled the Azores Islands, and eventually passed around Africa's Cape of Good Hope, making contact with India and the Africa-India-Middle East trade. According to some historians, as early as the 1480s sailors from Bristol, England, may have begun to exploit the rich fishing banks off Newfoundland, Canada. They preceded, or perhaps followed, French fishermen from Brittany. At the time, fishermen from various nations cooperated with each other without the national rivalries that would occur in the 1500s.

COLUMBUS LEADS SPAIN TO THE AMERICAS, 1492–1504   The Spanish, too, were interested in exploration. King Ferdinand V and Queen Isabella commissioned Christopher Columbus to sail west from Spain in search of a short route to Asia and its spices. On October 12, 1492, Columbus found instead what Europeans called the "New World." Mistaking the islands of the Caribbean for outposts off the Asian mainland, he called the area the "Indies" and the native peoples "Indians." Both names stuck, although people eventually renamed these islands the West Indies to distinguish them from the East Indies off the southeast coast of Asia.

Columbus's failure to recognize what he had discovered not only produced confusion but also cost this sailor from Genoa, Italy, some of his fame. When mapmakers first added the new continent to their maps, they named it "America" in honor of another early explorer, Amerigo Vespucci, who, upon reaching Brazil in 1499, had understood the true nature of his discovery almost immediately.

Spain had several advantages in the early exploration of the New World. The Spanish government did not publicize all the information gained from Columbus's four voyages between 1492 and 1504. In addition, compared to other European countries, Spain enjoyed both closer physical proximity to the New World and a more favorable sailing route. In 1492 Columbus had sailed out on the Canaries current and the northeast trade winds and returned by a northern route, aided by the Gulf Stream current and the westerly winds. England and France lacked easy access to this particular route, which became the lifeline to Spain's American empire.

THE RACE FOR CONQUEST BEGINS, 1493–1524   In the late 1400s Europe was in ferment. Trade flourished, economies grew, and demand soared for exotic imports such as pepper or cinnamon from faraway places like China or Asia's spice islands.

At the same time, Europeans recovered much learning from the ancient Greek world that had been lost for centuries. This rebirth of knowledge, called the Renaissance, led Europeans to gain self-confidence, to experiment with inventions, to create great art, to gain a belief in their own superiority, and to seek ways to impose their rule on other parts of the world.

Johann Gutenberg invented printing around 1456, and his invention promoted the use of everyday languages instead of Latin, spreading the idea that knowledge was not the sole property of the Church. Books published in Italian, French, German, or English bound together those who read the same language and led to a rising sense of nationalism.

Throughout Europe, fragmented and localized feudalism gave way to powerful, centralized monarchy in the form of the modern nation-state. Soon the Protestant Reformation, begun by Martin Luther in 1517, would shake the Catholic Church's hold on Europe. By the early 1500s, commercial interests, nationalism, and religious strife had unleashed unprecedented energies, many of which found expression in the conquest of the New World.

In 1493 the pope, under Spanish influence, used his power as head of the Catholic Church to issue an edict reserving the New World for Catholic Spain while recognizing the right of Catholic Portugal to explore Africa. A year later Spain and Portugal signed a treaty confirming this division, although an accidental shift of the dividing line westward gave Portugal the right to settle in what became Brazil. Other European countries, whether Catholic like France or in the process of becoming Protestant like England, ignored both the papal edict and the treaty. Actual possession was to be the only way to hold a claim in the New World.

Accordingly, other European nations almost immediately began exploration. In 1497 the English sent John Cabot, an Italian who had previously worked for the Portuguese, along the North Atlantic coast. He may have sailed as far south as Long Island Sound off New York. A year later Cabot was lost at sea while on another expedition. From 1500 to 1502 two brothers, Gaspar and Miguel Corte Real, explored the coast at Newfoundland and Labrador under the Portuguese flag. Both vanished at sea. In 1524 Giovanni da Verrazano, an Italian sailing for the French, followed the Atlantic coast from South Carolina to Rhode Island and en route discovered New York harbor.

BUILDING THE SPANISH EMPIRE, 1513–1542

Spanish explorers moved quickly to expand the empire and gain personal profit. In 1513 Vasco Núñez de Balboa became the first European to see the Pacific Ocean, and in 1519 Ferdinand Magellan began his journey around the world. Meanwhile, Hernando Cortés conquered Mexico, and Francisco Pizarro seized Peru. These Europeans brought diseases that killed millions of Indians. In 1540 Francisco Vásquez de Coronado explored the Southwest. Florida attracted Juan Ponce de León in 1521, Álvar Núñez Cabeza de Vaca in 1528, and Hernando de Soto in 1539.

CONQUISTADORS SEEK FAME AND FORTUNE   Despite the rival expeditions of European nations, the Spanish maintained their lead in exploring the New World. In 1513 Vasco Núñez de Balboa crossed the isthmus of Panama and became the first European to see the western ocean, which he named "Pacific" because it appeared to be so calm.

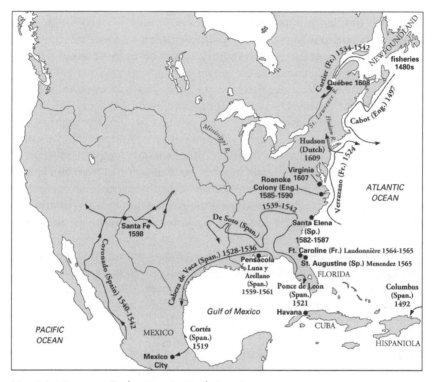

Map 1.2   European Explorations in North America

Six years later Ferdinand Magellan set out from Spain to find a route to Asia around the southern tip of South America. He did find a route, and his expedition became the first to sail around the world, but the rocky, stormy Strait of Magellan did not prove to be a viable trade route to Asia.

In 1519 Hernando Cortés and 600 men conquered the Aztec empire in Mexico. The Spaniards came with horses and guns; to the Aztecs, both were new and terrifying. The wealth of the Aztecs, especially gold and silver, quickly fell into Spanish hands and whetted the conquistadors' appetites for more riches. Then, in the 1530s, Francisco Pizarro conquered the Inca empire in Peru, gaining fabulous wealth in the form of silver mines.

Largely because of the silver and other valuables, the Spanish decided to colonize the New World. Although they sent out settlers, the Spanish were more concerned about protecting their valuable income-producing property from other Europeans, and so they sent many soldiers, as well as Jesuit priests to convert the native peoples to Christianity.

EUROPEAN DISEASES KILL INDIANS   The Indians, however, died in epidemics from exposure to diseases brought by the Spanish and other Europeans.

The native peoples had no resistance to measles, smallpox, or bubonic plague, and death rates in some epidemics reached 95 percent.

Sometimes, within a few days of first contact with Europeans, dozens of Indians in a village would sicken and die. Epidemics were physically debilitating, politically disruptive, and psychologically devastating, the more so because Europeans seldom died. The only disease that may have been passed from Indians to Europeans was syphilis, but evidence for this is inconclusive.

On the island of Hispaniola, which today contains the Dominican Republic and Haiti, the nearly four million Arawak whom Columbus found in 1492 had declined to 15,600 people in 1518, almost entirely disappearing within a generation. According to one estimate, the population of the Aztec empire, which covered much of present-day Mexico, fell from about 25 million at or just after Spanish contact to 750,000 a century later.

It would take hundreds of years for the native population to regain its precontact level. Although wars and Spanish mistreatment of Indians, which included enslavement, hastened population decline, the major cause was lack of resistance to European diseases.

PONCE DE LEÓN VISITS FLORIDA, 1521   Meanwhile, the Spanish had concluded that the easiest sailing route for sending silver and trade goods from the New World to Spain was through the straits between Cuba and Florida. However, this route proved dangerous, for ships sometimes went aground on coral reefs, and hurricanes were common. In consequence, the Spanish were keenly interested in establishing forts and settlements along the Florida coast.

Juan Ponce de León, who had first landed in Florida in 1513, led a major expedition to that peninsula in 1521. He had his own reasons for the trip. Although the commander told people he was looking for the fountain of youth, in reality he hoped to find wealth comparable to that previously discovered and plundered in Mexico. But no riches were found; wounded by natives in Florida, Ponce de León retreated to Havana, Cuba, where he died.

CABEZA DE VACA LIVES TO TELL QUITE A TALE, 1528–1536   Despite Ponce de León's failure, the Spanish sent another expedition to Florida in 1528. Led by Pánfilo de Narváez, it ended in disaster as a hurricane tore up the ships along Florida's northwestern gulf coast. A few survivors, including Álvar Núñez Cabeza de Vaca, made their way west along the coast through what became Louisiana and Texas. Cabeza de Vaca spent several years among the Indians in Texas first as a slave, then as a trader and medicine man.

Eight years after landing in Florida, Cabeza de Vaca and three other men from the original party, including a man of African descent, joined one of the southwestern Indian trading parties that routinely bartered with the Spanish in northern Mexico. From there the four traveled to Mexico City and then back to Spain, where they retold their bizarre adventure.

DE SOTO TOURS FLORIDA AND THE SOUTHEAST, 1539–1542   As other European powers became more interested in the New World, the Spanish grew uneasy. They saw Florida as a key base from which to protect the Spanish shipping lanes. Thus, in 1539 Hernando de Soto and 600 men set out to explore Florida more thoroughly. De Soto treated the inhabitants harshly, and because word of his movements preceded his expedition, he often found villages deserted. His troops lived off the land, eating much of the Indians' corn from their fields. He also brought pigs, which escaped and became Florida's wild boars.

In 1540, finding nothing of value on the Florida peninsula, de Soto moved northward. Wherever he wandered, the Indians assured him that they had no wealth but that rich tribes lived in remote places further inland. The natives told these stories to encourage de Soto to move on quickly, and he did so in eager pursuit of wealth. Frequently, he took captives, put them in chains, and made them carry his expedition's equipment or act as guides until he entered another tribe's land.

In what is now South Carolina, de Soto and his men were entertained by a great Indian queen whom the Spanish called the Lady of Cofitahequi. Amid elaborate ceremony, the Lower Creeks carried their queen on a litter into de Soto's presence. After exchanging gifts, de Soto decided to march into the mountains, but, as was his habit, he took the queen along as a captive. In the middle of the night, however, she escaped.

Finding little of interest in the Appalachian Mountains, de Soto headed west through present-day Alabama and Mississippi, where he wintered in 1540–1541. He reached the Mississippi River and built barges to cross, as thousands of Indians watched from canoes but disappeared without attacking. Moving west through Arkansas, de Soto sent scouts far enough west to encounter buffalo-hunting plains tribes.

De Soto and his dwindling band, reduced by disease, remained in Arkansas, where they wintered inside a stockade in 1541–1542. He retreated to the Mississippi and, after preparing barges, died of a fever. The remnants of the expedition then floated down the river and sailed along the Gulf to Mexico, which they reached in 1543.

CORONADO PLUNDERS THE SOUTHWEST, 1540–1542   Having established powerful bases in the West Indies and Mexico, the Spanish began to explore the vast interior of the North American continent. Francisco Vásquez de Coronado, who lived in Mexico and heard rumors of cities filled with gold to the north, marched into the American Southwest and remained there from 1540 to 1542. Unimpressed by the Pueblo villages in present-day New Mexico and Arizona, he nevertheless plundered awhile and then returned to Mexico. The major consequence of his expedition was to introduce horses to North American Indians.

FRANCE AND SPAIN BECOME RIVALS IN NORTH AMERICA

While the Spanish explored the Southwest and Southeast, the French investigated Canada. There they found neither gold nor a passage to China, but Indians were eager and willing to trade valuable furs. An early attempted settlement failed, however, and soon the French eyed Florida, which guarded the Spanish treasure ships. In 1564 the French colonized Florida, but the Spanish attacked the settlement and ruthlessly murdered the Protestant inhabitants. The Spanish then built a fort at St. Augustine. Some years later they moved north from Mexico to colonize New Mexico.

CARTIER EXPLORES CANADA, **1534–1542**   While the Spanish roamed the Southeast and Southwest, the French began to concentrate on the mainland further north, nearest to the Newfoundland fishery. In 1534 Jacques Cartier explored the St. Lawrence Gulf, hoping to find a passage to China. A year later he discovered and named the St. Lawrence River, explored the river as far as what is now Montréal (where more than a thousand natives greeted him), and then wintered at a well-constructed fort near present-day Québec city. Cartier traded knives and trinkets for the local Indians' furs. The high quality of the furs as well as the absence of gold or silver led the French to pursue explorations to extend trade with fur-gathering Indians in the colder parts of North America.

On a third expedition in 1541, Cartier explored the St. Lawrence valley beyond Montréal and again wintered near the site of Québec city. In 1542 he returned to France, and Jean François de la Roque, seigneur de Roberval, brought 200 settlers to the St. Lawrence valley. The winter proved more severe than anticipated, and many of the French died of scurvy. The following year the French abandoned the colony.

At the time, the area was inhabited by Iroquois-speaking Indians. When the French finally did establish a permanent settlement at Québec in the St. Lawrence valley under Samuel de Champlain in 1608, these Indians had been pushed out by Algonquin-speakers from the north. This major shift in Indian populations in less than a century shows the fluid and often hostile nature of relationships among native peoples prior to European contact. Indeed, Europeans often played off rival native peoples against each other. The Indians, in turn, learned to do the same to Europeans from different nations.

EUROPEANS FIGHT OVER FLORIDA, 1559–1587   Increasingly, Florida held the potential to create conflict among Europeans. To the Spanish, controlling the Florida peninsula was necessary to guarantee the safety of Spanish ships carrying wealth from the New World to Spain. To other Europeans, especially the French and English, Spanish control of Florida not only secured Spain's wealth and her role as a great power but also threatened the interests of other Europeans trading in furs and fish further north. As part of this contest, in 1559 Tristán de Luna y Arellano established a Spanish colony at Pensacola Bay, but it was abandoned two years later.

The English and French increasingly preyed upon Spanish shipping along the Atlantic trade route. This business was lucrative but dangerous. During wartime—and there were many wars throughout this century— well-armed private ships, called *privateers*, carried government letters authorizing them to seize enemy merchant ships. During peacetime many of these same ships operated without legal authority, as pirates.

In 1562 the French moved aggressively. Jean Ribault explored the Atlantic coast from the St. John's River in north Florida to Port Royal, South Carolina. He built a fort at Port Royal, but the soldiers mutinied and, starving, turned to cannibalism before being rescued by an English privateer in 1563.

The following year, the Frenchman René Goulaine de Laudonnière planted a colony of Huguenots (French Protestants) in Florida at a site on the St. John's River, near what is now Jacksonville. Although ostensibly peaceful in purpose, the Fort Caroline colony was clearly intended to provide privateers with a safe haven.

At first Fort Caroline appeared to prosper, but soon the settlers had trouble with the Indians, who may have resented the colonists' increasing appetite for Indian corn. Then the Spanish arrived under the command of Pedro Menéndez de Avilés. The ruthless Menéndez considered the Protestant French to be heretics who deserved only death; he created an international incident by slaughtering virtually all the French after they had surrendered.

In 1565 the Spanish under Menéndez built their own permanent settlement in Florida on the Atlantic coast at St. Augustine, which soon included a substantial fort. The Spanish designed this outpost, which was supported by Mexican revenues, both to protect their sea lanes from English and French privateers and to discourage the other European countries from trying to establish colonies on the North American continent. From 1572 to 1587 the Spanish also maintained the Santa Elena colony, at what is now Parris Island, South Carolina.

SPAIN COLONIZES NEW MEXICO, **1598** Somewhat later the Spanish also moved into the Pueblo Indian country in the Southwest. In 1598 they colonized the area around Santa Fe, New Mexico, and in 1610 they built an administrative capital at Santa Fe. They sent Jesuit missionaries to convert the nearby Indians to Christianity. In 1680 the Indians suddenly massacred the priests and settlers and drove the remaining Spaniards south to the Rio Grande. It was 1692 before the Spanish reconquered New Mexico.

ENGLAND COMES LATE TO THE PARTY

By the time the English were prepared to explore North America, they found the French and Spanish already there. Under the brilliant leadership of Queen Elizabeth, the English challenged the Spanish empire by sending privateers to seize Spanish treasure ships. Francis Drake used one such expedition to sail around the world and return home triumphantly. Spain retaliated with the Armada, an attempt to invade England that failed. The seafaring English also tried to seek the Northwest Passage to Asia. No such passage existed. In 1584 the English planned the Roanoke colony in today's North Carolina, but by 1590 intrigue, poor planning, and international politics had doomed the colony.

ENGLAND CHALLENGES SPAIN, **1560–1588** Queen Elizabeth of England hated Spain, perhaps with good reason. Her father, Henry VIII, had had a Spanish wife, Catherine of Aragon; when Catherine failed to produce a male heir, Henry decided to divorce her. The pope, under Spanish influence, blocked the divorce in 1529, and Henry responded by becoming a Protestant, declared himself the head of the Church of England, seized Catholic property in England, and annulled his own marriage. Five more wives followed, but the only male heir, the intensely Protestant Edward VI, proved sickly and barely outlived Henry.

In 1553 Mary, Henry's daughter by Catherine of Aragon and a staunch Catholic, gained the English throne. She married King Philip II of Spain and began to burn Protestants as heretics. When "Bloody Mary" died in 1558, the crown passed to her half-sister, Elizabeth, who was Protestant. The queen had little choice about her religion, since neither the Spanish nor the Catholic Church had ever recognized Henry's divorce and therefore considered her illegitimate.

Perhaps religion would not have mattered, or an accommodation might have been made, but Spain was then the world's greatest power, and its power appeared to be the direct result of the treasure extracted from its colonial empire. England, a poor, weak nation in comparison, became jealous; because the English as islanders were naturally a seafaring people, they hungered to gain an empire like Spain's or at least to plunder the Spanish. The brilliant, wily Elizabeth used every trick in the book to gain advantage, and during the course of her long reign (1558–1603), she raised her country to new prominence.

Queen Elizabeth considered Spain a threat to England's security. To weaken the Spanish while strengthening her own kingdom, she authorized expeditions by privateers, whom the Spanish considered pirates, against the Spanish silver shipments from the Americas. In the 1560s John Hawkins turned privateer in the West Indies and traded in African slaves. Sir Walter Raleigh, one of the queen's favorites, observed Hawkins's success and turned privateer, too.

Although Elizabeth enjoyed the benefits conferred by the "sea dogs," as the privateers were called, she did not wish England to be known as a nation of pirates. Thus, she kept her government's distance from the actions of her subjects and stood ready to condemn to the Spanish ambassador the very pirates she had approved in private.

Leaving England late in 1577, the privateer Francis Drake sailed along the South American coast, passed through the Strait of Magellan, and entered the Pacific Ocean. He then surprised and seized Spanish ships along the western coast of South America, explored as far north as Drake's Bay in California, and returned to England in 1580 via the Pacific. His ship's holds bulged with wealth; the voyage created a sensation and whetted appetites for more booty. The first Englishman to sail around the world—a task accomplished for Spain by Magellan's expedition in 1522—Drake was welcomed home as a hero and knighted.

King Philip II of Spain tired of Elizabeth's tactics. He decided to end the English harassment of Spanish shipping once and for all by invading England with a massed fleet called the Armada. The Spanish sailed in 1588 but failed disastrously due to better English ships and skills as well as stormy weather (sardonically called the "Protestant Wind"). The destruction of the Armada gained the English their strongest position yet from which to challenge the Spanish in the New World.

SEEKING THE NORTHWEST PASSAGE, 1576–1610 Much of the English effort in the New World went into the search beyond Newfoundland for a northern sea route to Asia called the Northwest Passage. Such an opening, everyone agreed, would enable England to bypass Spain's control of South America and would give the English an exclusive direct link to the profitable Chinese market. Martin Frobisher made three northern voyages between 1576 and 1578; Sir Humphrey Gilbert sailed in 1583 and in 1584, when he was lost at sea; and John Davis explored the far north between 1585 and 1587. These explorers experienced howling snowstorms and saw massive icebergs but found no Northwest Passage.

After 1600 faith in the existence of the Northwest Passage dwindled, but Henry Hudson pursued this quest in four voyages from 1607 through 1610. In 1609, on the only trip he made for the Dutch, he found the river that he named for himself and reached present-day Albany, New York. In 1610 he sailed much further north, to Hudson Bay, where his sailors mutinied and cast him adrift in a small boat, never to be seen again. Hudson's failure raised doubts but did not end the quest for the nonexistent Northwest Passage.

ESTABLISHING THE ROANOKE COLONY, 1584–1590   The English also tried to plant a colony in North America. In 1584 Queen Elizabeth granted Sir Walter Raleigh the right to establish a colony along the Atlantic coast. He sent out an exploring party and chose a spot for settlement at Roanoke on the Outer Banks, in what was then called Virginia but is now North Carolina. The location was chosen perhaps more for military reasons—its closeness to Spanish Florida and its convenient access for passing English privateers—than for its promise as a location for settlement.

In 1585, knowing that war with Spain was coming, the queen prohibited Raleigh from leaving England, and the Roanoke colony was started without its founder. That year Ralph Lane and about a hundred settlers, most of them soldiers, reached Roanoke and built a fort. Relations with the local Indians were uneven, and the colony nearly starved.

When Francis Drake visited the colony in 1586, he found it in poor condition. Lane prepared to evacuate part of the colony on Drake's ships, but a storm ruined this plan. In the end, Lane and a few colonists accompanied Drake to England. Raleigh sent a relief ship that same year, but it arrived after Drake's visit and found the settlers gone. The ship returned to England.

Later that year a new expedition brought 150 to 200 additional colonists, but no one was at Roanoke, and the expedition returned to England, leaving only 15 to 18 men at the fort. Later it was learned that Indians had attacked these men, who had then set sail in a small boat and were never seen again.

In 1587 another 110 colonists arrived, led by John White. Opposed by other leaders in his plan to relocate the colony to Chesapeake Bay, White reluctantly agreed to remain at Roanoke. Meanwhile, he cultivated good relations with the Indians at nearby Croatoan Island. The colonists suffered from both food shortages and diseases, and White returned to England to get supplies. He left behind, as a kind of guarantee for his own return, his daughter, his son-in-law, and his granddaughter, Virginia Dare, the first English child born in North America.

In 1588 an attempted rescue failed when pirates attacked White's small ships en route and forced the party back to England. Meanwhile, war had broken out between England and Spain, and in preparation for heading off the Armada, Elizabeth prohibited all English ships from leaving port.

In 1590 White took passage on a privateer that promised to stop at Roanoke. He found the fort abandoned. The only sign of the colonists came from two markings on a tree and a door: CRO and CROATOAN. There was no sign of the maltese cross, the agreed-upon sign for distress. According to a prearrangement with the colonists he had left behind, the markings indicated to White that the settlers had voluntarily abandoned the fort and moved to Croatoan Island, where friendly Indians lived. However, a storm prevented the English from landing at Croatoan, and the fate of the settlers remained unknown.

Years later, in the early 1600s, an English settler in the later Virginia colony reported a story that at least some of the Roanoke party had been given shelter by friendly Indians who had later moved to the Chesapeake. There, it was said, both Indians and settlers had been massacred in about 1607 under orders of the great Indian leader Powhatan.

CONCLUSION

The original inhabitants of the Western Hemisphere developed agriculture and complex cultures but lacked sophisticated technology, which put them at a compelling military disadvantage against the invading Europeans. Disease devastated millions of indigenous people, but probably even more important factors in the easy conquest of America were the self-confidence and zest that the Europeans, and especially the Spanish, brought to the task. They combined modern governmental organization, in the form of the nation-state, with an intense desire to convert the "heathen" to Christianity.

The European countries squabbled among themselves. In part, these quarrels were those of thieves fighting over booty, but they also involved controversies over religion, government, and the proper forms for colonialism. The Spanish empire exploited native peoples to extract wealth for export to Spain. The French had a more reciprocal relationship with the Indians, perhaps because the French had to cultivate the natives in order to maintain the fur trade, a renewable resource. The English arrived so late that they could only seize land that France and Spain did not want, and they had to plant permanent colonies in order to maintain possession.

Recommended Readings

DOCUMENTS: Álvar Núñez Cabeza de Vaca, *Cabeza de Vaca's Adventures in the Unknown Interior of America (1983)*; Richard Hakluyt, *The Principal Navigations, Voiages, Traffiques and Discoveries of the English Nation* (3 vols., 1598–1600); Paul Hulton, *America, 1585: The Complete Drawings of John White* (1984).

READINGS: (INDIANS) James Axtell, *The European and the Indian* (1981), *The Invasion Within* (1985), and *Beyond 1492* (1992); Colin G. Calloway, *New Worlds for All* (1997); William Cronon, *Changes in the Land* (1983); Alfred W. Crosby, *The Columbian Exchange* (1972); Brian M. Fagan, *The Great Journey* (1987) and *Ancient North America* (3rd ed., 2000); Ramón A. Gutiérrez, *When Jesus Came, the Corn Mothers Went Away* (1991); Charles M. Hudson, *The Southeastern Indians* (1976); Francis Jennings, *The Invasion of America* (1975); Alvin M. Josephy, Jr., ed., *America in 1492* (1993); Andrew L. Knaut, *The Pueblo Revolt of 1680* (1995); James H. Merrell, *The Indians' New World* (1989); Neal Salisbury, *Manitou and Providence* (1982); Bruce G. Trigger, *The Children of Aataentsic* (2 vols., 1976); (EXPLORATION) Kenneth R. Andrews, *Trade, Plunder, and Settlement* (1984); W. J. Eccles, *France in America* (rev. ed., 1990); Stephen Greenblatt, *Marvelous Possessions* (1991); Karen O. Kupperman, *Settling with the Indians* (1980) and *Roanoke* (1984); D. W. Meinig, *The Shaping of America* (vol. 1, 1986); Samuel E. Morison, *The European Discovery of America* (2 vols., 1971–1974); J. H. Parry, *The Age of Reconnaissance* (1963); William D. and Carla R. Phillips, *The Worlds of Christopher Columbus* (1992); David B. Quinn, *North America from Earliest Discovery to First Settlements* (1977) and *Set Fair for Roanoke* (1985); David J. Weber, *The Spanish Frontier in North America* (1992).

2

The Plantation South, 1607–1771

OVERVIEW Founded in 1607, Virginia survived and eventually prospered by growing tobacco as a cash crop. From 1642 to 1677 Governor Sir William Berkeley promoted the development of a hierarchical society based on inequality. The wealthy obtained land easily, the poor only with difficulty. For a time, white indentured servants provided labor, but Bacon's Rebellion (1675–1676) revealed the instability of this social system.

Virginia planters turned increasingly to black slave labor. During the 1700s the use of this self-perpetuating labor force led to the emergence of a wealthy, powerful, and stable elite. With minor variations, the other southern colonies—Maryland, South Carolina, North Carolina, and Georgia—were modeled on Virginia.

VIRGINIA'S EARLY DAYS, 1607–1624

Arriving in Virginia in 1607, the first English settlers nearly starved to death, and at first the colony barely survived. With instructions from the Indians, however, the colonists soon were able to harvest a substantial tobacco crop. But the colonists' success brought them into conflict with the Indians over land. In 1618 Virginia adopted the headright system, by which settlers could be granted free land by the government. This led to increased population, rampant speculation, and further conflict with Indians. In 1625 Virginia became a royal colony. The king appointed the governor, the governor appointed a council, and property holders elected the House of Burgesses. The state-supported Church of England, through its vestrymen, aided the poor.

FOUNDING THE COLONY OF VIRGINIA, 1607   In 1603 James I succeeded Elizabeth as England's ruler and quickly patched up the old quarrel with Spain. In return for England's ban on privateering, the Spanish accepted the presence of English colonies in North America. Accordingly, in 1606 James granted the Virginia Company of London, a private stock-holding corporation, the right to colonize North America; but in order to obtain title, settlers had to occupy the land. The company's shareholders planned to profit from land sales, from trade with Indians, and from gold or other valuable minerals found in Virginia.

In 1607, thirteen years before the Pilgrims landed at Plymouth, the company formed the first permanent English settlement in North America, at Jamestown, Virginia. Lured to America with promises of adventure and easy wealth, the 105 colonists instead fell prey to misadventure and bad health. Virginia held no gold; the local Indians had no furs to trade; and the combination of bad water, bad diet, and fevers killed two-thirds of the colonists within seven months.

The survivors begged, borrowed, or stole food from the Indians, awaited an overdue supply ship from home, and quarreled among themselves. Individual initiative was lacking: Few were interested in putting food into the common storehouse, but all eagerly withdrew supplies. Finally, sensing disaster, Captain John Smith took charge. "He that will not work shall not eat," he declared, ordering food to be given only to those who fished or planted corn. Smith even ordered one settler who stole corn to be tied to a tree until he starved to death, and a wooden pin was driven through his tongue. Hated by the colonists for his harshness, Smith left the colony in 1609. He spent the rest of his life promoting the settlement of New England.

The Virginia colonists, whose number included a few idealistic gentlemen but most of whom were poorer farm workers from southern and western England, continued to bicker. Leadership was poor or nonexistent; expectations far exceeded reality; the water was contaminated; and although more settlers arrived, hundreds died in the "starving time."

In 1610, a scheduled supply ship failed to appear. The sixty survivors, having eaten all the chickens and livestock (including their horses), packed their belongings and prepared to abandon Virginia. They boarded a ship and sailed down the James River to the sea, only to meet three ships bringing both supplies and new colonists. The colony revived.

However, Virginia still did not prosper. In 1616 it had only 380 English residents, and investors in the Virginia Company of London received no profits. With neither gold nor Indian trade, the colony's only hope was to discover a crop that could be grown in Virginia and sold at a handsome profit in England.

GROWING TOBACCO AS A CASH CROP   An Indian plant, tobacco, saved the colony. In the early 1600s middle-class merchants throughout Europe began to smoke tobacco in their coffeehouses. The weed became so popular in England that James I, who hated the smoke, published the world's first antitobacco pamphlet.

By 1614, with help from the Indians, the Virginians had discovered that the country produced excellent tobacco. There was a ready, growing market in England, and the price in the early years was so high that profits could be enormous. Tobacco gained such an importance in Virginia's economy that it became the colony's only currency. Residents paid court fines and property taxes in pounds of tobacco, and ministers received their salaries in the same form.

Profits, however, were not automatic. Although land was readily available for planting, labor was difficult to obtain. Tobacco, more than most crops, required intensive labor. A single worker could care for only

Europeans were fascinated by the large-leafed tobacco plant, shown here in the right foreground. In the left foreground a worker is picking leaves, while other workers prepare and hang the leaves in the curing shed. (Art Resource, NY)

three acres. The seed had to be started in a bed and then transplanted to a field. Weeding was constant, and tobacco worms had to be removed by hand. At a crucial stage of growth, the tobacco leaves had to be cut and then cured.

COLONISTS CONFRONT INDIANS   The success of tobacco farming meant that the settlers took over more and more Indian land. Although the area was largely unpopulated, the native inhabitants resented the colonists' land grab, even when the settlers' cows and hogs did not trample unfenced Indian gardens. The English experimented with enslaving the natives to work on the tobacco plantations, but the natives ran away into the woods.

Powhatan, the powerful local Indian chief, tried numerous strategies to deal with these English settlers, including trade, diplomacy, war, and withdrawal. He sent his daughter, Pocahontas, to make contact; several years later, in 1614, Pocahontas married one of the settlers, John Rolfe. This was one of the few English–Indian marriages. Englishmen preferred to bring over Englishwomen rather than marry natives as the Spanish and the French did.

In 1616 the Rolfes visited England, where Pocahontas died. John Rolfe returned to Virginia and was among those killed by Indians in a sudden attack in 1622. Of the colony's 900 white settlers, 347 died. The colonists used the massacre as an excuse to kill Indians and to drive away even nearby friendly natives. Reduced by war and disease, the Indian population of coastal Virginia had declined from 30,000 in 1607 to 2,000 by 1669.

REORGANIZING THE COLONY   Once the Virginia Company of London understood that the colony's future depended upon tobacco, it moved to attract settlers to Virginia to farm. In 1618 the company adopted the headright system, by which settlers from England who paid for their own passage and that of others were promised fifty acres of free land for each settler, family member, and imported worker. Wealthy settlers imported indentured servants, who contracted to work for a fixed period in Virginia in return for payment of their passage.

This system made no provision for servants to acquire land after gaining their freedom, and it allowed speculators to accumulate vast acreages. Reports reached England from the colony about how those in power exploited laborers; nevertheless, the headright system did lead to increased immigration to Virginia.

In 1619 a Dutch sea captain, active in the flourishing slave trade between Africa and the West Indies, sold the English settlers twenty or more

Africans. Although slavery came early to Virginia, many years passed before slaves were numerous or the slave system's legal structure established.

At this same time the Virginia Company of London tottered toward bankruptcy. Virginia's leading planters sought to shore up the company and protect their own landholdings by organizing an elected body to pass laws for the colony. Each elected representative was called a burgess and the body the House of Burgesses.

In 1624 the king revoked the company's charter, ending the House of Burgesses, and the next year Virginia became a royal colony. The king's new charter provided a model that other colonies later adopted. The king appointed a royal governor, who ran the colony. A powerful figure, the governor named numerous officers, including judges. He was assisted by a council, whose members he appointed for life. Council members were invariably the wealthiest men in the colony.

In 1628, after a brief period without an elected representative body, dissatisfied Virginians revived the House of Burgesses, and until the 1650s the burgesses and council met jointly. Landed property holders elected the burgesses, who tended to be wealthy. They were the colony's only elected officials. Laws had to be approved by the burgesses, the council, and the governor, whose veto was absolute.

Local government followed the English model, according to which the governor appointed justices of the peace. Exercising both judicial and executive power, these men were, once again, the leading tobacco planters of each locality. The governor also named county sheriffs, although justices recommended the appointees.

From the beginning, the Church of England (the Episcopal Church) was the official, tax-supported church in Virginia. All public officials were required to belong to it, and all residents had to attend services at least once a month. Exemption from attendance was granted to some colonists who belonged to other Protestant denominations, but as late as 1705 Virginia had only five dissenting churches. Throughout its history, the colony regularly recruited English-trained ministers. Poor pay and Virginia's remote location, however, contributed to vacancies. In contrast to New England's Puritan clergy, Virginia's ministers usually delivered short sermons.

Each church parish was governed by a body of men called the vestry, who managed church affairs, including the welfare of the poor, a church responsibility. Parish boundaries followed county lines. The vestry was a self-perpetuating body that filled its own vacancies. Drawn from the wealthiest and most politically powerful segments of society, vestrymen were often also justices of the peace.

GOVERNOR SIR WILLIAM BERKELEY'S VIRGINIA, 1642–1677

Believing that social order required hierarchy, Governor Sir William Berkeley sought to create an elitist society based on inequality. Land policy, in particular, favored the wealthy. White indentured servants provided labor. Many servants died before their terms of service had ended; those who survived found only limited opportunities to acquire land.

In 1675–1676 these resentments, combined with the greed and ambition of the newly arrived Nathaniel Bacon, led to rebellion against Berkeley's authority. Bacon and his land-hungry followers demanded that Berkeley drive the Indians from the frontier in order to open more land for settlement, but the governor did not want an Indian war. In the end Bacon's Rebellion and its aftermath became a turning point that left Virginia a stable, hierarchical society.

BERKELEY SHAPES VIRGINIA AS AN ELITIST SOCIETY   In 1642 Governor Sir William Berkeley arrived in Virginia, where he remained as governor for most of the next thirty-five years. Berkeley, more than anyone else, nurtured the colony and shaped its destiny during its most crucial years.

A member of an ancient, prominent, and powerful family in England's west country, Berkeley possessed all the prejudices of his class and region. A sometime student at Oxford University, a soldier with a record for valor, and a passionate royalist during the English civil war of the 1640s, Berkeley brought strong convictions to Virginia.

First and foremost, he held that social and political order required a chain of hierarchical authority. God, Church, and King were at the top of his system; the governor was only a little lower. Then came the gentry, followed by other free people and, on the bottom, indentured servants and slaves.

Those high in the hierarchy not only had the right to wield power but also bore responsibility for those below. In return for this patriarchal concern, inferiors owed duty and loyalty to their superiors. The lowly were expected to honor their betters constantly, to obey them cheerfully, and to show deference; for example, by lining up according to social rank to enter church on Sunday.

For Berkeley, his most important task in Virginia was to recreate English life, especially as he had known it in the west country. He designed laws to lure English gentlemen and merchants and their younger sons to Virginia. After the English Puritan leader Oliver Cromwell gained power and executed King Charles I in 1649, a number of English gentry did immigrate to the colony.

PRESERVING INEQUALITY   Virginia society was based on preserving and maintaining inequality. At the top, the gentry, about 10 percent of the population, held 50 to 75 percent of the wealth, including much of the land, most white servants, and nearly all the slaves. Small-scale farmers, another 20 to 30 percent of the population, owned their own land and perhaps one or two white servants. The rest of the population consisted of white tenant farmers, poor white laborers, white indentured servants, and black slaves.

As in England, Berkeley expected the gentry to lead society. He did not believe in or practice equal opportunity; rather, opportunity was a function of one's social standing at birth. These ideas enabled hierarchy to be established and order maintained in Virginia.

Berkeley once boasted that Virginia had neither schools nor a printing press. He believed both to be curses because education and information might lead ordinary people to challenge elite rule and the hierarchical social order. The gentry enjoyed better education than the masses; they hired private tutors, and some sent their sons to Oxford University in England. The poor and "middling" classes remained unschooled. Even among the landowners, half could neither read nor write.

As Berkeley intended, over time the Virginia elite accumulated power and wealth. The leading several dozen families who arrived after 1660, with names such as Byrd, Carter, Harrison, Lee, Randolph, and Taylor, became known as the First Families of Virginia (who are still referred to today as "the FFV") simply by having children who survived. They quickly married among themselves. In 1724 all twelve members of the governor's council were related to each other. By 1775 every member was descended from at least one council member who had served in 1660.

In the mid-1600s the gentry used their control of high office to enhance their positions, especially with regard to land grants. Members of the governor's council and the House of Burgesses regularly voted themselves large tracts of land from the colony's vast holdings. Back in England, King Charles I pursued a similar policy; in 1649, for example, he gave five million acres to one man. This grant, which covered five counties, eventually passed to Lord Fairfax, who became the wealthiest Virginian.

The elite protected their interests in other ways, too. Berkeley's government continued the headright system, which allowed anyone to claim fifty acres of land for each English settler brought to Virginia. By enticing settlers and paying their passage in return for a period of indentured servitude, the large planters gained not only labor but also free land. The servant, even at the completion of service, had no easy means to obtain land.

USING THE LABOR OF WHITE INDENTURED SERVANTS   During Berkeley's governorship the main source of labor on Virginia's tobacco plantations was white indentured servants. More than three-quarters were male, and most had migrated from southern and western England, where they had been tenant farmers. Only 25 percent could sign their names. Generally aged fifteen to twenty-four, few were artisans or tradesmen. Some had been kidnapped or transported for petty crimes. Many were boys or teenagers from poor families. In exchange for the cost of the ocean voyage, they usually agreed to serve a master in Virginia for five to seven years. Of the English immigrants to Virginia in the 1600s, 75 percent came as indentured servants.

In the early years climate, disease, hard work, and poor diet killed as many as 80 percent before they had been in Virginia a year. If they were lucky enough to survive the "seasoning" and lasted to the end of their service, they became free men with doubtful prospects. They neither owned land nor could they readily earn from their labor enough money to buy land. Unlikely to marry, due to the shortage of women, few of these early white male Virginians produced descendants.

In the 1630s and 1640s, during which 60 percent of indentured servants lived out their term of service, about half of the survivors became landowners. Later, the chance for survival grew, but land prices rose and tobacco prices fell, making it harder to save money to buy land. As it became harder for those on the bottom of society to rise socially or politically, the elite increasingly dominated. A number of Virginians, of course, moved to other colonies, where land was easier to acquire, and others settled on the frontier, where farms could be worked without formal ownership.

Many former indentured servants became tenant farmers who rented from the great landowners, just as in the English west country. This is what Berkeley intended, but it did not please the tenants. They dared not complain, however; deference required that poor people speak of their betters only with great respect. Loose talk by a poor man about a gentleman could bring thirty lashes for "contempt of authority."

Owning land made a man more attractive to a woman seeking a husband. Because so many immigrants were male and so few female, the marriage prospects of these men were poor. Some men did marry, but most marriages ended with the death of a spouse in less than ten years. Life expectancy was no more than forty years. Only after 1660, when families began to arrive, did the colony's population increase naturally.

For children, the prospect was equally bleak. Of white children born in Virginia, half died before age twenty. If a child survived, the parents probably did not; more than three-fourths of children lost at least one parent before the age of eighteen. The extended family was important; often orphans, half-siblings, nieces, and nephews lived together in the same household.

The contrast between Virginia and New England is striking. During the 1600s five times as many people migrated from England to Virginia and Maryland (125,000) as to New England (25,000). A milder climate, lucrative tobacco crops, and free passage for indentured laborers favored these southern colonies. Yet in the year 1700, healthful New England, where nuclear families flourished, had a white population of 91,000, almost as many as the 98,000 whites in the two southern colonies combined.

An even larger number of English settlers, more than 200,000, migrated to the West Indies; but the sugar cane–growing islands proved even less healthful than Virginia, and the population there remained small.

BACON REBELS AGAINST BERKELEY, 1675–1676   During the 1670s Governor Berkeley's elitist system increasingly came under attack. To avoid an expensive Indian war, the governor had restricted white settlement to areas near the seacoast. This policy not only sustained the lucrative Indian trade that the governor had developed for his personal profit, it also helped speculators by driving up the price of farmland.

Berkeley's land policy irritated indentured servants, former servants, and ambitious large planters who were not politically connected. The price of tobacco had dropped; the poor economy burdened many with debt and caused tempers to rise.

Finally, in late 1675 and early 1676 Berkeley chose to ignore a series of frontier battles between Indians and whites. The settlers were led by Berkeley's second cousin, the ambitious Nathaniel Bacon, who had only recently arrived from England. This twenty-nine-year-old member of the governor's council was a hothead, and when Berkeley refused to attack the Indians, Bacon raised his own army.

In May 1676, Berkeley publicly declared Bacon a traitor. When Bacon arrived in Jamestown, he was arrested. Then, at a legislative session, the governor forced Bacon to beg pardon on bended knee. Deference having been shown, pardon was granted.

Bacon returned home and raised an army of five hundred men. He marched his soldiers, who included landless free whites, indentured servants, and some slaves, into Jamestown and forced Berkeley to commission the troops to fight Indians. As soon as Bacon left the capital, the furious governor declared Bacon a rebel. But Berkeley could rally no troops, and so he fled.

Bacon then marched his force to the frontier, attacked the Indians, and returned to Jamestown in September 1676. After Berkeley and his supporters retreated, Bacon plundered and burned the capital city. By this time news of the rebellion had reached England, where an alarmed King Charles II decided to treat Bacon and his accomplices as traitors.

The king sent a thousand royal troops to Virginia; but before they arrived, Bacon died suddenly, perhaps of a fever or perhaps, as his supporters charged, by poisoning. Regaining power in 1677, Berkeley nullified royal pardons for the rebels and executed twenty-three of Bacon's most prominent supporters. Then, recalled by the crown, the elderly and exhausted Berkeley set sail for England, where he died shortly after landing.

Bacon's Rebellion marked a turning point in the colony's history. Afterward, no Virginia officials defended Indians, and officials promoted white settlement on the frontier. Opening more land drove down land prices, and the small-scale white farmer, whether formerly an indentured servant or not, was considered a positive element in Virginia society.

Hierarchy was preserved, however, as the great planters sought a more reliable and docile kind of labor to replace the unpredictable, unruly indentured kind.

THE GREAT PLANTERS TURN TO SLAVERY

Africans who arrived in Virginia before the 1660s were not necessarily slaves, and the differences between black slaves and white indentured servants were blurred. By the 1670s Virginia had adopted a clear policy of race-based slavery, and large importations of slave labor replaced indentured servants.

From 1700 to 1760 great planters used the stability provided by a permanent, naturally increasing slave labor force to gain and maintain enormous wealth, power, and social prestige. Planters displayed their wealth lavishly but also feared poor whites, slave revolts, and land-hungry frontier settlers. The elite kept control because they had all the wealth and power, dominated the society's existing institutions, and admitted talented white newcomers to their ranks.

VIRGINIA ADOPTS SLAVERY, **1619–1750**   Although the first blacks were brought to Virginia in 1619, as late as 1670 only 5 percent of the population were black slaves. Even in 1700 they made up only 20 percent. By 1750, however, slaves, mostly African-born, constituted more than 40 percent of Virginia's population.

In the early 1600s the words *slave* and *servant* were more or less inter-changeable. Both white servants from England and black slaves from Africa were sold to Virginia tobacco planters, and English colonists in the West Indies had previously used both types of labor.

Differences, however, put the two kinds of servants on an unequal ba-sis almost from the start. The English servants spoke the same language as the planters, deferred to them, conceived of themselves as free En-glishmen despite the temporary degradation of service, were protected by English law limiting terms of service, and practiced Christianity.

In contrast, the Africans spoke no English, were disoriented by their forced removal from Africa, were sold for whatever terms the market dic-tated, and were considered heathens. Because Africans were not Christian, whites thought, they did not have to be treated with Christian charity.

Remarkably, despite these disadvantages some Africans who arrived in Virginia in the early 1600s managed to attain their freedom. They did so by having their service sold by traders to planters for a short term of years rather than for life. Or they converted to Christianity; in early Vir-ginia a Christian lawfully could not be enslaved for life. Or they arranged with their masters to hire out their labor and use part of the proceeds to buy their freedom.

As late as the 1660s some free blacks had their own plantations. They bought land and worked it with bound labor. These black planters owned both white indentured servants and black slaves, brought lawsuits against whites, and testified against white planters in court.

AFRICAN SLAVERY BECOMES ROOTED IN VIRGINIA   As early as the 1640s, how-ever, Virginia began to change from a society that distinguished free per-sons (mostly white) from unfree persons (white and black) to a society in which whites were free and blacks were not. By the 1670s, race-based slavery had become entrenched in the colony. Laws banned interracial marriage, required all black slaves to serve for life, and declared the chil-dren of slave mothers to be slaves themselves.

The rising life expectancy of both whites and blacks may have played a role in the development of Virginia's particular slave system. The colony's elite feared that large numbers of white, formerly indentured servants could destabilize the colony and that their numbers would grow ever larger if they continued to immigrate, survive, marry, and have chil-dren. In contrast, the increased life expectancy of blacks made lifelong slaves a better investment for planters; slave children, even those born as a result of white masters' sexual exploitation of black slave women, prom-ised a perpetual, growing labor supply.

Also important to the rise of slavery in Virginia was the growth of the international slave trade, including the chartering of the Royal African Company in 1672. Between 1600 and 1800, European traders regularly called at ports in West Africa, buying as many as ten million slaves for shipment to the Western Hemisphere. During the horrifying Middle Passage, as the trip was called, people were packed so densely aboard ships that as many as one-sixth died.

Most slaves were destined for sugar plantations in Brazil and the West Indies. Because these plantations had to import food, planters tried to hold down costs by using only highly productive adult male slaves, who died quickly and were then replaced. In contrast, Virginia planters imported both men and women. Although only 4 percent of the Africans shipped to the Western Hemisphere were sent to North America, their descendants today outnumber the descendants of those sent to Brazil and the West Indies.

By the 1710s Virginia's slave population was increasing naturally. This reproduction pattern was found in South Carolina by the 1740s but never occurred in the unhealthful West Indies.

The most important reason for the new system, however, was white racism. Englishmen in Virginia believed that the white race was superior to all other races. This idea was not new but had existed throughout English and European history. To the English, Christianity and their own high rates of literacy, scientific invention, military prowess, and commercial success proved their superiority.

The relative disadvantage of Africans in Virginia also played a role in promoting the slave system. Lacking experience in living in an English society and without economic leverage, Africans were vulnerable to English exploitation.

By the end of the 1600s, few whites in England were willing to migrate to Virginia as indentured servants. The high death rates and the slim chances of acquiring land and becoming a planter had become well known in England. New colonies such as Pennsylvania offered better opportunities. In addition, the thriving English economy had created more jobs at home.

For Virginia's great planters, African slaves proved a boon. Vast acreages could be worked by a stable, reliable, permanent workforce, one that would never become free and would never be able to seek land ownership. The children of slaves would be slaves. If slaves multiplied as planters hoped and expected, then planters would grow ever richer. Virginia society would resemble English rural society, in which a permanent laboring class supported a landed aristocracy.

THE GREAT PLANTERS PROSPER, 1700–1760　　After 1700 the great Virginia planters acquired slaves in large numbers. The ruling elite established by Governor William Berkeley's land policies now sustained itself with a permanent labor force to work that land. The result was that the elite became permanent and self-perpetuating. And as the profits from slave-worked tobacco land increased, with larger acreages being worked, the planters bought more slaves and worked yet more land.

As late as 1700 the wealthiest planters in Virginia owned only a few slaves. Very, very few people owned more than twenty. Plantations were small and profits low. Ordinary planters lived in one- or two-room wooden houses, and even wealthy planters had only four- or six-room pine clapboard homes. When planters died, they left remarkably few personal possessions, in some cases only an iron skillet and an iron cooking pot. Even wealthy planters lacked china dishes or silverware. Furniture of local woods such as pine or cherry was crudely made on or near the premises.

By 1750 much had changed. The wealthiest planters often owned hundreds of slaves and worked several large plantations in various parts of the colony. Profits could be enormous, although the lifestyle of a great planter often led to debt. While ordinary planters continued to live in one- or two-room houses, the great planters were beginning to build the mansions that we associate with the South. Houses such as George Washington's Mount Vernon, beautifully situated overlooking the Potomac River, were designed less for comfort than to show off a family's wealth. Washington's house was built of local wood, but the wood was carved so that from a distance it looked like stone.

Planters furnished their new homes with fine mahogany furniture, much of it imported. They ate from the finest English china with silver knives, spoons, and forks. The three-pronged fork for eating was a recent innovation. House servants cooked increasingly elaborate meals and polished the family silver.

Planters' wives held an ambiguous rank. On the one hand, the mistress of the household instructed servants, supervised children, and doctored everyone. She had authority, but her authority was entirely derived from her husband, whom both law and custom required her to obey. To him, she must show the deference due to a superior being. Like her poorer sisters, she was often bearing and burying children.

PLANTERS INTRODUCE FREEWHEELING LIFESTYLES　　Great planters displayed their wealth to maintain their social and political status. They bestowed alms upon the poor, entertained lavishly, and continued the old English west country custom of keeping an open house, at which any respectable traveler could get food and lodging without charge. Some poor gentlemen lived by traveling from house to house.

Planters drank freely. When William Byrd II was a member of the governor's council in the early 1700s, the council frequently got drunk; sometimes members collapsed under the council table. Virginia gentlemen chased women, both white and black, and forced themselves on servants or slaves without feeling guilt.

They were also notorious gamblers. Horse races, in particular, provided entertainment and reinforced the gentry's high status. A race was usually between two horses ridden by their owners for a quarter mile on a dirt track. Gentlemen often raced after church on Sunday, frequently on a dare and without preparation. It was illegal for poor people to race horses or to bet on a horse race. In Virginia a man could sue to collect a gaming debt in court.

Gambling and ostentatious public display led many planters to live beyond their means. Fox hunting and lavish dancing parties were expensive forms of recreation. Although outwardly successful through ownership of land and slaves, a planter could easily squander his income.

Planters often had a cosmopolitan outlook. They kept in touch with the larger world through conversations with the captains whose ships landed at plantation docks. Most of the comforts of life and the goods that defined high social status came from England. The ships that picked up the tobacco and transported it to England for sale also brought English goods, especially fancy cloth, household articles, and books. For example, when George Washington married Martha Custis, who was considered the colony's wealthiest widow, he found it necessary to order a long list of imported items for the occasion.

A planter usually ordered goods through his tobacco factor, that is, the person in England who sold the tobacco for the planter's account. Factors sold goods to planters on credit and reimbursed themselves out of the following year's tobacco sales. As a result, many planters owed large debts to their English factors.

PLANTERS FEAR CHALLENGERS   Great planters maintained an uneasy hold on Virginia society. The immigration of white indentured servants in the 1600s had resulted in a substantial population of small-scale white farmers. Although some of these farmers acquired land, others were tenants. In 1676, 25 percent of free whites were landless. Ignorant and poor, they posed a threat to the gentry's rule. The elite, however, controlled Virginia by their insistence on deference from poor whites, coupled with a growing emphasis on white racial solidarity.

As Virginia's slave population grew, the great planters became afraid of slave revolts. In parts of the Tidewater region, nearest Chesapeake Bay, slaves made up more than 60 percent of the population. The colony passed laws to prevent slaves from owning guns, from congregating in groups, from moving freely about the country, and from learning to read, and slaveowners were discouraged from freeing slaves.

A third threat to planter rule came from the Virginia frontier. By the mid-1700s that region had developed its own culture. Although the great planters owned large tracts, the frontier was settled primarily by non-slaveholding white farmers, some of whom were squatters rather than owners. Many came from the Tidewater area, but others were Scotch-Irish or German settlers who had drifted down the Great Valley of the Shenandoah River from Pennsylvania.

Frontier culture was ethnically mixed and more egalitarian than in the Tidewater region. The area was also unstable; during any five-year period, 40 percent of all households moved. The English institutions that were strong in the Tidewater, especially the Church of England, did not take root. Indeed, most frontier parishes lacked ministers, and dissenting Protestants such as Scots Presbyterians and German Lutherans were allowed to form their own congregations.

PLANTERS KEEP CONTROL   Yet the great planters did maintain control of Virginia. They held most of the society's wealth and power, and they had the time and resources to serve in government office. Seeking public office was costly, and only the wealthy could afford to run. Elections to the House of Burgesses, for example, depended upon the custom of treating the voters to liquor. To save money, George Washington once ran without treating; he lost. He learned his lesson and at a later election in 1758 provided each voter with a half-gallon of liquor. This time, he won.

The gentry were flexible enough to admit newcomers into their ranks, particularly by marrying their daughters to promising, ambitious young men. Yet the gentry insisted on dominating all the institutions of society and went unchallenged because there were no other organized centers of power. This Virginia gentry produced ten presidents: Washington, Jefferson, Madison, Monroe, both Harrisons, Tyler, and, through remote, lesser branches, Taylor, Truman, and Carter.

Although the Virginians hated cities and built none, in 1699 they did relocate their colony's capital from swampy, mosquito-infested Jamestown to a more healthful place, Williamsburg. The new town, which had fewer than a thousand residents, was carefully planned to reflect planter values. The public buildings were built of brick. The dominant one was the Governor's Palace, not the Capitol. Also important were Bruton Parish Church and the College of William and Mary, which was founded in 1693. The broad, straight, empty streets were dotted with small wooden houses and a few taverns and inns that came to life when the fun-loving legislature was in session. Otherwise, the oaks, pines, squirrels, and songbirds of the peaceful countryside prevailed.

Virginia was founded on greed. To this lust for wealth, the great planters added an emphasis on politeness. In an often raw frontier society, the elite's good manners were perhaps the only way to hold the society together. These two traits, greed and politeness, became hallmarks of southern culture. They did not preclude exploitation in the form of slavery.

FOUNDING THE OTHER SOUTHERN COLONIES

With only minor variations, Virginia provided the model for the other southern colonies. Founded in 1632, tobacco-growing Maryland most closely resembled Virginia, but its small size discouraged land speculation, and its religious diversity contrasted with Virginia's uniformity. South Carolina, chartered in 1663, depended from the beginning upon slaves to grow rice. North Carolina, which split off from South Carolina in 1729, had fewer plantations and more small farms. Georgia, founded in 1732 as the last colony, at first restricted land ownership and prohibited slavery and rum, but these policies failed.

MARYLAND, 1632–1750   In 1632 Cecilius Calvert, Lord Baltimore, received a royal charter from King Charles I to establish the colony of Maryland. This was the first proprietary colony placed entirely under the control of a single person. The owner or proprietor, Lord Baltimore, was Catholic, and he established his colony as a refuge for Catholics seeking a haven from the religious turmoil then engulfing England.

Although many original settlers at St. Mary's City were Catholic, Maryland soon lost its Catholic character, as Protestants (including Scotch-Irish Presbyterians and German Lutherans) flooded into the colony. A handful of wealthy Catholic families, however, continued to exert influence.

In 1649 the colony passed the Toleration Act, which allowed all Christians to practice their religion freely. Five years later the Protestants, believing themselves protected by Oliver Cromwell's Puritan government in England, repealed the act. In 1658 Lord Baltimore restored a policy of toleration, but religious strife continued.

Like Virginia, Maryland produced tobacco; Maryland, too, was home to great planters, African slaves, English indentured servants, and former

Map 2.1   American Seaboard Colonies

servants who owned and operated small farms. Maryland imported large numbers of slaves even before Virginia did.

Maryland also adopted the headright system that gave fifty acres to each settler for a settler's family member or servant. This colony, however, provided free land to servants after they had completed their service. The result was more small farms than in Virginia.

Because of Lord Baltimore's lesser political influence and his religious views, Maryland's boundaries were restricted. The colony was too small in area to support the sort of land speculation common in Virginia. And because Maryland sprawled across both sides of Chesapeake Bay, providing access to Virginia and interior Pennsylvania as well as the Atlantic Ocean, the colony early gained commercial importance.

In its religious and ethnic diversity, Maryland was more like a middle colony such as Pennsylvania, but its cultivation of tobacco and widespread use of slave labor on large plantations rooted Maryland culturally in the South. There were long, stormy disputes with Virginia, whose citizens regarded Marylanders as latecomers who lived in a puny, inferior place.

SOUTH CAROLINA, **1663–1750**   In 1663 King Charles II, who had gained the throne after the collapse of England's Puritan government in 1660, granted eight wealthy supporters, called the lord proprietors, the right to colonize Carolina. Named to honor the king, the colony originally included what later became North and South Carolina.

Carolina was planned both to protect Virginia from Spanish movement northward from Florida and to add a distinctive semitropical agricultural area to the ever-expanding English empire. The philosopher John Locke helped write a bizarre, aristocratic constitution for the colony. The proprietors and settlers ignored most of its provisions, including plans for a titled nobility.

In 1670 settlers arrived near the site of Charles Town (now Charleston). Many great planters came from the English West Indian island of Barbados, where they used African slave labor to cultivate sugar at great profit. After a brief period of raising grain and cattle to sell to the food-short West Indies, the planters turned the hot, humid swamps along the southern Carolina seacoast into rice plantations. Slaves brought the knowledge of how to grow rice. Later, Carolinians grew indigo, a plant used to produce a widely used blue vegetable dye.

The climate of South Carolina was brutal. The English and other Europeans died from malaria and other fevers that affected neither the native Indians nor the Africans (who had gained immunities in Africa). From the beginning, the planters ignored white indentured servants and depended exclusively upon slave labor, both Indian and African.

In the early years native Indian slaves worked the plantations; however, they often ran away. Planters then purchased Indian slaves from friendly tribes and sold them to the West Indies in exchange for African slaves. The Indian slave trade was a major business, and the colony's population became mixed. In 1708 there were 5,300 whites, 2,900 black slaves, and 1,400 Indian slaves.

As the English encroached on Indian lands, tensions grew. Finally, in 1715 many of the local tribes revolted. The Carolinians, with support from the Cherokee, defeated the Yamasee and the Creek. In terms of the white casualty rate, the Yamasee War was the deadliest Indian war in colonial America. Of the six thousand whites in Carolina, four hundred died. At the end of the Yamasee War, the English in Carolina embarked on a long-term policy of pushing the Indians west, destroying any who remained behind.

South Carolina planters quickly turned to a massive importation of black slave labor. From the failure of Indian slavery until just before the American Revolution, a majority of South Carolina's population was black. In many coastal rice-growing areas, the African population exceeded 90 percent. In these areas slave communities succeeded in preserving patterns of African culture, including housing types, medicinal herbs, linguistic styles and words, conjuring, and music. Unlike Virginia, South Carolina plantations used the task system, which gave the slaves more control over their own time. Under the task system, each slave had a daily assignment, and when it was completed, the slave had the right to spin, weave, fish, or tend garden on his or her own account. In Virginia slaves worked for the master from sunup to sundown.

Planters were afraid of slave revolts. In the Stono Rebellion of 1739, a hundred slaves killed several whites and then marched toward Spanish Florida. They were defeated in battle by the white South Carolina militia allied with Indians.

During the malaria season, wealthy planter families fled their plantations and moved to the one healthful spot, Charles Town. Protected from malaria-breeding mosquitoes due to the steady flow of the Ashley and Cooper Rivers, Charles Town became a populous outpost of English culture and civilization. By 1750 its eight thousand people made it the only major town in the South, a center of urban culture with many accomplished white and black artisans, especially furniture makers.

NORTH CAROLINA, 1729–1771   In 1729 disputes among powerful land speculators forced Carolina to be split into two colonies. North Carolina developed slowly. Geographically isolated, its climate and soil were different from Charleston's. Its coastal areas were too swampy to be habitable, and its barrier islands and the storms off Cape Hatteras prevented ships from reaching much of the mainland, depriving the colony of good ocean transportation.

Attracted by good land on ocean-going sea routes, Virginia tobacco planters settled the extreme northeastern portion of the colony, on Albemarle Sound, as early as 1653. Some also came to North Carolina to escape legal problems. These planters controlled North Carolina until the American Revolution. The border with South Carolina was settled largely by South Carolinians. North Carolina, it was said, was "a valley of humility between two mountains of conceit."

North Carolina did not prosper until settlement reached the fertile interior. Scotch-Irish and Germans came down from Pennsylvania through Virginia's Great Valley. They were not slaveholders, and because North Carolina lacked numerous large plantations along its swampy coast, the colony always had a greater proportion of small-scale white farmers than its neighbors.

The Quakers who settled Greensboro brought commercial skills. In 1753 German Moravians from Bethlehem, Pennsylvania, founded Salem (now Winston-Salem). These highly skilled craftsmen worked iron, wood, and leather and developed an important pottery industry. They also opened the first bank in the South.

For many years these western Carolinians were dominated by the colony's eastern planters. Friction grew, but the planters kept control. During these years, they moved the colony's capital several times in search of a locale that had good water. Finally, the capital was fixed at New Bern, which had been founded by Baron de Graffenried as a German-Swiss colony in 1710. New Bern was an ocean-going seaport, even though it was 100 miles from the Atlantic.

In 1767 the royal governor, William Tryon, built a palace at New Bern. Tryon's Palace was conceived both as a governor's mansion like the one in Williamsburg, Virginia, and as a capitol building. Although Tryon provided a chamber for the governor's council, he did not include a meeting room large enough to hold the colonial legislature. The alarmed planters took this as a sign that the governor intended to rule without a legislature.

To pay for the palace, Tryon imposed a special property tax, to be paid in gold or silver. Lacking cash, frontier farmers grew furious; in 1771, after years of east-west tension, they revolted. Although Tryon used eastern militia to crush the Regulators, as they were called, many western North Carolinians had no further use for royal government. Later, during the American Revolution, the governor fled the palace to a British warship. Tryon's Palace was so hated that the new state legislature refused to use it, and in 1798, unmourned, it burned to the ground.

GEORGIA, 1732–1749   Georgia was founded in 1732, the last of the original thirteen colonies. General James Oglethorpe, an English reformer, obtained a charter to establish a colony for England's poor, including those in prison for debt, which was then a crime. The British government was willing to grant such a charter in order to beat the Spanish (or others) to settlement of the area.

To make the colony a success, Oglethorpe adopted several unique policies. First, all settlers, including the poor, were granted fifty acres apiece. Second, there were no large land grants; instead, actual settlers could own a maximum of five hundred acres. These policies encouraged widespread land ownership and retarded the establishment of the kind of elite that dominated Virginia and South Carolina.

Third, there were no slaves. Slaves, Oglethorpe believed, degraded the value of labor, forced poor whites to compete with slaves, and created an idle, slaveholding elite. Fourth, rum was banned because alcohol caused much poverty.

Oglethorpe built military fortifications at the mouth of the Savannah River and laid out Savannah as a planned city with handsome public squares. Lots were large so that homeowners could plant vegetable gardens and raise chickens.

Little came of Oglethorpe's plans except for the immigration to Georgia of a sizeable number of paupers and debtors, who did acquire land. Rum came in 1742. South Carolina planters began to move into Georgia, defying the law and bringing their slaves. When challenged, they answered that the climate required slave labor. Slavery became legal in 1749.

Although great planters dependent on slave labor quickly gained control of Georgia, the colony retained two features from its early days: Its white population formed a higher percentage than in South Carolina, which had a black majority through most of the colonial period; and Oglethorpe's land policy did enable many small-scale farmers to own land. Originally granted a twenty-year charter, Oglethorpe considered the experiment a failure and returned the colony to royal control before the charter expired.

CONCLUSION

Founding a colony was difficult and dangerous. To succeed, a colony had to attract settlers. Virginia's appeal was tobacco grown for overseas markets. Growing tobacco required land, which was plentiful in Virginia once the native inhabitants were pushed aside, and labor, which shifted over time from white indentured servants to black slaves. The planters, who made the crucial decisions and set land policy, accumulated acreage, wealth, and power for themselves.

After Bacon's Rebellion, when Virginia's rulers saw that an increasing population of poor whites might threaten their power, planters quickly turned to race-based African slavery. They used the slave system to dominate society by controlling land and labor and by rallying poor whites through the idea of white supremacy. Elite power, slavery, racism, and cash crops became the hallmark of all the southern colonies.

Recommended Readings

DOCUMENTS: William Byrd II, *The Secret Diary, 1709–1712* (1941); Landon Carter, *Diary, 1752–1778* (2 vols., 1965).

READINGS: (VIRGINIA) T. H. Breen, *Puritans and Adventurers* (1980), *Tobacco Culture* (1985) and, with Stephen Innes, *Myne Owne Ground* (1980); Kathleen M. Brown, *Good Wives, Nasty Wenches, and Anxious Patriarchs* (1996); A. Roger Ekirch, *Bound for America* (1987); David Galenson, *White Servitude in Colonial America* (1981); James Horn, *Adapting to a New World* (1994); Rhys Isaac, *The Transformation of Virginia* (1982); Edmund S. Morgan, *American Slavery, American Freedom* (1975); Ivor Noël Hume, *Martin's Hundred* (1982); Darrett B. and Anita H. Rutman, *A Place in Time* (2 vols., 1984); Daniel B. Smith, *Inside the Great House* (1980); Mechal Sobel, *The World They Made Together* (1987); Bertram Wyatt-Brown, *Southern Honor* (1982); (SLAVERY) Ira Berlin, *Many Thousands Gone* (1998); Philip D. Curtin, *The Atlantic Slave Trade* (1969); Alan Gallay, *The Indian Slave Trade* (2002); Winthrop Jordan, *White over Black* (1968); Herbert S. Klein, *The Middle Passage* (1978); Peter Linebaugh and Marcus Rediker, *The Many-Headed Hydra* (2000); Philip D. Morgan, *Slave Counterpoint* (1998); Gerald W. Mullin, *Flight and Rebellion* (1972); John K. Thornton, *Africa and Africans in the Making of the Atlantic World* (2nd ed., 1998); (FRONTIER) Richard R. Beeman, *The Evolution of the Southern Backcountry* (1984); M. Thomas Hatley, *The Dividing Paths* (1993); (MARYLAND) Lois G. Carr et al., *Colonial Chesapeake Society* (1989) and *Robert Cole's World* (1991); Paul G. E. Clemens, *The Atlantic Economy and Colonial Maryland's Eastern Shore* (1980); Allan Kulikoff, *Tobacco and Slaves* (1986); Gloria Main, *Tobacco Colony* (1982); Thad Tate and David Ammerman, eds., *The Chesapeake in the Seventeenth Century* (1979); (LOWER SOUTH) Joyce E. Chaplin, *An Anxious Pursuit* (1993); Margaret W. Creel, *A Peculiar People* (1988); A. Roger Ekirch, *Poor Carolina* (1981); Rachel N. Klein, *Unification of a Slave State* (1990); Daniel C. Littlefield, *Rice and Slaves* (1981); Betty Wood, *Slavery in Colonial Georgia* (1984) and *The Origins of American Slavery* (1997); Peter H. Wood, *Black Majority* (1974).

3

Religious New England, 1620–1760

OVERVIEW   An English religious group called Pilgrims rejected the Church of England and settled at Plymouth, in what is now Massachusetts, in 1620. At the time, England's rising middle classes demanded religious reform, and between 1630 and 1642 many reformers, called Puritans, moved to Massachusetts. Puritan society revolved around the church and its theology. After 1660 religion declined; Massachusetts officials and English officials quarreled, and 1692 brought the Salem witch trials. By 1700 commerce flourished, and religion revived with the Great Awakening in the 1730s and 1740s.

THE PILGRIMS FOUND PLYMOUTH COLONY, 1620

In 1620 the Pilgrims settled at Plymouth, Massachusetts. They were Protestant religious zealots who considered the Church of England hopelessly corrupt and, against government opposition, demanded the right to worship in their own way.

THE PILGRIMS MOVE TO PLYMOUTH, 1620   As early as 1602, Englishmen fished off the northeastern shore of North America. They sometimes traded with the local Indians, transmitting diseases in the process. As a result, most of the native inhabitants died before 1620 in a series of epidemics. Native American villages were abandoned after being depopulated so rapidly that the dead remained where they fell. In a few years once-productive cornfields were covered with scrubby brush. Many En-

44

glishmen concluded that God had killed the heathen Indians to enable the Christian English to replant the fields. It was all part of God's plan.

In 1620 English settlers sailed on the *Mayflower* to establish the first colony at Plymouth, in what is today southeastern Massachusetts. While on board, forty-one of the colonists signed the Mayflower Compact, an agreement that provided the colony with a government, which soon came under William Bradford's leadership.

The colony barely survived and did not prosper. Summers were warmer than in England and winters far more severe. Almost half the colonists died in the first year. They avoided starvation only by obtaining food from nearby friendly Indians. Squanto, the last surviving member of a local tribe, taught the English settlers how to plant corn. He fertilized each cornhill by burying a dead fish, a technique which the English thought to be Indian but which Squanto had learned earlier while living in England.

RELIGION LEADS THE PILGRIMS TO NEW ENGLAND   The Plymouth colonists called themselves Pilgrims because they had moved to New England for the sake of their religion. In truth, they were fanatics. In England, as in other Christian countries at that time, the government controlled religion and required people to participate in the state-run church. In the late 1500s the Pilgrims came to think that the Church of England was impure and corrupt. They disliked its leaders, its practices, and its principles. Rejecting bishops, they demanded local control by congregations and less ceremony in church services. Finally, they rejected the state church altogether and became separatists.

These fundamentalists thought icons, stained glass windows, and church music were evil. Opposed to all practices not found in the Bible, they wanted communion to be taken at a plain table, not at an altar covered with a fancy cloth. They wanted ministers to wear ordinary clothes and preach long, powerful sermons using the Bible as the text.

Nor were these dissenters silent. Because of their outspoken opposition to the state church, they came under suspicion of treason. The government told them to shut up and worship like everyone else, but some went underground instead, and in 1608 a number moved to Holland. The Dutch government tolerated them, but after twelve years they found the Dutch grating, and their own children had begun to lose the English ways. In 1620 they decided to resettle in North America.

For ten years the tiny Plymouth colony existed but barely grew. No new immigrants followed except some nonreligious settlers who set up Indian trading posts and fishing villages along the New England coast. The most famous of these settlements was Thomas Morton's Ma-re Mount, founded in 1627 in what is now Boston. In the eyes of the Pilgrims, it was devoted to drinking, gambling, and whoring; worse, Morton traded guns to the Indians. The Pilgrims raided Ma-re Mount in 1628 and shipped Morton to England.

ENGLAND IN 1620

In 1620 England was becoming modern but still retained many traditional ways, among them a rigid class structure in the rural areas. Many members of the rising middle classes demanded change, including reform of the Church of England. Because they wanted to purify the church, these reformers called themselves Puritans.

MAINTAINING THE POLITICAL AND CLASS STRUCTURES   In 1620 England was becoming what we would recognize as a modern country. But ties to olden times were still strong. For example, an elderly person born in 1550 might remember a grandparent born in 1480. In 1480 England had an overwhelmingly rural populace, numerous Catholic monasteries, feudal rules, no printing presses, little influence in Europe, and a weak government wracked by civil war.

During the 1500s royal government was strengthened. Henry VIII (reigning 1509–1547) declared the country Protestant, abolished monasteries, and confiscated the church lands. His daughter Elizabeth I (r. 1558–1603) defeated Spain's Armada, sent explorers to North America, and provided for the crowns of England and Scotland to be unified under her successor, James I (r. 1603–1625). The King James Bible was published in 1611; printing flourished; and commercial towns thrived, especially in East Anglia, the area northeast of London. The capital teemed with nearly half a million people.

Despite these changes, in the early 1600s England still retained many old ways. Social classes remained rigid, and people generally were born, lived, and died in the same class. At the top of the class structure were the king and the royal family. Just below were 16,500 high-ranking noble or gentry families, who owned most of the real estate. Another 85,000 farmers, called *yeomen*, owned their own land.

The remaining one million families included prosperous, nonlandholding craftsmen, farm tenants, farm laborers, servants, and the unemployed. About one-quarter of the five million people could find work only during planting and harvesting seasons. Thousands of beggars strolled along the roads.

Although 10 percent of the people lived in London and many others in thriving commercial distribution centers called market towns, about three-fourths of the people resided in traditional agricultural villages. English farmers rarely lived on individual farms; rather, 500 to 1,500 people lived together in a village, and each day residents walked to surrounding fields to labor. People rarely moved away and often became related through marriage.

Usually, one person owned an entire village, and this property was called a manor. Most villages had a manor house, where the owner, the lord of the manor, lived and actively managed its affairs. This static, traditional society was undergoing stresses and strains. For one thing, landowners in some areas were beginning to fence in the open fields where traditionally villagers had herded cows and gathered firewood. This policy of enclosure drove down rural living standards and led to emigration.

Life expectancy was only about thirty-five years, and two-thirds of all children died before the age of four. Nevertheless, high birth rates matched high death rates, and the population grew steadily. Increased population was difficult to absorb in a society with a rigid class structure, which provided rural residents few new opportunities. People saw England as overpopulated and looked to emigrate.

THE MIDDLE CLASSES RISE   England, however, was richer than most European countries. Although this wealth was highly concentrated, it did stimulate both crafts production and trade. The English wrought iron and wove woolen cloth. They also built ships, filled them with woolens, and sailed to trade with the world. Crafts and commerce encouraged the growth of market towns, especially in East Anglia, which became densely populated. London, too, thrived. Commercial prosperity in turn produced work for lawyers, bankers, and accountants.

Many people in these new commercial classes did not fit into the old social system. They owned no land, and their business did not require land, but without land the new middle classes lacked social status or political power. They formed a restless, rootless part of the society.

REFORMING THE CHURCH OF ENGLAND   If the Church of England had not been a state-controlled church dominated by lords of the village manors, perhaps the members of rising new classes might have expressed their discontent in other ways. But the elite used the church to maintain the rigid social structure. Village lords picked the ministers, whose main purpose often was to defend the lord's power. In other cases, a lord's younger son became the village minister, and religious taxes became yet another means to support the landlord's family.

Like other restless groups in other times and places, many people from the new middle classes turned to religion. But the traditional Church of England, which stressed preservation of the old ways, including the power of village lords, did not meet their needs. In the late 1500s and early 1600s, however, an occasional minister broke with tradition and captured the middle-class imagination by preaching long, inspirational sermons based closely on the Bible. The Bible, now easily available from the new printing presses, was the key to this movement.

A movement for reform grew within the Church of England. The reformers called themselves Puritans because they said that, unlike the Pilgrims, they did not wish to separate from the church; rather, they wished to reform the church by purifying its corrupt, worldly, and ungodly aspects.

As late as the 1620s the Puritans were optimistic. In many English towns, especially in East Anglia, prosperous middle-class residents had used their new wealth to install Puritan preachers in public lectureships. A number of Puritan lords of the manor had appointed reformers as ministers in their churches. Cambridge University had become a Puritan stronghold, and Puritans could be found in high office in London and among the Church of England's bishops.

Puritanism produced a backlash, however, and—unfortunately for the reformers—the opposition's leader was King Charles I (r. 1625–1649). The king understood keenly the danger of Puritanism. If the church were run by congregations from the bottom up rather than by the king's bishops from the top down, it would not be long before these same people, in the king's view, challenged the king's divine right to rule.

In 1629 the king dismissed Parliament, where support for Puritanism was strong, and ruled alone. Four years later he appointed William Laud as the Archbishop of Canterbury, the head of the Church of England. Laud aggressively purged Puritan ministers from the church.

In the short run this campaign succeeded, but Laud's zeal, together with financial problems that forced Charles I to recall Parliament, led to a growing dispute between Charles I and Parliament over royal power and taxes, resulting in a civil war between the king and Parliament in the 1640s. The Puritans, under General Oliver Cromwell (r. 1653–1658), won the war, executing Laud in 1645 and Charles I in 1649.

THE PURITANS FOUND MASSACHUSETTS BAY COLONY, 1629–1642

In 1629 the Puritans received a charter for the Massachusetts Bay Company. From 1630 to 1642 as many as 21,000 colonists migrated to Massachusetts, establishing America's first self-governing colony. Drawn largely from the middle classes, the Puritans stressed education. They recreated English ways, including living in villages with outlying fields, a system that discouraged land speculation. Life expectancy was long and families large. The Puritans constituted the largest single group of Europeans to immigrate to America and exercised more influence on America's development than any other single group.

THE MASSACHUSETTS BAY COMPANY GETS A CHARTER, 1629   In 1629, as the atmosphere in England began to turn nasty for the Puritans, a number of middle-class religious reformers used their political connections to obtain a royal charter for a private joint-stock company to acquire land and trading rights in Massachusetts. The Massachusetts Bay Company's planners selected Massachusetts as a place for settlement because of Indian depopulation and because the area lacked valuable resources that would attract rivals.

The English government saw the Massachusetts Bay Company as a way to claim land in North America that might otherwise fall to the French, the Dutch, or the Spanish. The colony also promised to remove from England a set of well-known, powerful troublemakers.

The charter had one curious feature: It did not specify the location of the company's annual meeting. The corporate colony's founders took the charter to Massachusetts and declared that the colonists themselves would meet to select the company's officers. Voters chose both the governor and legislators in annual elections. Thus, the colony was self-governing from the beginning, and later attempts to force the company to surrender its charter were hampered by the fact that the charter was physically in Massachusetts. Under English law physical possession of the original document guaranteed the holder the rights stated in that document. Courts were reluctant to overturn a charter unless it was produced in court.

THE GREAT MIGRATION, 1630–1642   The Puritan move to Massachusetts in 1630 was the largest single European migration to the New World. More than a thousand settlers arrived in seventeen ships. Unlike Virginia's settlers, the Puritan colonists included many women and children and even a few elderly people. Perhaps three-quarters came in family groups. The flow that started in 1630 continued through 1642, by which time 21,000 people had arrived in the area around Boston. Because of Puritan success in the civil war in England, few Puritans migrated after 1642.

These family-oriented immigrants reproduced in large numbers. The population doubled every generation, and today more than 16 million Americans can trace their ancestry to the great migration of the 1630s.

They include seventeen presidents: both Adamses, Fillmore, Pierce, Lincoln, Grant, Hayes, Garfield, Arthur, Cleveland, Benjamin Harrison, Taft, Harding, Coolidge, Franklin Roosevelt, and the two Bushes. This group, in terms of its effect on the development of American society, has played a larger role than any other single immigrant group in American history.

THE PURITANS EMPHASIZE EDUCATION   The Puritans were drawn principally from England's middle classes. Almost no titled nobility immigrated, and most of the gentry who came soon left. On the other hand, the Puritans barred the poor, drifters, laborers, and servants, except for those of a religious temperament with long service in a Puritan family. No indentured servants were sent to New England.

At the high end, the Puritans included some English landowners, essentially yeomen; a few men of greater prominence, like the longtime governor, John Winthrop, whose family had controlled a lesser English manor; and ninety well-educated ministers. At the low end, a majority of Puritans had been town-dwelling craftsmen; in New England most of these people gave up their trades for agriculture. Other settlers were farmers who had leased but did not own land in England.

They were remarkably well educated. Two-thirds of the adult males could sign their names—twice the number typical of Englishmen. Because the Puritans associated education with religion and particularly with Bible reading, they quickly established public schools for both boys and girls. In 1647 Massachusetts required every town with fifty or more families to levy taxes to maintain public schools. (Many towns, however, ignored the law.) School books reflected Puritan values. The widely used *New England Primer* opened with the line: "In Adam's Fall, We Sinned all."

One in every forty heads of family was a college graduate. This was a far higher proportion than in England. No other colony ever began with so many educated people. To maintain this level of learning, Harvard College was chartered in 1636 and opened in Cambridge, Massachusetts, two years later. Instruction was in Latin, and the students—all males—were required to study Hebrew, Greek, and theology. Half of the graduates became ministers.

In 1640 the Puritans established the first printing press, at Harvard College; they published sermons, catechism books, and school primers. It remained the only press in English North America until 1675, when a second printer set up in Boston.

RE-CREATING OLD WAYS OF LIFE   A disproportionate number of settlers were from East Anglia, a part of England that showed Scandinavian influences dating back to invasions and settlements of centuries earlier. This densely

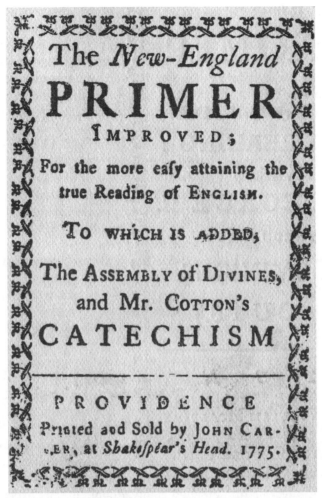

The *New England Primer* went through many editions and was the most common schoolbook in that region throughout the colonial period. (© Bettmann/CORBIS)

populated region combined agriculture, thriving market towns, and the weaving of woolens. East Anglians conducted a busy trade with Holland, and the area had long been noted for religious dissent and rebellion against authority.

East Anglians built wooden saltbox houses, that is, boxy houses with two stories in the front and one in the back, covered by a steeply pitched roof with a long rear slope; and so did the colonists. Like the Dutch, the East Anglians preferred to cook by baking, a tradition they carried across the ocean. Pies had been invented in East Anglia, where they were filled with meat. New Englanders filled their pies with fruit.

The Puritans replicated East Anglian life in many ways, but there were differences, including New England's severe winters and strange local foods, such as corn and pumpkins. Other differences included the absence of manor houses, less rigid social classes, and abundant land for new farms. Those who felt constrained by their neighbors could join with others to create a new town in the wilderness.

The colony's officials granted land in the form of a new town not to individuals but to groups of settlers. Settlers often came as a single congregation from England. The town, the basic unit of organization, then deeded property to individuals according to their needs and abilities as farmers. This system both discouraged land speculation and enabled officials to maintain careful control over who could live in a town. Towns governed themselves through annual town meetings.

Following the model of English villages, residents lived in a concentrated fashion. Each family was given a lot for a house and garden bordering on the common, near the meeting house, as well as several agricultural fields on the village's outskirts. Towns preserved pastures and woodlands for shared use and retained generous acreage for anticipated population growth.

THE PURITANS ENJOY LONG LIFE AND LARGE FAMILIES   New England turned out to be more healthful than England and far more so than Virginia or the West Indies. The soil probably had more nutrients, at least in the early years, and low population density discouraged the spread of contagious diseases. Severe winters killed more microbes than people. Few children died, and most adults who reached age twenty survived to sixty.

Of those who came in the Great Migration, the average life span reached seventy; one-fifth attained eighty, double the life expectancy in Virginia. New England may have been the first society in which it was normal to have living grandparents.

Puritan life revolved around families. Practically everyone married, and it was illegal to live alone. Divorce was rare but possible. Men headed households, but women enjoyed a higher status than in England. For example, in contrast with England, wife beating was a crime. The typical family had seven or eight children. Families consciously replicated themselves: 75 percent of first-born children were given the name of a parent.

The state watched family life closely. A couple who produced a child born less than seven months after marriage was fined or whipped. A woman who gave birth out of wedlock was pressured by the midwife during delivery to name the father. Courts usually accepted the answer, especially if the man named was able to provide child support. Adultery was a capital crime, but only one adulterous couple was ever executed, because juries declined to convict.

PURITAN LIFE REVOLVES AROUND RELIGION

Puritan society focused on religion. These newcomers restricted church membership and embraced a complex theology that balanced faith and works and stressed the conversion experience. Rejecting tolerance, Puritans banished dissenters like Roger Williams and Anne Hutchinson. Dissidents sometimes founded new colonies, such as Connecticut. Thus, Puritan beliefs were largely responsible for the spread of colonies around New England.

ESTABLISHING A SOCIETY BASED ON RELIGION   For the Puritans, religion was the key to life. All questions, big and small, had to be answered with reference to the Bible, to the church, to the minister, and to prayer. The colonists put the church at the center, and yet they did not create a theocracy, that is, a church-run government. Instead, their churches and their government operated along parallel, complementary tracks.

In England the Puritans claimed that they merely wanted to reform the corrupt, state-controlled Church of England. Once in Massachusetts, however, they created churches that resembled those of the separatist Pilgrims in Plymouth. Indeed, Massachusetts absorbed the Plymouth colony in 1691.

Most important was the concept of congregational church government: Each congregation selected its own minister. There were no bishops, and power flowed from the bottom up, not from the top down.

This democratic tendency was restrained in two ways. First, not everyone could be a church member, although everyone was expected to attend services. The right to membership had to be earned through religious devotion. Second, the ministers of the colony met collectively from time to time and monitored each other's behavior. It was difficult for a congregation to select a minister not generally approved by all the colony's ministers.

The church was separated from but connected to the government. For example, the Puritans by law prohibited as pagan the celebration of Christmas and Easter. Government officials, not ministers, performed marriages, which took place in public buildings rather than in churches. As in England, taxpayers supported the churches. All local residents paid for the services of the minister, whose income ranked high in most towns.

Dissent was not tolerated. There was no freedom of religion. During the 1600s the government ordered residents who did not wish to practice Puritanism to conform or leave. People who were banished but then returned to the colony ran the risk of being executed. Between 1659 and 1661 four Quakers, members of a radical Protestant sect that later settled Pennsylvania, were hanged.

MAKING RULES FOR CHURCH SERVICES AND MEMBERSHIP   Puritans kept the Sabbath, doing no work from sundown on Saturday until sundown on Sunday. Food had to be cooked ahead of time. Reports of work, play, or any unnecessary activity on Sunday brought condemnation from both the church and the government.

A church service was long, solemn, and serious, lasting at least two hours. It began with a long prayer, was followed by exposition of a Bible verse and the singing of a psalm without musical accompaniment, featured an hour-long sermon, and concluded with a short prayer and benediction. Settlers attended two services each Sunday.

Both men and women joined the church, and in most towns women formed a slight majority of members. To become a member, a person had to undergo a "conversion experience" in which he or she became convinced of personal, eternal salvation. Furthermore, this experience had to be recounted to the minister and often to the deacon, the leading layperson in the congregation. If these two found the experience convincing, the candidate then recounted the conversion to the entire congregation. Only then could membership be granted.

Among those who immigrated in the 1630s, about half joined the church. Almost every family had at least one member. Although members came from all social and economic levels, those higher up the scale were more likely to belong. Only a church member could have a child baptized or could be licensed to operate a tavern. Only a male church member had the right to vote in elections or hold public office. These practices preserved Puritan control over government, including the important task of land distribution.

THE PURITANS PONDER FAITH, WORKS, AND CONVERSIONS   At the heart of Puritanism was a concept developed by the Protestant reformer John Calvin: The world was divided into two kinds of people, those whom God intended to save for eternal life and those damned to eternal hell. The very small number of the world's people to be saved were called the Elect or, more commonly, the Saints. The Puritans conceded that they could not know for certain whom God would save. But the Puritans believed that they could devise tests to indicate who would probably be among the Saints.

The most important test was faith, that is, belief in God. Although God might save an unbeliever, the Puritans thought this unlikely. The chances were that those who were to be saved would come from among those who claimed to have faith in God. Through faith, God bestowed grace, and grace guaranteed salvation.

For the Puritans, however, this test posed problems. After all, a person could assert faith and, through self-delusion or lies, could falsely claim grace. So a second test was a matter of works, that is, one's deeds or how one lived one's life. The chances were that if one had received grace, one would be enabled to live a godly life of charity, honesty, and humility. The danger was that a person could live an outwardly blameless life yet lack true faith, be without grace, and be damned. Thus, works might lead to self-delusion and prevent salvation. Works, therefore, were insufficient.

Thus, the Puritans came to their third test, the conversion experience. A person born a sinner and wishing to be reborn of God and placed among the Saints not only had to have faith, receive grace, and do good works, but also had to undergo an intense, personal religious experience that could be convincingly related to others. Public ratification of this personal experience was taken as an indication that the conversion was real and that the person truly was a Saint.

The Puritans recognized that no person could know God's will, but they believed that they had devised a means to gain a likely understanding of the truth. Thus, no Puritan who had had a conversion experience and had been accepted into church membership could claim with absolute certainty to be a Saint, but the probability was high. Anxiety concerning a possible miscalculation, however, produced much tension.

ROGER WILLIAMS SEPARATES CHURCH AND STATE, 1636   The congregational system of church government made it difficult for colonial officials to restrain a minister who persuaded his congregation to go in a new direction. Roger Williams was such a minister. Williams began to suspect that many conversion experiences were false. After serious reflection and much prayer, he concluded that few people were truly Saints. His list of Saints kept shrinking until it included only his wife and himself.

At this point Williams suddenly saw the absurdity of a religious system with only two Saints. Therefore, he reversed himself and concluded that any person could go to heaven; one needed only to have faith and thereby receive grace. Williams's idea of universal salvation, which became the basis for the Baptist Church in America, alarmed the Puritan authorities. If Williams's idea were accepted, church membership, voting, and public office would have to be open to everyone. Massachusetts society might unravel. Williams's ideas would lead to a separation of church and state.

Worse, from a theological standpoint Williams's position destroyed Puritanism. Conversion experiences would have no significance, and in a world in which any person could claim salvation, how would self-deluders and liars be stopped? Individual claims of righteousness would lead to the organization of strange new churches. Attempts to stop these churches would fail because members of each new church would claim to be true believers.

Williams had other unorthodox ideas. He declared that the colonists should buy land from the Indians, not just occupy it. This idea challenged the legitimacy of the colony's charter, under which public officials gave land to towns. In 1636 Massachusetts authorities forced Roger Williams to flee. He founded a new colony at Providence, Rhode Island, which was chartered by Parliament in 1644 and by the king in 1663. Williams recognized that others did not share all his views, and he soon advocated religious freedom. Thus, Rhode Island became the first American colony founded on the basis of personal religious choice.

ANNE HUTCHINSON EMBRACES ANTINOMIANISM, **1638**   The Puritan religious system contained contradictions that caused trouble. In England the Puritans had attacked Archbishop Laud for putting too much emphasis upon works. Such a belief was called Arminianism, after the theologian Arminius. But in Massachusetts the threat came from the opposite direction, from Puritans who ignored authorities' warnings and put too much emphasis on faith. This belief was called Antinomianism, derived from a Latin word that means "opposing works."

A principal Antinomian challenge came from Anne Hutchinson. She had migrated to Boston with her husband and began to hold prayer meetings and religious discussions in her home. Although such activities were a normal part of Puritan life, the ministers and government officials grew uneasy when hundreds of people, including many women, began to attend Mrs. Hutchinson's meetings. To the men who ran the government and the churches, her sessions also seemed unwomanly.

As in all the colonies, women in Massachusetts were legally subordinate to husbands and could not own property. Although women could be church members, they could not be ministers or play a leading role in the church.

Authorities became gravely concerned about Hutchinson's message. She found the Holy Spirit present at her meetings. Though that statement did not challenge Puritan doctrine, church authorities investigated; she took the witness stand and claimed a direct, personal line to God. He spoke to her "by an immediate revelation."

No Puritan could accept that belief. Such an idea meant that each person, under God's direct input, could declare what was religiously acceptable. The church would lose control of its members, and each individual would constitute a personal church. Religious order would collapse and, since religion was the basis of the state, so would social order. In 1638 Massachusetts authorities banished Anne Hutchinson. She moved to Rhode Island and then to an English settlement on Long Island, New York. In 1643 she was killed by Indians.

FOUNDING CONNECTICUT, **1636**   The Puritan system was fragile and religious disputes common. The easiest way to keep the peace was to encourage outspoken people to leave. In 1636 Thomas Hooker, a respected but opinionated Puritan minister, led a group into the Connecticut Valley and founded a colony at Hartford. Other Puritans, considered to be the most religiously fervent, arrived from England and founded a colony at New Haven in 1638. In 1662 these colonies, having secured a royal charter, merged as Connecticut.

Not everyone in New England shared the uniform religiosity of Massachusetts. Religiously diverse settlements could be found in Rhode Island (which attracted Baptists, Jews, and Quakers); on the Massachusetts frontier, for example, William Pynchon's secular colony at Springfield; and in remote areas of Maine and New Hampshire. Massachusetts controlled Maine from 1652 to 1820, but New Hampshire succeeded in organizing separately in 1680.

TROUBLES COME TO MASSACHUSETTS, 1660–1692

After 1660 religion waned, despite the Half-Way Covenant and sermons called jeremiads that were designed to induce conversion experiences. King Charles II challenged Massachusetts, and the Indian King Philip led the last Indian war against whites in New England, 1675–1676. In 1684 England revoked the Massachusetts charter and in 1686 merged the colony into the Dominion of New England, which lasted three years. In 1691 Massachusetts was rechartered as a royal colony, which limited the colonists' self-government. The next year, in an incident that began in Salem Village and that revealed political, social, and psychological instability, nineteen witches were hanged.

PURITAN RELIGION DECLINES   John Winthrop, the long-time early governor
of Massachusetts, had spoken of founding a godly community, a "city
upon a hill," and the first generation of Puritans had devoted itself to that
cause. But their children, born in Massachusetts, began to drift away from
religion. As the number of conversion experiences fell, the percentage of
adults in the church dropped from about 50 to 20 percent. Because the
founding members' children failed to join, and since only members could
have their children baptized, the number of infant baptisms plummeted.

   In 1662 some congregations adopted the Half-Way Covenant. An
adult child of a church member who had faith and lived a godly life

John Winthrop, the long-time governor of the Massachusetts colony;
earnest and serious, he wears the starched collar of a gentleman. (Culver
Pictures, Inc.)

could, without a conversion experience, receive communion, which was normally restricted to church members, and could have children baptized.

Amid religious decline, ministers preached sermons called jeremiads, after the Old Testament prophet Jeremiah. These sermons bewailed the woes that were befalling an ungodly people and demanded mass repentance and multiple conversion experiences as the price for saving Massachusetts from utter destruction as an ungodly society.

The first great New England poet, Anne Bradstreet, had written warmly of family, love, and religion. In her work the three were entwined aspects of a godly whole. In 1662 Michael Wigglesworth, the next great poet, gloomily predicted New England's doom for its sins in "God's Controversy with New England."

CHARLES AND PHILIP MAKE ROYAL TROUBLE, 1660–1676 During Oliver Cromwell's Puritan regime in England, Massachusetts had been left alone, but the installation of the distinctly unpuritanical King Charles II in 1660 put the colony on the defensive and complicated its politics. The English government took an increasing, unwelcome interest in New England's affairs. While Massachusetts fared poorly, Connecticut, under the politically shrewd John Winthrop, Jr., obtained a royal charter in 1662 that provided for self-government. This document lasted until 1818.

On the New England home front troubles grew. In 1675 the Indian leader Metacom, called King Philip by the settlers, led the Wampanoag tribe in war against the colonists. For years, ever since the minor Pequot War of 1637, relations between whites and Indians in New England had been peaceful, but by the 1670s the remaining Indians recognized that white population growth was destroying the Indian way of life, which depended upon hunting.

In King Philip's War (1675–1676) Indians attacked fifty-two of ninety towns in New England, destroyed twelve of them, killed six hundred whites, and took many captives. One of them, Mrs. Mary Rowlandson, wrote a popular account of her ordeal that became a model for many later narratives.

The colonists fought ruthlessly, losing one of every sixteen men of military age. They took advantage of old tribal rivalries and hired Indians to kill other Indians. At the end of the war in 1676, many natives fled west. The remainder settled on reservations. King Philip's War was the last Indian–white war in New England.

THE DOMINION OF NEW ENGLAND RISES AND FALLS, 1684–1691 In 1684, long frustrated by Massachusetts's snubs, lack of cooperation, and smuggling, the English government annulled the old charter and imposed direct royal rule. The colony's prospects worsened the following year, when King James II (r. 1685–1688) came to power. A practicing Catholic, James II antagonized Parliament in all sorts of ways, including the appointment of Catholic officers in the army and aggressive management of the country's colonies.

In 1686, under the king's newly appointed governor, Sir Edmund Andros, Massachusetts was merged with New Hampshire and Maine as the Dominion of New England. Organized in the name of greater administrative efficiency, the Dominion's main effect was to increase both Andros's power and the king's opportunity to exploit America. The next year Andros's Dominion took over Plymouth and Rhode Island, and the governor visited Hartford for the purpose of annexing Connecticut. The clever Yankees, however, defied Andros by hiding their charter in an oak tree.

In 1688 Andros added New York and New Jersey to the growing, unwieldy, and unpopular Dominion, an act that irritated almost everyone. Land speculators in England and the colonies, as well as farmers, worried about a consolidated system under which only the most influential could extract concessions, including confirmation of land titles.

New Englanders also feared an attempt to use taxes to establish the Church of England. The brusque Andros heightened these anxieties when he ordered an Anglican church set up at his administrative capital at Boston. Andros also questioned the legitimacy of the Massachusetts General Court as a governing legislature and the legality of the colony's land grants to towns. That threatened property rights.

In late 1688 James II fled from the throne and was succeeded in the bloodless and hence Glorious Revolution by William III (r. 1689–1702) and Mary II (r. 1689–1694), both Protestants. When word of this event reached Boston in early 1689, the local residents overthrew Andros's regime. Many yearned for a return of the godly days of their old charter government.

The English, however, refused to give Massachusetts its former privileges. In a political compromise, a royal charter was granted in 1691. It called for the king to appoint a royal governor, for the people to elect the General Court to pass laws, and for the General Court to elect a council to advise the governor.

Power was to be shared. Although the governor was influential and, along with the council, controlled spending, the legislature retained the sole right to levy taxes. This system produced much conflict during the 1700s. The right to vote was extended to nonchurch members, based on property as in England; and Massachusetts was allowed to retain control of both Plymouth and Maine.

MASSACHUSETTS HANGS WITCHES, **1692**   Amid the unraveling of Puritan society and following immediately on the political chaos of 1684–1691, there occurred one of the strangest episodes in American history, the Salem witch trials. Witchcraft accusations and trials had occurred regularly in Europe for centuries, and at least thirty witches had been executed earlier in colonial New England. What set the events that began in Salem apart from earlier episodes were mass accusations, mass hysteria, and mass hangings.

Salem Village, today the town of Danvers, Massachusetts, was an agricultural area geographically remote from but politically controlled by the seaport town of Salem. The farmers who lived in the village had long been bitterly divided, and one important issue had been the attempt to establish a separate church in Salem Village.

In 1692 two young girls who lived in the household of the town's minister, Samuel Parris, suddenly became hysterical, even convulsive. Parris, as well as the local physician and others, quickly became convinced that a witch afflicted the girls. Accusations of witchcraft were made, accused witches were examined and jailed, and the number of afflicted girls grew to ten. Whenever a witch was jailed, the outcries stopped; but then they returned as yet another afflicted girl claimed to be possessed by a new witch.

Eventually, as the craze spread to other towns, more than 150 persons were jailed as accused witches, and nineteen were tried, convicted, and hanged. All but five were women. One man was pressed to death with stones for refusing to enter a plea in court. When the accusations marched up the social scale and included the wife of the Massachusetts governor, officials suddenly halted the proceedings.

As in earlier New England witchcraft proceedings, accused witches in Salem and the other towns tended to be elderly women, especially those without husbands or sons. In some cases inheritance of family property seemed to be an issue. In almost all cases the suspected witch came from a family where witchcraft had been charged or suspected earlier, had engaged at some time in unseemly or immoral behavior (such as having a child out of wedlock), or was on poor terms with church members.

The Salem trials became so notorious that they inhibited further legal prosecutions of witches. Folkways die slowly, however, and New Englanders continued to believe in witches, an idea rooted deep in the folk culture of East Anglia.

AWAKENINGS, COMMERCIAL
AND RELIGIOUS, 1700–1760

New Englanders increasingly participated in the larger world, including three wars against France. After 1700 the colonists traded inside the British Empire. Shipbuilding and sailing flourished, and urban merchants grew wealthy. The 1730s and 1740s brought a series of religious revivals later called the Great Awakening, led by the Reverend Jonathan Edwards. These revivals replaced the traditional emphasis on community with an emphasis on individual religion.

NEW ENGLAND THRIVES ON COMMERCE AFTER 1700   After 1700 New England became a more secular society and gained greater contact with the broader world. New Englanders fought alongside England in global conflicts against France in King William's War (1689–1697); against both France and Spain in Queen Anne's War (1702–1713); and again in King George's War (1744–1748), during which New England soldiers captured Louisbourg, Nova Scotia, in 1745. The Louisbourg expedition was so plagued by illness that it gave Massachusetts the dubious distinction of having the deadliest war in American history on a per capita basis.

As the British Empire developed, extensive trade grew among England, New England, Virginia, and the West Indies. New Englanders played a prominent role in this trade. Felling great trees in abundant forests, they built and sailed ships. They raised grain and horses for export to the West Indies, where these items were in short supply. New Englanders netted fish for overseas markets and imported both rum and molasses, from which they distilled their own local rum. They carried rum to Africa, where they traded it for slaves, whom they sold in the West Indies and along the southern seacoast.

Commerce became a major part of the New England economy, and, as is always the case in commercial societies, merchants in the leading seaports gained great wealth. By the 1750s the richest 5 percent of Boston's population owned half the city's wealth.

Boston and, to a lesser extent, Salem and Newport, Rhode Island, became filled with the mansions of the newly rich. People who cared more about making money than saving souls dominated the seaport's economy, society, and politics. The Church of England even erected a building in a prominent location in Boston, while the Revere family turned out silver cups and plates as elegant as any crafted in London. Among the new luxuries were forks, table linens, and mirrors.

Rural New Englanders looked upon these changes with awe and suspicion. Although the glitter of Boston attracted ambitious young people, farm folk suspected that Boston's worldliness and wealth were proof of the city's ungodliness. As late as 1735 fewer than 4 percent of New Englanders dissented from the established congregational churches.

Sticking to the old ways was what farmers and farmer–craftsmen in the countryside did best, and they continued to plow their fields, ply their trades, and lay plans for providing farm lands for their children, if not in the immediate vicinity (which had filled up), then on lands along the frontier.

Meanwhile, if they saw an opportunity to build a mill, to sell some grain to strangers, or to swap some local produce for imported earthenware plates, they took the main chance. They were in transition from devout, otherworldly Puritans to sharp-eyed, hard-bargaining Yankees.

RELIGION RETURNS WITH THE GREAT AWAKENING, 1741–1742   In the early 1700s New Englanders lacked the intense religious feelings of their ancestors. This began to change as early as 1733, when the Reverend Jonathan Edwards stirred people with his preaching at Northampton, Massachusetts. During the rest of the decade the revival spread throughout the colonies. From 1739 to 1741 the great English evangelist George Whitefield preached from the South to New England. Everywhere he traveled, large crowds turned out. In Boston nineteen thousand people— far more than the city's population—heard him.

Whitefield preached in a new style, extemporaneously and without notes. His message had great emotional appeal. Among his listeners at one New England meeting was Jonathan Edwards, who wept. After Whitefield's visit, a wave of revivals in 1741 and 1742 flooded across New England in both rural and urban settings.

Soon ministers and others disputed the meaning of these events. Conservatives, or "Old Lights," became suspicious and were especially upset by outbursts of emotion at the revivals. Liberals, called "New Lights" because they believed the revivals brought forth God's light, looked approvingly upon the large number of converts.

In New England the Great Awakening's most important figure proved to be Jonathan Edwards. Although his written sermons showed the dryness, quiet logic, and rich use of scripture associated with Puritanism, his oral delivery was closer to Whitefield's. Edwards gazed out across his congregation, his eyes transfixed on the far end of the meeting house, and preached as if the spirit of the Lord were pouring forth from his mouth. Members of Edwards's congregation in Northampton, Massachusetts, burst out in screams of religious ecstasy, and dozens surged to the front of the church to declare their conversions. Edwards rarely challenged these claims. He harvested hundreds of church members.

Important people in Northampton were appalled. Edwards offended their sense of order and threatened their status. The creation of a mass, popular church on a wave of emotion might overturn the town's political, social, and economic order. So Edwards was dismissed. He went into the wilderness, ministered to Indians, and wrote several volumes explaining his theology. In 1757 he moved to Princeton, New Jersey, where he became the president of a college, now Princeton University, founded by Presbyterians in 1746 to train "New Light" ministers. He died in 1758.

The revivals also led Baptists to found the College of Rhode Island (Brown University) in 1764, the Dutch Reformed to begin Queen's College (Rutgers University) in 1766, and Congregationalists to start Dartmouth College as an Indian mission school in 1769.

The Great Awakening was the single most important event in the history of American religion. Although it took place in all the colonies, its most pronounced effect was in New England. Those who rejected the revival, if they tried to maintain orthodox Puritan views, were left with an emotionally dead, rigid system of predestined salvation for only a handful of Saints, which did not appeal to Americans living in and developing a more egalitarian society. John Winthrop, John Calvin, and old-fashioned Puritanism were long dead.

New Englanders as well as other Americans were now divided religiously not so much by denomination as by how they regarded the revival. To accept the revival was to admit the possibility of free grace; that is, all people who had faith could receive grace and be saved. This was the Antinomian idea that Anne Hutchinson had articulated.

As the Puritans had warned, this sort of evangelical religion emphasized emotion over reason, heart over intellect, and individual sentiment over communal decisions. Such a religion ran the dangers of emotional excess, personal eccentricity, and social disintegration; it was also inherently anti-intellectual. Jonathan Edwards, a transitional figure who tried to combine the old theology with the new style, struggled to maintain a theological balance.

Boston merchants embraced a more comfortable, rational, and socially cohesive religion. They drifted toward the Arminian belief in works. Smugly confident that wealth was a sign of God's favor and reinforced in this belief by charitable acts that suggested salvation through works, they rejected both predestination and the revival. During the 1700s their branch of congregational religion evolved into Unitarianism, which stressed reason and social justice evidenced through works. They clung to intellect without emotion.

Since the Great Awakening, no one in America has been able to put the two halves of religious experience—theology and reason versus faith and feeling—together again, and the country has more or less regularly oscillated between periods of rational, secular activity and periods of intensely emotional religious revivals.

CONCLUSION

Puritan religion shaped both New England society and America as a whole. The Puritans were unusual immigrants—middle class, educated, resourceful, and fanatical. While trying to replicate English village life, they emphasized church and family. The church and state together monitored, regulated, and controlled people's lives, imposing conformity as well as high standards.

After 1660 formal ties between church and state began to loosen, religion lost preeminence, and New Englanders became commercially engaged with the rest of the world. During these years friction between England and Massachusetts led the colonists to assert local, democratic rights and to distrust authorities in faraway London. By the early 1700s England's benign neglect and the colonies' prosperity had temporarily cured these resentments. During the Great Awakening, religious fervor returned, providing the foundation for modern American religion and indicating the development of a belief system that reflected a truly American psyche.

Recommended Readings

DOCUMENTS: William Bradford, *Of Plymouth Plantation* (1952); Anne Bradstreet, *Works* (1967); Samuel Sewall, *Diary* (2 vols., 1973).

READINGS: (PURITANISM) Francis J. Bremer, *The Puritan Experiment* (rev. ed., 1995); Charles L. Cohen, *God's Caress* (1986); Stephen Foster, *The Long Argument* (1991); Richard Godbeer, *The Devil's Dominion* (1992); Philip F. Gura, *A Glimpse of Sion's Glory* (1984); David D. Hall, *Worlds of Wonder, Days of Judgment* (1989); Edmund S. Morgan, *Visible Saints* (1963); David Stannard, *The Puritan Way of Death* (1977); Harry S. Stout, *The New England Soul* (1986); (NEW ENGLAND) Virginia D. Anderson, *New England's Generation* (1991); Jon Butler, *Awash in a Sea of Faith* (1990); David W. Conroy, *In Public Houses* (1995); David Cressy, *Coming Over* (1987); Richard L. Dunn, *Puritans and Yankees* (1962); Stephen Innes, *Creating the Commonwealth* (1995); Susan Juster, *Disorderly Women* (1994); John F. Martin, *Profits in the Wilderness* (1991); Roger Thompson, *Sex in Middlesex* (1986); Laurel T. Ulrich, *Good Wives* (1982); (COMMUNITIES) Richard L. Bushman, *From Puritan to Yankee* (1967); John Demos, *A Little Commonwealth* (1970); Philip J. Greven, Jr., *Four*

Generations (1970); Christine Heyrman, *Commerce and Culture* (1984); Stephen Innes, *Labor in a New Land* (1983); Kenneth A. Lockridge, *A New England Town* (1970); Daniel Vickers, *Farmers and Fishermen* (1994); Michael Zuckerman, *Peaceable Kingdoms* (1970); (INDIANS) Russell Bourne, *The Red King's Rebellion* (1990); Jill Lepore, *The Name of War* (1998); Calvin Martin, *Keepers of the Game* (1978); Ian K. Steele, *Warpaths* (1994); Richard White, *The Middle Ground* (1991); (EMPIRE) Michael G. Hall, *Edward Randolph and the American Colonies* (1960); Richard R. Johnson, *Adjustment to Empire* (1981); (WITCHCRAFT) Paul Boyer and Stephen Nissenbaum, *Salem Possessed* (1974); John Demos, *Entertaining Satan* (1982); Carol F. Karlsen, *The Devil in the Shape of a Woman* (1987); Richard Weisman, *Witchcraft, Magic, and Religion in Seventeenth Century Massachusetts* (1984).

4

The Diverse Middle Colonies, 1624–1760

OVERVIEW   The Dutch established New Netherland in 1624, but forty years later the English captured this diverse, unstable colony and renamed it New York. That colony's political quarrels continued, as did its ethnic diversity. In 1681 William Penn founded Pennsylvania for the Quakers, who were joined by Germans and Scotch-Irish. Philadelphia became the most important city in the American colonies in the 1700s. New Jersey and Delaware were closely tied to New York and Pennsylvania, respectively.

THE DUTCH FOUND NEW NETHERLAND, 1624–1664

In 1624 the Dutch founded New Netherland, but few Hollanders wished to immigrate, and so in 1629 the Dutch adopted the patroon plan to settle the colony. This plan failed, and by the 1640s Governor Pieter Stuyvesant's colony held an increasingly diverse population of Dutch, English, Germans, Africans, Jews, Italians, French, and New Englanders.

THE DUTCH SEEK A FUR-TRADING COLONY, 1624–1647   In 1600 tiny Holland (also called the Netherlands) was one of the richest and most powerful countries in the world. Its wealth came from the hand manufacture of textiles and from worldwide trading and commerce. Dutch merchants' ships carried spices to European markets from the East Indies (Indonesia, which became a Dutch colony); shipped slaves from the African coast to the West Indies; and sent Dutch, French, and German textiles, knives, and other products throughout the world.

Wealthy Protestant merchants had long dominated Holland. In 1588 they ended the Catholic Spanish king's control over the northern Netherlands and established the Dutch Republic. For a time, the Protestant Dutch and English were allied against the Catholic French and Spanish, but the Dutch competed commercially against the English, and this rivalry grew during the 1600s.

After the English began to settle North America, the seafaring Dutch decided to found their own colonies. They were especially interested in trading European goods for Indian furs. Around 1614 the private Dutch East India Company built a fort at what became Albany, New York, to trade with the Mohawk, a tribe in the Iroquois confederation.

In 1624, using Henry Hudson's exploration of the Hudson River under Dutch sponsorship as the basis for their claim, the Dutch founded the colony of New Netherland on the site of what is now New York. The Hollanders knew that the English would not recognize this claim, so in drawing New Netherland's boundaries, they made the colony as large as possible to enhance their negotiating position with the English.

The Dutch West India Company planted their main colony on the lower tip of Manhattan Island at a place they called New Amsterdam (today, New York City). In 1625 they built a crude wooden fort that offered little protection against possible attack by an English fleet. Soon the Dutch decided to farm the whole of Manhattan Island, and in 1626 their leader, Pieter Minuit, bought the island from the local Indians for $24 worth of trading goods.

To capture the interior Indian fur trade, the Dutch built another settlement 140 miles up the Hudson River at the site of the previously established Fort Orange (today's Albany). Outposts were also constructed on the eastern tip of Long Island, on the western bank of the Connecticut River, and on the eastern shore of the Delaware River nearly opposite present-day Philadelphia.

THE DUTCH ADOPT THE PATROON PLAN, 1629   The Dutch realized that, unless their own people migrated to the colony, they would lose control of it. In 1629 the Dutch government authorized a plan for the colony that gave huge land grants to men called patroons. To keep ownership of the land, each patroon had to settle fifty Dutch immigrants within a few years. The immigrants would never gain the right to own their land but would remain tenants and pay a small annual rent to the patroon.

As it turned out, only one Dutchman ever met all the terms for establishing a patroonship. The Van Rensselaer family gained control of an area of more than one million acres near Albany. However, the manor, called Rensselaerswyck, limped along, much of its land remaining empty as tenants shrewdly realized that they could buy nearby land rather than remain as tenants. Nevertheless, the Van Rensselaers became a wealthy, powerful family through land sales and rent.

Despite the patroon plan, few Hollanders wanted to leave home, and the colony quickly gained a mixed population. Only half were Dutch. By 1643 the colony's 1,600 residents spoke eighteen languages among them. There were no churches, but seventeen taverns. Dutch and English merchants, especially in New Amsterdam, joined Jews, Scots, Italians, slaves from Africa, Huguenots (French Protestants) in Westchester County, Germans along the Hudson River, and New Englanders on eastern Long Island.

PIETER STUYVESANT GOVERNS NEW NETHERLAND, 1647–1664   In 1647 a one-legged military veteran named Pieter Stuyvesant arrived to become the

Pieter Stuyvesant, the canny, shrewd Dutch governor of New Netherland, was forced to surrender his colony to the English in 1664. (North Wind Picture Archives)

governor of New Netherland. A shrewd if ruthless politician, Stuyvesant both ignored the impractical instructions that he received from Holland and discouraged ethnic conflict. Against all logic, he declared that Lutheran services conformed with the Calvinist Dutch Reformed church, a policy that enabled the Germans to claim equality with the Dutch. He also allowed Jewish immigrants to remain, as long as they held religious services in their homes and not in a synagogue.

He even made border compromises with the New Englanders, who were known to be difficult negotiators. In the Hartford Treaty of 1650, Stuyvesant gave the New Englanders control of eastern Long Island, where they had already settled, and established Connecticut's present western boundary. Stuyvesant joined his New England rivals to fight a series of wars against their common foe, the Indians.

Fearing the colony's long-term insecurity, in 1655 Stuyvesant led an expedition to seize the Swedish and Finnish settlements on the Delaware River. He quickly incorporated them into New Netherland. The fur-seeking Swedes, caught up in the mania for American possessions like other Europeans, had first colonized that area at Fort Christina in 1638. They introduced the first log cabins.

THE ENGLISH ADD NEW YORK
TO THEIR EMPIRE, 1651–1750

Mercantilism led the English government to regulate colonial trade by means of several Navigation Acts. In a related move, in 1664 the English seized New Netherland and renamed it New York. There the English manor system created a wealthy, powerful elite, which the popular Jacob Leisler nearly toppled in 1689. From 1700 to 1750 New Yorkers quarreled in this ethnically diverse and politically fragmented colony. In 1734 the trial of the newspaper editor John Peter Zenger for libel established the precedent for a free press.

THE ENGLISH USE NAVIGATION ACTS TO REGULATE TRADE, 1651–1725   During the 1600s Europeans did not believe in free trade between nations. Instead, they thought that a country's prosperity depended upon controlling colonies and restricting access to markets. According to this system, called mercantilism, a mother country could best prosper by giving exclusive trading rights to colonies that produced a wide variety of raw materials. Government could use chartered monopolies, fixed prices, and quotas to bring power to bear upon economic activity, especially overseas trade.

In 1651 the English government under Cromwell passed the first of a series of Navigation Acts. This law required that American colonists trade only with English ships. To be considered English, not only did the ship have to fly an English flag—easy enough to change before arriving in port—but at least half the vessel's crew had to be English.

The restoration of Charles II (reigned 1660–1685) brought more Navigation Acts. In 1660 the law required the shipping trade to use only ships built either in England or in its colonies and crews three-fourths of whom were English. Colonists could market certain products, including tobacco and rice, only in England or in other English colonies. In 1663 the English government tried to stop smuggling by requiring European goods destined for America to be offloaded in England to pay duties. Ten years later duties were charged on some American exports.

In 1675 the English systematized the commercial and political regulation of the American colonies by establishing an agency, the Lords of Trade and Plantations, which sent officials to the colonies to monitor trade and to ensure payment of customs duties. This agency, however, proved inefficient, and in 1696 the last of the Navigation Acts created the Board of Trade to regulate the colonies' commerce. It functioned vigorously until 1725, when enforcement became lax.

THE ENGLISH CAPTURE NEW NETHERLAND, 1664   The Dutch and English battled to control both the world tobacco market and the African slave trade. The English hated New Netherland, sandwiched between New England and Virginia, and disliked the Dutch tendency to undercut English merchants by trading with England's American colonies at lower prices. The growing commercial rivalry between Holland and England led to a series of wars between the two countries.

In 1664 an English fleet sailed into the harbor at New Amsterdam and captured New Netherland without a shot. At the time, the population was about nine thousand, of whom two thousand were New Englanders. The English sought to win over the Dutch settlers by allowing them to practice their own religion and retain their property. King Charles II gave the colony to his brother the Duke of York, the future James II. In honor of the duke, the colony and its capital were renamed New York.

The English found New York difficult to digest. In 1673 the Dutch briefly recaptured the colony, but the English regained control the following year. Unlike New England with its fanatical Puritans and Virginia with its iron rule by the gentry, New York lacked a stabilizing focus. It was a colony destined to be dominated by quarrels.

English authorities did not seek to evict any of New York's mixed population. More English merchants did settle in New York City, which became largely English, but the area around Albany remained over-whelmingly Dutch, as did much of the Hudson River valley, and the fur trade remained in the hands of Dutch traders.

New Englanders who settled on Long Island and in Westchester County found the new English authorities scarcely more accommodating than the Dutch. The colony's proprietor, the Duke of York, sent a series of political hacks to govern the colony. These governors were autocrats who used their offices to gain as much wealth for themselves in as short a time as possible before retreating to the comforts of England. From 1664 to 1682 the Duke refused to allow New York's elected assembly to meet.

THE ENGLISH ADOPT THE MANOR SYSTEM   The only way to gain wealth in New York was by controlling land. The Dutch patroon system failed, but it inspired the English. Governors, their councils, and the elected assembly eventually established by the English adopted the Virginia practice of granting large acreages to themselves. The usual trick was to write the boundaries of the grants so vaguely that a later, friendly court might interpret what had at first appeared to be a grant of 2,000 acres to be a grant of 200,000 acres.

The English laid out a series of large estates, called manors, along the fertile banks of the Hudson River, especially on the eastern side. By 1703 five families held half the land between Albany and New York City. Land made the Schuylers, Livingstons, and Van Cortlandts the wealthiest and most powerful families in New York. By 1750 these large landholders formed a colonial elite second in wealth only to South Carolina's rice planters.

Although they tried to keep tenants on the land, landowners were freewheeling capitalists, a characteristic that became a hallmark of New York society, and were willing to sell land outright if that was more profitable. As long-term speculators, they kept enormous blocks of land off the market, thereby discouraging settlement, and in the end caused New York's economic development to fall behind that of other colonies. Discouraging newcomers, however, had the effect of preserving this elite's power.

The use of vague descriptions in land grants had another consequence. From the beginning, New York was awash in lawsuits. In many cases original grantees literally did not know what had been granted, and in other cases claims conflicted. The government sometimes gave the same land to two or more sets of people. Sales of land with clouded title to settlers only compounded the problem. Lawyers benefited handsomely. Courts showed little respect for evidence or justice and usually sided with the politically well connected.

JACOB LEISLER REBELS, **1689**   Many New Yorkers hated their government, dominated as it was by an appointed governor, an appointed council of wealthy and powerful land speculators, and a weak, tiny, elected assembly composed of the same sorts of people. New York's absorption into the Dominion of New England in 1688 did not make the government more popular. When James II was overthrown in England in 1688, some New Yorkers also feared that local officials would betray the colony to France, to which the Catholic James II had fled. Accordingly, colonists moved to replace their government.

In 1689, with support from German and Dutch farmers as well as a good many New York City laborers and merchants, a wealthy German merchant and intense Protestant named Jacob Leisler deposed Lieutenant Governor Francis Nicholson and declared himself the acting governor. Generally popular, he ruled for more than a year until, much to Leisler's surprise, an English officer arrived in 1691 and demanded his surrender. Leisler hesitated before capitulating, and the new governor, Colonel Henry Sloughter, found Leisler's tardy obedience treasonous.

The new government charged Leisler and seven supporters with treason, and they were convicted. Six were pardoned, but Leisler and his son-in-law were hanged, drawn, and quartered. Jeered at the public execution, Leisler warned his enemies that they would live to regret their actions.

Leisler's prophesy proved correct. Four years later Parliament pardoned Leisler and restored his confiscated property to his family. Thousands attended his reburial. For more than a generation the lingering bitterness over the execution of the popular Leisler dominated New York politics. In addition, the anti-Leislerians discovered that they not only lacked popular support but in time lost the influential friends in England who had made them powerful.

NEW YORKERS QUARREL, **1700–1750**   Throughout most of the 1700s, New York did not thrive. The colony's constant political bickering was not helped by a series of incompetent or corrupt governors. One, Lord Cornbury, was accused of transvestism, and another, Sir Danvers Osborn, hanged himself within a week of his arrival. A third, George Clarke, arrived poor and retired to England with a fortune of £100,000.

Other issues also produced tension. In 1733 John Peter Zenger established a new newspaper, the *Journal,* in opposition to the government-sponsored *Gazette.* A year later Governor William Cosby, long annoyed by Zenger's barbed attacks, ordered Zenger arrested for libel. The judge, whom Cosby controlled, disbarred Zenger's lawyers, and the desperate Zenger finally had to import a brilliant trial lawyer, Andrew Hamilton, from Philadelphia. Hamilton argued a new and important legal theory, namely that criticizing the governor was not libel so long as Zenger had told the truth. The jury acquitted Zenger and thereby established truth as a defense against the charge of libel, setting the precedent for a free press.

Slavery presented another troublesome situation. In 1741 New Yorkers discovered a plot by the city's many black slaves—nearly 20 percent of the city's total population of eleven thousand—to revolt against their white masters. Riding a wave of hysteria against the alleged slave plot, New York executed twenty-nine slaves and banished seventy others. In this quarrelsome and socially fragmented colony, slavery never seemed firmly established, and white New Yorkers gradually turned against the institution.

Clouded land titles, large landowners who refused to sell, and the resultant high prices discouraged people from settling in New York. Without interior settlement the marvelous port at New York City was largely a wasted asset. The city stagnated as Philadelphia grew far more rapidly.

MULTIETHNIC EXPERIMENTING IN PENNSYLVANIA, 1681–1760

In 1681 William Penn founded Pennsylvania as a refuge for Quakers. Members of this militantly pacifist sect were few, however, and the colony quickly became diverse with Germans and Scotch-Irish. A Quaker–German alliance long controlled Pennsylvania, which had lush farms that produced a high standard of living.

THE QUAKERS FOUND PENNSYLVANIA, **1681**   Quakers, a Protestant group more formally called the Society of Friends, founded and settled Pennsylvania. In 1681 a wealthy English Quaker named William Penn received from his friend and debtor King Charles II a charter for a new colony in North America. Penn became the colony's proprietor, a position that gave him great power and influence in Pennsylvania. The king named the colony for Penn's father, an admiral.

Penn planned his colony carefully in order to avoid the mistakes made in earlier settlements. To avoid disputes with other colonies, he had the boundaries surveyed. Carefully negotiating treaties with the various Indian tribes, including the friendly Lenni Lenape who lived in the Delaware River valley, Penn insisted that whites could settle only on land that he had purchased from the Indians. Showing great respect for native culture, Penn even learned the local Indian language in order to avoid interpreter's errors.

The founder of Pennsylvania, the Quaker William Penn, took the unusual position that the colonists should buy land from the Indians instead of merely seizing it. Penn signed treaties with a number of Indian tribes. These events have long fascinated American artists. (North Wind Picture Archives)

The founder placed the government in the hands of a governor (the proprietor's designated deputy), an elected assembly, and a council chosen by the assembly. The council sat as a court, and it also initiated all laws, which had to be ratified by the assembly. This structure failed, and in 1701 Penn's Charter of Privileges established a government with a weak governor, a powerful one-house legislature, and a strictly advisory council. Political bickering, however, continued.

THE SOCIETY OF FRIENDS SEEKS INNER LIGHT   Penn thought of his colony primarily as a refuge for English Quakers, who had suffered from much religious persecution in England. This sect, founded by George Fox during the English civil war in the 1640s, rejected the formal, hierarchical religion of the Church of England but also opposed the gloomy Calvinism of New England's Puritans. To the Quakers salvation came from an inner light, and religious conversion was mostly an individual experience. This particular doctrine led to the sect's tolerance of outsiders, to diverse practices within the group, and to their tendency toward pacifism.

Quakers rejected family hierarchy, holding all members equal before God. Because men and women were spiritually equal, the sect recognized female preachers. Family life was child centered, and family members

The Society of Friends, founded in England, was among the first religious groups to allow women to preach. Quakers, as they were usually called, also insisted upon plain, undecorated gray clothing. (North Wind Picture Archives)

took meals together. Quakers stressed the work ethic, dressed simply in gray, kept austere houses, and ate plain food. In the eyes of others their very simplicity was a form of ostentatious display.

Other practices annoyed their neighbors too. Quakers refused to bow, kneel, or take off their hats in the presence of their social betters. Quakers insisted on using *thee* and *thou* instead of *you*, a term they believed to imply spiritual inequality. They declined to swear oaths in court and refused to bear arms. In England their pacifism often landed them in jail.

PENNSYLVANIA SHOWS ETHNIC DIVERSITY   Penn recognized that the Quakers were not numerous enough to populate an entire colony. To attract other settlers, he promised that Pennsylvanians would pay no taxes to a state church and could worship with few restrictions.

The colony was begun in 1682 with the arrival of two thousand Quakers personally led by William Penn, but only in the beginning were Quakers a majority, and their proportion of the population constantly declined with further immigration. Mainly from England's northern Midlands, the Quakers were joined by other English immigrants as well as by people from Germany, Wales, Scotland, and Ireland.

By 1755 Pennsylvania was 42 percent German, 28 percent English or Welsh, and 28 percent Scotch-Irish. Despite this polyglot population, or perhaps because of it, the Quakers remained influential beyond their numbers. Until the American Revolution they dominated Pennsylvania society, politics, and business.

Quaker control was based on an alliance with Pennsylvania's large German community. The first Germans settled in 1683 at Germantown (now within Philadelphia). They not only farmed but also engaged in crafts, which thrived in a colony blessed with the timber, iron ore, and coal important to heavy industry. Germans preserved their culture by the early establishment of a printing press at Germantown.

In the early 1700s tens of thousands of Protestant Germans migrated to the colony. Some were Lutherans, but many belonged to small Protestant religious denominations that were persecuted in Germany. Their English neighbors called them the Pennsylvania Dutch, a corruption of *Deutsch*, the German word for "German"; they had nothing to do with Holland. The Pennsylvania Dutch included Calvinists; Moravians, who founded a large colony at Bethlehem; Mennonites, who preached pacifism; the Amish, who clung to tradition; and Dunkers, who baptized by immersion.

Most were farmers, but they avoided the frontier. Instead, they bought out pioneer farms and then greatly improved these farmsteads. Occupying the best land in southeastern Pennsylvania, they became famous for neat farms, large barns, productive orchards, molasses-based shoofly pie, a certain stinginess, and a crabbed suspicion of outsiders. They had little interest in politics, often quarreled among themselves, and stubbornly clung to the German language.

SCOTCH-IRISH SETTLE THE FRONTIER   The other large immigrant group were Scotch-Irish Presbyterians from northern Ireland. More than 100,000 Ulster Protestants emigrated (one-seventh of Ulster's total population), mostly between 1750 and 1800. Disdainful of the Quakers and the Pennsylvania Dutch, they usually headed for the frontier, which they came to dominate not only in Pennsylvania but also in Virginia and the Carolinas.

Scotch-Irish culture stressed hard drinking, a warrior's ethic of physical courage, egalitarianism within a system of masculine domination, and the preeminence of the extended family as a clan. Rowdy and raucous, they hated Indians, explored the wilderness, lived off wild game, distilled whiskey, cut trees to make farms, and then floated the timber downstream to market. Many remained poor backcountry farmers for generations.

The Scotch-Irish had an eye for the main chance, frequently went into business, and quickly took to politics, where they became the main rivals of the Quaker–German alliance. During the American Revolution the Scotch-Irish were intensely patriotic and with the American victory gained political control of Pennsylvania, which they kept for generations.

The arrival of large numbers of immigrants destroyed Penn's policy of harmonious relations with Indians. For one thing, these new white settlers often neglected to buy land. They became "squatters," as they were called, and simply occupied whatever frontier space that they wished. During the mid-1700s, as immigrants encroached on native lands, the Indians resisted with increasing violence.

PENNSYLVANIA AS THE BEST POOR MAN'S COUNTRY   Although settled late, Pennsylvania proved remarkably successful during the 1700s. William Penn's policies provided a firm foundation. Religious toleration encouraged the migration of clannish groups who were as devoted to hard work and thrift as to piety. Penn's generous land policies, which eventually bankrupted Penn and put him in debtors' prison, made land readily available to settlers and discouraged large-scale speculation. Penn's policy of buying land from the Indians instead of merely taking it reduced military expenses and led families to take up isolated farms scattered across the countryside.

Farmland within fifty miles of Philadelphia was unusually rich and productive, by far the best land for general agriculture along the Atlantic seaboard. The soil was better and the growing season longer than in New England. Winter feed for animals such as horses and cows was minimal, while the hot summers were shorter, more healthful, and more bearable than further south.

Even small farms yielded bountiful crops, which led Pennsylvanians to be well fed. Living standards in the middle colonies were about 40 percent above the average for all the American colonies, ranking considerably above the South and more than double the level in New England, then the poorest region. Overall, Americans enjoyed a standard of living higher than Scotland's or Ireland's and similar to England's.

Because this lush agricultural area lay close to Philadelphia, farmers easily sold their surplus in that city's public market, which grew to occupy five blocks under a covered roof along Market Street. One could buy fresh meat, fish, and produce, as well as clothing, imported clocks, and other luxury goods.

In addition, Pennsylvania exported wheat, beef, pork, and lumber to the West Indies. In the 1750s Americans built, owned, and operated one-third of the ships sailing under the British flag; by 1770 Philadelphia ranked as the second busiest port in the British Empire, behind London.

PHILADELPHIA GROWS AND PROSPERS, 1682–1760

William Penn carefully planned Philadelphia, and his ideas influenced later American cities. During the 1700s this boomtown became the second most populous English-speaking city in the world. Its leading citizen was Benjamin Franklin. Although merchants prospered, laborers, including those with skills, often did not. Many arrived as indentured servants as signs of poverty increased. The Quakers turned against slavery, but free blacks faced harsh discrimination, and women fared poorly.

PHILADELPHIA AS A PLANNED CITY   From the beginning William Penn's colony was dominated by Philadelphia, America's first planned city. In 1682 Penn carefully picked the site between the Delaware and Schuylkill Rivers. He hired a surveyor to lay out a town that was two miles in each direction, with broad, straight streets at regular intervals. Two exceptionally wide streets, Market and Broad, crossed at a square at the center, while each of the city's four sections also held major squares.

The grid concept became a model for most later American cities. Even New York, founded with narrow, twisted streets, eventually adopted a grid that covered Manhattan Island. So did later cities, such as flat Chicago, Salt Lake City, Denver, Phoenix, and Miami, and, improbably, hilly San Francisco and Seattle.

Philadelphia's large blocks enabled householders to combine the advantages of both urban and rural life by having deep lots with gardens, chickens, and fruit trees. Despite the plan, Penn's settlement grew mostly along the Delaware River, where good drinking water could be readily obtained and where ocean-going ships could easily dock.

To prevent a fire like the one that had destroyed most of London in 1666, Philadelphians built houses and shops of brick. Tall, narrow, and deep, most buildings contained a basement with storage, a ground floor with a shop in front and a living area behind, two upper floors with rooms rented to boarders, and an attic for servants.

CULTURE AND SCIENCE FLOURISH IN PHILADELPHIA   Although founded much later than Boston or New York, Philadelphia grew rapidly during the 1700s, becoming the most populous city in America by the 1760s, by which time it had about 25,000 people. Philadelphia was then probably second only to London in population in the English-speaking world. The city's rich agricultural hinterland provided an unrivaled supply of cheap, plentiful food.

Philadelphia's culture owed much to its most famous resident, Benjamin Franklin. This native Bostonian and former runaway apprentice made his fortune as a printer and retired at age forty-two. Turning to invention and public service, he invented the Franklin stove and bifocal lenses, tested for electricity with a kite, and founded the first property insurance company and the first volunteer fire department.

·He also helped start a private lending library, which became the basis for the idea of a public library; set up a debating club called Franklin's Junto; and organized the American Philosophical Society, which gave the city intellectual prestige, sponsored scientific experiments, and published the results.

Franklin's city was also home to David Rittenhouse, a self-taught astronomer, who invented the orrery, a wooden model that showed how the moon revolved around the earth as the earth revolved around the sun. Newspapers, pamphlets, and almanacs—including Franklin's witty *Poor Richard's Almanac*, which became America's first self-help book—made Philadelphia an important early publishing center.

The Quakers established free schools so that even poor children could get an education. Like the Puritans, the Quakers expected people to read the Bible. Unlike the Puritans, however, the Quakers had uneducated lay ministers and believed that higher education was unnecessary to preaching, a hindrance to getting the inner light, and destructive of good business habits. Other Philadelphians established the University of Pennsylvania and a medical school.

DIFFERENCES IN WEALTH GROW   Although Philadelphia thrived throughout the colonial era, as evidenced by its rapid population growth, not everyone shared the prosperity. At the top of society, wealthy Quaker merchants did well; they devised business networks of trustworthy fellow Quakers both in England and in other colonies. Merchants also profited from local real estate speculation. Just 10 percent of the populace owned more than half the city's property.

Craftsmen and other skilled workers had mixed experiences. Some, like Ben Franklin, became self-employed as masters and gained fortunes. Others became master craftsmen, went bankrupt, and had to seek work as journeymen, that is, employees. Although most apprentices still expected that they would complete the journeyman stage and eventually become masters, the odds of success declined after 1760.

Unskilled laborers were usually hired in the morning for one day's work. If a man could not find work after a few days, he was likely to leave

Philadelphia and seek his fortune elsewhere. Laborers did not prosper, but so few stayed in Philadelphia that their lack of success made little impact on the city.

INDENTURED SERVANTS ARRIVE   During the colonial period many residents of both Philadelphia and the rest of Pennsylvania were indentured servants. These servants, unlike Virginia's single indentured males in the 1600s, often arrived in family groups. Perhaps one-third of the arriving Germans immigrated this way. By 1729 about one-fifth of Philadelphia's workforce consisted of indentured servants.

Men and women who wanted to migrate to North America were often too poor to pay the passage. Some ship captains transported people in exchange for the right to sell the person's labor upon arrival. Usually, these immigrants were teenagers or young adults who were bound as servants for four to seven years.

They were generally not taught trades, and they ended their service as unskilled laborers or servants. About 10 percent successfully ran away. After completing their service, many moved to rural areas. Of those who immigrated to Pennsylvania during the early years, about one-third eventually became landowners.

Over time, the number of indentured servants declined. In the 1770s such servants made up only 11 percent of the Philadelphia workforce. Servants who came in these later years fared poorly. Within twenty years of finishing their service, almost half ended up on public assistance—a rate four times that of the population as a whole.

From 1730 to 1753, booming Philadelphia had little poverty, with fewer than 1 percent of the city's residents considered poor. Labor shortages led to a growing use of indentured servants. The poor enjoyed cheap food and housing—rent was often only 5 percent of income—but firewood became increasingly expensive because it had to be brought from greater and greater distances. The preferred wood was walnut, which made a hot fire with little effort.

By the 1760s, when poverty clearly had increased in Philadelphia and other American cities, private charitable assistance and taxes to aid the poor rose substantially. Urban poverty, however, remained rare because more than 90 percent of Americans lived on farms. Fewer than 5 percent of the country's populace lived in the five largest cities: Philadelphia, New York, Boston, Charleston, South Carolina, and Newport, Rhode Island.

DIVERSITY INCREASES   Like other ports, Philadelphia attracted sailors, who came from many nations and shared a common language of the sea. Risking their lives on long, dangerous voyages that often lasted many months, they came into port to unwind and to boast of their adventures, bringing both salty talk and curiosities from every part of the world, as well as a little money in search of liquor and women. Jack Tars, as they were called, kept the city from being dull.

Philadelphia also had a number of black slaves. In 1729 they made up about one-fifth of the workforce; most were house servants or unskilled laborers. In 1758 the Quakers' yearly meeting agreed to oppose slavery, and wealthy Quaker merchants eventually freed their slaves. Free blacks in colonial Philadelphia found few occupations other than servant or laborer open to them, however; the newly freed blacks usually remained servants. By the 1770s the number of slaves in the workforce had declined to 5 percent.

Women lived and worked in their own sphere, marrying, raising children, cooking, cleaning, and sewing clothes. They were not taught male trades. Widows faced difficulties, since only a handful could earn enough money through their labor to support a family. A few lucky widows operated businesses left behind by their husbands. There were female printers and tavernkeepers, but all were widows, and the businesses eventually passed into the hands of sons. Many widows remarried as quickly as possible. Others ended up living on the charity of relatives or made their way to the poorhouse.

FOUNDING THE OTHER MIDDLE COLONIES

In 1664 the Duke of York carved New Jersey out of New York without informing the governor of New York. The result produced so much confusion that for a long time New Jersey was split into East Jersey and West Jersey and reunited only in 1702. Delaware fell under the control of William Penn, who recognized it as a separate colony in 1704.

CARVING NEW JERSEY OUT OF NEW YORK, **1664**   New Jersey, originally part of New Netherland, became an English colony in 1664 when the Duke of York named two followers, Sir George Carteret and John, Lord Berkeley, as its proprietors. Sharing characteristics with both New York and Pennsylvania, New Jersey was trapped between its two more prominent neighbors. It lacked a good harbor and a major city, which weakened its sense of identity.

Unfortunately for Berkeley and Carteret, the governor of New York— who incorrectly assumed that New Jersey was still part of his province— granted land west of the Hudson River to New Englanders. He also promised them a representative assembly. Amid this confusion, neither

Berkeley nor Carteret made much money, and in 1674 Berkeley's share in the colony passed to the Quakers. In 1676 the dispute among the proprietors caused New Jersey to be split formally into two colonies, East Jersey and West Jersey. They were reunited in 1702 as a single royal colony.

East Jersey, the northeastern portion adjacent to New York, had a polyglot population like the one on the other side of the Hudson River. New Englanders, who had a habit of multiplying and spreading in all directions, made several important settlements, including one at New Ark (Newark). To produce ministers, they founded a college at Princeton.

East Jersey's politics were so controlled by New York that the local residents were relieved when the two Jerseys were rejoined to form a more vigorous, independent colony. From 1702 to 1738 the royal governor of New York was also commissioned separately as the royal governor of New Jersey.

West Jersey, the southwestern portion nearest to Philadelphia, was long dominated by Quaker settlers at Burlington, who had arrived in 1677. The Quakers retained their local influence longer in that area than in Pennsylvania.

Much of New Jersey had a poor, marshy, and sandy soil little suited to cultivation—the later famous cranberry bogs. Settlers preferred Pennsylvania's better land, and New Jersey remained sparsely populated by poor farmers.

DELAWARE BECOMES INDEPENDENT OF PENNSYLVANIA, 1704   Delaware, a tiny colony just below Philadelphia, was originally part of New Sweden and then of New Netherland, becoming part of New York in 1664. Because of its small size and generally poor soil, which made it unattractive to land speculators, Delaware quickly fell under the influence of neighboring William Penn. He gained control in 1682 and recognized it as a separate colony in 1704.

Until the American Revolution the governor of Pennsylvania served as the governor of Delaware. Because Delaware had never been technically annexed to Pennsylvania, during the Revolution Delaware escaped Pennsylvania's domination and reasserted its separate status.

CONCLUSION

Unlike the plantation South or religious New England, no single group or idea prevailed in the middle colonies. In both New York and Pennsylvania, ethnic diversity produced disputes about core values, making strong, stable government difficult. Bitter party politics prevailed in these two colonies. New York's quarrels, painfully illustrated by Jacob Leisler's execution, both reflected and reinforced the wealthy manor elite's control. Often politically weak and unstable, this elite nevertheless ran the colony as it pleased. Pennsylvania settled for the gentler if less effective solution of giving little power to the government.

New York's land policies, in particular, retarded development and kept New York City poor and sleepy. Philadelphia benefited from Penn's policies as well as from a rich agricultural hinterland that supplied the city with cheap food and provided commodities for export. The integration of agriculture into the commercial economy and the increasing importance of Philadelphia as a world port inside the growing British Empire marked the beginning of sophisticated economic development. By 1760 Americans engaged in such activities showed an increasing unwillingness to be governed from London. They were no longer rude, primitive colonists who automatically did the mother country's bidding.

Recommended Readings

DOCUMENTS: Daniel Horsmanden, *The New York Conspiracy* [1744] (1971); Peter Kalm, *Travels* [1750] (2 vols., 1937).

READINGS: (GENERAL) Patricia U. Bonomi, *Under the Cope of Heaven* (rev. ed., 2003); Jack P. Greene, *Pursuits of Happiness* (1988); John J. McCusker and Russell R. Menard, *The Economy of British America, 1607–1789* (2nd ed., 1991); Gary B. Nash, *Red, White, and Black* (4th ed., 2000) and *The Urban Crucible* (1979); Marcus Rediker, *Between the Devil and the Deep Blue Sea* (1987); Alan Tully, *Forming American Politics* (1994); (NEW YORK) Patricia U. Bonomi, *A Factious People* (1971); Joyce D. Goodfriend, *Before the Melting Pot* (1992); Stanley N. Katz, *Newcastle's New York* (1968); Donna Merwick, *Possessing Albany, 1630–1710* (1990); Daniel K. Richter, *The Ordeal of the Longhouse* (1992); Oliver A. Rink, *Holland on the Hudson* (1986); Robert C. Ritchie, *The Duke's Province* (1977); (PENNSYLVANIA) David H. Fischer, *Albion's Seed* (1989); James T. Lemon, *The Best Poor Man's Country* (1972); Barry Levy, *Quakers and the American Family* (1988); Sharon V. Salinger, *To Serve Well and Faithfully* (1987); Sally Schwartz, *A Mixed Multitude* (1987); Billy G. Smith, *The Lower Sort* (1990); Stephanie G. Wolf, *Urban Village* (1976); (IMMIGRATION) Bernard Bailyn, *Voyagers to the West* (1986); J. M. Bumsted, *The People's Clearances* (1982); Jon Butler, *The Huguenots in America* (1983); Ned Landsman, *Scotland and Its First American Colony* (1985); A. G. Roeber, *Palatines, Liberty, and Property* (1993).

5

The American Revolution, 1750–1783

OVERVIEW   From 1750 to 1763, the American colonists, satisfied with the British Empire, helped drive the French out of North America. To pay for that war, the British Parliament then imposed taxes in the form of the Sugar Act (1764), the Stamp Act (1765), the Townshend Acts (1767), and the Tea Act (1773). The colonists rebelled. Their most dramatic protest, the Boston Tea Party, prompted the British to punish Massachusetts with the Coercive Acts (1774), which led to war in 1775. A year later the Americans declared independence. Financing the war proved even more difficult for the Americans than raising an army. The British won many battles but lost two armies, one at Saratoga in 1777 and the other at Yorktown in 1781. Britain recognized American independence in 1783.

AMERICANS HELP MAINTAIN THE
BRITISH EMPIRE, 1750–1763

In 1750 the American colonies belonged to the British Empire, prospered commercially, and grew rapidly in population. The colonists, protective of their liberty and wary of concentrated political power, developed a democratic politics based on English Whig principles. The colonists hated Britain's rivals, the French, and joined Britain in war against them in 1754. During the war, George Washington learned a military tactic that would later help him defeat the British in the Revolutionary War. In 1763 Britain won and, to Americans' relief, acquired French Canada. Britain's subsequent attempts to force the colonists to help pay for the war set the stage for the revolution.

THE COLONIES IN 1750   By 1750 nearly one and a half million Americans lived along the seacoast in thirteen English colonies from Maine (then part of Massachusetts) to Georgia. About one-fifth were slaves of African descent. Another one-sixth were white servants indentured to labor for terms as long as to seven years in return for payment of their passage.

Although economic growth had been slow and life hard during the 1600s and early 1700s, the years after 1730 had brought both increased immigration and greater prosperity. Americans then enjoyed the fastest economic growth of any society in the world.

The population doubled every twenty-two years, with a high birth rate, a relatively low death rate, and continued immigration. Half to two-thirds of the growth came from natural increase. Benjamin Franklin shrewdly calculated that in the next century the colonies would have more people than England. In the long run English control appeared doubtful. In 1750, however, no one expressed such doubts.

The composition of the population was also changing. Whereas in the 1600s most immigrants to mainland British North America were English, of the roughly 600,000 who arrived from 1700 to 1775, half were African, nearly a quarter were Scots or Irish, and one-seventh were German.

The British Empire was increasing in size, wealth, and prestige, with opportunities for commerce and trade expanding on a global scale. As part of the empire, the colonists shared in its benefits. Americans already supplied it with numerous raw materials, raising grain and horses or cutting timber for sale to the West Indies. In time America, too, promised to become a major market.

Thanks to Indian corn, food was cheap and plentiful in America. The colonists also found land and timber for housing easy to come by. Skilled laborers usually worked for high wages, but the picture was not entirely rosy; the poor were likely to remain poor.

Table 5.1   Estimated Immigration to British North America, 1700–1775

Africa	300,000	Scotland	35,000
Germany	85,000	England	45,000
Northern Ireland	65,000	Wales	30,000
Southern Ireland	42,000	Other places	6,000
TOTAL	608,000		

Immigrants looked for opportunities for their children. In England a rigid social class system limited the prospects of a poor man's son. In many parts of America, education was more readily available than in England, and throughout the colonies a poor boy had a better chance than in England to gain an apprenticeship to a trade without paying a fee.

AMERICA IS RIPE FOR SELF-GOVERNMENT   In each colony the most powerful person was the governor. While Connecticut and Rhode Island retained ancient charters that allowed the settlers to elect the governor, by 1750 the king appointed the governor in all of the other colonies. A governor, in turn, named officials, controlled the military, and spent legislative appropriations as well as funds provided by Britain. Although a governor had an absolute veto on legislation, he could find himself in political trouble if he ignored public opinion. Increasingly, Americans looked to self-government.

White male Americans enjoyed more actual political rights than their English or European counterparts. Although in both England and America a man could vote only if he owned property, the colonists found it easier to gain the small amount of real estate needed to qualify. In most colonies a majority of the adult white males could vote, but in England fewer than 10 percent were eligible.

In England both the poor and the middle class were dominated by a wealthy, landholding aristocracy. Dukes, earls, and lords had titles, special privileges, and great wealth. Nobles and knights, who had inherited both titles and money, had little reason to migrate to America. Almost none did.

America lacked titled nobles and, as a new country, had little inherited wealth. Indeed, only a handful of colonists, mostly a few landed families in New York and rice growers in South Carolina, had truly great wealth. Even George Washington, reputed to be the richest American at one point, lived in a relatively modest wooden house, not an ornate stone palace like Versailles.

The colonial middle class—mainly owners of small farms, self-employed craftsmen, and storekeepers—felt much closer to the wealthy, and, indeed, many of the newly rich in America had been born middle class. From the viewpoint of an English duke, colonial society lacked the leadership provided by aristocrats. From the viewpoint of a colonist, America offered a unique possibility for ordinary people to develop their own political leadership.

AMERICANS ADOPT WHIG POLITICAL IDEAS   Throughout the 1700s both Americans and Europeans embraced the Enlightenment, a widespread philosophical movement characterized by a devotion to reason, including science; by a desire to promote learning, including mass education; by an

insistence upon testing ideas concretely and empirically; and by a growing skepticism toward religion. In America Benjamin Franklin, a man
both practical and philosophical, epitomized the Enlightenment, as did
Thomas Jefferson and John Adams.

As part of the Enlightenment's emphasis on the dispassionate exploration of ideas, both the British and Americans discussed the nature of a
just government. Much of this discussion grew out of a general acceptance
of the English philosopher John Locke's theory that people came together
under a compact of their own making to create a government. All government, in this view, was based on natural law, that is, on certain rights that
all human beings share. This concept of rights led most English-speaking
people on both sides of the Atlantic to conclude that government must be
based on the rule of law; otherwise, rulers would trample on rights and become tyrants.

They also agreed that power led to corruption, and they sought to establish a mixed political system in which power was not concentrated but
diffuse. In particular, they sought to maintain checks and balances, even
though executive, legislative, and judicial powers were not separate.

In Britain, especially after the Glorious Revolution of 1688, power was
shared among the king, Parliament, and the courts, which became increasingly independent. In the colonies power was shared by the governors (appointed by the king's government), governor's councils (usually
appointed by the governor), legislative assemblies (elected), and local
courts (appointed).

Some Englishmen, however, worried that, even with built-in safe-
guards, the political system favored the rich and powerful—especially the
king and the aristocrats. Warning their countrymen that they must be ever
vigilant lest the government stamp out the liberties of the people, these
Englishmen, many of whom, ironically, were aristocrats, called themselves Whigs.

Not everyone in England agreed with the Whigs. For one thing, some
people pointed out, too much liberty could lead to disorder—even to civil
war. The purpose of government was to maintain order, and everyone
owed allegiance to the government. This allegiance prevented disorder. In
this view the king and especially the Church of England symbolized
proper order. These Englishmen, among whom were many wealthy merchants and powerful rural gentry disinclined toward change, called themselves Tories.

Most Americans were Whigs. Indeed, in a new country where change
was common, few people feared disorder. Instead, Americans became ob-
sessed with liberty. They took to heart such English Radical Whigs as John
Trenchard and Thomas Gordon, who, in *Cato's Letters* (1720), warned that,

unless people were vigilant, a corrupt government would trample on people's liberties. Long before the American Revolution, Americans had adopted this position.

Widespread property ownership and voting, the absence of a wealthy aristocracy, and the fluid nature of a rapidly changing society also gradually led Americans to accept the idea of equality. In the 1700s equality did not mean that the wealth should be shared, nor did it mean that each person should have an equal opportunity. Equality meant that the same law applied to all people—or at least to all adult white males. The colonists did not consider slaves or Indians equal, and in 1750 few would have argued that the concept applied to free blacks or women. Generations would pass before the idea of equality would be expanded to mean equal opportunity for everyone.

FIGHTING THE FRENCH AND INDIAN WAR, 1754–1763   In the mid-1700s Britain's empire had a great rival: France, which also had an empire, including the important colony of New France (today's Canada). French control extended west to the Great Lakes and south down the Mississippi River valley, which Robert Cavelier, sieur de La Salle, had explored and claimed for France in 1682.

In the early 1700s the French traded furs with Indians on the frontier and started slave-worked sugar plantations along the lower Mississippi River. Slaves built impressive levees along the river to prevent fields from flooding. The French founded New Orleans in 1718, and the city developed a Creole culture of mixed French, African, and West Indian influences. In 1755 the British expelled French-speaking Acadians from Nova Scotia; they relocated in Louisiana, where they became known as Cajuns.

Both the French and the British wished to crush each other's empires and to take valuable colonies. The two countries were at war from 1689 to 1697, from 1702 to 1713, and from 1744 to 1748. In America, these wars retarded frontier settlement, driving up land prices and worsening Indian–white relations (since both sides used Indians to attack colonists).

The British believed that New France threatened the British colonies along the North American seaboard. The French had cultivated good relations with many tribes both to gain beaver skins for the fur trade and to join the Indians in attacking English frontier settlements. Especially in New England, which was geographically closest to New France, the colonists feared the French and clung to England's protection.

The settlers' views were echoed by land speculators both in England and in the colonies. Land grants were of uncertain or little value if they could not be sold, and few people wanted to buy property that was likely to become a battleground the next time Britain and France went to war.

In 1754 Britain and France did go to war again in North America. Two years later the war spread to Europe. In most of the world the war was called the Seven Years' War (even though it lasted nine years), but in England's American colonies it became known as the French and Indian War.

Because the British navy controlled the Atlantic Ocean, the American colonies did not face a French threat from the sea. Instead, the French and their Indian allies attacked interior frontier areas with sudden, violent surprise.

The British and the colonists agreed that these raids must cease and that the only way to guarantee peace on the frontier was to remove the French permanently from North America. The British supplied the officers, some of the soldiers, and heavy weapons. The Americans provided armed men and food.

That same year, 1754, colonial leaders met at Albany, New York, to consider defense matters, including a possible coordinated attack on Canada. Nothing came of that scheme. They also discussed a Plan of Union, presented by Benjamin Franklin. Neither the colonies nor British authorities, however, wanted a single, unified American government, and the idea died.

In 1755 an expedition under Britain's General Edward Braddock marched through the woods to take France's Fort Duquesne (later renamed Fort Pitt by the English; today, Pittsburgh). At the Battle of the Wilderness, the French surprised and defeated the British. Although Braddock's soldiers maintained impressive discipline, the French fought Indian-style by shooting from behind the trees. Braddock died from wounds received in this battle. His aide, George Washington, observed the superiority of French methods.

After the French had repulsed attacks against New France, a British army in 1759 defeated the French on the Plains of Abraham at Québec city in New France. The commanding generals of both sides were killed in the battle. In 1760 the British took Montréal and gained control of all New France.

THE BRITISH WIN THE WAR, 1763   In 1763, when Britain and France made peace, the British held a strong negotiating position. They demanded and got New France, which they renamed Canada. The numerous French settlers were allowed to remain in Canada under British rule.

Settlers in the American colonies celebrated, especially in New England. The French threat had been permanently removed. Indian–white relations promised to be more stable and the frontier made safe for settlement; land speculators looked forward to profits. The British, however,

In 1755 the French and their Indian allies defeated the British, led by General Edward Braddock, at the Battle of the Wilderness. (Brown Brothers)

looked at matters somewhat differently. The French threat had encouraged the British to treat the colonies well, and over the years they had humored the colonists in many small ways. Now that that threat had been removed, the British expected the Americans to show their gratitude by helping their mother country in two major ways.

First, the war had been very expensive, doubling Britain's national debt. British taxpayers, including wealthy aristocrats, resisted further tax increases. Taxes in the colonies were low; surely, thought the English, the colonists should pay a portion of the cost of a war that had benefited them so much.

Second, there were the Indians. English frontier settlers had constantly battled Indians, and this problem did not end with the war. From 1763 to 1766 Pontiac's Rebellion swept across western Pennsylvania, Maryland, and Virginia. After Pontiac, the chief of the Ottawa, failed to take key British strongholds at Detroit and Fort Pitt, he signed a peace treaty.

Threats of Indian attack had forced the British to post a very expensive army on the frontier. Without the French threat, the English saw no need for a large frontier army. If the Indians could be placated, then the army could be withdrawn. The natives would be peaceful, thought the English, without French guns and without American settlers encroaching on their territory.

In 1763 the British government issued a proclamation that prohibited frontier settlement beyond the ridge of the Appalachian Mountains. Americans reacted with anger and disbelief; some settlers already lived beyond the proclamation line, and many land speculators saw their dreams of fortune evaporate. Besides, America's population was growing rapidly, and how could the increase be provided for within the coastal area left for settlement?

The French and Indian War changed the map of North America. It also changed the political relationship between Britain and the American colonies. Instead of the beginning of a long peace, the end of the war heralded a new age of strife. Seldom has a peace failed so utterly.

THE MOTHER COUNTRY ABUSES
HER CHILDREN, 1764–1774

The British Parliament passed a series of acts to tax the colonists to help pay for the French and Indian War. After the Sugar Act (1764) raised little revenue, Parliament passed the Stamp Act (1765). The colonists rebelled. Benjamin Franklin explained that Americans would pay import duties on goods they bought but not general taxes levied by a Parliament in which they were not represented. Contrary to Franklin's argument, Parliament's Townshend Acts (1767) found Americans unwilling to pay even import duties. The Tea Act (1773) led to the Boston Tea Party, for which Parliament punished Massachusetts with the Coercive Acts (1774).

LAWS ABOUT SUGAR, CURRENCY, AND QUARTERING, **1764–1765**   In 1764 the British Parliament decided to tax the American colonies. Actually, some small taxes had been levied for years in the form of import duties. The amounts were minor, wealthy merchants mainly paid them, and smugglers frequently evaded them.

The Sugar Act (1764), which covered many items in addition to sugar, reduced duties for some goods, increased charges for others, and extended levies to a number of items. To make sure that these duties were paid, Parliament authorized the appointment of many new customs officials and provided for disputes to be sent to special British admiralty courts that did not use juries. (American juries had routinely declined to convict smugglers.)

In another sign of meddling, Parliament passed the Currency Act (1764), which restricted the ability of the American colonies to issue paper money. Because the colonies always ran short of gold and silver, they had long used paper money to supply the credit necessary to keep commerce alive. This measure worsened a postwar depression.

A third measure, the Quartering Act (1765), required the colonies to provide barracks and provisions for the thousands of British soldiers stationed in America. If the colonies did not provide barracks, the law allowed soldiers to use inns or vacant buildings, including barns. New York's assembly defied the law, and Parliament ordered it to comply or be dissolved.

THE STAMP ACT OUTRAGES THE COLONISTS, 1765 The British government found that, due to widespread smuggling, the Sugar Act's import duties were raising little money. So Parliament looked for a way to gain additional revenue from a broad-based tax. A stamp tax seemed the answer. England already had such a tax, and Parliament reasoned that the colonists should not object to any tax also levied in the mother country.

The Stamp Act (1765) required all colonial court papers, deeds, licenses, pamphlets, or newspapers to be stamped by a government official for a small fee. This measure showed no political sensitivity; it affected most colonists, regardless of class, and its impact on licensed taverns and newspapers guaranteed a noisy response. The colonists reacted with outrage to the Stamp Act and to the changes in the enforcement of import duties.

The truth was that Americans hated taxes. This hatred, a peculiarly American idea, was rooted both in practice and in theory. In a new country built largely on credit, it was difficult to find the cash to pay taxes. More important, Americans, drawing on popular Whig ideas about power, concluded that the Stamp Act was part of a scheme to deprive Americans of their liberty. Americans were afraid that, if the British had the power to tax, the power of elected colonial assemblies would weaken and the power of appointed royal governors would increase.

In May 1765, a young Virginia legislator named Patrick Henry introduced resolutions declaring that only the elected House of Burgesses could tax Virginians. Speaking for the Virginia Resolves, as the resolutions were called, Henry, it was said, compared George III to Caesar and Charles I (who had been beheaded). Shouts of "Treason!" led Henry to reply, "If *this* be treason, make the most of it."

When British officials in America tried to enforce the duties and the new stamp law, they were met with smuggling and defiance. To oppose British policy, Americans, including many wealthy merchants, created a secret organization called the Sons of Liberty. In the larger towns the Sons of Liberty forced officials to swear that they would not enforce these laws. Crowd action in the streets marked a new kind of politics; officials who held the public in contempt soon learned that ignoring mobs could be expensive in terms of broken windows and ransacked stores.

Printed propaganda from ever more plentiful presses also became important in shaping issues, in rallying opinion, and in organizing protests. Single-sheet broadsides posted on walls announced meetings and denounced enemies, while pamphlets and newspapers presented longer, rational political arguments. Collectively, these activities tended to ridicule and weaken British authority.

Newspapers defiantly printed a skull and crossbones in the space where the Stamp Act required a stamp. In Boston the Sons of Liberty compelled the local Stamp Act collector to resign, and a mob sacked Chief Justice Thomas Hutchinson's house.

No duties could be collected if no goods were imported: Americans organized a boycott of English imports and resolved to do without them. This insistence upon self-sufficiency coincided with economic hard times; it was easy for colonists to swear not to buy imports when they lacked the means to buy much of anything. At the same time, as Americans dressed in homespun clothing, their pride swelled at the realization that they were capable of producing everything they needed for themselves.

In October 1765, nine colonies sent representatives to the Stamp Act Congress in New York. At the suggestion of James Otis, the delegates petitioned both the king and Parliament to repeal the Stamp Act. They argued that only colonial assemblies had the right to levy taxes.

The protests, resistance, violence, and petitions surprised the British government. The Prime Minister, George Grenville, was of two minds. On the one hand, he did not want trouble from the colonies. On the other hand, he was not prepared to capitulate to American mobs.

FRANKLIN DISTINGUISHES BETWEEN DIRECT AND INDIRECT TAXES   Benjamin Franklin, then a colonial agent in London, and other Americans devised a theory both to explain American anger and to offer a solution. According to Franklin, Americans drew a distinction between indirect taxes, such as import duties, and direct taxes, such as the Stamp Act. The colonists had never objected to Parliament's small import duties, because they were a valid charge to maintain the benefits of the British Empire's trading system. Besides, they were easy to evade.

Direct taxes like the Stamp Act, however, were another matter. The colonists, said Franklin, believed strongly that Parliament had no right to levy such taxes. Americans were not represented in Parliament; as Whig political theory had long held, there could be no taxation without representation. Therefore, only the popularly elected colonial assemblies could impose direct taxes on Americans.

Many members of Parliament found Franklin's position appalling. Parliament, including Grenville, believed that it alone held supreme legislative authority throughout the empire. As for the argument that the colonists were not represented in Parliament, members stated that the colonists did enjoy representation. Their virtual representation, like that of any other nonvoters, was derived from the fact that the members of Parliament collectively represented the entire empire. According to the theory of virtual representation, *some* voters elected Parliament, which then represented *everyone.*

This controversy continued, but in 1765 Grenville's Whig government fell, for other reasons. The new prime minister was another Whig, the Marquess of Rockingham. The new government was more sympathetic to American concerns, and it sought compromise.

In 1766 Rockingham's government repealed the Stamp Act. Even a Whig-led Parliament, however, rejected the American notion that Parliament had no right to impose taxes on the colonies. The Declaratory Act (1766), which accompanied the repeal of the Stamp Act, made this point specifically. In addition, although Parliament removed import duties from many products, it kept small duties on sugar, tea, and a few other items.

The colonists paid these duties without complaint, and the controversy subsided. Under the surface, however, both sides seethed. Parliament noted that very little revenue arrived from the colonies. Sooner or later, ways would have to be found to make the Americans pay more. And the colonists realized that, despite the repeal of the Stamp Act, the Declaratory Act threatened American liberties. Besides, British officials began to enforce import duties more vigorously.

AMERICANS BATTLE THE TOWNSHEND ACTS, 1767–1772   Lord Rockingham's government soon gave way to another Whig government under the Earl of Chatham. When Chatham fell ill, the administration was run by Charles

Townshend. In 1767 Townshend decided that the time was ripe to make the colonists pay more taxes. Paying careful attention to Franklin's distinction between direct and indirect taxes, Townshend persuaded Parliament to impose new and higher import duties on the colonists for paper, glass, paint, and tea.

The Townshend Acts (1767) produced an outcry in America. For one thing, Americans perceived correctly that the royal governors intended to use the revenues so that they would not have to seek appropriations from the elected colonial assemblies.

Americans then resumed the boycott of imported goods. Women played an important role in organizing this campaign by urging other women to honor the boycott, by admonishing people who used imported goods, by advocating and wearing homespun clothes, and by refusing to serve tea or other imports at home. Little revenue was collected, and smuggling thrived. John Dickinson's widely read *Letters from a Farmer in Pennsylvania* (1767) denied that Parliament had any right to tax Americans. "No taxation without representation" soon became a popular American slogan.

In 1768 British customs officials in Boston who were looking for smuggled goods seized the *Liberty,* a ship owned by the wealthy merchant John Hancock that carried goods without the required customs manifest. A mob attacked customs officials, who fled to an island in the harbor. The British then stationed two regiments of troops in Boston.

In 1770 Lord Frederick North, a Tory, became the head of the British government. He recognized the futility of trying to enforce the Townshend Acts. North's government, however, was unwilling to surrender parliamentary power. Besides, the American reaction to the import duties had shown that Franklin's distinction between direct and indirect taxes, even if it had once been true, was no longer accepted by most colonists. From the English viewpoint, the Americans were ungrateful upstarts, cantankerous children who needed to be taught a lesson. In 1770 Parliament repealed the Townshend Acts, but North's government insisted on showing the Americans who was boss. Therefore, the tax on tea was reduced but retained.

That same year British soldiers, popularly called redcoats, angered New Yorkers by cutting down their Liberty Pole. In Boston, where fights between soldiers and local crowds had become common, the redcoats fired into an angry mob. Five people died in the Boston Massacre, including Crispus Attucks, who may have been a runaway slave of mixed African, Indian, and white ancestry. At the time of his death, he was probably a sailor. Ten thousand or more Bostonians joined the funeral procession.

In 1772 a British customs ship, the *Gaspée*, went aground in Rhode Island. After nightfall a mob led by the wealthy merchant John Brown attacked the ship and set it afire. A British investigation failed to uncover what had happened, because local residents refused to cooperate.

TEA TIME IN AMERICA, 1773   The following year the British government decided to aid the nearly bankrupt East India Company by passing the Tea Act (1773). This law reduced the import duty on tea sold in America but gave the East India Company a monopoly on American tea sales. Ordinary Americans worried less about the price of tea than about the British show of power. Wealthy merchants who had long sold Dutch tea, whether obtained legally or not, faced ruin.

In 1773, to the surprise of North's government, the tea tax became a political issue in America. In Charleston, South Carolina, a tea ship was allowed to unload its cargo only after officials agreed not to collect customs duties. The untaxed tea was put into storage. In New York and Philadelphia residents persuaded tea ships to depart without docking.

In Boston the royal governor, Thomas Hutchinson, insisted that the tea be unloaded. He arranged special protection for the tea ship to enter the harbor. Once docked, however, the ship fell prey to a protest organized by Samuel Adams and John Hancock, leaders of the Sons of Liberty. Disguised as Indians, 150 angry colonists went aboard and threw 342 chests of tea into the harbor in an episode that came to be called the Boston Tea Party.

PARLIAMENT COERCES MASSACHUSETTS, 1774   The Boston Tea Party outraged the British government, which decided to make the people of Boston pay for their bad joke. Parliament passed a series of laws designed both to punish Boston and to deter other colonists. Collectively, they were called the Coercive Acts (1774).

The harshest provision closed the port of Boston. Because Boston was essentially a commercial city devoted to trade, closing the port for an indefinite period threatened to wreck the city's economy. This measure, more than any other, united residents in opposition to England.

Closing the port required a naval blockade to prevent smuggling, and, given the history of Boston, unrest was likely inside the city. So the British sent several thousand soldiers to Boston and in a new Quartering Act required that the city's residents house and feed them, even if it meant that civilians had to take soldiers into vacant rooms in their homes.

The English knew that widespread popular opposition throughout the colony of Massachusetts would cause further trouble. The center of that opposition was the colony's popularly elected assembly and town meetings. Therefore, Parliament ordered that the governor's council be appointed by the Crown rather than chosen by the assembly. The royal governor was to control the courts, and town meetings were to be restricted.

The colonists had long used the local courts to harass British officials. Massachusetts juries rarely convicted smugglers and routinely ruled against colonial officials. To prevent these kinds of decisions, Parliament provided that cases could be tried in England rather than in Massachusetts.

The four Coercive Acts were joined by a fifth measure, the Québec Act (1774). This law provided Canada with a government that lacked an elected assembly. In addition, Parliament gave Canada generous boundaries and allowed the French inhabitants to keep their Catholicism and their language. To the English colonists, the harsh treatment of Boston contrasted with the generosity shown to the French settlers. Furthermore, the tolerance of nearby Catholics did not set well with many Americans, especially in New England.

AMERICANS MAKE A REVOLUTION, 1774–1783

In 1774 the crisis intensified, and the next year war began in Massachusetts at Lexington, Concord, and Bunker Hill. In early 1776 Tom Paine proposed independence, which the Continental Congress adopted in July. The Americans' victory at Saratoga in 1777 raised American morale and convinced the French to provide crucial help to the Americans, who desperately needed help, lacking money to finance the war and feed their hungry soldiers. The British army moved south, where they got support from local sympathizers. After a costly campaign in the Carolinas (1780–1781), Lord Cornwallis surrendered to George Washington and the French at Yorktown in 1781. The peace treaty, signed in 1783, left America independent—and financially ruined.

SEEKING A POLITICAL SOLUTION, 1774   By 1774 many Americans had adopted a new view of the proper relationship between Britain and the colonies. According to this view, Britain and the colonies were distinct political entities. Britain was governed by the king and Parliament. The colonies were to be governed by governors acting as the king's representatives and by popularly elected colonial assemblies. Parliament had no role to play in governing the colonies. Until the 1760s, in fact, the colonies had been governed this way. The sole connection between the colonies and Britain was to be allegiance to the same king. Many years later, the British government would adopt this formula for the British Empire, but in 1774 few people in England accepted the idea of colonial self-government.

In response to the Coercive Acts, leading colonists organized Committees of Correspondence, which created a network to exchange information about current events throughout the thirteen colonies. These leaders urged the colonies to stand together; otherwise, they believed, the British government would play colonies off against one another and, as evidenced by Boston's recent experience, conquer them one at a time.

Correspondence, however, was not enough. The hated British laws had to be opposed vigorously. For this purpose self-appointed leaders, such as Boston's fiery Samuel Adams, created Committees of Safety. These committees organized mass support and began to arrange with elected legislative leaders and militia officers to provide military force if needed against the British.

To coordinate these activities, twelve colonies (excluding Georgia) sent representatives to the First Continental Congress in Philadelphia in September 1774. This congress pledged to continue the trade boycott, authorized coordinated military preparation, and sent a conciliatory petition to the king. The atmosphere, however, was anything but tranquil, as Samuel Adams and Patrick Henry raged, John Adams brooded, and George Washington carefully observed. It became clear that, however the controversy with Britain might end, the congress would play a major role in shaping the colonial response to the British challenge.

FIGHTING AT LEXINGTON, CONCORD, AND BUNKER HILL, 1775   In 1775 British officials in America watched events with growing alarm. The greatest threat to British rule came from popular defiance backed by local militias. To maintain authority, the British had to crush the colonists' organized opposition.

Boston, which the British correctly perceived to be the center of the rebellion, offered an important test case. A crackdown there might serve as a warning to rebels elsewhere. The closing of the port had only worsened relations between the people and the occupying British army; furthermore, the arming of the militia in nearby towns threatened to leave the British soldiers, called redcoats, trapped inside Boston.

So on April 19, 1775, the British army marched from Boston to Lexington and Concord to challenge the local militia companies and to seize the arms and ammunition stored there. Instead, on Lexington's village green the redcoats met the local militia, who had been warned of the British approach by the midnight rides of Paul Revere and William Dawes. Ordered to disband, the militia at first refused, then began to disperse. Someone let

On April 19, 1775, the Revolutionary War began when the British army and the American militia exchanged fire on the town green at Lexington, Massachusetts. (© CORBIS)

go a single shot—the "shot heard round the world"—and the British opened fire. The war was on.

The British soldiers did take some arms from Concord and Lexington but found themselves so unwelcome that they beat a hasty retreat back to occupied Boston. Snipers harassed them along the way. The Americans saw this episode as a great victory.

The redcoats were stuck in Boston. The American militia had the city surrounded. Both sides agreed that a pitched battle could lead to a big victory and end the dispute one way or another. When General Thomas Gage, the British commander, prepared to attack Americans outside Boston, the local militia suddenly felt weak.

On June 17, 1775, British troops left Boston by crossing the Charles River and moved toward Bunker Hill in Charlestown. Americans met the redcoats at Breed's Hill in the first great battle of the war. Although fought on Breed's Hill, it was remembered as the battle of Bunker Hill.

The redcoats marched in formation up the hill toward the Americans, who hid behind logs and hastily thrown up dirt breastworks. The Americans held; the British seemed stunned and recoiled twice under a hail of fire. Running low on ammunition, the Americans withdrew, and the redcoats captured the hill. Because of the heavy British casualties, the Americans claimed a great victory and celebrated.

The residents of Massachusetts appealed for military assistance from the other colonies, which raised troops and sent them to Massachusetts. They became the Continental army and were put under the command of a Virginian, George Washington, to demonstrate to the English that the Americans were united.

The British, however, remained in control of Boston. They could repel any direct attack upon their stronghold but were too weak to control the surrounding countryside. Similarly, the Americans could not drive the redcoats out, although they retained control of areas not under British occupation. Throughout the war the British found it impossible to occupy the entire countryside, while the Americans lacked the ability to take British-controlled cities. These two facts predicted a military stalemate.

AMERICANS DISCUSS INDEPENDENCE, 1775–1776   Meantime, the First Continental Congress had given way to the more militant Second Continental Congress. Meeting in May 1775 in Philadelphia—after the shooting had started—delegates for the first time began to question the fundamental political theory of the British Empire.

Why should a tiny island govern an entire continent? And did it make sense for Americans to fight a war in order to gain the right to be a self-governing part of an empire that had such contempt for Americans that it would not recognize their right to self-determination? In late 1775 the Congress debated these matters even as it scrambled to provide men and arms for Washington's army.

Meanwhile, Parliament decided to get tough with the rebels by passing the Prohibitory Act (1775). This law allowed the British to impose a naval blockade on the colonies and seize American ships on the high seas. Such economic warfare did not hold out the possibility of compromise, reconciliation, and a peaceful settlement.

In January 1776, Tom Paine, a tailor who had recently moved from England to Philadelphia, anonymously published a radical pamphlet entitled *Common Sense*. It swept through the colonies like wildfire, selling many thousands of copies in three months. Paine argued that Americans had a natural, God-given right to independence. Ridiculing monarchy as an archaic system of government, he embraced liberty. Paine believed that America had suffered rather than benefited from its ties with Britain. It was time to part and to preserve liberty through a republican form of government.

By June 1776, public opinion clearly supported independence. Congress prepared to act by authorizing a small committee chaired by Thomas Jefferson to draft a declaration setting forth the reasons why the colonies should be independent.

DECLARING INDEPENDENCE, 1776   Jefferson's Declaration of Independence, adopted by Congress on July 2, 1776, and proclaimed publicly two days later, mainly condemned King George III's conduct. Attacking the king was necessary in order to win over to the idea of independence those Americans who still clung to the notion of self-governance within the British Empire. The document was also designed to gain foreign support, especially from France.

The Declaration, however, did far more. It stated clearly that "all men are created equal." Even though the sentiment did not apply to slaves and women, it was a bold assertion, far more radical than anything in any other major political document of its era. Even today, the concept sends shivers of fear down the spines of elitists around the world.

Jefferson defended the right of revolution, maintaining that people have an innate right to overthrow their government any time they decide that the government is unworkable and tyrannical. This, too, was a radical concept—and one frequently cited by later revolutionaries. Linked to the right of revolution was the right of people to form a government based on rules of their own choosing. In other words, as John Locke had suggested, the people had an intrinsic right to draft a constitution in order to frame a new government in place of the one they had overthrown.

Finally, the Declaration stated that people have a right to "life, liberty, and the pursuit of happiness." The right to life and liberty had long been part of the Whig political philosophy. Whigs, however, generally joined these rights with the right to own property. Jefferson instead saw a right to pursue happiness. Property might be one form of happiness, but Jefferson's vision clearly contained the idea that people could seek out whatever made them happy. This notion resonated with a peculiarly American desire for personal satisfaction. Society was to be based on fulfillment of the self.

Not every American accepted the Declaration of Independence. The projected break with the British Empire terrified 10 to 20 percent of the colonists. To the Tories, as those who remained loyal to British authority were called, the power and order represented by the empire seemed necessary, the link to monarchy wise, and the British restraint on the democratic power of the American rabble desirable.

Tories, or Loyalists, as they called themselves, came from all social classes but were especially prevalent among officeholders and recent immigrants to America. Although found in all geographical regions, they were most numerous in northern port cities and the Carolina backcountry. By the end of the war about a hundred thousand Tories, some 3 percent of the population, left the colonies, mostly for Canada. One-quarter of the lawyers fled. The states usually confiscated their property.

Many more Americans, however, were Whigs, as the revolutionaries called themselves. They believed in the political ideas expressed in the

Declaration of Independence and were determined to make the revolution a success. About 30 to 40 percent of the colonists actively embraced independence, while most of the remainder, the silent near-majority, either gave lukewarm support or simply acquiesced.

THE BRITISH WIDEN THE WAR, 1776–1777 The British came to realize that their military occupation of Boston was meaningless, since a naval blockade could (and did) keep the port closed. The English decided to carry the war to the other colonies that had supported Boston's resistance.

So in March 1776, the British evacuated Boston, regrouped their forces, and returned in July under General Sir William Howe in a massive attack on Long Island, New York, by 32,000 troops, including 9,000 hired Germans. This was the largest military force ever assembled in North America; in contrast, Washington had only 19,000 soldiers, including militia.

The British strategy was to occupy the major cities—New York, Philadelphia, and Charleston—and to choke off the foreign trade that had seemed so necessary to sustain the American economy. Redcoats could make punitive raids into rebel areas near the seaports.

In 1776, after a string of minor defeats, Washington's Continental army retreated from the New York area. During this campaign the British

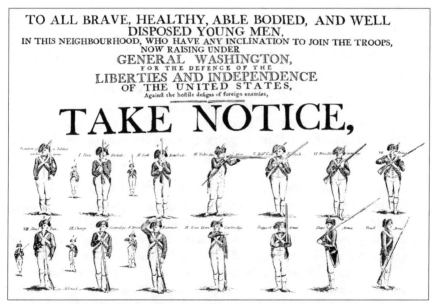

During the American Revolution, the Continental army used recruiting posters to encourage young men to enlist. Both glamour and patriotism were promoted by the uniform and drill suggested in this poster. (North Wind Picture Archives)

captured and executed the schoolmaster Nathan Hale as a spy. Facing superior British forces, Washington retreated across New Jersey.

As the year closed at Christmas 1776, a small number of Washington's troops crossed the Delaware River to capture an unimportant British garrison at Trenton. The nine hundred British-paid German soldiers who occupied Trenton were surprised amid their Christmas celebrations. This incident, as well as a similar minor victory at Princeton in January 1777, gave the Americans heart and suggested that the passionately committed colonists could defeat hired foreign troops who cared little about the war one way or the other.

In 1777 the British planned to march through upstate New York from Québec, which had remained loyal to Britain. This force would give comfort to New York's many Tories and would link up with another British army that moved north along the Hudson River from New York City. America would be cut in half, and, if the colonists were so stupid as to fight a battle, they would find themselves surrounded by two British armies.

This British strategy failed on two counts. First, it overestimated Tory support in upstate New York. Second, it depended on two British armies moving toward one another in a situation without communications. As it turned out, General Howe went south from New York to capture Philadelphia instead, leaving half the pincers missing.

Consequently, the Americans under General Horatio Gates surprised General John Burgoyne's British army coming from Canada. In October 1777, Gates's army surrounded Burgoyne's at Saratoga, New York. The British surrendered.

Saratoga boosted American morale. It also made it possible for Benjamin Franklin, then the American representative in Paris, to negotiate French support for the American cause. In 1778, the French agreed to send a navy, an army, and military supplies to assist the Americans. This help from a great power proved crucial to American victory.

WEAK FINANCES THREATEN RUIN AT VALLEY FORGE, 1777–1778   With the British in control of New York and Philadelphia, euphoria over Saratoga quickly faded, and the revolutionaries became demoralized by the lack of further success. Even the Continental Congress had been forced to flee. Congress found it increasingly difficult to raise money to support the war. The Congress continued to issue paper currency, but its value began to decline rapidly, partly because many expected a British victory and partly because the sheer quantity of paper money caused inflation to accelerate.

The financier Robert Morris valiantly tried to stabilize the government's finances in 1781. But by the end of the war Congress had issued

$240 million in paper money and the states another $200 million; the Continental dollar had lost 98 percent of its value.

George Washington's army suffered mightily. During the harsh winter of 1777–1778, they camped at Valley Forge just twenty miles from the British in Philadelphia. Although the valley was agriculturally rich, the local German farmers saw little reason to sell their produce to the revolutionaries for worthless paper currency when they could sell provisions for good British money to the redcoats occupying Philadelphia.

Washington's patience and courage provided the leadership that kept the army and the idea of nationhood alive. While others wrung their hands in despair, Washington stoically wrote letters begging Congress to find the money to continue the war. He promised that he would not quit if the means to sustain the cause could be found.

THE FRONTIER WAR   Throughout the war both sides sought allies among the Indians on the frontier. The British were more successful in this strategy because they had better trade goods and because they could promise tribes generous land grants after victory that would push back or retard white western settlement.

In central Pennsylvania and western New York Indian raids became so common that settlers were forced to abandon farms and flee into specially constructed forts. To stop these raids, in 1779 General George Washington sent General John Sullivan to invade the Iroquois lands in western New York. Sullivan routed the Indians at a pitched battle at Newtown and then burned villages and crops. The following year the Iroquois counterattacked along the frontier, but at the war's end that tribe was forced to yield vast acreage.

THE WAR MOVES SOUTH, 1778–1781   Meanwhile, the British turned to the South, where they played the race card, sometimes by threatening to start a slave uprising and sometimes by promising freedom to slaves who would support their cause. A few blacks took up the offer, but most remained suspicious either about British victory or about the prospects for actually attaining freedom. The British increased these suspicions by seizing rebel planters' slaves and selling them to the West Indies and by settling Loyalist planters and their slaves outside the United States.

Patriots confiscated Tory planters' slaves and removed their own slaves to remote areas beyond British control. When both sides contested a place, local whites fled. Slaves left to fend for themselves sometimes faced starvation, but they also imbibed the revolutionary idea of freedom. Southern slavery all but collapsed. Of Georgia's fifteen thousand prewar slaves, two-thirds ran away, were seized, or were left with the British at the end of the war. During the conflict as many as a hundred thousand slaves in the South may have deserted their owners.

At the end of the Revolution, thousands of southern slaves departed the United States. They had either sided with the British for a promise of freedom or left with their Loyalist masters. Some went to the Bahamas or Jamaica, others to Nova Scotia or Britain. In 1787 the British founded the Sierra Leone colony for blacks in Africa, most settlers of which were former American slaves from Britain and Nova Scotia.

Beginning in 1778, the British tried a direct southern strategy. After sending forces under Lord Cornwallis to occupy Georgia, they seized Charleston in May 1780, capturing three American generals and 5,000 troops, the greatest patriot loss of the war. Both sides used forced slave labor to build fortifications.

In parts of the southern backcountry, Tories were so numerous that more fought for the empire than with Washington's Continental army. In North Carolina, home to Tory Highland Scots long hostile to the Whiggish Scotch-Irish, local bands of Loyalists and revolutionaries marauded, burned, looted, and killed each other. This backcountry civil war was by far the most vicious campaign during the revolution.

White southerners, however, generally backed independence. British disruption of the slave system helped unite whites as patriots. Support was especially strong among Virginia's wealthy tobacco planters. Many were heavily in debt to London merchants, and the revolution provided them with a convenient opportunity to default.

Some revolutionary planters allowed their slaves to enlist under terms that provided for freedom at the end of the war. About 5 percent of the soldiers who fought on the American side in the revolution were black. After the war, Virginia had a large free black population due to this policy. Other states acted differently; South Carolina refused to arm any slaves, even at the risk of military defeat.

Responding to the loss of Charleston, Congress sent troops south under Horatio Gates, the hero of Saratoga. On August 16, 1780, Gates met the British, commanded by Cornwallis, in a major battle at Camden, in western South Carolina. Had the Americans been able to defeat the British so far from Cornwallis's coastal supply base, the war surely would have ended. Instead, Gates relied too heavily upon militia units, and, as the battle began, the militia fled. They retreated seventy-five miles, but Gates rushed away even faster and was finally located 160 miles north at Hillsboro, North Carolina.

More trouble followed. A month later the American General Benedict Arnold sold out to the British. His plan was to deliver the key post at West Point, New York, to the British. Only the timely capture of a British spy, the unfortunate Major John André, prevented Arnold from carrying out his betrayal. André was hanged. Arnold commanded British troops before retiring to London on a fat pension.

In the South, Washington replaced Gates with General Nathanael Greene, a onetime Rhode Island Quaker and blacksmith. Greene divided his forces, as did Cornwallis. A portion of Greene's army defeated a part of Cornwallis's at King's Mountain, North Carolina, in October 1780, and at Cowpens, South Carolina, in January 1781. Both backcountry battles left the British far from their supply lines. After a costly victory over Greene at Guilford Court House, North Carolina, in March 1781, Cornwallis headed for the coast.

THE BRITISH SURRENDER AT YORKTOWN, 1781   In 1781 Cornwallis's redcoats marched north into Virginia toward Yorktown in what turned out to be a major mistake. The Americans controlled the rivers on both sides of Cornwallis's position, and Washington placed his army alongside the Comte de Rochambeau's French army on the neck of land, cutting Cornwallis off from escape through Virginia.

British supply ships arrived late and faced a naval battle with the Comte de Grasse's French fleet. The French won and thereby prevented either resupply or retreat by sea. After a time, Cornwallis came to see the hopelessness of his situation. On October 19, 1781, he surrendered his army to Washington while, according to tradition, the British band played "The World Turned Upside Down."

By 1781 the British government had lost interest in the American war, which was part of a world struggle that had gone poorly for the British. Maintaining the empire by military force had little appeal because of the expense. A face-saving formula for withdrawal from America, however, could not be found, and peace negotiations dragged on, even after British troops had been evacuated from most of America.

Finally, in 1782, after the Marquess of Rockingham's Whig government replaced North's Tory government, negotiations grew serious. In September 1783, both the Americans and the British signed a peace treaty in Paris as part of a global settlement that recognized American independence. Shortly afterward, the last British troops left New York.

The western boundary of the new republic was generously fixed at the Mississippi River. The British, no doubt, had concluded that American settlers would soon reach the river anyway. To the British, it was more important to keep the Mississippi out of the hands of their enemies, the French, than to resist the encroaching Americans. The French gained nothing from the war except the satisfaction of seeing the British lose.

The United States began with a bright future—and with massive war debts, a ruined economy, no trade with the British Empire, weak political organization, and internal disputes between Tories and revolutionaries.

CONCLUSION

The British Empire did not meet America's needs. When the colonists protested against Parliament's arbitrary decisions, their actions had little effect in London except to produce more bad policies. Once war began, Americans realized that they had grown into a separate people, and their capacity for resistance became the basis for declaring independence. This independence existed in Americans' minds long before it was won on the battlefield and finally recognized in a peace treaty.

The war forced a clean break with Britain and gave national identity a heroic mold. The heroes of the American Revolution became both legends in their own time and heroes for all time. Jefferson's idealism and Washington's stoicism proved inspirational, just as the victory at Yorktown appeared providential. "God helps those who help themselves," Franklin had said; the revolutionaries lived out Franklin's admonition, convincing themselves that they thereby confirmed both their own worthiness and God's favor upon their enterprise. No other nation was ever born in such self-righteousness.

Recommended Readings

DOCUMENTS: J. Hector St. John de Crèvecoeur, *Letters from an American Farmer and Sketches of Eighteenth Century America* (1963); John Dickinson, *Letters from a Farmer in Pennsylvania* (1767); Peter Oliver, *Origin and Progress of the American Rebellion* (1961).

READINGS: (VALUES) Bernard Bailyn, *The Ideological Origins of the American Revolution* (1967) and *The Origins of American Politics* (1968); Ruth H. Bloch, *Visionary Republic* (1985); Jack P. Greene, *Peripheries and Center* (1986); Nathan O. Hatch, *The Sacred Cause of Liberty* (1977); Jean B. Lee, *The Price of Nationhood* (1994); Henry F. May, *The Enlightenment in America* (1976); Edmund S. and Helen M. Morgan, *The Stamp Act Crisis* (rev. ed., 1995); Alison G. Olson, *Making the Empire Work* (1992); Jack N. Rakove, *The Beginnings of National Politics* (1979); Gordon S. Wood, *The Creation of the American Republic, 1776–1787* (1969) and *The Radicalism of the American Revolution* (1991); (FRENCH AND INDIAN WAR) Fred Anderson, *A People's Army* (1984) and *The Crucible of War* (2000); Gwendolyn M. Hall, *Africans in Colonial Louisiana* (1992); Daniel H. Usner, Jr., *Indians, Settlers and Slaves in a Frontier Ex-*

change Economy (1992); (REVOLUTION) Joy D. and Richard Buel, Jr., *The Way of Duty* (1984); Edward Countryman, *The American Revolution* (1985); Robert A. Gross, *The Minutemen and Their World* (1976); Linda K. Kerber, *Women of the Republic* (1980); Pauline Maier, *From Resistance to Revolution* (1972), *The Old Revolutionaries* (1980), and *American Scripture* (1997); Mary B. Norton, *Liberty's Daughters* (1980); Kenneth Silverman, *A Cultural History of the American Revolution* (1987); Hiller B. Zobel, *The Boston Massacre* (1970); (WAR) Michael A. Bellesiles, *Revolutionary Outlaws* (1993); Colin G. Calloway, *The American Revolution in Indian Country* (1995); E. Wayne Carp, *To Starve the Army at Pleasure* (1984); Gregory E. Dowd, *A Spirited Resistance* (1992); David H. Fischer, *Paul Revere's Ride* (1994); Sylvia R. Frey, *Water from the Rock* (1991); Don Higginbotham, *The War of American Independence* (1971); Ronald Hoffman et al., eds., *An Uncivil War* (1985); Robert Middlekauff, *The Glorious Cause* (1982); Charles Royster, *A Revolutionary People at War* (1979); John W. Shy, *A People Numerous and Armed* (1976).

6

The New Nation,
1783–1800

OVERVIEW   A new country must first devise and then develop an appropriate political system. The 1780s began with a weak federal government under the Articles of Confederation, which proved inadequate, and ended with the adoption of the Constitution, which created a much stronger government. In the 1790s President George Washington set the tone and established crucial policies that came to define the American political system. From 1797 to 1801, his unlucky successor, John Adams, was embroiled in almost constant controversy, including foreign troubles and increasingly bitter partisan battles. The century ended with lusty political parties competing for power, a presidential election crisis, and the peaceful passage of power from Federalists to Democrats.

LIVING UNDER THE ARTICLES OF
CONFEDERATION, 1783–1787

Economically devastated by the Revolutionary War, the new nation entered a depression, which sparked Shays's Rebellion in 1786. The new state governments experimented with democratic constitutions that proved much more effective than the Articles of Confederation, which had provided a weak federal government throughout the 1780s. Congress accomplished little but did pass major ordinances governing the western territories. National leaders finally decided to overhaul the federal government.

Map 6.1   The United States in 1783

AMERICANS SUFFER DEPRESSION, INFLATION, AND DEBT   The 1780s brought both economic and political troubles. Massive public debt, worthless paper money, low economic growth, and high unemployment caused political crises, while the inability of the political system to respond worsened these economic problems.

The economic difficulties had many causes. The British government punished the United States by cutting off American trade with the British West Indies. Before the revolution, Americans had sold agricultural produce to the West Indies and in return had imported molasses and rum.

Much of this profitable trade had been carried in American ships. As these markets were lost, both trade and shipbuilding declined.

On the other hand, Americans were to blame for much of the trouble. They had paid for the very expensive Revolutionary War largely by borrowing, usually by issuing paper money. The money supply had increased much faster than had the economy, and the result was tremendous wartime inflation.

By 1783 most wartime paper money was worthless. State governments generally ceased to issue new paper money, and economic activity declined. People who had borrowed money during the war were now unable to pay their debts. As the dwindling money supply brought a general decline in commerce, artisans and farmers found it hard to sell their goods. Economic production dwindled, and the standard of living fell, creating a depression.

State governments seemed incapable of solving these problems. Rhode Island continued to issue paper money, even though its paper was held in contempt. This money did not circulate outside Rhode Island, but it was legal tender for all debts inside the state and had to be accepted. When debtors approached their creditors with Rhode Island paper, creditors fled to Massachusetts to avoid having to accept the stuff.

States quarreled and pointed accusing fingers across state boundaries. They imposed high tariff duties on goods from adjacent states. Although popular locally, this practice caused overall trade to decline.

SHAYS'S REBELLION CAUSES PANIC, **1786**   Massachusetts tried to pay off its war debts too fast. The state raised taxes on land and demanded that the new taxes be paid in specie, that is, gold or silver. Farmland owners in the western part of the state found few markets for their produce. Therefore, they had no access to specie with which to pay these burdensome taxes.

Threatened with the loss of their land, these farmers, led by Daniel Shays, rebelled in 1786. They sought to prevent the courts from meeting to hear suits brought against debtors. Although Shays's Rebellion failed and thereby showed the state government's soundness, it produced panic among Boston's wealthy merchants, who incorrectly saw the revolt as an attack on private property. Wise politicians understood that the real problem was a bad economy combined with an unresponsive federal government.

ESTABLISHING THE NEW STATE GOVERNMENTS   In the mid-1780s political leaders began to examine the political structure. In contrast to the anemic national government under the Articles of Confederation, most state governments established during the Revolutionary War seemed popular and robust. They had been constructed with written constitutions that largely confirmed the colonial practice of dividing power among independent executive, legislative, and judicial branches. The legislative branches had been made more powerful and had been divided into two houses.

In place of royal governors with absolute veto power over legislation, governors were now elected either by the voters or by the legislators; the governors had only limited vetoes, which the legislatures could override. Only Pennsylvania's radical constitution had broken with this concept. Pennsylvania provided for a plural executive council instead of a governor.

Most states had expanded the right to vote, although it was usually restricted to adult white males, and many states still required voters to own property. The minimum amount of property needed to qualify, however, declined. Property requirements for officeholders had also been reduced. Some states maintained religious requirements for voters. Personal rights, too, had been expanded. Virginia, for example, no longer used tax money to support churches and in 1785 guaranteed all citizens freedom of religion.

CONFRONTING THE WEAK ARTICLES OF CONFEDERATION   In contrast, in 1781 the states had created a weak central government through the Articles of Confederation. This government, which consisted of little more than a congress appointed by the states, was generally considered a failure; the states had retained too much power, including the right of taxation. The Confederation lacked power to collect taxes. It could only beg money from the states, which often ignored its pleas. The Confederation also could not control interstate commerce.

At the same time, the executive branch was virtually nonexistent. Congress was supposed to run the government, but the delegates seldom agreed on a policy and then only after long debate. Each of the thirteen states had one vote in the Congress, and important laws required the consent of nine states. It was hard to find nine votes.

THE CONFEDERATION MAKES PLANS FOR THE WEST   The Confederation's only success concerned land policy west of the Appalachian Mountains and north of the Ohio River. The Land Ordinance of 1785 had provided for surveying these federal lands in townships six miles wide by six miles long, for selling land at modest prices to settlers, and for providing one section per township to be sold or leased for the support of public schools.

The Northwest Ordinance of 1787 further provided for the organization of territorial governments in the same area. The territories were to be admitted to the Union eventually as five states (Ohio, Indiana, Illinois,

Michigan, and Wisconsin) on an equal standing with the original states. Furthermore, slavery was prohibited in this area.

NATIONAL LEADERS DEBATE THE ARTICLES   The Articles of Confederation had one fatal flaw. The Articles could be amended only with the consent of all thirteen sovereign states. As a practical matter, amendments were almost impossible. Maryland had blocked the settlement of western land claims, in which it had no interest, in order to gain political advantage, and Rhode Island's rum distillers had single-handedly prevented the Confederation from imposing a duty on imported rum.

Political leaders concluded that the Confederation was unworkable and that the ability of one state to block any changes made revision of the Articles unlikely. The Articles, unlike the state constitutions, had been too experimental. Not enough attention had been paid to organizing the government in ways supported by political experience. Many concluded that the central government needed to be made more like the successful state governments.

In 1786, therefore, at a meeting in Annapolis, Maryland, Alexander Hamilton persuaded a dozen delegates from five states to call for a general convention to deal with this political problem and, by implication, with the economic problem as well.

PLANNING THE UNITED STATES CONSTITUTION, 1787–1789

In 1787 state legislatures elected delegates to the Constitutional Convention, which drafted a plan for a new federal government. The new Constitution included a number of important compromises. Ratification by the states during 1787–1788 was difficult and controversial. As a condition for ratification, several states demanded that a bill of rights be added.

THE CONSTITUTIONAL CONVENTION MEETS, 1787   Twelve state legislatures sent fifty-five delegates to meet at a convention in Philadelphia during the sultry summer of 1787. (Rhode Island, still sulking over the attempt to tax rum, declined to send representatives.) It was generally expected that the convention would revise the Articles of Confederation. Although representing different states and diverse interests, these delegates were similar in several respects. All were white males, most owned considerable property, and a large number held slaves. Many were planters or large-scale commercial farmers, while others were wealthy merchants; some were both. A number practiced law. Almost all were politicians with much experience in government.

At the convention the delegates sought to protect their own property interests, but they also showed a remarkable capacity for dealing with larger issues. They understood that future prosperity, both for themselves and for the country as a whole, required boldness, a grand vision, and a willingness to sacrifice petty personal concerns to larger, national needs.

Above all, they wanted to create a national government that would last. If the new government succeeded, the failure of the Confederation would be overlooked. However, if the new government failed, most Americans would conclude that a strong continental government based upon republican principles was impossible. The country then would either become a centralized despotism or quickly disintegrate into a collection of warring states.

George Washington chaired the convention, and at crucial moments he acted to resolve angry disputes. An old and ill Benjamin Franklin, carried to the convention every day in a litter, retained his wit and kept the other delegates laughing. Alexander Hamilton of New York constantly pushed for a stronger new government, while two Virginians, George Mason and James Madison, continually drew upon political experience in their home state. Two prominent leaders were missing: Ambassadors John Adams and Thomas Jefferson were, respectively, in London and Paris.

DEBATING REPRESENTATION, SLAVERY, AND ELECTIONS   The Virginia delegates proposed a new constitution with a strong federal government divided among the executive, legislative, and judicial branches. The Congress was to have two houses, both based on state population. The lower house was to be elected by the people, while the upper house was to be elected by the lower house from among men nominated by state legislatures. The Congress was to elect the chief executive, who would resemble a prime minister. The executive and judiciary jointly were to have the right to veto legislation.

The Virginia plan drew much support, but delegates from lightly populated states opposed it. They were afraid that a powerful legislature controlled by a handful of populous states would dominate the new government. Delegates from New Jersey, then small in population, proposed modifying the Articles of Confederation. Congress would gain the power to tax, to regulate interstate commerce, to name a plural executive who would have no veto power, and to pick a supreme court. Each state, regardless of population, would continue to have equal representation in Congress.

Most delegates found the New Jersey plan's revisions too modest. They liked the Virginia plan's boldness, although they were uncomfortable with the details. Delegates from Connecticut then proposed a compromise, which was adopted. Representation in the lower House of Representatives would be based on population. Each state would have equal representation in the upper house, which the delegates decided to call the Senate.

Another compromise was contained within this compromise. Delegates from the South wanted representation to be based upon total population, but delegates from the North opposed counting the South's slaves, who did not participate in the political process. Finally, it was decided that three-fifths of the slaves were to be counted for the purpose of representation.

The convention also struggled with how to elect the president. Delegates were determined that the chief executive should be politically independent; they thus rejected election either by Congress or by state legislators. Nor did they trust popular election. Ignoring the methods proven effective in the states, they instead provided for an electoral college to choose the president.

THE CONSTITUTION'S CHECKS AND BALANCES   The Constitution was an extraordinarily clever political document. It ingeniously set forth a basic framework for government that kept power divided among the executive, legislative, and judicial branches. At every turn, checks and balances prevented hasty action and the aggrandizement of power by any single branch.

To become law, a bill had to pass both the House and Senate and then be signed by the president. However, the president's veto could be overridden by a two-thirds vote in each chamber of Congress. The president appointed the cabinet and all judges, but the Senate had to approve the appointments. Federal judges were independent because they served for life, but both judges and the president could be removed from office by Congress by means of the impeachment process. The president negotiated all treaties, but they had to be ratified by the Senate.

The Constitution also promised to settle the decade's economic problems. The new government would have the sole right to coin money, interstate tariffs would be prohibited, and an overseas tariff would help protect American manufactures. At the same time, the new federal court system offered merchants engaged in interstate commerce a practical way to resolve disputes that crossed state lines.

The document was written broadly so that it could evolve as the country evolved. Basic rules were stated emphatically, but specific details were left to later generations of Americans to debate and negotiate in the new political arena. Frequently amended and constantly reinterpreted in the light of changing political and economic conditions, the United States Constitution is today the world's oldest basic government document.

FEDERALISTS BATTLE ANTIFEDERALISTS, 1787–1788   Not all of the delegates to the convention approved of the new Constitution. Only thirty-nine of the fifty-five delegates signed it. They called themselves Federalists. Most objections came from those like George Mason who feared that the document created too powerful a central government at the expense of the state governments and of individual freedom. They took the name Antifederalists.

Proponents were well organized. Hamilton, Madison, and John Jay defended the Constitution in a series of widely circulated newspaper articles, later collected as the *Federalist Papers*. They argued that the Constitution would create a vigorous government that would represent the majority while protecting minority rights.

The convention had provided that the new Constitution would go into effect when ratifying conventions in nine of the thirteen states had approved it. The battle for approval moved to the state level. In a few states ratification was quick and easy. Fast approval came from Delaware, afraid of being swallowed by Pennsylvania, and from Pennsylvania, where Philadelphia merchants saw the new Constitution as the key to prosperity. New Jersey, Georgia, and Connecticut rapidly followed.

The first battle over ratification occurred in Massachusetts. The memory of Shays's Rebellion remained fresh, and western Massachusetts sent many delegates to the state convention who opposed the Constitution. Opponents, led by the war hero Sam Adams, feared a tyrannical federal government.

Proponents persuaded Adams and a narrow majority in the convention only by promising that the first Congress to meet under the new Constitution would submit nine amendments restricting the power of the new federal government. The most important amendment reserved to the states all powers not specifically mentioned in the new Constitution.

Rhode Island voters rejected the Constitution in a popular referendum, while the Maryland, South Carolina, and New Hampshire conventions approved. New Hampshire was the ninth state to ratify, but both sides recognized that, without support from populous Virginia and New York, the Constitution could not work.

The debate in the Virginia state convention was heated. Patrick Henry's opposition was brilliantly met by James Madison's arguments, although to win a narrow victory Madison had to agree to a set of twenty proposed amendments, including a bill of rights. Alexander Hamilton used political pressure to push ratification, 30 to 27, through the New York state convention.

North Carolina did not ratify until late in 1789, after the new government was established, and Rhode Island was coerced into the Union in 1790 by the threat to impose United States import duties on Rhode Island products.

POPULAR OPINION OPPOSES THE CONSTITUTION   Had the Constitution been put to a popular vote, it would have failed. The document had strong support from planters and from merchants and artisans in the towns and cities along the seacoast, where trade was crucial to economic health. But further inland, and especially among subsistence farmers, the predominant view was that the Constitution merely created a new, useless, and expensive layer of government.

To many, this new federal government seemed remote and alien. The average person lived too far from such a government to have any chance to shape its action. Only the socially, economically, and politically prominent were likely to have influence. Such a government seemed suspiciously like the British government that the revolution had overthrown. Americans worried that the new government could not be trusted to respect the liberties of the people.

ADDING THE BILL OF RIGHTS   In 1789, as the Antifederalists demanded, the first Congress passed a series of constitutional amendments called the Bill of Rights. Twelve amendments were sent to the states, and within a short period ten were ratified. (The two that failed concerned detailed provisions about representation and the salaries of members of Congress. In a strange twist, the salary amendment was declared ratified in 1992.)

The most important amendment, the First, provided that Congress could interfere neither with religious freedom nor with freedom of speech, including that of the press and of assembly. The Second Amendment provided for the right of militiamen to keep and bear their own arms. The Fourth through Eighth Amendments required search warrants, legal due process, a speedy trial, trial by jury, and reasonable bail. The Tenth Amendment, never much observed in practice, reserved powers not specifically in the Constitution to the states or the people. (See the U.S. Constitution in Appendix II.)

GEORGE WASHINGTON'S PRESIDENCY, 1789–1797

In 1789, as the first president, George Washington established many precedents, setting the tone, organizing the government, and adopting financial policies. Soon, much to Washington's disgust, cabinet members Alexander Hamilton and Thomas Jefferson bickered.

The administration was shaken by the Genêt affair in 1793, when the French ambassador's indiscretions raised anti-French sentiment, and by the Whiskey Rebellion in 1794, which tested the government's credibility. In 1795 Washington had mixed results, gaining only a poor commercial treaty with England but signing treaties in which Indians ceded land in the Great Lakes region and in which Spain confirmed America's southern border. After two terms, Washington retired in 1797.

SETTING A SERIOUS, DEMOCRATIC TONE   In early 1789 the first Electoral College, appointed by legislatures in some states and elected by the voters in others, met and unanimously elected George Washington the first president. There was no contest. To give geographical balance, John Adams of Massachusetts was made vice president and New York City the capital.

George Washington achieved a unique status as the living embodiment of the American Revolution. The powdered wig, prominent nose, straight mouth, and set jaw conveyed a sense of republican leadership. (National Portrait Gallery, Washington, D.C./Art Resource, NY)

Washington's popularity was matched by the respect accorded him by important political leaders. In the Revolutionary War, Washington had demonstrated an unusual capacity for humoring quarrelsome rivals, for settling both military and political disputes, and for handling vast flows of bureaucratic paper. These were good qualities in a president.

The new president's first and most important task was to set the tone of the government. Washington strongly believed in republican government as opposed to monarchy or aristocracy, but he also believed in order and decorum. He wished to steer a middle course between those like Alexander Hamilton who saw the president as an elected monarch and those like the Constitution's opponents who wanted no authority symbol at all.

Washington believed that republican government could only succeed if it were based on virtue, which he defined as a solemn, self-sacrificing devotion to duty. He sought to create a government that combined seriousness of purpose with a quiet dignity. The new federal government was to have integrity, to be taken seriously, and never to be a joke. To this day, the federal government has a solemnity found at no other level of government in the United States and in few other governments in the world.

Symbolism was important. Thus, Washington took his oath of office before the public on the balcony of the federal building in New York. A public oathtaking helped make the president a man of the people, but standing on the balcony, above and beyond the masses, surrounded by government officials, also conveyed the president's status as a uniquely important national leader.

Washington carefully considered how people should address the new president in person. He agreed with those who held that some title was necessary to show proper respect for the office, but he also understood that most Americans would ridicule any title that smacked of monarchy. So he decided that he and his successors should be addressed as "Mr. President."

ORGANIZING THE GOVERNMENT   The administration's first task was to organize the government. Since the Constitution was vague about the internal operations of the executive branch, Washington found it necessary to get Congress to set up the various departments.

The first cabinet had four members. Most important were Secretary of State Thomas Jefferson and Secretary of the Treasury Alexander Hamilton. President Washington took his cabinet seriously. In his view, the president should not make personal decisions. Rather, the president's main duty was to get the cabinet to reach collective judgments that then would become the basis of government policy.

The first Congress provided the Supreme Court with six justices as well as a system of lower federal courts. From the beginning, then, this extensive judicial system signaled that the new government was to be actively involved in people's everyday affairs.

THE NEW GOVERNMENT TAKES OVER WAR DEBTS, 1790   In 1790 the Washington administration tackled one of the main issues which had led to the creation of the Constitution: the old war debts and the now worthless paper money left over from the days of the Confederation.

Alexander Hamilton wanted the new federal government to take over the Confederation's foreign and domestic debts as well as most of the state war debts. To pay off these debts, the new government would issue bonds backed by new federal revenues. The policy would revive economic activity and generate confidence in the new government. It would also encourage bondholders from Boston to Charleston to back the new government.

Assumption of the Confederation debt was generally accepted, although James Madison, then the administration's floor leader in the House of Representatives, protested that many debtholders were speculators who had bought the nearly worthless debt at two cents on the dollar and now stood to make a huge profit. He proposed that the government pay only original debtholders at the full rate. Congress rejected this plan.

The proposed takeover of the state debts unleashed regional rivalries. The southern states had largely paid off their Revolutionary War debts and now faced having to pay higher federal taxes to help pay the debts of the northern states. Virginians were outraged; Madison, with his eye on the next election, permanently broke with the administration over this issue and became the opposition leader.

Finally, Thomas Jefferson arranged a dinner, at which a compromise between Madison and Hamilton was reached. The state debts would be assumed, which the North wanted. In return, the permanent national capital, which Hamilton had hoped would stay in New York, would be built as the South wanted, on the Potomac River between the southern states of Maryland and Virginia. In the meantime, the capital was to move to Philadelphia for ten years. Many Pennsylvanians gambled that the government would never leave Philadelphia.

MEETING THE GOVERNMENT'S BANKING NEEDS, 1791   In 1791 Hamilton proposed that the federal government charter the Bank of the United States. A public–private partnership, this mixed venture was to have both government and private directors. Under the control of wealthy private shareholders, this bank was to handle the government's banking needs, which had been greatly enlarged by the assumption of the debts and the issuance of federal bonds.

In the cabinet Thomas Jefferson protested vigorously. He saw nothing in the Constitution that permitted the federal government to charter a bank. Jefferson developed what became known as a "strict construction-ist" doctrine of the Constitution: The government could do only those things specifically listed among its powers.

Hamilton took a contrary view. The government, said he, had to be able to carry out its duties. The Constitution could not anticipate all the de-tails that would be needed to deal with different crises. Besides, the Con-stitution did grant a general power to the federal government in the "nec-essary and proper" clause, which gave the government the right to promote the general welfare.

Although Washington had reservations, he sided with Hamilton's "broad interpretation" on this issue. The bill to establish the bank was passed by Congress and became law.

Hamilton found that the government needed more revenue than import duties could provide. Tariffs on molasses and rum had led rum distillers to protest that such duties were unfair because they made rum more expensive than American whiskey. In 1791 Hamilton persuaded Congress to tax whis-key. Internal revenue agents were sent throughout the country to collect the tax. They met resistance in areas where people lacked money to pay.

HAMILTON AND JEFFERSON FEUD   Hamilton and Jefferson began to quarrel vigorously. Hamilton wrote nasty anonymous articles in John Fenno's *Gazette of the United States,* and Jefferson replied in kind in Philip Fre-neau's *National Gazette.* Washington wrung his hands in despair. Much of this dispute involved clashing personalities and a natural rivalry for po-litical leadership, but Hamilton and Jefferson also held quite different views about national purpose and about shaping the country's future.

Hamilton, as suggested in his *Report on Manufactures* (1791), believed that government power should be used to develop cities, industries, and trade. Government-subsidized manufacturing might provide employ-ment for the poor, and a totally self-sufficient American economy would guarantee national greatness.

This vision appalled Jefferson. In *Notes on the State of Virginia* (1787), he had championed rural life. Personal experience, especially in Paris, had taught him that cities generated disease, poverty, and corruption. The backbone of any republic was the independent, small-scale, landholding yeoman farm family.

Although Washington was reelected in 1792, his second term brought him much unhappiness. The Hamilton-Jefferson feud continued despite

Washington's attempts at mediation. Because Washington usually sided with Hamilton in policy disputes, in 1793 Jefferson, now firmly allied with Madison, finally resigned from the cabinet.

CITIZEN GENÊT CREATES A FOREIGN POLICY CRISIS, **1793**   Meanwhile, the United States became entangled in foreign affairs. The French Revolution, which started in 1789, had turned bloody, and the new French republic was at war with Britain and Spain. Hamilton sought to bring the United States into a closer relationship with Britain, which Jefferson opposed. Washington pursued a neutral course.

In 1793 Edmond Charles Genêt became the French ambassador to the United States. Warmly received, Citizen Genêt, as he called himself in revolutionary fashion, mistook a vague American popular endorsement of the French Revolution for support for himself. The politically indiscreet Genêt then violated American neutrality by commissioning privateers to attack British ships off the American coast.

Amid a rising tide of anti-French sentiment whipped up by Hamilton, the administration ordered Genêt to return to France. (Before he could leave, Genêt's enemies came to power in France, and he was allowed to remain in the United States as a political refugee.)

THE WHISKEY REBELLION TESTS THE GOVERNMENT, **1794**   At home, frontier settlers grew restless, and in 1794 farmers in western Pennsylvania openly revolted. They defied the federal government's attempts to enforce the whiskey tax. The tax was hated because people who lived on the frontier perceived the federal government as remote and useless and because frontier residents lacked the cash with which to pay the tax.

Prodded by Hamilton, Washington declared an insurrection and called fifteen thousand militiamen from adjacent states to crush the rebellion. Hamilton, in a panic, saw the event as a crucial test of the federal government's credibility. He drew up plans to lead the military expedition—and to become a military dictator of the country if necessary.

The military expedition, however, was led not by Hamilton but by Henry ("Lighthorse Harry") Lee with Hamilton's assistance. This massive show of force caused the resistance to collapse, and defiance of the whiskey tax resumed its more benign form—hidden stills. Several insurrectionists were charged with treason. Two were convicted and sentenced to be hanged. Washington shrewdly pardoned them.

MAKING THREE TREATIES, **1795**   Domestic turmoil led the administration to seek conciliation abroad. In 1794 Washington decided to obtain a commercial treaty with Great Britain and sent John Jay as special envoy to

Britain. The British, however, showed little interest in trade. They also refused to negotiate about the impressment of American seamen, which was the British practice of manning its navy by seizing American sailors from American ships on the high seas. The British offered a mediocre treaty, gaining access to the American market while keeping American goods out of Britain and the West Indies. Jay signed anyway. Jay's Treaty created a furor, and the Senate approved the treaty only reluctantly after an extensive debate in 1795.

The administration had better luck in the Great Lakes region. In 1794 General Anthony Wayne defeated several Indian tribes at Fallen Timbers in Ohio, and the following year twelve tribes signed the Treaty of Greenville, which led the native inhabitants to cede much of the area to white settlement.

In late 1795 Washington scored a triumph with Pinckney's Treaty with Spain. Thomas Pinckney persuaded the Spanish to confirm America's southern boundary and to give western American farmers the right to ship produce down the Mississippi River to New Orleans, then in Spanish hands.

WASHINGTON RETIRES WITH A FAREWELL ADDRESS, 1796   Despite these successes, by 1796 Washington was tired and frustrated. Yearning for the tranquility of his beloved estate at Mount Vernon, he announced that he would not accept a third term; this precedent was unbroken until Franklin Roosevelt's third election in 1940. Washington is one of only a few world leaders who ever gave up power voluntarily.

Washington decided to issue a Farewell Address. In it he lamented the rise of political parties, which he saw as against the public interest. His view was ignored. He also warned against permanent foreign alliances. Such alliances, he believed, led inevitably to war, and the United States would be better off remaining neutral. This warning more or less became the basis of American foreign policy for the next hundred years.

JOHN ADAMS'S PRESIDENCY, 1797–1801

Elected in 1796 in a bitterly partisan election, John Adams steered a middle course between Hamilton and Jefferson. Enraged by the XYZ Affair, in 1798 he found himself entangled in the Quasi-War with France but refused to ask Congress to declare war. His support of the Alien and Sedition Acts in 1798 revealed his foolish vanity, and despite an economic boom, he was defeated for a second term in the strange election of 1800. That election resulted in the Twelfth Amendment, which changed the way presidents were elected.

An intelligent and educated minister's daughter, Abigail Adams was an equal partner with her husband, John. (Brown Brothers)

THE ELECTION OF 1796   The drafters of the Constitution had not intended to create political parties and, indeed, generally looked upon such parties with suspicion as political combinations devoted to special interests rather than to the common good. However, the creation of a single powerful office, the presidency, had spurred the creation of parties as the means to that prize, and the electoral college system drove political leaders into a two-party system.

By 1796 two distinct parties had taken shape. The Federalists, led by Hamilton and John Adams, were strongest among merchants in the cities and throughout New England. The Democratic-Republicans, led by Jefferson, Madison, and Aaron Burr (in New York), were strongest among artisans in the cities and throughout the South.

A fierce fight to succeed Washington occurred. In 1796 Adams defeated Jefferson for the presidency by 71 to 68 electoral votes. Under the constitutional provisions then in effect, the runner-up Jefferson became vice president.

ADAMS FACES THE XYZ AFFAIR, 1797–1798   John Adams was temperamentally ill-suited for the presidency. Talented and hard-working, he had risen from a small farm to the top of the legal profession, but his perfectionism, obsession with detail, Yankee gloom, and sour suspicion of most of his contemporaries made him neither liked nor likable. His only joy seemed to come from his marriage to Abigail, which was a lifelong romance and a true partnership. She once teased John that, if the new country did not give women their rights, they would lead a revolution.

Almost from the beginning, Adams found himself trapped between the extreme views of Thomas Jefferson and those of Alexander Hamilton. Hamilton had deeply alienated many people inside his own party and had left the cabinet. This only made matters worse for Adams, because Hamilton received inside reports about the cabinet meetings and then used this information to undermine Adams.

Adams's first crisis was the XYZ Affair in 1797. The French government had been so angry at the pro-British Jay's Treaty that they had refused to receive Adams's ambassador. The president then sent three special envoys to make amends and to negotiate a trade treaty with France.

The French foreign minister, Talleyrand, sent three special agents to meet the American delegation. The French agents demanded a bribe of $240,000 to present the American case to the French government. The American envoys resisted, negotiations collapsed, and in 1798 a furious, righteous Adams presented the facts, with the names of the French agents identified only as Messrs. X, Y, and Z, to Congress.

American public opinion turned against France. Adams had copied Washington's policy of maintaining neutrality in the ongoing Franco-British war and now faced a severe test. Mobs surged through city streets demanding war with France, and the Hamiltonian wing of the Federalist Party vilified Adams.

The fear of war with France drove the pro-French Democratic-Republicans, the followers of Jefferson, into a frenzy. Worried that Adams was plotting such a war in order to crush his domestic political opponents, the Jeffersonians used their newspapers to denounce war, England, and Adams.

PASSING THE ALIEN AND SEDITION ACTS, 1798   In 1798 Adams and all the Federalists, temporarily united, used their majority in Congress to strike at the Jeffersonians with four laws. Many leading Jeffersonian newspaper editors were foreign born, and the Federalists now enacted a new Naturalization Act. It increased the period of residency required for citizenship from five to fourteen years. The implication was that noncitizen editors who attacked the government faced deportation.

A companion Alien Act gave the president the authority to deport any noncitizen deemed a threat to public safety. Both laws lasted until 1802. An Alien Enemies Act gave the president the right, during a declared war, to arrest and imprison any person from a country with which the United States was at war.

The Sedition Act was intended to prevent an internal insurrection. It prohibited meetings to plot treason. It also barred "malicious writing" that attacked the reputation of any government official. The law was so loosely drawn that it could be applied to almost any dissent.

In some parts of the country, especially New England, Federalists used the law to crush their political opponents. Ten prominent Jeffersonian newspaper editors were fined or imprisoned. Matthew Lyon of Vermont became a hero in jail and was elected to Congress.

ADOPTING THE KENTUCKY AND VIRGINIA RESOLUTIONS, 1798   The Jeffersonians attacked the Alien and Sedition Acts as despotic and unconstitutional. In their view, these laws violated both the First Amendment's protection of free speech and the Tenth Amendment's limitation of federal power. In 1798 Thomas Jefferson secretly drafted a series of resolutions, which the Kentucky legislature adopted. That same year Madison framed a similar set for Virginia. The Kentucky and Virginia Resolutions denounced the Alien and Sedition Acts as unconstitutional.

Both sets of resolves insisted that each state should judge for itself how to redress such grievances. Virginia suggested that a state might "interpose" itself to resist such a law, while Kentucky held that a bad law might be "nullified" by a state declaring a federal law invalid inside its borders. Other politicians would adopt these terms in later years.

The underlying issue was difficult and complex. The Constitution had not spelled out clearly how a law might be declared unconstitutional. The Kentucky and Virginia Resolutions suggested one method, but it could produce the awkward result that some federal laws might be enforced only in part of the country. Some people suggested as an alternative that the Supreme Court might rule upon a law's constitutionality. The court later adopted this idea.

ADAMS PURSUES QUASI-WAR WITH FRANCE, 1798–1800   From 1798 through 1800, the United States fought an undeclared naval war against France.

The Quasi-War, as it was sometimes called, grew out of American anger over the XYZ Affair combined with American insistence upon the right of neutral American merchant ships to trade with whomever they wished.

Adams opposed a declared war because it might provoke a French invasion. National defenses were decrepit, and the American army was too small to prevent a French landing. Adams did organize a modest navy, and the navy fought well against the French in several battles.

To pay for the war, the federal government imposed taxes on real estate and luxuries such as carriages. Opposition to these taxes was intense, especially from those who opposed war with France. In 1799 John Fries led hundreds of Pennsylvanians in open revolt. Caught, tried, convicted, and sentenced to death for treason, Fries was pardoned by Adams.

In 1800 Adams made peace overtures to the French, and the French accepted. Although Adams's action pleased and surprised the Jeffersonians, his decision angered the Hamiltonian faction of the Federalist Party. Adams had badly split the party, which appeared likely to lose the next election.

AMERICANS ENJOY AN ECONOMIC BOOM IN THE **1790s**   Adams's political troubles played against a booming economy. Throughout the 1790s the economy had done well. Once the Constitution was put into operation, opposition to it all but disappeared, in large part because of prosperity. How much of the improvement was due to Hamilton's refunding of the debt and how much to lucky timing is uncertain.

Real income per person increased during these years for almost everyone, or at least for everyone who participated in the moneyed economy. (It is difficult to believe that the living standards of slaves changed very much, although a prosperous master might have fed his slaves better.)

Because of war in Europe, American farmers enjoyed record exports at high prices. Much of this profit was recycled through the American economy, which became more self-sufficient in manufacturing due to Hamilton's tariff and to British and French anti-American trade policies.

Seaport merchants found the decade especially profitable. Urban artisans, unless they produced luxury goods, did less well than merchants. Many craftsmen concluded that Hamilton's policies favored wealthy merchants, and these mechanics split with the merchant-dominated Federalists to create their own labor unions and Democratic-Republican Societies, which moved into the Jeffersonian political camp.

PROSPERITY PRODUCES FEDERALIST CULTURE   Prosperous, self-confident Federalists frequently adopted British culture that matched pro-British politics. Federalist merchants built mansions that borrowed details from London's houses as portrayed in contemporary pattern books. The style was neoclassical, featuring Greco-Roman columns made of delicately carved wood, with modest, graceful, and restrained detail.

Furniture, too, was produced in the same style. American made from native walnut or cherry or from imported mahogany, wooden chests of drawers and sideboards were gracefully curved, delicately inlaid, beautifully polished, and carefully positioned upon thin, tapered legs. Gilded mirrors topped with fierce, patriotic eagles completed the typical Federalist merchant's drawing room.

As is often true during an economic boom, literature also flourished. Charles Brockden Brown published a series of novels in which he wrestled with the problem of class in an avowedly democratic society. Hugh Henry Brackenridge, an attorney and an active Jeffersonian, wrote *Modern Chivalry,* a scathing satire about Irish immigrants on the western Pennsylvania frontier. A youthful William Cullen Bryant amused himself turning out sarcastic anti-Jeffersonian verse.

THE ELECTION OF **1800**   Federalist smugness was smashed in the election of 1800. Although the party was split, Federalists saw no alternative to renominating the unpopular Adams. The Democrats, as they increasingly called themselves, had come close to winning with Jefferson in 1796, and so they renominated the Virginian.

It was a dirty campaign. Both the Alien and Sedition Acts and the Quasi-War with France had left bitter feelings. On the other side, the Federalists worried that a Jefferson administration would be too democratic, would pander to the popular will, and would lead the country back toward the chaos of the 1780s.

Jefferson's personal life became an issue. He believed in God but in no particular church and had little to say about Jesus Christ. New England ministers condemned his deism. Federalist newspaper editors raised questions about Jefferson's relationship with his slave Sally Hemings, who was three-fourths white and was his dead wife's half-sister. Jefferson denied any wrongdoing. Nearly two centuries later, genetic tests suggested that Jefferson might well have fathered Hemings's children.

The election was decided on regional lines. The South, along with New York (under Burr's control), voted for Jefferson. Adams got few electoral votes outside New England.

The Constitution had not anticipated a party system, and each member of the electoral college was to vote for two candidates for president. The person with the highest number, provided it was a majority of the electors, was to become president. The runner-up was to be vice president. In

1800 the disciplined Democrats in the Electoral College all voted for both party candidates. The result was a tie between Jefferson and his running mate, Aaron Burr.

The Constitution provided that, in the event of a tie, the House of Representatives would elect one of the top candidates from the Electoral College. Each state cast one vote, and a majority of states was necessary to win.

The Federalists in the House backed Burr, but the Democrats remained loyal to Jefferson, and a deadlock ensued. To avoid a constitutional crisis, Hamilton told friends that Jefferson should be picked. Burr never forgave Hamilton for this decision and later killed Hamilton in a duel. Finally, on the thirty-sixth ballot, Jefferson was chosen.

To prevent a similar problem in the future, the Twelfth Amendment to the Constitution was adopted in 1804. Each elector was to vote for two people separately, one for president, the other for vice president.

Although no one knew it then, the election of 1800 marked the end of national power for the Federalists. The party continued to hold power for another decade in some parts of the country, especially New England, but never regained the presidency or control of Congress. In 1801 power passed peacefully from one political party to another. Although relationships were strained, a major accomplishment had taken place. The ability to transfer power without revolution or revolt is one of the hallmarks of democratic government.

CONCLUSION

Any new nation can expect growing pains. The trick is to overcome present obstacles in ways that provide for healthy, long-term success. The sick economy and weak Confederation of the 1780s gave way to vigorous economic growth and a robust new federal government in the 1790s. Much of this transformation was due to the wisdom contained in the United States Constitution, the oldest fundamental government charter still in use.

A blueprint can succeed, however, only with expert builders. Washington not only set the tone but shrewdly adopted policies in the nation's long-term interest. Hamilton's financial genius was matched by Jefferson's understanding of the American psyche, while Adams sacrificed personal ambition to govern the way he believed necessary for the new nation's survival. By 1800 no one doubted that the founders actually had created a nation.

Recommended Readings

DOCUMENTS: Thomas Jefferson, *Notes on the State of Virginia* (1787); Thomas Paine, *The Rights of Man* (1791); Clinton Rossiter, ed., *The Federalist Papers* [1788] (1961).

READINGS: (GENERAL) Joyce Appleby, *Capitalism and a New Social Order* (1984) and *Inheriting the Revolution* (2000); Richard Beeman, et al., eds., *Beyond Confederation* (1987); Richard Buel, Jr., *Securing the Revolution* (1972); Saul Cornell, *The Other Founders* (1999); Stanley Elkins and Eric McKitrick, *The Age of Federalism* (1993); Joseph J. Ellis, *Founding Brothers* (2000); Jackson T. Main, *The Antifederalists* (1961) and *Political Parties before the Constitution* (1973); Peter S. Onuf, *The Origins of the Federal Republic* (1983); Jack N. Rakove, *Original Meanings* (1996); James R. Sharp, *American Politics in the Early Republic* (1993); David P. Szatmary, *Shays' Rebellion* (1980); Laurel T. Ulrich, *A Midwife's Tale* (1990); Shane White, *Somewhat More Independent* (1991); Rosemarie Zagarri, *A Woman's Dilemma* (1995); (WASHINGTON'S PRESIDENCY) Harry Ammon, *The Genêt Mission* (1973); Richard Brookhiser, *Founding Father* (1996); Jerald A. Combs, *The Jay Treaty* (1970); Felix Gilbert, *To the Farewell Address* (1961); Thomas P. Slaughter, *The Whiskey Rebellion* (1986); David Waldstreicher, *In the Midst of Perpetual Fetes* (1997); (ADAMS'S PRESIDENCY) Joseph J. Ellis, *Passionate Sage* (1993); John E. Ferling, *John Adams* (1992); Peter Shaw, *The Character of John Adams* (1976); William C. Stinchcombe, *The XYZ Affair* (1980); Lynne Withey, *Dearest Friend: A Life of Abigail Adams* (1981).

7

❦

Thomas Jefferson's
America, 1801–1829

OVERVIEW   By 1801 Thomas Jefferson had captured America's heart, at least outside New England, by advocating a minimalist federal government and a nation of small-scale, landowning, family farmers. Reality, however, never quite matched Jefferson's vision, and much of the anger toward Indians and the British that produced the War of 1812 had its origins in his vision's limitations. By 1816 Americans embraced a harmonious but nonvisionary Era of Good Feelings. Happy talk could not last, however, and from 1825 to 1829 John Quincy Adams failed to persuade Americans to seek national greatness in new ways.

THOMAS JEFFERSON ENVISIONS
A GREAT, EXPANDING NATION

Thomas Jefferson's values had been forged in the American Revolution but tempered under attacks from Alexander Hamilton in the 1790s, and by 1801, like a fine French wine, they were mature. Jefferson's high idealism contrasted with the ugly, undeveloped swampland of Washington, D.C., the nation's new capital. His vision of democracy rested upon the idea of a republic of small farmers stretched across the continent, in territory that promised the end of slavery, which Jefferson abhorred but did not know how to end. His vision of a great, expanding nation depended on the West. In 1803 he purchased Louisiana and then sent Lewis and Clark to explore what had been bought. Aaron Burr, too, had a western dream, but it was neither Jefferson's nor democratic.

Best known as the author of the Declaration of Independence, Thomas Jefferson was also an architect, inventor, university founder, and third president of the United States. (National Portrait Gallery, Smithsonian Institution, the Thomas Jefferson Memorial Foundation, and the Enid and Crosby Kemper Foundation. Monticello/Art Resource, NY)

Jefferson found it increasingly difficult to maintain American neutral rights in the Franco-British wars. In 1807 he tried cutting off foreign trade to stop the British and French from interfering with American ships, but the embargo only hurt America's own economy and was repealed in 1809. By the time Jefferson retired as president in 1809, his vision seemed terribly limited, an anchor to the Revolution rather than a predictor of the future. Passing his last years amid a stream of visitors to his home at Monticello, he was curiously silent about the nation's prospects, except when he shuddered about slavery.

JEFFERSON TAKES OFFICE IN A PRIMITIVE CAPITAL, 1801   On March 4, 1801, Thomas Jefferson was inaugurated as the third president of the United States. He took the oath of office inside the unfinished Capitol building in

Washington, D.C., the new capital city. In an attempt to heal wounds, he said, "We are all Federalists, we are all Republicans."

Earlier in the day, John Adams had fled to Massachusetts. Still smarting over losing the election, Adams was relieved to be leaving swampy, humid, and uncivilized Washington. Abigail Adams had frequently hung out the family's wash to dry in the still unfinished East Room of the Executive Mansion.

More than a mile separated the Capitol from the president's house. Although Pennsylvania Avenue had been partially cleared, travelers on horseback still had to pick their way through swamp and forest and sometimes got lost. Most people refused to make the trip after dark. Washington was called, sarcastically, "the city of magnificent distances." There was little magnificent about it.

The city's sprawling layout, planned by the French immigrant Pierre L'Enfant, physically separated the branches of the government. Congress met only a few months each year, and congressmen lived in ramshackle boarding houses within walking distance of the Capitol. They usually voted with their boarding housemates rather than with fellow party members or other representatives from the same state. After all, a vote against the majority view within the boarding house could cause severe repercussions when dishes were passed at table.

The Supreme Court's boarding house, too, was near the Capitol, and Chief Justice John Marshall governed both meals and the Court in patriarchal fashion. Marshall, a staunch Federalist, tolerated no dissenting opinions. Much to Jefferson's annoyance, the chief justice had been appointed to this lifetime post in the last days of Adams's term.

Jefferson's cabinet and other members of the executive branch lived near the president's house, where Jefferson conducted the affairs of state with a personal staff composed of one secretary. The president employed few servants and once shocked the British ambassador by personally opening the front door wearing his houserobe.

Jefferson's dinner parties became famous. He served fine food, French wine, and ice cream, which was a novelty in the United States. Guests included members of the cabinet, congressmen, diplomats, and visiting dignitaries. Conversation could turn to any subject, since Jefferson's interests ranged from politics to philosophy, from agricultural experiments to Indian languages, from the violin to architecture.

JEFFERSON'S FAITH IN DEMOCRACY   Jefferson's life was rooted in paradox. A wealthy, slaveholding Virginia tobacco planter, this complex man insisted that poor farmers and mechanics were the backbone of society. The sole heir to a fortune in land accumulated by his speculating father, he favored equal inheritance among all children and insisted that effort rather than luck brought the greatest rewards.

Jefferson was a democrat in part because he was an incurable optimist. The world was improving and progress inevitable. Everywhere he saw barbarism, superstition, and ignorance yielding to civilization, reason, and enlightenment.

Because of his democratic values, he believed that education could transform people's lives. He strongly supported public schools and late in life founded the University of Virginia. He hired its faculty and designed its campus, his greatest architectural achievement.

His faith in democracy came from two observations. One was that talented people often emerged from poor backgrounds. Democracy gave such people opportunities to improve themselves, and it gave society as a whole the benefit of their talents. No other system enabled talent to be developed so readily. He sometimes said that he favored an aristocracy of talent, or in other words, a meritocracy.

At the same time, democracy prevented a permanent ruling class from aggrandizing power and wealth solely for its own benefit. Monarchy, aristocracy, and dictatorship were inherently flawed because they kept power in the hands of a few people who were disconnected from the masses and could easily grow out of touch with society's needs. The French Revolution had resulted from just such a situation.

Democracy served the common good because it gave power to those who enjoyed popular support and shared the values of the masses. Power was held only so long as the people approved, and since public opinion was inevitably fickle, there would be no permanent ruling class.

Jefferson also saw democracy as the greatest protector of liberty. The temporary nature of democratic leadership made leaders respect liberty, since, if they fell from power (which was likely), liberty would protect them from their successors. Moreover, liberty celebrated the right of the average person to property, opportunity, and personal advancement based on merit.

Jefferson expressed his devotion to democracy and liberty in his architecture. The Virginia State Capitol at Richmond was the first neoclassical public building in America. Jefferson modeled the structure on an ancient Greek temple because Greece was the birthplace of democracy. This style, with its memorable columns, became the predominant one for American public buildings.

Jefferson's democratic ideas resonated with the public mood, especially along the western frontier. The Democratic Party expressed Jefferson's values, and the West became staunchly democratic and Democratic. In that most egalitarian region, depopulated of Indians and devoid of wealthy planters and their slaves, small-scale white farm families lived out the dream of a free, democratic society that Jefferson envisioned.

JEFFERSON HATES SLAVERY—IN THE ABSTRACT   On no subject was Jefferson more eloquent than on slavery. He hated it. He thought the institution degrading and inhumane, applauded its abolition in the North, and fought successfully to ban it in the Northwest Territories. He urged Virginia to consider gradual emancipation and supported ex-slaves voluntarily moving to Africa.

At the same time, race both fascinated and terrified him. He speculated that skin color might change with exposure to a different climate over several generations. Perhaps someday the South's slaves might turn white! Meanwhile, he believed, one must keep the races legally separate. Suspecting black inferiority, he believed that the white race had the right to dominate. He was a racist.

He was also a slaveowner who may have fathered children by his slave Sally Hemings. Although he freed a few of his own slaves in his will, most remained in bondage. Worse, he had accumulated massive debts in his last years, mortgaging his slaves in order to maintain the rural hospitality for which he was famous. Slaves had to be sold and their families broken up in order to settle the estate. This prospect tormented him.

For Jefferson, however, slavery was a given, a fixture of life, an age-old institution only beginning to crumble. Like others of his generation, he believed in halfway measures. Results were less important than intentions. He believed that slavery would fall in the fullness of time. He worked for its doom even as he received its fruits.

THE SUPREME COURT TAKES ON A NEW ROLE   Jefferson's presidency began with his enemies, the Federalists, in firm control of the judiciary. After the failure of an attempt to use the Constitution's impeachment powers to remove a Federalist Supreme Court justice, Jefferson and his supporters reluctantly backed down. As a result, the judiciary became independent of the executive branch in practice as well as in theory.

In 1803 John Marshall's Supreme Court issued a landmark ruling. At the end of his term in 1801, President John Adams had appointed William Marbury as a justice of the peace for the District of Columbia. Secretary of State James Madison, however, had held up the commission on President Thomas Jefferson's instructions.

When Marbury sued for his commission, the Supreme Court issued a remarkable ruling. John Marshall dismissed the suit on the grounds that the court lacked jurisdiction. This result pleased Jefferson. Marshall, however, went on to assert that the law under which Marbury had been commissioned contained an unconstitutional provision. Thus it was held for the first time, in *Marbury v. Madison,* that the Supreme Court could pass on the constitutionality of federal laws.

JEFFERSON PURCHASES LOUISIANA, 1803   Jefferson's most notable achievement as president was the Louisiana Purchase. He had sought to buy New Orleans and the right of western farmers to navigate and ship produce on the Mississippi River. The French, shrewdly observing the ongoing American migration to the western frontier, decided instead to sell all their American holdings. Besides, the sale would deprive the British of the territory.

For $15 million, the size of the United States was doubled. Exactly what had been purchased beyond New Orleans was not known. Louisiana had vague boundaries running westward as far as the imagination could roam. Jefferson had enough constitutional misgivings about the purchase to ask Congress to enact a constitutional amendment allowing it. Congress, however, ignored this request and merely appropriated the purchase funds.

Jefferson believed that enough land had been acquired to allow his beloved country of small-scale subsistence farmers to multiply for fifty or one hundred generations by expanding into the West. When thinking in this fashion, Jefferson gave little thought to the West's native inhabitants. Thus, the Louisiana Purchase was part of the long-term strategy of building and nurturing white democracy.

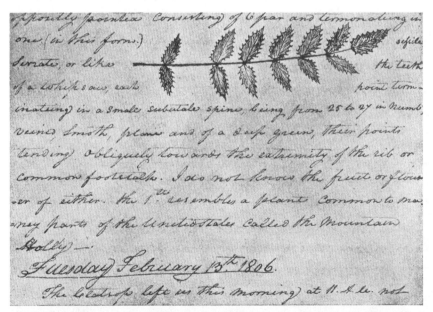

Several members of the Lewis and Clark expedition, including William Clark, kept meticulous journals describing everything they found during their exploration. (North Wind Picture Archives)

LEWIS AND CLARK EXPLORE THE WEST, 1804–1806   Intrigued by the mystery of the new territory, in 1804 Jefferson sent a large exploring party into the western region, led by Meriwether Lewis and William Clark. They were instructed to make sketches, to collect soil, plant, and animal specimens, to befriend Indians in order to build future trade relations, and to seek a water or land route across the region to the Pacific Ocean.

Setting out from St. Louis, the expedition made its way up the Missouri River. Much of this region was well known to fur traders. Lewis and Clark found a woman from the western Shoshone tribe, Sacajawea, who interpreted for them and guided them to her ancestral home in the Rocky Mountains.

The expedition then crossed the mountains and floated down the Columbia River to its mouth at the Pacific Ocean. After wintering on the coast, Lewis and Clark split into two parties for further explorations on their return trip. In 1806 they reached St. Louis and, soon after, personally reported to President Jefferson, who bubbled with excitement and enthusiasm.

BURR PLOTS TREASON IN THE WEST, 1806–1807   Not all was tranquil at home. In 1804 Aaron Burr, Jefferson's vice president, killed Alexander Hamilton in a duel. Burr, as interested in the West as Jefferson, withdrew from electoral politics and began to plot the establishment of a new western republic in the Mississippi River valley, with himself at its head.

Burr sought support from the British, the Spanish, and the American western military commander. In 1806 Burr and an adventurer named Harman Blennerhasset, who lived on an island in the Ohio River, organized a military expedition. The plot failed. Burr was caught; at Jefferson's orders he was tried for treason in 1807 in Richmond, Virginia. Although acquitted under Chief Justice John Marshall's strict definition of treason, Burr was ruined, and the West, for the time being, belonged securely to the United States.

ASSERTING NEUTRAL RIGHTS AND THE EMBARGO OF 1808   In 1807 Britain and France were again at war, and the fighting threatened American neutrality. Americans, especially farmers, had profited from selling surplus goods, including grain, to overseas customers. These goods were carried in American ships, which also profited from the trade.

Both the French and the British seized American ships that they suspected of trading with the enemy. The French, however, had a small navy and caused less trouble. The British stopped American vessels in the Atlantic Ocean, confiscated cargo that they believed destined for France, and took American seamen whom they claimed were British. Some were, but many were not; through this device of impressments, the desperate British had found a reliable way to man their fleet.

In 1807 a British frigate, the *Leopard*, stopped an American frigate, the *Chesapeake*, just outside American territorial waters. When the American ship refused the British the right to search for four deserters, the British attacked, won the battle, killed three Americans, and removed the alleged deserters. The *Chesapeake* incident soured relations and was not settled until 1811.

Unprepared for war with Great Britain, Jefferson decided to reduce the risk of war by cutting off American overseas shipping. In late 1807 Congress passed an embargo on all foreign trade. The Embargo Act was a disaster. During 1808 prices plummeted as foreign markets disappeared. Shipping merchants in the seaports went bankrupt, and their collapse dragged down other businesses. Urban unemployment soared, and people faced starvation. This manmade catastrophe provoked a political backlash.

JEFFERSON RETIRES TO MONTICELLO   In 1809 Jefferson followed Washington's example and retired after two terms. He returned to his beloved mountaintop plantation, Monticello. There he performed agricultural experiments, including an unsuccessful attempt to grow French wine grapes.

Many guests came to visit the Sage of Monticello. He showed them his inventions: his collapsible music stand, his chair with a built-in writing desk, his dumbwaiter for bringing wine from the cellar to the dining room, his eight-day clock in the central hall, and his three-panel windows that opened into doors. On a clear day he could see for forty miles around, including the University of Virginia and James Monroe's house at Ashlawn.

Jefferson's presidency did not live up to the grandeur of his vision. Perhaps Jefferson simply was at his best in theoretical speculation, or perhaps he was shrewd enough to understand that one cannot try to implement a grand vision and remain successful in politics.

FRICTION WITH BRITAIN LEADS TO THE WAR OF 1812

James Madison, who succeeded Jefferson in 1809, also had trouble staying neutral, especially when the British seizure of American seamen was matched by Indian attacks in the West.

In 1812 Congress pushed Madison into war against Britain and her Indian allies. The Americans crushed the Indians, but the British burned Washington, D.C., and antiwar New England threatened to secede. The peace treaty produced no gains, but Andrew Jackson won a victory at

New Orleans, which made him a hero. An odd consequence was the ruin of the nation's finances and the establishment, contrary to Jeffersonian principle, of the second Bank of the United States.

MADISON TAKES OVER, 1808   The embargo disaster took place just as the Democratic Party quarreled over Jefferson's successor. In those days the party's members of Congress picked the nominee. Some favored James Madison; others, James Monroe or George Clinton. Jefferson wanted Madison, and Madison got the nod. Despite the embargo, he won the election of 1808 against Charles Pinckney and a dying Federalist Party.

Jefferson and Madison had been political collaborators for two decades. Their philosophies were complementary but not identical. Jefferson was more theoretical, more ethereal, more other-worldly. Madison preferred concrete things, and he viewed politics more pragmatically as the art of the possible. Encumbered by a dark, brooding distrust of those who held power, he also profoundly respected the law. Nevertheless, he shared Jefferson's democratic vision.

In early 1809 Congress repealed the embargo and enacted the Non-Intercourse Act. Trade was resumed with all nations except Britain and France, which could regain trade rights by promising to respect American neutrality. Regardless of the risk of war, the United States had learned that it could not afford a policy of total isolation.

GROWING DISPUTES WITH BRITAIN, 1809–1811   In 1809, as American foreign trade resumed after the embargo's failure, the dispute with Britain turned bitter. Madison reopened trade with Britain after the British ambassador indicated that Britain would soon revoke its Orders in Council (1807), which had banned American or other neutral trade with France. Unfortunately, the ambassador misspoke, the Orders continued, and he was recalled. Madison then reinvoked the Non-Intercourse Act against Britain.

In 1810 Congress passed Nathaniel Macon's Bill No. 2, which authorized the president to reopen trade with either Britain or France. If either country repealed its laws against neutral commerce by early 1811, then the president could temporarily ban trade with the other country, which had three months to follow suit to gain back its trade.

France's Emperor Napoleon played a double game. He used the excuse of the Non-Intercourse Act to seize American ships in French ports. At the same time, he indicated that he was prepared to accept the terms laid down in Macon's bill. Madison rushed to reopen trade with France. Only later did he learn that Napoleon had not actually changed his policy with regard to neutrals.

During 1811 Madison pressured Britain to withdraw the Orders in Council, but Britain resisted the appearance of giving in to American pressure. British impressment of American sailors continued, and American relations with Britain grew steadily worse. An American frigate, the *President*, attacked a smaller British ship, the *Little Belt*, mistaking it for a ship that had impressed an American seaman.

BRITAIN SUPPORTS INDIAN RAIDS, 1811   That same year, 1811, the Indians of the Old Northwest, with promises of military help from the British, grew restless. The Shawnee chief Tecumseh, assisted by his brother, the Prophet, began to unite diverse native peoples over the issue of white encroachment on native lands. Tecumseh dreamed of creating a powerful Indian political and military combination that stretched from the Northwest to the Southwest. Indian frontier raids increased, and white settlers became frightened.

William Henry Harrison, the governor of Indiana Territory, moved to take the Indian capital on Tippecanoe Creek. Just before Harrison's troops reached the settlement, the Indians launched a surprise attack. Neither side won a decisive victory at Tippecanoe, but the battle raised Harrison's military stature and persuaded many frontier residents that war with Britain, which had backed the Indians, was necessary.

CONGRESS DECLARES THE WAR OF 1812   The new Congress that met in late 1811 included a large number of new, young members. Cocky, proud, and fiercely patriotic, these "war hawks," as they were called by John Randolph, clamored for war against Britain. The hawks included Henry Clay, John C. Calhoun, and Felix Grundy. Although a minority, these southerners and westerners were able to elect the charismatic Clay as speaker of the house.

In 1812 Madison found it impossible to resist the pressure for war. The hawks demanded war as a matter of honor, and the only way to avoid war, a British repeal of the Orders in Council, took place too late for news of it to reach the Congress before war was declared.

It was a sorry war. The United States had no military objective except to seize Canada. The British captured parts of the United States in order to gain political influence. The American army, led by elderly officers from Revolutionary War days, was incompetent. The government suffered the same lack of bureaucratic capacity as it had in the earlier war, and finances again created a problem.

In 1812 Detroit surrendered without firing a shot, and Indians under British direction massacred the garrison at Fort Dearborn (Chicago). The American invasion of Canada failed, in part because of a battle lost when the New York militia refused to cross the border. As the humiliated soldiers retreated across upstate New York, they were greeted with hoots and jeers.

The *U.S.S. Constitution* was nicknamed "Old Ironsides" for its ability to withstand British shells during the War of 1812. (Brown Brothers)

In contrast, the navy enjoyed surprising success against the renowned British fleet. Stephen Decatur and Oliver Hazard Perry became war heroes, and the *Constitution* was dubbed "Old Ironsides" for taking hits so well. In 1813 Perry took control of Lake Erie and declared, "We have met the enemy and they are ours."

INDIANS JOIN THE WAR, 1813–1814   In 1813 General William Henry Harrison defeated a combined British–Indian force in Canada at the battle of Thames River. Colonel Richard M. Johnson of Kentucky distinguished himself in the attack, but the battle's major event was the death of Tecumseh, which ended the dream of a pan-Indian western empire.

By 1814 the action shifted to the South. General Andrew Jackson led the Tennessee militia in a war against the Creek nation, whom Tecumseh had brought into the British–Indian alliance. After Jackson's victory at Horseshoe Bend, Alabama, the Creeks surrendered. The Treaty of Fort Jackson ceded more Indian land than any treaty in history. Most of what became Alabama and Mississippi passed into white hands.

THE WAR ENDS SLOWLY, 1814–1815   The British marched on Washington and humiliated Madison, who was forced to flee. The president's wife, Dolley, managed to save a favorite portrait of George Washington. The Capitol and the president's house were torched. Afterwards, the Executive Mansion, its stone stained by smoke, was painted white and renamed the White House.

Baltimore was the next British target, but the local residents had, unlike Washington's, arranged proper defenses. Fort McHenry's guns kept the enemy at bay. A nighttime bombardment failed, although the spectacular sight did move Francis Scott Key to write "The Star-Spangled Banner." Key's poem was later set to the music of a popular Anglo-American drinking song.

Meanwhile, sentiment against the war had grown ever stronger in New England. Generally Anglophilic and hostile to the frontier war hawks, Yankees wanted and needed British trade. Smuggling thrived. As the war continued and threats of invasion grew, many people in the Northeast questioned the value of the federal Union.

In late 1814 disaffected New England Federalists met secretly in Hartford, Connecticut. The Hartford Convention called for new laws and constitutional amendments to restrict federal power. Privately the group threatened secession if the war continued. Their meeting, considered treasonous by many, destroyed the already waning influence of the Federalist Party.

At that same time, American and British negotiators meeting in Ghent, Belgium, reached agreement to end the war. The American delegates, John Quincy Adams and Henry Clay, disliked the terms, but Clay at least had the satisfaction of beating the British delegates at poker. Neither country gained territory, impressment and neutral rights were not mentioned, and the United States lost the use of the fisheries off the Newfoundland coast.

Before news of the treaty could reach the United States, General Andrew Jackson won a spectacular victory at the battle of New Orleans on January 8, 1815. Repelling a British attack across an open field, Jackson hid his troops behind carefully made breastworks and waited until the British were quite close before raking the enemy with murderous fire. British casualties were 2,036, including the commander. Eight Americans were killed. Jackson became a hero.

The war left the country a shambles. By the time it ended, New England was talking secession, the federal government had proved barely capable of survival, and the economy was a mess. War debts threatened to create the same kind of economic trouble that had prevailed in the 1780s.

THE ERA OF GOOD FEELINGS, 1816–1824

The luckiest of presidents, James Monroe presided over a period so tranquil it became known as the Era of Good Feelings. Successful treaties in

1818 with Britain and in 1819 with Spain were matched in 1823 by the vigorous Monroe Doctrine, which asserted American supremacy in the Western Hemisphere. At the same time, John Marshall's Supreme Court upheld the sanctity of contracts, encouraged commerce, and increased the Court's own power.

The Missouri Compromise of 1820 proved that the political system could even deal with the nation's most difficult problem, slavery. Only a debate about the constitutionality of the federal financing of internal improvements disturbed the calm, at least until the election of 1824 produced a five-way battle for the presidency, which ended the good feelings.

MONROE DRAWS NEW BOUNDARIES   Virginia's domination of the presidency continued in 1816 with the election of James Monroe against a weak Federalist Party. Monroe's constitutional views were more flexible than Madison's, and his desire for political compromise and harmony caused his eight years in office to be called the Era of Good Feelings.

Foreign affairs took a decided turn for the better. In 1818 the United States and Britain fixed the Canadian boundary at the 49th parallel as far west as the Rocky Mountains. The two countries also agreed to joint occupation of the Oregon country (today's Oregon, Washington, Idaho, and British Columbia).

The next year Spain turned over Florida to the United States in return for the American government's assumption of American citizens' claims against Spain. In the Adams-Onís Treaty, Secretary of State John Quincy Adams and the Spanish ambassador drew a boundary between the United States and Mexico all the way to the Pacific Ocean. Spain gave up claims to the Pacific Northwest in return for American recognition that Texas was not part of Louisiana.

One of the most significant events of Monroe's presidency was the Monroe Doctrine. In 1823 the United States declared that no new European colonies could be established in the Western Hemisphere. The breakup of Spain's empire in Mexico and Latin America had whetted appetites. Although issued under Monroe's name, this militant, nationalistic document had actually been crafted by Secretary of State John Quincy Adams.

MARSHALL'S SUPREME COURT MAKES MAJOR RULINGS, 1819   On the domestic front the Supreme Court issued two important rulings in 1819. In the *Dartmouth College Case*, in which the eloquent Daniel Webster represented the college, Marshall's Court held that New Hampshire could not revoke a college charter that it had granted years earlier. The state must continue to honor its contracts. This ruling strengthened private entities, including businesses, that had received special charters from state legislatures.

Marshall's Court also considered banking. The Bank of the United States had come to an end when its charter expired in 1811, but the War of 1812 had proved so difficult for government finances that Congress and Madison chartered the second Bank of the United States in 1816.

In *McCulloch v. Maryland* the court ruled the Second Bank constitutional through a broad, Hamiltonian interpretation of the general welfare clause. The court also prohibited Maryland from taxing the federally chartered bank. "The power to tax involves the power to destroy," declared Marshall.

THE MISSOURI COMPROMISE LIMITS SLAVERY, 1820   The good feelings even extended to Congress. In 1819 Missouri petitioned to be admitted to the Union. A northern congressman persuaded the House to adopt an amendment to the admission bill. It prohibited the introduction of new slaves into Missouri and provided that the present slaves' future children born after statehood would become free at age twenty-five. The Senate, however, rejected this amendment.

The debate continued into 1820. Finally, Congress compromised. Missouri was to enter the Union as a slave state, but to maintain the balance in the Senate between slave and free states, Maine was to be set off from Massachusetts and admitted as a new free state. In addition, slavery was to be barred in the remaining Louisiana Purchase territory north and west of Missouri above 36°30' latitude. This compromise barely passed the North-dominated House.

Despite the Missouri controversy, Monroe's popularity remained high, and in 1820 he was reelected with only one electoral vote cast against him. (The dissenting elector explained that Washington deserved to be the only president elected unanimously.) The Federalist Party had totally disappeared.

CONTEMPLATING INTERNAL IMPROVEMENTS   Although Monroe was more willing than Madison to approve laws giving the federal government broad powers, he shared the general Jeffersonian suspicion of the federal government. Thus, in 1822 he vetoed the Cumberland Road Bill on the grounds that the Constitution did not specifically give the federal government the right to build highways. Monroe cheerfully proposed a constitutional amendment allowing federal funding of national improvements. Members of Congress chafed, wondering what the difference was between the Second Bank, which the Supreme Court had upheld, and the Cumberland Road. Monroe declined to offer an explanation.

THE FIVE-WAY ELECTION OF **1824**   The collapse of the Federalist Party, along with Monroe's erratic course of trying to please everyone, created political confusion. The result was a bitter five-way battle to succeed Monroe as president in 1824.

The leading candidate was Secretary of State John Quincy Adams. Tradition favored Adams, since both Madison and Monroe had served as secretary of state immediately before becoming president. Adams, on the other hand, was personally cold and aloof. Nor was he fully trusted, being the son of a Federalist and a Yankee suspected (correctly) of opposition to slavery. He said little about policy but could be considered a supporter of Monroe's approach.

Another strong candidate was Secretary of the Treasury William H. Crawford of Georgia. Southerners, especially those devoted to Jefferson's doctrine of a strict interpretation of the Constitution, liked Crawford, who called himself a states'-rights man. He had strong support in Congress, and the Jeffersonian Democrats traditionally had picked their presidential candidate in a congressional caucus.

Secretary of War John C. Calhoun also enjoyed support. He, too, appealed to white southerners, since as a South Carolinian he was considered sound on slavery. Unlike Crawford, however, in this phase of his career Calhoun was a broad constructionist, an enthusiastic nationalist, a federal road builder, and a proponent of a large military establishment.

Crawford's supporters undermined Calhoun, whose friends retaliated. The jousting among Monroe's cabinet officers gave outsiders a chance. Henry Clay, the charismatic House speaker from Kentucky, calculated that he might prevail, especially, as seemed possible, if the Electoral College did not produce a majority and the House decided the outcome.

Clay countered Crawford's Jeffersonian views with his own American System. He proposed a high tariff to protect American manufacturing, which pleased the East, along with massive federally financed internal improvements, which pleased the West.

Eager for Clay to be the western candidate, Clay and his friends urged the Tennessee legislature to support his election. To everyone's surprise, the Tennesseeans instead nominated General Andrew Jackson, a war hero and a man almost totally unknown in Washington politics.

Calhoun, playing the Scotch-Irish ethnic card, carefully engineered a large convention in Pennsylvania, where the Scotch-Irish dominated politics, to endorse his candidacy. Much to his amazement and consternation, the convention instead backed Andrew Jackson, who was also Scotch-Irish.

Calhoun then reassessed his chances. Adams had a lock on the nationalist constituency in the North, and Calhoun seemed destined to lose the South to Crawford over states' rights. Clay and Jackson were likely to divide the West. Calhoun withdrew and announced that he would accept the vice-presidency. He was unopposed.

The previously important congressional caucus endorsed Crawford, but so few representatives attended that the action was meaningless. More significantly, Crawford suffered a paralyzing stroke, which his friends unsuccessfully tried to keep secret. The stroke ruined his chances, but he refused to withdraw.

Legislators picked electors in some states; voters did so in other states. When the electoral vote was counted, Jackson had 99; Adams, 84; Crawford, 41; and Clay, 37. The popular vote was similar, although Clay had a slight edge over Crawford.

Since no candidate had a majority in the Electoral College, the election went to the House of Representatives, as Clay had calculated. Crawford's third-place Electoral College finish, however, destroyed Clay's chances, since the Constitution provided that the House could only elect one of the top three electoral vote getters, and Clay had placed fourth.

Clay found it easy to ignore Jackson's claims. Although clearly popular, Jackson lacked a majority. More voters had cast ballots for other candidates. Besides, Clay suspected Jackson of states'-rights views, and both were rivals for leadership of the West.

Adams, on the other hand, appealed to Clay. The two had utterly different personalities but shared a common political vision of a great national republic bound together by a vigorous federal government exercising strong political leadership. Besides, Clay's West and Adams's North could provide a long-term political combination every bit as strong as Jefferson's South and Burr's New York.

Clay's support for Adams in the House guaranteed Adams's election. It also enraged Jackson and his supporters, who charged that Jackson should have been picked because he got the largest number of both popular and electoral votes. After Adams appointed Clay as his secretary of state (and heir apparent to the presidency), Jackson charged that Adams had bought the presidency in a "corrupt bargain." The Era of Good Feelings was over.

JOHN QUINCY ADAMS'S PRESIDENCY, 1825–1829

John Quincy Adams's yearning for national greatness yielded nothing, in part because the cold, impersonal Yankee lacked the common touch and in part because the country was confused. Parochial Americans still insisted on borrowing almost everything from others—from the ancient

Greeks, from the modern British, from their own decaying revolutionary heroes. Adams's policies never rose above this confusion and quickly descended into pork-barrel politics, producing the Tariff of Abominations in 1828. In the end he fell before Andrew Jackson, who created a new, popular vision of America.

ADAMS PROMOTES NATIONAL GREATNESS   John Quincy Adams was out of touch with the nation's mood. When he asked Congress to establish a National University in Washington, he was merely ignored. But when he suggested a National Observatory, which he unfortunately called a "lighthouse of the skies," his poetic whimsy brought scorn and ridicule.

Adams was a wealthy, urbane, cosmopolitan man. An avid book collector, he read fourteen languages and conversed in eight. He had lived abroad much of his life. More than most Americans of his era, he understood the vast potential of the United States; he also recognized that the realization of national greatness required determination, effort, and the ability to transcend the limits imposed by past visions, including Thomas Jefferson's.

To Adams facts were facts, and the nostalgic longing for a republic of small-scale farmers replicating themselves ever westward to the Pacific represented a refusal to face facts. The world was changing, and the rise of industry was a reality. The only question for the United States was whether the country would remain predominantly rural and hence backward while under Britain's economic domination, or whether Americans would harness the continent's vast resources for national prosperity, strength, and glory.

Adams hated slavery because it discouraged slave initiative while it promoted slaveholder indolence. Worse, the defense of slavery caused slaveholders to fear all change. The Jeffersonian vision of rural virtue, small farms, and states' rights condoned and even celebrated the dominance of slaveholding planters as society's natural leaders. National greatness, to Adams, meant renouncing this outmoded institution. Just as Europeans, in order to make progress, would have to give up monarchy for democracy, Americans would have to replace slavery with a free market labor system.

Adams found only his native New England ready for the modern age. There, government provided mass public education, industry flourished, banks were sound, cities grew, and commerce thrived. Surplus rural population moved west, as in the South, but it was also drawn to the cities, and the rural birthrate was falling. All of this could be a model for the rest of the country, which was at least a generation behind New England.

AMERICANS BORROW CULTURE   Although Adams talked of national greatness, like most Americans he remained within the Jeffersonian tradition. He, too, admired neoclassical architecture, the prevailing style of public buildings in the 1820s. Even more than before, Americans modeled themselves consciously on the citizens of the ancient Greek democratic city-states. The fact that the Greeks had held slaves did not go unnoticed in the South.

For many visitors the American tendency to borrow cultural values was the country's least endearing trait. Americans seemed, in this era, peculiarly incapable of expressing a uniquely American vision. Even a genius as bold and as bright as Thomas Jefferson had not been able to provide a sustainable vista. Having all but invented modern republican politics in the revolutionary era, Americans of the next generation—represented by John Quincy Adams, Clay, and Calhoun—found it impossible to construct a culture that both resonated with and built upon the values of the founders.

In 1820 the *Edinburgh Review,* a well-known Scottish magazine, ridiculed American pretensions. "In the four quarters of the globe," asked the author sarcastically, "who reads an American book? or goes to an American play? or looks at an American picture or statue?" Indeed, who did?

JOHN QUINCY ADAMS PURSUES CONTRADICTORY POLICIES   The visionary but impractical Adams nearly drove Henry Clay crazy. Adams refused to remove any federal employees from office unless they were guilty of corruption. This policy, Clay pointed out, both deprived the administration of a patronage network and left in place Jackson–Crawford supporters who actively used their positions to destroy the administration.

In 1826 the Senate, under the influence of Vice President John C. Calhoun and Senator Martin Van Buren, confronted Adams over a projected American delegation to a Western Hemisphere conference in Panama. Although Congress eventually approved American participation, it humiliated Adams in the process.

Tariff policy concerning imports became controversial during Adams's presidency. To raise revenue, Jefferson had established modest tariffs instead of high protective tariffs that kept out foreign goods, protected American manufacturers, and raised no money.

With the rise of American manufacturing during and after the War of 1812, especially textiles, producers had gradually succeeded in getting tariff duties increased. An attempt to raise duties on wool and textiles failed in 1827 because other interests felt left out.

In 1828 Congress considered higher duties on many items, including textiles, wool, hemp, and iron. By lumping many special interests into a single bill, proponents were able to pass it. Opponents, mainly southern cotton exporters, called it the Tariff of Abominations. It became a major issue in the 1828 presidential election.

ADAMS LOSES, 1828   Adams lost to Jackson in 1828. The incumbent Adams carried New England and other parts of the Northeast; Jackson, the South and West. The election was decided by Jackson's success in Pennsylvania among his fellow Scotch-Irish and in New York. Jackson narrowly won New York because of the Albany Regency, the political machine of Martin Van Buren and William L. Marcy. In 1824 Van Buren had backed Crawford. Jackson was to reward Van Buren handsomely for his political conversion.

CONCLUSION

Circumstances change, and no political vision—even one from a thinker as brilliant as Thomas Jefferson—lasts more than a generation. Jefferson advocated economic and geographical expansion under the watchful eye of a federal government always more active than in Jefferson's rhetoric. The War of 1812 did little damage to the Democratic Party, and the so-called Virginia Dynasty of Jefferson, Madison, and Monroe marched on. The Jeffersonians temporarily resolved the controversy over slavery in Missouri in 1820, but rising sectional discord gradually dissolved the Era of Good Feelings amid the bitter personal rivalries of the presidential election of 1824. John Quincy Adams failed to build on the Jeffersonian past, and Andrew Jackson waited in the wings.

Recommended Readings

DOCUMENTS: Lester J. Cappon, ed., *The Adams-Jefferson Letters* (1959); Merrill D. Peterson, ed., *The Portable Thomas Jefferson* (1975); John A. Schutz and Douglass Adair, eds., *The Spur of Fame: Dialogues of John Adams and Benjamin Rush, 1805–1813* (1966).

READINGS: (GENERAL) Lance Banning, *The Jeffersonian Persuasion* (1978) and *The Sacred Fire of Liberty* (1995); Doron Ben-Atar, *The Origins of Jeffersonian Commerical Policy and Diplomacy* (1993); Joseph J. Ellis, *After the Revolution* (1979); Joanne B. Freeman, *Affairs of Honor* (2001); Annette Gordon-Reed, *Thomas Jefferson and Sally Hemings* (1997); John C. Miller, *The Wolf by the Ears* (1977); Jeffrey L. Pasley, *The Tyranny of Printers* (2001); (JEFFERSON'S PRESIDENCY) Stephen Ambrose, *Undaunted Courage* (1996); Richard E. Ellis, *The Jeffersonian Crisis* (1971); Richard Hofstadter, *The Idea of a Party System* (1969); Linda K. Kerber, *Federalists in Dissent* (1970); Drew R. McCoy, *The Elu-*

sive Republic (1980) and *The Last of the Fathers* (1989); R. Kent Newmyer, *The Supreme Court under Marshall and Taney* (1968); Merrill D. Peterson, *Thomas Jefferson and the New Nation* (1970); Norman K. Risjord, *The Old Republicans* (1965); Robert E. Shalhope, *John Taylor of Caroline* (1980); Marshall Smelser, *The Democratic Republic* (1968); (WAR OF 1812) Ronald L. Hatzenbuehler and Robert L. Ivie, *Congress Declares War* (1983); Donald R. Hickey, *The War of 1812* (1989); J. C. A. Stagg, *Mr. Madison's War* (1983); Steven Watts, *The Republic Reborn* (1987).

8

The Market Revolution, 1790–1850

OVERVIEW   From 1790 to 1850, approximately the length of a single lifetime, the United States underwent a startling transformation. This period of sudden, rapid change is called the Market Revolution. After a century of slow economic growth during the colonial period, the economy grew so rapidly that per capita income doubled in a single generation.

This economic "take-off" was marked by drastic changes in the way the economy worked. Subsistence agriculture increasingly gave way to sales of produce in the market, handcraft production was reorganized, factories were built, transportation was improved, and great cities emerged. A high birthrate and, after 1840, increasing immigration caused the population to soar from four million in 1790 to twenty-three million in 1850.

Most important to the Market Revolution was the idea of change itself. Prior to 1790 Americans, like people throughout history, had modeled their lives on those of their ancestors. Tried and true patterns of behavior worked best. By 1850 everyone knew that change was the only constant, that old ways had little value, and that each generation faced new challenges.

TEXTILE MANUFACTURING STARTS
THE MARKET REVOLUTION

Before the Market Revolution, clothing was both scarce and expensive; rural women spent much time spinning yarn by hand and weaving cloth.

In the 1790s water-powered mechanical spinning, a new technology that Samuel Slater brought from England, began to reduce fabric prices. Then the Boston Associates introduced water-powered weaving in 1813 at Waltham, Massachusetts, and in 1823 at Lowell. These mills provided industrial employment for young women and produced ever greater quantities of low-priced cloth. By 1860 cheap fabrics, made increasingly by poorly paid Irish immigrants, sold in a national market. In textiles, the Market Revolution was complete.

MAKING TRADITIONAL CLOTHING   From the beginning of settlement, white Americans clothed themselves as well as their slaves in European fashion. They wore shirts, trousers, dresses, and stockings hand cut and hand sewn from cloth. The making of clothes was a time-consuming task for females in almost every household. Only the well off could afford professionally tailored clothing.

The process began with yarn made at home. Women and girls in farm families devoted much of their time to converting raw linen plant fibers and fluffy bits of sheep's wool into yarn on their spinning wheels. Many families owned spinning wheels, but if they did not, one of these lightweight, portable devices could be borrowed. Women spent so much time spinning that an unmarried older woman became known as a spinster.

Cloth, commonly a combination of linen and wool called linsey-woolsey, was usually professionally woven on large handlooms. Both men and women did weaving. Because looms were expensive, took up much space, and required special skills, few people tried home production. Weavers usually accepted yarn from a neighborhood and provided cloth in exchange, retaining a portion of the output. This surplus could then be sold or traded outside the community.

Weavers sometimes dyed the fabric they made. Butternuts, for example, made a rich golden brown fabric. In some places professional dyers, often women, provided this service, taking their commission in the form of a percentage of the material, while in other areas cloth buyers dyed it themselves, often using ancient, secret family recipes.

Keeping a family in clothes was burdensome and expensive in terms of labor. Wool wore out quickly, and children outgrew their clothes. Even though a large amount of household labor went into the production of garments, few people owned many clothes. Adult slaves, for example, had only the coarse, simple clothing on their bodies, and slave children sometimes were kept naked to save the expense.

In an ordinary white family, each person usually had two sets of clothes. A man's set included underwear, a shirt, trousers, long stockings, and a neckerchief (a hat and shoes were extras). A woman's set included underwear, a skirt, a blouse, and an apron. The best set was for Sunday use, and after a year's wear it then became the set worn during the work-week the following year. Thus, clothes were supposed to last two years in annual rotations.

SAMUEL SLATER INTRODUCES MECHANICAL SPINNING, 1790

In the mid-1700s the English invented water-powered machinery that could spin high-quality yarn cheaply at enormous profit to the manufacturer. The inventors jealously guarded their machinery. No strangers could see it, and Britain allowed no skilled workers to leave the country.

But one workman, Samuel Slater, disguised himself as a sailor, left England, and moved to Pawtucket, Rhode Island. Carrying the plans for a spinning mill inside his head, in 1790 Slater opened the first American water-powered spinning mill. It was an enormous success.

Other spinning mills soon opened elsewhere in New England and in the Philadelphia area. Professional weavers, many of them English or Irish immigrants, settled near the new spinning mills. Meanwhile, the English had kept their technological lead in textiles by perfecting the more difficult task of using water power for mechanical weaving.

In the early 1800s many American families began to find it cheaper and easier to sell raw wool and buy yarn or cloth to make clothing. The time saved could be spent more productively on other tasks. Indeed, some families quit keeping sheep altogether and produced other items for sale, such as grain, eggs, or honey, from which they could gain a larger profit. Some of the purchased fabric was made from yarn spun at Slater's and other American mills, but much of it, and especially the highest quality that sold for the highest prices, came from the new English mechanical weaving mills.

THE BOSTON ASSOCIATES ESTABLISH THE WALTHAM MILL, 1813

A group of wealthy Boston merchants decided to set up a mechanical weaving mill. Organized as the Boston Associates, they sent one of their number, Francis Cabot Lowell, to England, where he toured the new mills and memorized the closely guarded machinery that he saw. Lowell returned to New England and perfected his own machinery, which improved upon the English devices. In 1813 the Boston Associates opened the first American combined water-powered spinning and weaving mill at Waltham, Massachusetts, near Boston.

During the War of 1812 the United States lost access to British fabrics. Waltham, as well as the rest of the American textile industry, prospered mightily. Cloth was sold at a high profit as fast as it could be produced. Indeed, within a few years Waltham's production had reached the maximum possible with that site's available water power.

FOUNDING THE LOWELL MILLS, 1823   In 1823 the Boston Associates established a series of textile mills at the new town of Lowell, Massachusetts. Growing rapidly, by 1850 it was the second most populous city in Massachusetts, with 33,000 people. Whereas Slater and other early mill owners had employed poor families as workers, the Boston Associates tried a different strategy. They recruited teenaged, single women from New England farm families. Wages for such workers were quite low—only $3.50 a week, about half the rate paid unskilled adult male laborers, who generally earned $1 a day for a six-day week.

To reassure parents that their daughters were safe, the company built boarding houses connected to the mill buildings. The young women lived under enforced curfews and various moral restrictions, including mandatory church attendance on Sunday. To reinforce the virtuous atmosphere, the employers sponsored a morally proper magazine, *The Lowell Offering*, written by and for the workers.

The workers considered the twelve-hour days and six-day weeks tending textile machinery easier than the farm work at home. Few, however, worked for more than several months, although many returned for additional periods. Women were attracted by the adventure of living in a town and by the chance to find a husband among the mechanics and carpenters employed at the mills and thus escape permanently from farm life. Many also saved a sum of cash, which could be used as a dowry, to attend school, to pay family debts, or to buy fancy clothes.

After turning to mechanical spinning and weaving, by the 1830s textile mills were beginning to add the capacity to print designs on cotton cloth. High-speed calico printing revolutionized fashion and taste. (Culver Pictures, Inc.)

TEXTILE MILLS SPREAD From 1830 to 1860 textile mills popped up wherever water power could be harnessed. Overall production soared, and as output rose, competition increased and prices fell. Consumers found cheaper cloth at higher quality. Careless, shoddy producers closed, as did smaller mills that lacked sufficient capital or water power to add new machinery.

By midcentury a national market had developed. Textile production became concentrated in places like Lowell that had access to large sums of capital, abundant water power, sophisticated technology, and cheap labor. Mills were located in rural areas, away from big cities that lacked water power and had expensive labor. Such production centers could and did manufacture more fabric at cheaper prices. Even when shipping costs were added, it was usually cheaper to buy Lowell cloth than to make it locally.

Although the economy as a whole benefited, as did consumers and owners, mill workers did not. Thin profit margins led Lowell's managers constantly to speed up production rates, reduce wages, or raise boarding house fees, all of which amounted to the same thing. When Lowell workers protested by striking, as they did in 1834 and 1836, they were replaced.

By 1860 few farm girls worked at Lowell. Instead, the workforce increasingly was composed of desperately poor Irish immigrant families. The men were paid no more than the farmers' daughters had been, and all members of the family had to work in order to make ends meet. They did not, however, live in company boarding houses, and owners no longer required workers to attend church.

Irish immigrants did not complain about their treatment as much as had the New England farm women. The Irish had been abused for centuries in their own country, and most were grateful to be in the United States instead of in famine-ridden Ireland.

KING COTTON DRIVES THE ECONOMY

The textile industry needed a raw fiber to spin and weave. Mechanization and vast increases in cloth production were based on a shift from linen and wool to cotton, which became practical only after Eli Whitney invented the cotton gin in 1793. After 1800 high demand for cotton produced both high prices and the march of new cotton plantations rapidly westward across the South.

More than any other crop, cotton was identified with slave labor. Cotton planters boasted that slaves made possible both King Cotton and the nation's prosperity, which depended heavily upon cotton exports to England. Cotton was, in fact, the key to the transatlantic economy, stimulating plantations in the South, textile mills in England and New England, food production in the Midwest, and the export of English capital to America's North and West to finance railroads.

WHITNEY'S COTTON GIN TRANSFORMS PRODUCTION, 1793   In the 1790s a small number of planters along the South Carolina seacoast grew a specialty crop called sea island cotton. This particular cotton plant, which did not grow inland, developed an oversized boll filled with loose strands of long, thick, fluffy white fibers that could be picked from the boll and spun into a yarn to make a luxury cloth. As late as 1800 only eight million pounds of sea island cotton were produced for export.

Inland, planters experimentally planted short-fiber cotton. This plant produced a small, hard boll tightly packed with short white fibers from which the seeds were difficult to remove. One laborer, usually a slave, could pick, deseed, and sort only about one pound of cotton a day. At that rate, short-fiber cotton cost too much to prepare to make cloth.

In 1793 Eli Whitney, an inventor from Connecticut, visited Georgia and, learning about the problem of processing short-fiber cotton, designed a small device to deseed cotton, the cotton gin. Whitney's gin, about the size of a breadbox, enabled one worker to process about fifty times more cotton than by hand.

The device was ingeniously simple. A worker placed raw cotton in the top and then hand-cranked two comblike metal pieces that separated the fibers from the seeds. The loosened strands of cotton could be prepared for machine spinning, while the irksome seeds dropped to the bottom, later to be pressed into cottonseed oil.

THE DEMAND FOR COTTON ENCOURAGES SLAVERY   Whitney's gin made processing raw cotton practical, and the new textile mills increasingly demanded cotton, which soon displaced wool as the leading fiber in cloth. Raw cotton production soared:

1810	171,000 bales
1830	731,000
1850	2,133,000
1859	5,387,000

Increased production required two main ingredients: land and labor. The land came from the Cotton Kingdom that spread itself westward across the entire lower South from South Carolina to Texas. Cotton could not move north of this area of mild winters because it required an exceptionally long growing season.

Slaves provided the labor. Had blacks been free, they might have preferred growing food for their own use in subsistence agriculture, or they might have been reluctant to move so rapidly toward or even beyond the Mississippi River. But the slaves had no say in the western migration of planters and their plantations. Slave labor made it possible to settle the cotton belt rapidly and to expand production quickly.

As a crop, cotton almost perfectly matched the needs of the slave system. Cotton required little specialized agricultural knowledge; provided near year-round labor, including months of backbreaking weeding; and could employ families, including children of all ages. No other crop in the United States ever made such full, effective use of slave labor.

In the early 1800s cotton prices were high, and the newly plowed land returned fabulous crops that made planters rich for relatively small investments. By the 1830s increased production, lower cotton prices, and higher land prices brought about by speculation gradually made cotton less profitable. The price of slaves also rose sharply, and unless a planter had inherited slaves, it became increasingly difficult to find the money to buy or hire the slaves needed to enter the business.

COTTON LEADS THE TRANSATLANTIC ECONOMY   Much of the cotton was exported to England, where it was made into cloth and returned to the United States. White southerners gradually became aware that they were part of a vast transatlantic commercial system, and they came to realize that they were engaged in the least profitable part of the business.

The planters made less money than did the cotton brokers (many of them Yankees), the shippers (almost all Yankees), or the textile manufacturers, whether in England, in Lowell, or in the South. Furthermore, planters, whose cotton exports to England provided the positive balance of trade that made imports to the United States possible, had to buy many manufactured goods, which came from either Britain or the Northeast. Duties on imports kept prices high.

Southern cotton exports to the North and to England stimulated manufacturing in both those areas. Although the South grew much of its own food, and many large plantations were self-sufficient, southerners often found cotton so profitable that they preferred to import food from the Midwest, which also shipped food to the Northeast. The English invested in railroads and manufacturing in the Northeast and the Midwest. Every section of the transatlantic economy prospered from this increased regional specialization and trade.

Southern planters boasted that both the American and British economies were beholden to King Cotton. And the key to the success of cotton, white southerners believed, was the institution of slavery. This latter idea was not entirely true, because cotton could be grown without slavery; but much northern guilt about slavery grew out of the perception that the entire nation owed its prosperity to the enslaved producers of cotton. No one asked the slaves for their views.

IMPROVED TRANSPORTATION STIMULATES COMMERCE

Improved transportation was a key ingredient in the Market Revolution. Only when goods could be shipped cheaply, efficiently, and reliably over long distances could an integrated national economy emerge. The first significant change was the invention of the steamboat in 1807, which opened trade in the continent's interior. Then came canals, which enlarged markets in the 1820s by enabling heavy, bulky goods, particularly grain and coal, to be moved at low cost. After 1830 railroads, which were built where steamboats and canals did not go, made it fast, easy, and profitable to ship perishable goods to national markets.

ROBERT FULTON INVENTS THE STEAMBOAT, 1807   The idea of applying steam power to boats was tested in the 1780s, but only in 1807 did Robert Fulton's *Clermont* make a convincing demonstration on the Hudson River between New York and Albany. The idea quickly caught on, and by the 1820s large numbers of steamboats plied America's rivers.

These boats revealed much about the emerging entrepreneurial spirit. Quickly constructed from cheap, plentiful green lumber, the average steamboat lasted less than five years. It survived long enough for an owner to make a fortune. Crude but fast boats rode high on the water. They could puff their way up the shallowest streams in search of new business. Boilers were gigantic but inefficient because wood, used for fuel, was cheap, and the technical knowledge for constructing engines was primitive. Captains were often incompetent even when sober, and the boilers frequently blew up, sinking the boats and killing the passengers with steam.

STEAMBOATING IN THE MISSISSIPPI AND OHIO VALLEYS   Nowhere did the steamboat make a larger difference than in the Mississippi and Ohio River valleys. Previously cut off by the Appalachian Mountains from the important trade that flowed along the Atlantic seacoast, residents of the interior had developed a self-sufficient, isolated culture.

Although Kentucky and Ohio had good soil and a climate favorable to corn, the lack of a market gave residents little incentive to produce. Lacking both towns and transport to the East, western farmers simply planted less corn and took life easy or turned their corn into whiskey, a form of liquid asset that could be stored easily. Farmers needing cash floated their produce down the Ohio and Mississippi rivers on wooden rafts. At New Orleans they usually sold in a glutted market at low prices, often watched their produce rot on the wharf, and always had to walk home, which took an average of six weeks along robber-infested trails.

The steamboat changed everything. Some farmers found it profitable to load produce on a boat and sell it upstream in drought-stricken areas or in places to the north where crops had not yet come in. Others continued to float produce to New Orleans, but now they returned home safely on a steamboat in less than a week. They also carried goods home on the boat.

Economic activity grew. For example, western farmers long had planted apples and peaches, but these crops had been strictly for home use. Fruit previously had had no economic value. Locally, everyone's fruit ripened at the same time and would spoil if shipped to faraway places. The steamboat marked the beginning of sales to distant places where fruit did not grow or where it ripened at a different time.

From 1817 to 1855 the number of steamboats on western waters rose from 17 to 727. As a result, numerous cities along the heartland's major rivers became inland ports. The Atlantic seaports of Boston, New York, Philadelphia, Baltimore, and Charleston now had western rivals in Pittsburgh, Cincinnati, Louisville, St. Louis, and New Orleans.

Cincinnati, in particular, grew to be the leading city in what was then the American West. Founded with Yankee capital, its location just across the Ohio River from Kentucky gave it a southern flavor. Its main fame, however, came from its processing of the numerous hogs that in free, democratic fashion roamed its unpaved streets. Barrelled salt pork and soap were the most famous products of the city that was nicknamed "Porkopolis."

BUILDING CANALS   Canals also improved transportation. Heavy, bulky products such as grain could be shipped cheaply—at 10 percent of wagon rates—on barges that floated on canals while being pulled by horses or mules walking along the bank. The speed was barely faster than a person walked, but the animals required little feed, and canals could be kept open more predictably than the rivers that dried up in droughts or flooded in storms.

In the early 1800s the Atlantic seaport cities, recognizing that the population was pushing inland, tried to keep control of inland trade and dominate the hinterlands by building canals. Boston did benefit from the Middlesex Canal, but Washington, D.C., profited little from the canal along the Potomac River. An attempt to build a canal above Richmond along the James River into West Virginia failed due to the high cost of building locks in the mountains.

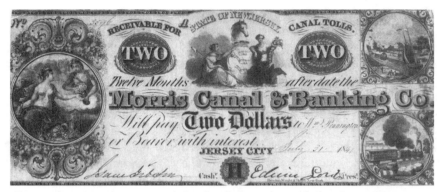

All sorts of private paper money circulated in the United States before the Civil War. Here a canal company's money was based on the prospect of future canal tolls. How much was it worth? A good question. . . . (© Bettmann/CORBIS)

THE ERIE CANAL OPENS, 1825   By far the most successful waterway was New York's three-hundred-mile-long Erie Canal, built by Governor De-Witt Clinton. Begun in 1817, this canal crossed the flat area between Albany and Buffalo north of the Appalachian Mountains. When it opened in 1825, it connected New York City, which already enjoyed excellent access to Albany along the Hudson River, with the Midwest's Great Lakes at Buffalo.

The Erie Canal set off a major boom in New York City. Population, manufacturing, and commerce soared, as New York quickly eclipsed Philadelphia as the most important city in America. The canal brought cheap western food to New York, where it replaced more expensive, locally grown food. New Yorkers also reshipped food at a profit to other eastern seaports.

Raw materials also came cheaply from the West, and New York manufacturers benefited from that too. Increased availability of produce and locally made products led more ships to call at the port, and New York boasted the only regularly scheduled ships sailing to England. That, too, led to increased business. Finally, the profits made from trade and manufacturing made New York the center for capital, which could be attained more easily and at lower interest rates than in other cities. New York quickly became the nation's banking center.

Upstate New York was also transformed. Sleepy towns along the canal route blossomed into a string of important cities that included Utica, Syracuse, Rome, and Buffalo. Rochester, settled almost entirely by New Englanders, underwent rapid change. Flour millers who had started with modest mills became, much to their surprise, wealthy owners of major works.

Rapid economic change was accompanied by the collapse of Rochester's political system, long dominated by the founding families, and a religious upsurge, in which the newly successful suddenly praised God for their fortunes and encouraged their workers to join. Those who did were more likely to be promoted to junior partners in business.

Philadelphia, New York's desperate rival, planned its own canal system. Central Pennsylvanians, however, favored using the Susquehanna River to connect to the port at Baltimore. Although several interconnecting canals were built across Pennsylvania, the high cost of crossing the Appalachian Mountains made an effective system impossible.

RAILROADS FORM A NATIONAL TRANSPORTATION NETWORK   Baltimore and Charleston also recognized the importance of the Erie Canal. These cities were determined not to be left behind. Geography, however, made canals impossible, and so in 1830 both cities borrowed an English invention and opened the first American railroads. Despite the early start, neither became a major rail center.

Railroads could be built far from water, where steamboats or canals could not go, and rail routes could be laid through mountains. The Pennsylvania canal system was eventually completed with a railroad. Railroads, however, posed their own problems. They were hideously expensive to build. During the 1840s one-tenth of all the new capital invested in the United States was spent to build railroads. By 1850 the nation had 8,879 miles of track.

Construction was difficult and frequently dangerous. In the North, Irish immigrants provided most of the labor, as they had for digging canals. Many died from disease and accidents. In the South some slave labor was used, but the Irish also worked there because many slaveowners were reluctant to risk the lives of their valuable slaves in such dangerous construction.

Part of the problem in the early years was the brittleness of the iron rails, which frequently broke while being laid or later in use. The railroad industry tried desperately to solve this technical problem, at first in the 1840s by using a rolling method to make iron rails, and later in the 1860s more successfully through Bessemer's process for making steel, which led to the replacement of iron rails with steel ones. By 1850 the railroads had created a vast iron industry that was rapidly consolidated into large-scale enterprises centered in Pennsylvania.

Railroads were also inherently political. Although some were government sponsored, including the principal line in Georgia, most were built with private money, often from England. Even with private financing, railroad companies required legislative approval both for incorporation and for the acquisition of rights of way. As a practical matter, a railroad company had to be able to place its track wherever it wished, even if a property owner opposed the route. Thus, railroads had to be given the right of eminent domain, that is, the right to take over private property and pay a fair price for it, whether or not the owner wished to sell.

By the 1850s two vast regional railroad systems, one northern and one southern, had been built. Trains could not leave their home system, however, because most of these two systems used different track widths—the southern gauge was three and a half inches wider—and they met at only two points: Louisville, Kentucky, and Washington, D.C. Cities along rail lines had prospered, and towns passed by, like Georgia's capital, Milledgeville, were beginning to dwindle. Some rail junctions, such as Atlanta and Chicago, were already boomtowns.

Railroads both reinforced and changed trade patterns. Overall, commerce grew even more rapidly, as many perishable goods were now shipped quickly to market. Between 1817 and 1852 the time for shipping goods from Cincinnati to New York dropped from fifty-two days by hand-poled keelboat and overland wagon to six days by rail. Since trains often followed the earlier canal and steamboat routes, trade frequently flowed in familiar ways. But not always.

In 1850, for example, 80 percent of Cincinnati's trade floated on the Ohio River to southern markets. Local political and business leaders dared not offend the South and refused to discuss slavery. Ten years later 80 percent of the city's trade moved on railroads to northern markets. Local leaders then expressed open hostility to slavery.

THE MARKET REVOLUTION TRANSFORMS SOCIETY

Technology, invention, capital, and improved transportation combined to create an economic revolution in the United States during the early 1800s. Even before the organization of the large industrial corporation or the use of large-scale factories, economic life was transformed. The key was specialization, whether by farm women who lived near Philadelphia and entered the butter business, by Cincinnati's pork processors, or by Rochester's flour millers.

The topsy-turvy national market produced both losers like Philadelphia's traditional shoemakers and winners like Lynn's shoe entrepreneurs. Success came to those who had access to capital. Skilled workers sought protection through labor unions, which generally failed. Limited social mobility drew little protest, because immigrants who arrived on the bottom pushed those born in the United States up the scale. Cities grew rapidly and contained vast, new wealth and appalling poverty. Everyone angled to make a dollar.

ADOPTING NEW WAYS OF BUSINESS   People gave up old ways, even though they had been followed for centuries, and took up new ones. Inventors played a major role in this change. After Eli Whitney invented the cotton gin, he and Simeon North independently manufactured firearms using standardized, interchangeable parts. Their idea depended upon fine tolerances that helped develop the machine tool industry. In the 1820s Thomas Blanchard's gunstock lathe allowed mass production copied from a single, hand-carved model. New Englanders patented the largest number of inventions, but one of the most successful inventors was the Virginian Cyrus McCormick, who pioneered the mechanical grain reaper in 1831.

Farm families became less likely to produce at home all that they consumed. They tried to specialize in whatever their particular farm could produce best and then traded or sold some of the surplus in order to obtain the items they no longer produced. For many families, the first item to be bought was cloth, which was produced cheaply and efficiently in the new textile mills.

Farm women played a major role in this change. For example, in the rural townships nearest Philadelphia, farm wives and their daughters kept cows and made vast quantities of butter for sale in the Philadelphia market. Many of these women took the butter into the city and sold it at the market on their own account. By tradition, women kept the money from the sales of their own production.

Residents of towns and cities were even more likely to find a special niche in the economy. Different places had different advantages, and local production became highly targeted for sale in a national market. Thus, the numerous hogs in the vicinity of Cincinnati made that city the center for pickled pork and soap. Similarly, the wheat belt of northern New York led Rochester to become the Flour City. The entire lower South, with its long growing season and its slave labor, became the Cotton Kingdom.

For some Americans the national market offered extraordinary opportunities for economic success. Matthew Baldwin, a modest master ironmonger in Philadephia, began to produce railway locomotives just as that industry was developing. By the 1850s Baldwin had expanded his small shop to more than five hundred employees, which made him one of the leading employers in the country. Baldwin's workers, however, had no prospect for following in their boss's footsteps. The capital required to enter the business had grown enormously in just a few years.

While the masses bought cheap shoes from Lynn's factories, well-off ladies like this one continued to buy handmade shoes at fancy shoe stores. (Culver Pictures, Inc.)

FROM SHOEMAKERS TO SHOE ENTREPRENEURS   Philadelphia shoemakers were among the major losers. In this ancient craft, an apprentice learned the trade and then became a journeyman who temporarily worked for wages. After saving money, a shoemaker then became a master with his own shop. Traditionally, journeymen had been able to earn decent wages of up to $2 a day, which had enabled most to become masters. Amid the Market Revolution, however, Philadelphia proved to be a poor place for making shoes from scratch by hand in competition with the new system. By the 1840s local shoemakers faced bankruptcy.

The winners were the shoe entrepreneurs of Lynn, Massachusetts. They divided the labor of making a shoe into multiple parts and assigned many of these tasks, such as sewing the shoes or polishing them, to women and children, who performed the work cheaply at their own homes. This system, called out work, reduced the need for highly skilled, highly paid master shoemakers. Awash in capital, Lynn's shoe masters also bought vast quantities of leather cheaply and hired expert cutters to use the leather efficiently.

The subdivision and deskilling of labor, combined with national marketing, led Lynn's shoe entrepreneurs to dominate the American shoe business. The consumer, of course, benefited, since Lynn shoes were incredibly cheap, less than half the price of shoes made by traditional methods. By the 1840s shoemaking had been destroyed as a craft. Only after 1850 did shoe entrepreneurs gradually begin to build factories and use machinery and unskilled immigrant labor to make cheap shoes. The crucial change that made such manufacturing possible was the national market created by the Market Revolution.

PRINTING BECOMES AN INDUSTRY   The printing industry provides another example of how the Market Revolution changed America. In 1816 James Harper finished his apprenticeship to a New York printer. A year later, with $1,000 saved from his work as a journeyman and $1,000 borrowed from his father, a Long Island farmer, James Harper and his brother founded a printing company.

The technology was similar to that Benjamin Franklin had used a century earlier. Printers set type by hand and hand-pulled printed sheets of paper for books or newspapers from presses at a maximum speed of 250 copies per hour. By the 1850s Harper Brothers was the largest printer and book publisher in the country, and although typesetters still worked by hand, the firm produced more than a million volumes a year on high-speed steam presses that operated at the rate of 18,000 sheets of paper per hour.

In the 1830s Horace Greeley finished his apprenticeship as a printer and went to New York to seek work. Because of a temporary glut of journeymen printers, he barely made enough to avoid starvation. Eventually, conditions improved, and he saved $1,000, but it took political connections to put together the $10,000 necessary to buy a power press to start the *New York Tribune* in 1841. Greeley became a famous editor.

Ten years later, in 1851, Henry J. Raymond, who had worked for Greeley, founded the *New York Times*. To compete, Raymond needed the expensive high-speed press invented by Richard Hoe in 1846, and the firm had to be capitalized at $100,000. Able to contribute only $1,000, Raymond never had control and was later forced out of the company. Thus, in one generation between 1817 and 1851, the amount of capital required to succeed in printing and publishing had multiplied by fifty.

CAPITAL FLOURISHES   The Market Revolution created unprecedented opportunities for capital. A relatively small investment, if combined with favorable local conditions, good transportation, and luck, might generate an overwhelming comparative advantage. An entrepreneur could charge lower prices and make higher profits, with the profits providing the new capital that enabled the business to gain further advantage and yet more market share.

Attempts were made to measure entrepreneurial activity, and particularly to evaluate businessmen who wanted to borrow money or make deals. The emergence of a national economic market led to the need for a fair measure of individual worth. In 1841 Arthur and Lewis Tappan, two New York City merchants, sent agents to every county in the United States to evaluate all local businessmen. Their credit rating service, the forerunner of Dun and Bradstreet, played a crucial role in economic development by assisting the expansion of credit.

LABOR PROTESTS AS INEQUALITY INCREASES   For skilled labor, the Market Revolution produced mixed results. Some trades, such as iron molding and machinery, prospered enormously, with wages rising for scarce skills to as much as $4 a day. In other trades, like printing, work was usually plentiful, but typesetters had to recognize that they would never make more than $2 a day, might be laid off in economic slumps, and could not save enough money to open their own shops. Still other trades, such as shoemaking, simply disappeared. Factory shoeworkers earned about $1 a day, the rate for unskilled labor.

In large cities, the distribution of wealth became more uneven. In 1825 the wealthiest 1 percent in Boston, New York, and Philadelphia, including manufacturers as well as merchants, owned about a quarter of the wealth; by 1850, they owned half. A new, educated middle class of doctors, lawyers, and specialized managers also prospered. Small shopkeepers did about as well as before, while skilled artisans shrank in relative wealth and as a percentage of the population. The ranks of the unskilled, mostly poor and all without property, increased from about one-fifth to two-fifths of the population.

These changes did not take place without objection. As early as the 1790s, skilled artisans had sneered at nonproducing "drones" such as merchants, bankers, and attorneys. As craftsmen's status and relative income fell in the 1820s and 1830s, the comments grew more bitter. Proclaiming a "producer ideology," artisans denounced people who did not make tangible things for a living. They promoted the "labor theory of value," that is, that only labor created economic value.

Some artisan spokesmen, such as William Leggett and Robert Rantoul, entered politics, often as Democrats. Other radicals broke with mainstream politics to organize the anemic Workingmen's parties in the 1820s. In the long run, skilled workers found that the greatest political influence came through participation in mainstream parties and elections. After 1850 in some cities artisans were elected to high office. For example, the mayors of New Orleans and Lynn, Massachusetts, were respectively a printer and a skilled shoeworker.

Artisans also organized labor unions to promote their interests. Unions were created in the booming 1790s, but few survived past 1800. In the 1830s skilled workers in some trades organized both local and national unions, which advocated a ten-hour day. In Philadelphia these unions succeeded in setting up a citywide trades council, but no national unions from this period lasted, and the failure to organize beyond local areas proved fatal as the economy became national. Few unions survived the economic Panic of 1837. Organized labor did well during boom years but faded during economic downturns.

Labor's protests were surprisingly ineffective. For one thing, many artisans, perhaps a third, continued to follow custom. These traditionalists drank heavily, skipped work on Monday, which they celebrated as "St. Monday," and cultivated close relationships with their masters—a name the oldtimers preferred to the modern term *employers*. Other craftsmen, perhaps half, embraced modern values, including a strong work ethic, but did so through the transforming power of evangelical Christianity. Only about a sixth of skilled workers adopted radical political or labor ideas.

AMERICANS FACE LIMITED SOCIAL MOBILITY   In reality, there was little social or economic mobility. Most American children grew up to belong to the same class as their parents. Merchants, artisans, and laborers begat, respectively, merchants, artisans, and laborers. Of those who were wealthy, 90 percent had wealthy parents; only 2 percent were born poor. Relative to others, people were as likely to move down as up.

Few complained, for a variety of reasons. For one thing, the poor, unskilled workers on the bottom were unsettled. They contributed little either to politics or to community consciousness. Most of these unpropertied masses moved from town to town looking for work by the day. They signaled that they wanted jobs by standing in front of the courthouse early in the morning; if they could get no work for a few days, they moved on. In most cities as many as half the people had lived in town less than a year.

Then, too, the Market Revolution had produced a growing economy. Per capita income doubled within a generation, and many people whose *relative* socioeconomic standing was no higher than their parents' nevertheless did enjoy higher living standards. For many, even though their *share* of the economic pie stayed the same, their *piece* of pie still grew, because *overall* the pie had doubled in size.

On the whole, Americans preferred to believe that the United States was a country of opportunity. Matthew Baldwin, James Harper, and Horace Greeley were heralded as proof that people could succeed on their own. This ideology was reinforced by evangelical Protestantism, which held that people were primarily responsible for looking after themselves. Any success was visible proof of holiness and God's favor.

Many ambitious artisans abandoned their crafts for greater opportunities in commerce. If they were too old to change, then they tried to provide suitable training for their children. In the early 1800s, the principal demand for the expansion of public education, including high schools, came from urban artisans. A high school diploma led to employment as a clerk in the booming commercial sector.

Finally, immigration pushed native-born Americans up the social and economic ladder as thousands of unskilled and impoverished newcomers entered at the bottom. To immigrants, especially the Irish, the standard of living in the United States was higher than at home, even if for some people it had declined from what it had been in the United States in earlier years.

LARGE CITIES GROW RAPIDLY   Urban populations, defined as communities with at least 2,500 people, rose from 3 percent in 1790 to 15 percent by 1850. Although the country remained rural, the emerging national economy quickly led to the creation of several large cities. In a single lifetime the scale and magnitude were transformed. In 1790 New York's 33,000 people vied with Philadelphia's 42,000 for national leadership. Each of the next three most populous cities, Boston, Charleston, and Baltimore, had fewer than 20,000 residents. By 1850 New York had 515,000 people and its thriving suburb Brooklyn, another 97,000. Philadelphia's metropolitan population was 409,000, while the populations of Baltimore, Boston, New Orleans, and Cincinnati were each over 100,000.

Rapid growth and large populations created enormous urban problems. Water was often contaminated, and not until the middle of the century was good water from reliable sources piped in, at great expense. Sewer systems were primitive or nonexistent and epidemic diseases widespread, such as the cholera that struck in 1832, 1849, and 1866. Every year more city dwellers died than were born.

Public safety measures did not keep pace with rapid growth. City residents resisted higher taxes to replace unpaid volunteer night watchmen with a professional police force. In the 1840s only the rise of marauding gangs, highly organized vice, and street robberies finally led to hiring uniformed officers on call day or night. Fire protection long remained a private matter until people became disgusted by the volunteer fire companies who frequently fought each other while buildings burned to the ground.

The principal method of getting around the city was on foot. Since most people could not walk more than three miles to work, there was little sprawl. Construction techniques, however, limited building height to about six stories. Poor transport and low buildings led to incredible congestion and high rents. Large families sometimes lived in a single room, and ten thousand people might live on one block.

As cities grew and became more congested, wealthy residents moved from the commercial centers, where they had traditionally lived behind or above stores, to outlying areas, where they built mansions on landscaped lots and kept horses in private stables. The suburbs flourished, and by the 1850s the middle classes followed the wealthy in commuting to the city by horse-drawn streetcar or steam railway.

Neighborhoods became identified with particular social classes, and this tendency increased when massive immigration began in the 1840s. Class and ethnicity were linked; the Irish in most cities were unskilled laborers; the Germans, skilled craftsmen. Few immigrants were middle class. No one, it appears, wanted to live near the Irish—sarcastically ridiculed as the "Great Unwashed"—and Germans formed neighborhoods where everyone spoke their language. One could live in New York's Kleindeutschland or Cincinnati's Over the Rhine without knowing or hearing a word of English.

The American city demonstrated both what was right and what was wrong with the country. Fabulous wealth was generated next to the grimmest poverty. Intense local pride led private donors to establish numerous museums and charities, but public money could seldom be found to improve urban life. Democratic political rights degenerated into corrupt political machines, and the ideal of equality contrasted with frequent ethnic riots. Every city puffed itself with expectations of even greater glory in the future, and yet almost no one pondered the price of success.

Meanwhile, there was always a dollar to be made. In the final analysis, that was the message of the Market Revolution.

CONCLUSION

The Market Revolution produced the single most dramatic change in American history. Textile manufacturing based on slave-produced cotton marked the beginning of an industrial revolution that over the long run transformed people's lives in multiple ways. Transportation improvements in the form of steamboats, canals, and railroads accelerated economic growth by creating national markets. Business began to be conducted in new ways, as products such as shoes and books were produced on a massive scale. Inequality in wealth increased, labor protests failed, and large cities grew rapidly. That all these changes took place simultaneously is why the total result is called the Market Revolution.

Recommended Readings

DOCUMENTS: Joseph G. Baldwin, *The Flush Times of Alabama and Mississippi* (1853); *Lowell Offering* (1840–1845); Frances Trollope, *Domestic Manners of the Americans* (1832).

READINGS: (GENERAL) Richard D. Brown, *Modernization* (1976); Thomas C. Cochran, *Frontiers of Change* (1981); John L. Larson, *Internal Improvement* (2001); Charles Sellers, *The Market Revolution* (1991); (TEXTILES) Thomas Dublin, *Women at Work* (1979); Jonathan Prude, *The Coming of Industrial Order* (1983); Philip Scranton, *Proprietary Capitalism* (1983); Cynthia J. Shelton, *The Mills of Manayunk* (1986); Anthony F. C. Wallace, *Rockdale* (1978); Gavin Wright, *The Political Economy of the Cotton South* (1978); (LABOR) Mary H. Blewett, *Men, Women, and Work* (1988); Jeanne Boydston, *Home and Work* (1990); Alan Dawley, *Class and Community* (1976); Herbert G. Gutman, *Work, Culture, and Society in Industrializing America* (1976); Joan M. Jensen, *Loosening the Bonds* (1986); Alexander Keyssar, *Out of Work* (1986); Bruce Laurie, *Artisans into Workers* (1989); David Roediger, *The Wages of Whiteness* (rev. ed., 1999); W. J. Rorabaugh, *The Craft Apprentice* (1986); Mary P. Ryan, *Cradle of the Middle Class* (1981); Merritt R. Smith, *Harpers Ferry Armory and the New Technology* (1977); Peter Way, *Common Labour* (1993); (COMMUNITIES) Christopher Clark, *The Roots of Rural Capitalism* (1990); Timothy J. Gilfoyle, *City of Eros* (1992); Paul A. Gilje, *The Road to Mobocracy* (1987); Bruce Laurie, *Working People of Philadelphia* (1980); Suzanne Lebsock, *The Free Women of Petersburg* (1984); William H. and Jane H. Pease, *The Web of Progress* (1985); Howard Rock, *Artisans of the New Republic* (1979); Steven J. Ross, *Workers on the Edge* (1985); Winifred G. Rothenberg, *From Market-Places to a Market Economy* (1992); Ronald Schultz, *The Republic of Labor* (1993); Christine Stansell, *City of Women* (1986); Charles G. Steffen, *The Mechanics of Baltimore* (1984); Alan Taylor, *William Cooper's Town* (1995); Sean Wilentz, *Chants Democratic* (1984).

9

Evangelical Religion and Reform, 1790–1850

OVERVIEW In 1790 most Americans had little interest in religion. During and after the American Revolution, many people put political principles above religion. Despite this, religion was not dead; going to church remained a favorite activity for many people. Of those Americans who did profess faith, probably 98 percent called themselves Protestant Christians. Catholics and Jews were few.

Between the late 1790s and 1830, intense religious revivals swept across the United States. This evangelical upsurge, similar to the revivals of the 1740s, became known as the Second Great Awakening. The movement began on the southern frontier, where residents developed a religion that combined a belief in universal salvation with emotional display. The northeastern revivals shared these traits, but evangelical Calvinists also stressed reform. Northerners established Sunday schools and missions; gave up gambling, premarital sex, and liquor; built hospitals, prisons, and schools; and considered women's rights. Not everyone thought that such reforms went far enough, and idealists advocated communes, adopted romanticism, embraced transcendentalism, or worshipped nature.

SOUTHERNERS EMBRACE REVIVALS BUT DISDAIN REFORM

The Revolutionary War had destroyed the Church of England as an effective force in the South, and afterward the region became largely churchless. In the 1790s traveling Baptist and Methodist preachers—uneducated representatives of new denominations—provided some services and began to hold camp meetings on the frontier. These meetings created a new evangelical style in which, contrary to Calvinist ideas, worshippers accepted the belief in universal access to salvation and the need for intense emotional display, which included rolling on the ground. In the early 1800s southerners became devout but adopted a form of Protestantism that disdained moral or political reform.

SOUTHERN RELIGION DECAYS AFTER THE REVOLUTION   In no region of the country had organized religion suffered more losses than in the South. Before the Revolution most southerners, white and black, had at least nominally belonged to the Church of England (i.e., the Episcopal Church). In Virginia it had been the legal, tax-supported state church. In cities and long-settled areas near the seaboard, the church had functioned well, providing not only worship services but also charity for the poor. In inland frontier areas the church existed only in theory. There, even before the Revolution, Baptist, Methodist, and Presbyterian ministers had preached, although few congregations were organized formally.

The Church of England's ministers had been routinely supplied from England, and during the Revolution many of its clergymen were Tories. They returned home. Financial support from England was cut off, and wartime inflation destroyed the value of church investments in America. All of the southern states withdrew their tax support of the church.

The Episcopal Church, as it was renamed, emerged from the war with few ministers and meager resources. Although the church continued strong in towns and along the seacoast, it lacked the means to maintain inland missions. Frontier areas went largely without organized religion.

TRAVELING PREACHERS SERVE THE FRONTIER   Beginning in the 1740s, during the period of religious revivals later called the Great Awakening, wandering Baptist and Methodist preachers, many with little or no religious training, circulated throughout the colonies. In the 1790s leaders of these new denominations, along with some Presbyterians, crisscrossed the otherwise churchless wilderness.

Although the frontier lacked regular churches, once every few years a circuit rider might show up at a farm, have dinner, perform a marriage ceremony for a young farm couple, and baptize their children. The preacher, who carried news and good stories, would read from the Bible and lead a family prayer. He would then move on to repeat his mission with the next family.

Sometimes neighbors would learn about the pending visit of a travel-ing minister. A makeshift religious service might be held, almost certainly out of doors, as frontier cabins could not hold more than a few people. Such services were popular, and the preachers, who learned the ways of ordinary people as they traveled around, decided that organized events that brought people together would strengthen religion.

HOLDING CAMP MEETINGS   In the late 1790s frontier preachers in western North Carolina, Tennessee, and Kentucky began to hold camp meetings. Weeks in advance the organizers posted signs on trees for miles around, and at the appointed time thousands gathered to hear preaching, pray, and sing hymns. In 1801 the largest camp meeting, held at Cane Ridge, Kentucky, attracted an estimated twenty-five thousand people.

Camp meetings were often interdenominational. Baptists, Method-ists, and Presbyterians preached and prayed together. Although these evangelicals competed to see who could gain the most converts, this co-operation marked a new attitude among American Protestants.

The camp meeting ground was laid out in a rectangle. Participants placed the horses and wagons in which they traveled and the tents in which they slept along the outside perimeter. In front of each tent, facing

In the early 1800s evangelical Protestants' camp meetings often led to outpourings of emotion, which were seen as a sure sign of the beginning of a religious conversion. (Li-brary of Congress)

the preaching field in the center, each revivalist built a fire for cooking and light. At some camp meetings, rival preaching platforms were built at each end, and ministers vied to get and hold the biggest audience. Sometimes logs served as benches, but many people sat on the ground.

The meetings lasted three to seven days. Every morning, bugles called people from their tents, and the preaching started. After breakfast, there was more preaching and prayer, then a dinner break followed by more religious activity. This pattern continued all day and, with campfires burning brightly, often all night as well.

Camp meetings frequently became mass exercises in pandemonium. Participants—including both whites and blacks of all ages, perhaps three-fourths of them female—did not listen politely to cogent, logical sermons. Rather, the preachers exhorted their listeners to accept Christ into their lives, to feel their newfound religion, and to express their agony or their joy openly. People responded with shrieks, fainting, praying aloud, rolling in the dirt, and speaking in tongues (that is, by making unrecognizable sounds).

SOUTHERN EVANGELICALS PREACH UNIVERSAL SALVATION   The revivalists specifically rejected the Calvinist idea that God planned to save only a few people whom He had selected. Salvation, these evangelicals preached, was open to all. God freely gave everyone the right to be saved. This was a democratic, egalitarian religion.

Furthermore, the camp meeting preachers stressed that salvation required no education, no special religious study, and no visible good deeds. Salvation required only faith in Christ as the savior. Faith and faith alone guaranteed eternal life.

This simple doctrine had broad appeal, but it posed one problem. How could anyone, even a preacher, tell whether a person was sincere in proclaiming faith? The ministers looked for outward signs consistent with faith. Hence, the shouts, faintings, and loud prayers became the means by which a person proved faith and rebirth in Christ.

Southern evangelicals' staunch belief in the primacy of faith and their insistence upon measuring faith through visible signs of religious fervor had a profound consequence: This emotionally self-contained kind of religion had little concern for, or connection with, events in the secular world.

Southern churches looked upon secular reform with suspicion or hostility. Attempts to define social issues as moral problems offended southern evangelicals, since morality was the province of the church, and southerners knew that universal faith, repentance, and rebirth for salvation were all that were required to make a perfect society.

The frontier revivals first spread eastward, then throughout the South, and eventually northward into the Midwest. By 1840 the South's leading denomination was Methodism. After the Civil War, the region became the "Bible Belt," the section of the United States where religion was (and still is today) most important. Furthermore, the evangelical Protestantism established during the Second Great Awakening of the early 1800s has prevailed. As late as the 1920s, about 98 percent of southerners outside Louisiana were evangelicals, most of them Baptists, Methodists, or Presbyterians.

NORTHEASTERNERS UNDERTAKE REVIVALS WITH REFORMS

In the early 1800s the Second Great Awakening also reached rural New England, but local traditions caused the revivals to take a different form. New England had been founded by Calvinist Congregationalists, who believed that God offered salvation through grace to only a small number of people. During the early 1700s, this idea lost its popular appeal, and by the time of the Great Awakening in the 1740s, it was largely ignored.

By 1800, orthodox Calvinists had lost ground both to Edwardseans (followers of Jonathan Edwards), who believed in universal salvation, and to Unitarians, who emphasized behavior. Then the Calvinists regained the initiative by adopting evangelicalism. The "Burned-Over District" of western New York, settled by New Englanders, produced much religious fervor as well as new denominations. Throughout the Northeast, evangelicals sponsored Sunday schools and missions. Faced with a large Irish Catholic immigration, they also expressed a biting anti-Catholicism.

EDWARDSEANS, UNITARIANS, AND ORTHODOX CALVINISTS   The followers of Jonathan Edwards, the great revivalist of the 1740s, moved away from the early colonists' Calvinism, which had held that only the select few who had had conversion experiences could be saved. These Edwardseans, as they were called, gravitated, like the southern revivalists, toward a doctrine of salvation open to all. In this egalitarian religion, faith and fervor displaced doctrine, although the Edwardseans were never as outwardly emotional as southern evangelicals. (Yankees can't "get down," southerners say to this day.) By the early 1800s many of these Congregationalists had become Baptists, especially in poorer rural areas such as the Maine seacoast.

In the seaports wealthy merchants and professionals had increasingly drifted from Calvinism to Unitarianism, which became the creed of John

Adams. Unitarians argued that moral conduct was more important than faith. Their most famous minister, William Ellery Channing, advocated the "perfection of human nature." Wealthy church members gave considerable money and devoted much energy to solve social problems that they believed were rooted in immorality. Over time, Unitarians drew away from Jesus Christ, whom they admired as a noble man but denied as a manifestation of God.

Thus, by 1800 the orthodox Calvinists found themselves under attack from two directions. Increasingly defensive, the ministers of New England's established, tax-supported Congregational churches looked on with incredulity and rage as local congregations hired Unitarians or Edwardseans to replace retiring Calvinist ministers.

In 1804, the wealthy and socially prominent Unitarians gained control of the Harvard Divinity School, which, along with Yale, had traditionally educated New England's Calvinist clergy. If Harvard were to produce only Unitarians for a generation, Calvinists realized, old-style Congregationalism would die. The Calvinists were desperate.

EVANGELICAL CALVINISTS LEAD THE NORTHEASTERN REVIVALS   In the early 1800s a large number of Calvinists suddenly caught the spirit of the Second Great Awakening. Borrowing the revival techniques of the Edwardseans, the evangelical Calvinists, as they now styled themselves, decided to confront both Edwardseans and Unitarians.

Like the Edwardseans, the evangelical Calvinists accepted salvation through faith. Although they declined to emphasize salvation's universal availability in their preaching, their revival was designed to gain mass converts. Like the Unitarians, the evangelical Calvinists emphasized doing good in the world. Deeds, however, were not to be valued for their own sake but as visible outward signs of true faith. Thus, for evangelical Calvinists, unlike southern evangelicals, moral issues, including those from the secular world, had great religious significance.

The leading figure in this movement was Timothy Dwight, a grandson of Edwards and the president of Yale. Dwight trained a generation of evangelical Calvinist ministers, who spread these ideas not only across New England but also into those parts of New York and the Midwest where Yankees settled. Among Dwight's students was Lyman Beecher. He became the leading evangelical Calvinist of the next generation, as well as the father of the abolitionist author Harriet Beecher Stowe.

Evangelical Calvinists in Massachusetts were galled at having to send divinity students to Yale, which was in the rival state of Connecticut, and so in 1808 they founded their own seminary at Andover, Massachusetts. Students at Andover found the atmosphere exciting. They talked about establishing foreign missions, publishing Sunday school tracts, cooperating across traditional denominational boundaries, and organizing moral societies to deal with the nation's leading social problems.

REVIVALS SCORCH NEW YORK'S BURNED-OVER DISTRICT   No part of the United States was more influenced by evangelical Calvinism than western New York. Settled almost entirely by New Englanders in the years just after 1800, the region from Utica to Buffalo witnessed so many revivals that it became known as the "Burned-Over District." Lacking the stability of New England's long-settled towns and without older Edwardseans, Unitarians, or traditional Calvinists, western New York was ripe for evangelicals of all types.

One of America's great revivalists, Charles Grandison Finney, carried the evangelical message across the region with incessant travel. In 1830–1831 he spent six months in Rochester and claimed 100,000 conversions. Finney combined charisma with a shrewd sense of organization. Wherever Finney went, he recruited local talent to organize a church after he left.

He also had an eye for technique and published a manual on how to conduct a revival. For example, he advised the preacher to leave the pulpit and exhort among the people. As the minister passed by, he ought to lay hands on people. Amid the great tension of a revival, this physical act would often cause the touched persons to scream, sending waves of emotion through the entire gathering. Many converts would follow.

The intensity of feeling in the Burned-Over District led many converts to seek new ways to express religion. Joseph Smith, originally from a poor farm family in Vermont, was converted to Methodism during the revivals in western New York. Dissatisfied with that church's loose doctrine and gripped by a passion for religion, by 1830 he had founded the Church of Jesus Christ of Latter-Day Saints. Early followers came from among the residents of New York's religiously scorched region. Smith's adherents, called Mormons, lived semi-communally; they developed their own economic institutions, practiced a ritualized religion given more to good deeds than to faith, and eagerly sought converts. The Mormons moved to Kirtland, Ohio, and, after alienating non-Mormons, to Missouri and then to Nauvoo, Illinois.

After an Illinois mob murdered Joseph Smith in 1844, leadership passed to Brigham Young, a Vermont native who had been converted in western New York. This brilliant organizer sent missionaries to Europe to make converts and recruit immigrants. In 1847, after careful planning, he took more than ten thousand Mormons to Utah (then part of Mexico). The most controversial early Mormon doctrine was polygamy. Young had sixteen wives and fifty-seven children. The methodical Young maintained each wife in a separate household and visited them in rotation.

Also in the Burned-Over District, William Miller, an uneducated Baptist minister, preached that Christ was about to return to earth. Miller unwisely indicated a precise date, in 1844. His followers bought white robes to ascend to Heaven in proper attire and gathered for the appointed day. (Some purchased their robes on credit, rationalizing that Judgment Day would cancel the debt.) When nothing happened, many became disillusioned, but others merely concluded, as did Miller, that his calculations were incorrect. Out of the Millerite movement came the Seventh-Day Adventist Church, which rose to prominence under the influence of the religious and dietary prophetess Ellen White.

Western New Yorkers did not always express their religious yearnings by founding new denominations. If people felt confused, they could turn to advice from their ancestors. So said the Fox sisters, two residents who in the 1840s claimed that they had made contact with the dead through séances. They invented the crystal ball. The popular press reported excitedly on spiritualism, which most people eventually came to see as a hoax. To understand the popularity of spiritualism, one must remember the context of the times; spiritualism was scarcely more fantastic than the newly invented telegraph, which carried sounds over wire for hundreds of miles.

The Burned-Over District's peculiar religious zeal had several causes. The area was newly populated and hence unstable. It just happened to be settled at the moment when the Second Great Awakening overtook the entire country. Its residents, native New Englanders, had grown up in a culture that stressed religion. The opening of the Erie Canal also played a role, as rapid economic growth brought drastic economic, social, and political upheaval to the region. As in other parts of the North, by 1840 Methodism had become the leading denomination.

CREATING SUNDAY SCHOOLS, TRACTS, AND MISSIONS   Northeastern evangelicals were keen to spread their version of the Christian gospel. One innovation was the organization of children's Sunday schools. Reformers designed programs, including children's religious literature that was sent all over the country, to entice young people to the revival. Evangelicals adopted the practice of rewarding children who memorized large numbers of Bible verses by presenting them with Bibles.

Revivalists also produced millions of adult religious tracts, many distributed by more than one denomination. A sharp decline in the cost of printing in the 1830s made free distribution possible. Tracts not only explained the Bible but also offered advice about personal and social problems.

They praised churchgoing and condemned taverns, lauded family life and warned that those who rejected religion would go to hell.

Determined to save the entire world, in the early 1800s evangelicals organized foreign missions to Africa, India, China, and Hawaii. Husband-and-wife missionary teams were sent overseas, and women in American churches provided the cash and goods that kept the missions going.

Only after overseas missions were established did evangelicals turn to the many churchless people on the American frontier. Giving special attention to Indians, evangelicals set up missions, such as the one at Walla Walla in the far Northwest, which was founded in 1836 by the Reverend Marcus and Narcissa Whitman. In 1847 the Whitmans were murdered by native Americans who blamed the missionaries for bringing fatal diseases into the country.

Some of the most important missions took place in large cities. In the 1820s the Unitarians appointed Joseph Tuckerman as a street missionary in Boston. Walking all over the city made Tuckerman familiar with its wretched sailors' drinking halls, its houses of prostitution, and its children living on the street. He organized hot meals and beds in shelters, but his efforts seemed paltry beside the grim and growing needs of the poor.

In New York during the 1850s, Charles Loring Brace set up a cheap boarding house for orphans and newsboys, poor children who earned barely enough to eat by hawking newspapers on the streets. The Ladies' Five Points Mission was one of the first large settlement houses, located at the center of New York's grimmest Irish slum. The mission offered meals, shelter, second-hand clothes, advice about jobs, emergency travel money, and Protestant tracts. The founders were especially pleased that the site was an abandoned brewery.

Catholic and Jewish immigrants had mixed feelings about these Protestant missions. Although the missions stressed charity, the message of salvation through conversion to evangelical Protestantism was seldom left out, and the missionaries were often condescending if not insulting. Catholic and Jewish religious leaders were downright antagonized. Not only were Protestants trying to steal their members, but the missions suggested that Protestants did not believe other groups capable of providing for themselves. As quickly as possible, immigrants organized their own charities.

NORTHEASTERN EVANGELICALS ATTACK CATHOLICISM   Anti-Catholicism appealed to northeastern evangelicals. Rallying Protestants against the Pope as the Antichrist was an old custom that united people from different denominations who might otherwise have quarreled among themselves. But more was at stake: Protestants worried that Catholic and Jewish immigrants would change the character of the United States. After all, evangelicals believed that their form of Christianity was uniquely suited to America. Their religion nurtured self-improvement, the moral reform of society, and wholesome, democratic politics.

Deeply ignorant about and darkly suspicious of Catholics, a Protestant mob in Boston, egged on by the Reverend Lyman Beecher, left church in 1834 to cross the Charles River and burn down the Catholic convent at Charlestown. Boston's wealthy merchants forced Beecher to resign, and he moved to Cincinnati, which he was determined to save. The pope, according to Beecher, was settling Catholics in Cincinnati in preparation for moving the Vatican there.

In 1836 a visibly pregnant prostitute arrived in New York and persuaded several leading Protestant ministers that a Jesuit had impregnated her while she was being held against her will in a monastery in Montréal. Calling herself Maria Monk, she became a celebrity, told her story on stage, and was the subject of a best-selling book. Only later was her story generally dismissed as false.

In 1844 Philadelphians burned a Catholic church, and the same thing might have happened in New York, but Archbishop John Hughes vowed that, if any Catholic church was torched, the financial district would be set ablaze. When the pope donated an inscribed building block to be placed inside the Washington Monument, then under construction in the nation's capital, an anti-Catholic mob saw evil in the papal stone and dumped it into the Potomac River. In 1854 an official representative from the Vatican, Archbishop Gaetano Bedini, had to flee New York in the middle of the night to avoid being lynched.

REFORMERS TACKLE SOCIAL PROBLEMS

The Second Great Awakening, especially in its northeastern evangelical Calvinist form, combined with the impact of the Market Revolution to unleash an unprecedented era of reform, particularly in the Northeast. As economics, politics, and society changed rapidly, reformers rushed with fervor and enthusiasm to reorganize both the country's morals and its ways of doing business. Improvement, both individual and social, became the watchword of the day. Optimistic and self-confident reformers believed that society's problems could be solved only if sufficient reform took place.

EMPHASIZING MORALS AND URGING SEXUAL RESTRAINT   Northeastern evangelicals were determined to remake society in a moral fashion. They lobbied for a law to prohibit the mail from being carried or distributed on Sundays, and they succeeded in establishing stage lines and steamboat companies that refused to operate on the Sabbath. Under this attack, state lotteries were abolished. Gambling was immoral because winnings were an un-earned windfall. To evangelicals, who believed that faith rather than works was the basis of salvation, winning at gambling was as obscene as attaining salvation without making the effort to gain the faith necessary for re-birth.

Sexual practices were also subject to new restrictions. Reformers vig-orously attacked prostitution, even in the seaports where it had long been tolerated, and homes for unwed mothers were opened. In addition to shelter, the young women received more than ample moral and religious advice. The percentage of women who were pregnant at the time of mar-riage dropped from 30 percent in 1790 to 10 percent by 1850.

Much of the effort to restrain sex was directed at young men. Advice books warned against prostitution, which led to disease, and masturba-tion, which, according to reformers, produced insanity. The only safe so-lutions for a young man were self-restraint or early marriage. In the ab-sence of a virtuous woman and the financial means for marriage, reformers recommended vigorous physical exercise and cold baths.

Sex within marriage was also subject to restraint. Reformers believed that frequent sexual activity caused the male to lose vigor, to become both sexually and economically lethargic, and to decline into an alarming, non-productive, premature old age. The female had to protect her mate from this fate by declining his advances.

Reformers also taught that sex excited women, which made them un-fit mothers. Besides, childbirth exhausted women, and in congested cities or in long-settled rural areas with scarce, expensive land, where most Americans lived, children had ceased to be economic assets. Coitus inter-ruptus, that is, early withdrawal, was recommended as a form of birth control. (Condoms existed in Europe but were unknown in the United States.) In the rural Northeast, family size had declined to only three chil-dren by 1860.

Not all reformers shared these views. In the 1830s Frances Wright, an advocate of labor's rights and founder of a failed abolitionist commune, preached the doctrine of free love to New York audiences. According to the Scots-born Wright, men had designed the institution of marriage to control women. If marriage were abolished, a perfect harmony and equal-ity between the sexes might result. Protestant clergymen, almost all of whom were men, denounced her from their pulpits. Few people dared to put Wright's theories into practice.

FIGHTING ALCOHOL   The most important reform, both in the eyes of evangelical leaders and in the number of people involved, was the campaign against alcohol. The temperance movement, as it was called, combined a religious idea with a secular practice. A born-again Protestant who gave up liquor offered visible outward proof of the proclaimed inner faith. To break a lifelong habit in this fashion provided strong evidence of a true conversion.

At the same time, giving up drink had practical consequences. The ex-drinker no longer wasted time and money sipping whiskey in a tavern, with its temptations to fights, gambling, and prostitution. The abstaining male was expected to work harder and with more enthusiasm, to be more devoted to family, and to use leisure time for self-improvement, Bible reading, or prayer.

Heretofore, the United States had been one of the hardest-drinking countries in the world, with the typical adult white male drinking about a half pint of whiskey a day. Between 1825 and 1850 alcohol consumption dropped by half. This did not mean that the average American drank half as much; rather, it meant that the evangelical half of the population took the "teetotal" pledge to stop drinking altogether.

" FATHER, DEAR FATHER, COME HOME WITH ME NOW,
THE CLOCK IN THE STEEPLE STRIKES ONE.'

In the mid-1800s, T. S. Arthur's play *Ten Nights in a Bar Room* enjoyed popularity throughout the United States. This story of a drunkard and his daughter conveyed well the temperance movement's antiliquor message. (Culver Pictures, Inc.)

At first, evangelicals were delighted with the progress of the anti-alcohol campaign, but in the 1830s they came to realize that the reform was no longer spreading. The nonreligious, as well as Catholics and Episcopalians, never accepted abstinence.

Evangelicals then proposed laws to prohibit the sale of alcohol. The first such law, passed in Massachusetts in 1838, outlawed the sale of hard liquor in quantities under fifteen gallons. The theory was that only respectable people could afford to buy that much liquor. Retailers quickly found ways to evade the law. One enterprising seller charged 6 cents for the right to see his blind pig; viewers got a free drink. This is the origin of the expression "blind pig" to denote an illegal drinking establishment. Within two years the state repealed the law.

In the 1840s, many states allowed voters to ban alcohol sales in cities or counties, and in 1851 Maine became the first dry state. Pushed through by Neal Dow, the dry Quaker mayor of Portland, the Maine law provoked such a backlash that it was repealed in 1856. Although several states tried prohibition in the 1850s, none kept it for long. The evangelical war against liquor would be resumed after the Civil War; by 1850, however, evangelicals had managed to make abstinence a requirement of middle-class respectability.

PROMOTING HEALTH   In the 1830s the antiliquor campaign led to a more modest movement to ban meat. Vegetarians argued that alcohol and meat made people animalistic and that spirituality could be enhanced with an all-grain diet. To ensure that such a diet was balanced, the Reverend Sylvester Graham, a leading temperance lecturer turned vegetarian, invented Graham flour, a nutritionally balanced blend of several grains. That flour today is the basis of the graham cracker.

Many reformers rejected orthodox medicine, which depended heavily upon laudanum, that is, opium dissolved in alcohol, and bleeding patients with leeches. Instead, reformers sought to restore proper bodily balance through water cures, which meant visiting mineral springs, or through homeopathy, an unorthodox branch of medicine that advocated minimal doses of a large variety of natural drugs designed to restore balance.

Another reformer was Amelia Bloomer, who rejected the tight, unhealthful, whalebone corsets worn by fashionable middle-class women. Bloomer designed, made, and wore a short skirt combined with loose trousers gathered at the ankles. Although some radical women took to wearing bloomers, as the new costume was called, it would be more than a century before respectable women wore pants.

Others thought that health and destiny could be read in the shape of one's head. After an examination, a phrenologist would declare the subject's susceptibility to specific diseases, the nature of his morals, and his financial prospects. Phrenology remained popular until it was discredited by science in the late 1800s.

OPENING ASYLUMS FOR THE POOR AND THE MENTALLY ILL   After 1830 many aspects of the reform movement were secular and institutional. Cities and states used profits from the growing economy to build poorhouses. Whereas most poor people, usually old and infirm, had previously received what was called outdoor relief, that is, sporadic, small quantities of food or cash, the poor were now provided with permanent shelter and hot meals. The system cost more money, but it was expected that some of the poor could work indoors and thereby help support themselves. Also, some vagabonds might be discouraged from seeking assistance if they had to live in a government institution without liquor or bawdy activities.

Mental hospitals were also built in large numbers. Previously, families had chained disturbed relatives in the cellar or attic. Now, people with mental problems were considered ill and therefore capable of receiving treatment. Treatment began by placing the person in a clean, sanitary, comfortable institution, where doctors and staff could look after their needs and help them adapt to normal life. Much of the credit for this new policy goes to Dorothea Dix, a tireless reformer who successfully lobbied numerous state legislatures and city councils to build asylums.

BUILDING PRISONS   Prisons were another innovation. Prior to 1800 criminals were executed, whipped, or fined, but rarely imprisoned. Jails were used only to hold people awaiting trial. By 1830 reformers conceived of prisons as a more humane form of punishment. They were expensive, but reformers believed the expense worthwhile, because prison provided the best way to reform the criminal. Criminals, like sinners, could be reborn and saved.

Exact methods varied. At the Pennsylvania Prison in Philadelphia, prisoners served relatively short sentences in solitary confinement. Jailers pushed food into the cell through a trap door; the prisoner, who had been given a number and ordered to observe total silence, had nothing to do in the cell except read the Bible and contemplate the error of his ways. On Sundays the doors were opened a crack, and the prisoners, whether they wanted to or not, heard an evangelical sermon in the hallway. The theory was that lack of contamination by other inmates would enable a large number of criminals to reform their characters. Instead, a high percentage went insane.

New York's Auburn Prison was cheaper to operate than Pennsylvania's because the prisoners slept alone in tiny cells but spent their days working in a large common room. To avoid criminal contamination, the prisoners were not allowed to talk with each other, and to enforce this rule, guards with six-foot-long whips circled the working inmates. Despite brutal beatings, the productive work and the contact with other human beings made the Auburn prison more successful than the one in Philadelphia.

SETTING UP PUBLIC SCHOOLS   Around 1830 reformers demanded the establishment of public schools. Under the reform governor William Henry Seward, New York provided schools upstate and reorganized the charity schools in New York City into a true public school system. Pennsylvania overcame resistance from Germans who believed, correctly, that their language would die out, and set up public schools across the state. Even in the South the movement for public schools made some headway. Wealthy planters, however, resisted paying higher taxes to educate poor white children. Their own children were often privately tutored.

Massachusetts, under its brilliant commissioner of education, Horace Mann, set the pace for school reform. Mann concentrated on the quality of education. He stressed that children had to be prepared for a rapidly changing society, one in which industry and commerce demanded workers who were sober, cheerful, obedient, resourceful, and disciplined. Mann expressed a keen interest in the new high schools, which promised to provide clerks and skilled managers to run the emerging industrial economy. He also urged that women be hired as teachers. Women were supposed to improve morals and could be paid lower salaries.

ADVOCATING WOMEN'S RIGHTS   The Market Revolution had upset old ways, and one consequence was that women began to question their role in society. The early 1800s brought the first generation of educated women. In 1821 Emma Willard founded Troy Female Seminary, where women were taught serious, college-level subjects. In 1833 Oberlin College became the first American college to admit female students, and four years later Mary Lyon opened Mount Holyoke as a women's college. Many leaders of the women's rights movement came from this first generation of formally educated women.

The women's rights movement had its origins in certain evangelical churches. Although only a few churches allowed women to preach, most evangelical congregations were preponderantly female. Furthermore, as almost every male minister recognized, women ran church activities, and the pressure of women on husbands, fathers, and sons kept money flowing into church coffers.

The can-do evangelical spirit, combined with everyday experiences of tending to church business, led women to become involved in moral and secular reform movements. Women were active in all the reform movements, especially temperance and the abolition of slavery, which is discussed in chapter 11.

Eventually, some women came to believe that their own position in society should be changed. Started by two breakaway radical religious groups that had given women the right to preach, the Hicksite Quakers and Wesleyan Methodists, the women's rights movement was publicly scorned and mocked during the 1830s. When Sarah and Angelina Grimké dared to become the first women to speak before "mixed" audiences, that is, audiences of both men and women, riots nearly occurred. In 1837 Angelina Grimké broke new ground by debating a man in public. The press generally agreed that she won the debate.

Still, little was accomplished, and in 1848 Lucretia Mott and Elizabeth Cady Stanton organized a women's rights convention at Seneca Falls, New York. At this meeting the delegates, including women and men, adopted the Female Declaration of Independence. It placed men in the position of a George III, the hated tyrant, and it mockingly threatened revolution unless male oppression and domination came to an end. Although the Declaration drew some attention, it would be two generations before the women's rights movement became a major force in the United States.

IDEALISTS SEEK CHANGE

Some Americans thought that reformers focused too narrowly on changing society's existing institutions and ways. These idealists, often influenced by evangelicalism even when they rejected formal religion, advocated a larger, more philosophical approach that promised to restructure society radically. Some idealists, such as evangelicals in the peace movement, believed that the change of heart required to make a born-again Christian could so transform the human personality that war would become impossible. Pacifism, however, failed. Others, usually more secular, looked to communalism as a way to restructure society that would solve all the problems created by the Market Revolution while providing moral uplift. Still others turned to romanticism as an alternative to religion and reform, and yet others embraced the semireligion of transcendentalism or simply worshipped nature. Many women influenced these movements through their writings.

PRACTICING COMMUNALISM   Idealism took many forms, including the advocacy of a shared, communal way of life. Many communes were religious. "Mother" Ann Lee, an English immigrant, had brought the Shakers, or Shaking Quakers, to America in 1774. Noted for the simplicity and grace of their architecture and furniture, they thrived during the Second Great Awakening. In more than a dozen colonies, they farmed, worked, and lived communally, with men and women occupying separate dormitories. The Shakers denounced sex, and the men and women saw each other only at religious services, where they did shaking dances. They recruited new members primarily by raising orphans. By far the most successful of the communes, the Shakers survived into the twentieth century.

Other religious communes rarely outlived their founders, and secular communes seldom lasted long. One of the exceptions was the Oneida Community, founded by John Humphrey Noyes in 1848. Strong personal leadership and business sense made the difference. Noyes's advocacy of multiple sexual partners in group marriage gave the colony a scandalous reputation, but Oneida eventually gained economic security through the sale of its well-made, elegant silverware.

The most famous commune was the secular one at New Harmony, Indiana, founded in 1825 by the Scottish immigrants Robert Owen and his son, Robert Dale Owen. The elder Owen had owned a textile mill in Scotland, and the horrors of the sweatshop had revolted him. Selling out, he had founded New Harmony on the theory of communal, socialist ownership and operation. Although both Owens were brilliant speakers, neither could make the commune work. It ended in disharmony within a few years.

Some people argued that the existing communes had failed either because of shallow theory or because of inadequate attention to detail. The French philosopher Charles Fourier proposed fully self-sustaining socialist communities with about ten thousand people per commune. Each commune, which Fourier called a phalanx, was conceived as a giant circle with a village at the center and fields radiating outward like spokes. The large size enabled the commune to employ people efficiently at specialized work. Land use and economic production could be carefully planned.

The reformer Horace Greeley, publisher of the *New York Tribune* and an enthusiast for many "isms," adopted Fourier's ideas in the 1840s. He envisioned settling frontier America with a series of these large, circular communes marching across the landscape toward the Pacific Ocean. Greeley provoked much talk but little action, since most Americans, even evangelical reformers, scorned the planned, "beehive" model of society.

ADOPTING ROMANTICISM   Not all Americans responded to the Market Revolution by adopting evangelical Protestantism, by joining various reform movements, or by advocating communalism. Some people became romantics. The romantic movement, most closely identified with the English poets Byron, Keats, and Shelley, was a global reaction in the early 1800s to the Enlightenment's stiff, logical emphasis on reason.

Romantics believed that life could be understood best and lived to the fullest only by recognizing that emotion rather than reason was the key to personal contentment. Only through living "on the edge" could a person discover the true self. Critics found this attitude both dangerous and self-indulgent, but romanticism had a growing appeal, especially to those in literature and the arts, amid the radical change and cultural confusion caused by the Market Revolution.

Writers such as the southerners Edgar Allen Poe or William Gilmore Simms, whose work defended the South and slavery, adopted a romantic attitude. Romanticism could also be seen in the widespread popularity in the South of the novels of Sir Walter Scott, who set his formulaic tales of heroes rescuing heroines from villains in the Middle Ages. Indeed, southern planters, escaping from a reform-minded present that they did not much like, held mock medieval festivals complete with jousts on horseback.

In northern hands, romanticism often included a moral element. By the 1850s women authors were turning out numerous novels, poems, and magazines for women. Both authors and readers were northern, urban, upper-middle-class women. The magazine *Godey's Lady's Book* had the name of the male publisher in the title, but it was truly the work of its editor, Mrs. Sarah J. Hale. The widowed Mrs. Hale was probably the first woman in America to make her living by the pen.

The poet Lydia Sigourney wrote verse on topics as diverse as nature and, more darkly, the soul. No matter the subject, she presented an emotional, romantic attitude. Lydia Childs was one of the few authors to mix openly a demand for reform with sentiment, and she sold distinctly fewer copies of her books than did Fanny Fern or Mrs. E.D.E.N. Southworth. The latter two's novels, early versions of gothic romances, sold millions of copies. Although little was serious in the works of either Fern or Southworth, their villains inevitably hated evangelical religion, and their heroines never deviated from conventional evangelical morals.

ADVOCATING TRANSCENDENTALISM   Ralph Waldo Emerson and other New Englanders embraced the love of nature, called it transcendentalism, and turned it into a religion which incorporated the romantic movement and rejected evangelicalism. Through the study, contemplation, and admiration of nature, Emerson argued, people could *transcend* reason and the manmade world in order to approach and commune with God. Nature was, in this view, God's noblest work. Emerson, the most popular public lecturer of his day, expressed his views in small-town lyceums, that is, educational lecture series, all over America.

In 1841 some transcendentalists pursued their ideas by founding an experimental commune called Brook Farm, located just outside Boston.

The literary Alcott family lived there for a time, and although the commune was a commercial and agricultural failure abandoned in 1847, it did produce a stunning literary magazine, *The Dial,* edited by the talented Margaret Fuller.

EMBRACING NATURE   Some Americans, like Henry David Thoreau, coped with modernity by escaping to embrace nature. In 1845 Thoreau retreated to Walden Pond in Concord, Massachusetts, and when the train whistle intruded there, he moved to the remote Maine woods. Less interested in reforming a rapidly changing society than in escape, Thoreau found America so corrupted by the Market Revolution that only total personal isolation brought him solace. Communing with nature restored the soul and freshened thought, but Thoreau realized that his personal experience had no social significance unless he shared it with others. He did so in *Walden* (1854). His minimalism, his love of nature, and his jaundiced suspicion of capitalism found wide appeal in later years.

The appeal to nature was also expressed through the growth of the cemetery movement. Before 1830 Americans were typically buried in small, simple graveyards next to churches. Often ill-kept and overgrown with weeds, churchyards had little natural beauty. After 1830 increasing numbers of urban, middle-class Americans were buried in spacious suburban cemeteries. These parklike burial grounds, such as Mt. Auburn Cemetery outside Boston, were professionally landscaped with trees, shrubs, flowers, meandering walks, and occasional ponds. Families spent Sunday afternoons walking through the grounds, often picnicking near their loved ones.

The obsession with nature led to the new profession of landscape architect. Andrew Jackson Downing, the first professional in this field, not only laid out spacious grounds around suburban and rural estates, but he also published books encouraging others to do so. To Downing, the setting was as important as the house, and trees and plants could be used to create a natural environment that pleased the eye, shaded the house, and soothed the spirit.

Wealthy residents in congested, growing cities could not bask in a natural setting, so as a substitute they increasingly hung pictures of nature on their walls. Some of America's greatest oil painters, such as Frederic Church, Thomas Cole, Asher Durand, and George Inness, turned out so many fine landscapes that they became known, because of their favorite subject, as the Hudson River School. These paintings celebrated the grandeur of nature, and any manmade elements they included, such as a railroad, were always dwarfed by the mountains, the trees, and the sky. There is no greater clue to Americans' feelings about the industrial age, even as they partook of its profits.

CONCLUSION

The Second Great Awakening's revivals accompanied the Market Revolution's economic changes. In the South, the revivals produced a type of evangelical Protestantism that embraced universal salvation while rejecting reform. In the North, evangelical Calvinists adopted both revivalism and reform. Reformers tackled social problems by advocating such new ideas as abstinence from alcohol, building public schools, and women's rights. Idealists, some of whom had little use for evangelicalism, experimented with communes, romanticism, transcendentalism, and the worship of nature. By 1850 the country's ideals and institutions had been transformed.

Recommended Readings

DOCUMENTS: Lyman Beecher, *Autobiography* (1864); Horace Greeley, *Recollections of a Busy Life* (1868); Elizabeth C. Stanton, *Eighty Years and More* (1898).

READINGS: (RELIGION) Robert H. Abzug, *Cosmos Crumbling* (1994); John B. Boles, *The Great Revival* (1972); John L. Brooke, *The Refiner's Fire* (1994); Richard L. Bushman, *Joseph Smith and the Beginnings of Mormonism* (1984); Paul K. Conkin, *Cane Ridge* (1990); Jay P. Dolan, *The Immigrant Church* (1975); Nathan O. Hatch, *The Democratization of American Christianity* (1989); Christine L. Heyrman, *Southern Cross* (1997); Paul E. Johnson, *A Shopkeeper's Millennium* (1978); Donald G. Mathews, *Religion in the Old South* (1977); Stephen J. Stein, *The Shaker Experience in America* (1992); James Turner, *Without God, without Creed* (1985); (REFORM) Carl F. Kaestle, *Pillars of the Republic* (1983); Michael B. Katz, *The Irony of Early School Reform* (1968); Walter D. Lewis, *From Newgate to Dannemora* (1965); Steven Mintz, *Moralists and Modernizers* (1995); W. J. Rorabaugh, *The Alcoholic Republic* (1979); David J. Rothman, *The Discovery of the Asylum* (1971); Ian R. Tyrrell, *Sobering Up* (1979); Ronald G. Walters, *American Reformers* (1978); (WOMEN) Norma Basch, *In the Eyes of the Law* (1982); Barbara J. Berg, *The Remembered Gate* (1978); Ellen C. DuBois, *Feminism and Suffrage* (2nd ed., 1999); Lori D. Ginzberg, *Women and the Work of Benevolence* (1990); Nancy A. Hewitt, *Women's Activism and Social Change* (1984); Nancy Isenberg, *Sex and Citizenship in Antebellum America* (1998); Mary Kelley, *Private Women, Public Stage* (1984); (COMMUNES) Carl J. Guarneri, *The Utopian Alternative* (1991); (CULTURE) Charles Capper, *Margaret Fuller* (1992); Mary K. Cayton, *Emerson's Emergence* (1989); Ann Douglas, *The Feminization of American Culture* (1977); Drew G. Faust, *A Sacred Circle* (1977); Leo Marx, *The Machine in the Garden* (1964); Anne C. Rose, *Transcendentalism as a Social Movement* (1981).

10

Andrew Jackson of the West

OVERVIEW   A product of the self-reliant, egalitarian frontier, Andrew Jackson brought western democratic principles to national
politics. An advocate of voting rights for all white males, frequent
elections, and term limits, Jackson adopted policies that rearranged
the political landscape and greatly expanded presidential powers.
In the 1830s he eliminated the presidential hopes of John C. Calhoun, ended the idea that states could nullify federal laws,
wrecked the economy by destroying the second Bank of the United
States, and removed Indians from the East.

Jackson isolated Henry Clay, his western rival, as the leader of
the hapless Whig Party, and named Martin Van Buren as his successor in 1836. Ironically, Jackson's banking policies helped bring
on a depression that ruined Van Buren and resulted in the election of the Whig William Henry Harrison in 1840. By then, however, even the Whigs accepted many of Jackson's democratic
ideas.

THE FRONTIER WEST GIVES BIRTH
TO JACKSONIAN IDEALS

In the early 1800s frontier culture became nationally important as Americans increasingly moved into the landlocked area west of the Appalachian
Mountains in the Ohio and Mississippi River valleys. Pioneer families engaged in gender-divided subsistence agriculture in a society where pos-

Map 10.1   Water versus Land Transportation

sessions were few and where most people enjoyed rough equality. Ideals of self-reliance and equality marked the West, and frontier figures such as Andrew Jackson naturally embraced these principles.

THE ISOLATED FRONTIER WEST PRACTICES DEMOCRACY   In 1790 only one in forty Americans lived west of the Appalachian Mountains. By 1810 one in seven did, and twenty years later nearly one in three did. This massive population growth in the Trans-Appalachian West led to growing political power as new states entered the Union. In 1787, thirteen states hugged the Atlantic seacoast. Fifty years later, the twenty-six United States stretched as far west as Missouri.

In one sense, this migration merely continued the movement of people inland from the seacoast that had begun in the 1600s. In another sense, however, Americans who settled west of the Appalachian Mountains encountered new challenges. No rivers crossed the mountains, which formed a crucial barrier to trade. A farmer's horse could not carry grain across the mountains worth as much as the horse's feed. Trade often went the long way around. For example, from Bedford, Pennsylvania, to Philadelphia, it cost more to ship goods using the 200-mile overland route than the 2,100-mile water route via Pittsburgh, the Ohio and Mississippi Rivers, and New Orleans.

Although western settlers brought their culture from the East, the isolation of the West allowed people to develop their own economy, society, and politics. Freed from eastern influence, westerners stressed principles and practices that had been present in weaker form in the East. Over time they shaped a society that, without colonial or English tendencies, was peculiarly American.

Democracy may not have been born on the frontier, but it certainly reached an earlier maturity there than in the East. A stubborn insistence by white males upon equality among themselves, a giddy expression of the love of freedom, distrust of government and organized institutions—especially those suspected of elitism—and an enthusiasm for popular participation in politics became hallmarks of the West.

In 1800 the frontier stretched from Maine to Ohio, through Kentucky and Tennessee to Georgia, and to southern outposts along the Mississippi River. Its exact location is impossible to describe, since the frontier was never a fixed place; it moved continually westward at a varying rate of twenty, fifty, or one hundred miles a year.

The "frontier" was less a particular place than a state of mind. Beyond the frontier was the "wilderness," where Indian tribes hunted game, planted corn, and moved restlessly, often in conflict with each other. The only whites who lived in the wilderness were fur trappers and traders. To the east of the frontier was "civilization," where white settlers farmed and often shipped their produce to cities for sale, where land had to be bought or rented, where a sheriff might seize a man for failing to pay a debt, where churches, schools, and towns thrived, and where, in the South, slave labor might be used to grow cash crops.

Frontier Americans farmed, too, but they had begun by taming the land. They cut and burned the trees and hacked away the stumps in order to gain a field to plant. This backbreaking labor gave the settlers an intense relationship to the land, even though, paradoxically, the land had been only recently acquired, and many were "squatters" rather than landowners. Lacking any market for their crops, these farmers grew only what they could consume. Nor could they consume anything that they did not grow or make. They were independent, autonomous, subsistence farmers.

THE FRONTIER FAMILY AND GENDER-BASED LABOR   Frontier life meant hard physical labor, and this labor was divided according to gender. Men and boys hunted game, planted, weeded, and harvested the corn and other crops, took care of the family horse, cleared fields, built cabins, barns, and fences, chopped vast quantities of winter firewood, and engaged with the outside world, including swapping produce, goods, and stories.

Women and girls tended chickens, fed hogs, milked cows, made butter, prepared food, kept house, spun thread, arranged for the weaving of cloth, made clothes, and watched the children. The log cabin, although said to be a man's castle, was the wife's domain, as was the medicine cabinet. Except for periods of intense specialized labor, such as harvest, males and females seldom saw each other during the workday.

Because of this division of labor, a farm required the presence of both a man and a woman. This was a family way of life. Furthermore, young people were encouraged to marry early. By the age of seventeen or eighteen, a young man was fully trained and, if strong enough to plow, ready for marriage and a farm of his own. Such a youth might marry a young woman fifteen or sixteen years old. Parents tried to provide land for the young couple, although sometimes the marriage had to be delayed until the youth had cleared it. While waiting, the young woman might sew clothes for her "hope chest."

Early marriages and economic incentives led to large families. Children cost little to feed in a society based upon subsistence agriculture, and their labor was highly valued in a culture where hired labor virtually did not exist. Even two-year-olds could weed gardens. In fact, they were the only people who actually enjoyed weeding.

Families had eight, ten, or a dozen offspring, each of whom expected someday to live on his or her own farm. For example, James K. Polk—a product of the frontier, Andrew Jackson's friend, and later president— was typical in having more than a hundred first cousins. The inability of Polk and his wife to have children caused Polk considerable embarrassment. Children were considered to be a sign of God's blessing.

PRIMITIVE WAYS PREDOMINATE   Frontier life could be unpleasant. Imagine a dozen people living in a typical one-room log cabin no larger than eighteen feet by twenty-four feet. The window openings lacked glass windows and could be only open or shuttered. The floor was dirt, the roof leaked, and wind howled through the cracks between the logs where the mud filler had fallen out. Insects crawled and flew everywhere. There was no plumbing and only two paths, one to a spring perhaps a quarter-mile away and the other to an outhouse, which froze in the winter.

Scarce furniture might consist of a crude, homemade table, a few three-legged stools, and a chest in which the wife kept her few treasures. There was probably one bed, which took up most of the space in the cabin. The parents slept in it with the younger children. Older children climbed a ladder to sleep upstairs in the loft, where the cured hams hung.

Cooking was done over an open hearth that smoked up the entire cabin. The same foods appeared at breakfast, midday dinner, and evening supper. The women prepared hominy from corn, the main crop, or hand ground the corn into a crude flour. When combined with water, this flour was made into johnnycakes and fried in pork lard along with pieces of salted pork. To wash down this greasy, salty food, the settlers drank whiskey, distilled from corn. Hogs ran wild in the woods and were lured back to the farm with corn, which they loved. Except for venison or rabbit from the woods, seasonal peaches or apples, or eggs and milk, this was the diet. People rejected many foods; tomatoes, for example, were considered poisonous.

Pioneers needed practical skills. Shooting straight with a hunting rifle was more useful than being able to read the Bible. Chopping wood quickly yielded more prestige than spelling words correctly. Raising a log cabin with a group of neighbors as a cooperative venture while under the influence of whiskey showed character. Curing an illness with herbs and roots plucked from outside the cabin door had more value than did proper medical knowledge based on medicines that could only be bought in Philadelphia.

CREATING DEMOCRATIC PRINCIPLES   Self-reliance led pioneer Americans to a special devotion to liberty, which they defined as a family's right to make its own way in the world. They expected little help from others, especially from the government. Assistance, when offered, was rejected as an interference with basic rights. Sometimes this attitude took extreme forms, as in the case of one woman eating dinner in a frontier tavern. When offered a dish on the other side of the table, she declared, "I helps myself," adding as she reached across, "I don't want no waitin' on." Much of America's devotion to rugged individualism can be traced to frontier culture.

Pioneers also loved equality. An essential social equality pervaded frontier life. Capital was unimportant, and even land had little value without access to labor. Nor were sophisticated skills that might be valuable in more settled areas very useful. The frontier way of life depended upon simple skills easily learned by almost everyone. This reality of equality was matched by an intense devotion to the ideal of equality. Residents resented anyone who put on airs, and they used practical jokes to cut people down to size.

According to the settlers, taking land and turning it into farms not only improved the earth but constituted a moral duty. God had made the land for those who could use it best, and frontier Americans believed that God wanted them to carve farms out of the forest for themselves and their plentiful descendants. Because the population doubled about every twenty years, it was necessary to bring ever more acreage into cultivation. God had willed it, and these pioneers were determined to carry out God's will.

THE FRONTIER PRODUCES ANDREW JACKSON   Andrew Jackson was born in 1767 in a Scotch-Irish settlement along the western North Carolina–South Carolina border. Jackson's father died before his birth; his mother and two older brothers died supporting the Revolution. In the war, a British officer ordered the teenaged Jackson to clean the officer's boots. When the youth refused, the officer nearly killed Jackson with a sword blow to the head. Jackson wore the scar as a lifelong badge of honor.

After the war young Jackson moved to frontier Tennessee, practiced law, speculated in land, and eventually acquired a plantation and many slaves. He married Rachel Robards, whom he believed to be divorced from Lewis Robards. When this proved to be untrue, the Robardses divorced, and the Jacksons remarried. Jackson, a sensitive man with a hair-trigger temper, resented Charles Dickinson's gossip about Rachel's marital problems, and in 1806 Jackson challenged Dickinson to a duel. Both men were crack shots. When ordered to fire, Dickinson quickly did so, hitting Jackson, who, while suffering intense pain, calmly and deliberately took aim at Dickinson and killed him.

Frontier experiences shaped Jackson's politics. Involved in a local bank whose paper money proved worthless, Jackson nearly went bankrupt and began to hate banks and especially paper money. He also had little use for Indians. Although kind to individual Native Americans and himself the father of an adopted Indian son, Jackson believed Indians to be a doomed people who used resources unproductively and primitively. When Jackson encountered Indians who had adopted white ways, he shifted the argument. Then, he said, racial animosity and cultural differences made it dangerous for whites and civilized Indians to live in the same vicinity.

JACKSON BRINGS FRONTIER DEMOCRACY TO THE NATION

As the first western president, Andrew Jackson brought frontier values to the federal government. The Jacksonians promoted egalitarianism, at least among white males. Strong proponents of equal opportunity, they urged such democratic policies as frequent elections, term limits, and the rotation of bureaucrats in and out of office.

JACKSON BECOMES THE FIRST WESTERN PRESIDENT   Riding a wave of popularity, especially in the South and West, that followed military victories over both the Creek Indians and the British during the War of 1812, Andrew Jackson defeated John Quincy Adams in the 1828 presidential election.

This victory marked a turning point. For the first time, a man whose adult life had been spent west of the Appalachian Mountains entered the White House. Although a planter and a slaveholder, Jackson was much more closely identified, both in his own mind and in the public's, with the western frontier.

He fervently preached his region's rugged individualism and equality. Speaking in a twang—he invited guests to "set in this hare cheer"—and writing an uneducated hand riddled with misspelled words, Jackson unnerved many wealthy, powerful people, who shuddered at his ascension to power.

Jackson, like earlier presidents, had a cabinet composed of political leaders from many states. The new president, however, felt uncomfortable with his cabinet's political philosophy and formal, eastern ways. The cabinet ceased to meet, and Jackson instead turned to a group called the "Kitchen Cabinet." These behind-the-scenes political operators included the frontier newspaper editors Amos Kendall, Francis Preston Blair, and Isaac Hill.

JACKSONIAN DEMOCRATIC IDEALS   Jackson and his friends began to articulate a new political philosophy. Building on Jefferson's ideas, the Jacksonians called themselves Democrats and then refined the term's meaning. To Jefferson, democracy meant a written constitution, the rule of law, equality of persons before the law, and broad participation in the political process. Jackson found these conditions necessary but insufficient to guarantee a democratic society. In refining Jefferson's vision, the Jacksonians looked to the essential equality of frontier life.

The Jacksonians insisted upon adult white male equality. The law must give all white men the same rights. Thus, the law must apply equally to all, and to guarantee this equality, all white men must have the right to vote. Property, literacy, or religion must not be considered, because they tended to produce a privileged, elite electorate. On the other hand, the Jacksonians opposed extending the vote or any other rights to women, minorities, or children, because Jacksonians believed these people to be inferiors who lacked the essential equality found among all white men.

Jacksonian Democrats wanted equal opportunities rather than equal outcomes. Blaming the actual inequality that existed among white men on laws that favored the few, Democrats wanted to use the political system to make life into a fair race, with each white youth in an equal position at the starting line. Although the Jacksonians excluded women and minorities, their concept of equal rights could theoretically be expanded to include everyone. Thus, they favored constructing canals that any farmer might use and operating public schools for the masses, but they often opposed state universities, which only the well-to-do attended.

JACKSONIAN POLICIES   At the state level, Jacksonians ended medical licensing, because that system gave wealthy, educated people an advantage in becoming physicians. Any person should be able to hang out a shingle, claim to be a doctor, and practice medicine. The public, not elite government officials, would decide a doctor's competency. Similarly, Democrats opposed federal or state bank charters. Any person should have the right to operate a bank without a charter or any other regulation.

Democrats believed that frequent elections kept public officials close to voters and preserved democracy. They advocated the election of all officials, including judges, for short terms of office. They also favored limitations on terms, so that officeholders would not look upon elected positions as lifetime jobs. Beginning in 1832, they organized national party conventions in place of congressional caucuses to select presidential candidates.

They practiced "rotation in office," a policy of replacing all appointed government officials after a few years' service. Such a policy ensured that even unelected bureaucrats did not grow arrogant in their positions, and because the Jacksonians believed that all white men had an equal right to any public position, the policy of rotation gave more people the chance to hold office.

Winning an election, Democrats held, gave them the right to replace all government employees. "To the victor belong the spoils," said William L. Marcy of New York. Under the "spoils system," critics charged, talent and merit counted for less than political connections.

JACKSON FIGHTS TO PRESERVE THE UNION

As South Carolina began to assert states' rights, so did Vice President John C. Calhoun. In 1828 he viewed himself as Jackson's successor, but they quarreled over whether states had a right to nullify federal laws, over Calhoun's role in an attempt to courtmartial Jackson in 1818, and over Peggy O'Neale Eaton's social standing. By 1833, when South Carolina threatened to defy federal authority, Jackson and Calhoun had become such bitter enemies that the president threatened to hang Calhoun.

CALHOUN'S TUNE CHANGES   During the War of 1812, John C. Calhoun of South Carolina had been a strong nationalist. Later, as secretary of war, he advocated increasing military preparedness, including the use of federal funds to build roads and to dredge harbors. Such expenditures could be defended constitutionally as providing for the national defense. In 1824 Calhoun was elected vice president under John Quincy Adams. Four years later, he gambled that Adams would lose to Jackson, that Jackson would retire after one term, and that he might replace Jackson in 1832. So Calhoun allied himself with Jackson and successfully ran for vice president under Jackson in 1828.

The political climate in Calhoun's native South Carolina, however, had changed during the 1820s. Cotton prices fell, and so did yields on land that was wearing out. Planters' incomes declined, but the prices of manufactured goods rose due to higher tariff duties on imports. South Carolinians demanded a lower tariff, and Calhoun took up the issue. Congress, however, was under the influence of northern manufacturers more than ever, and in 1828 it passed an even higher tariff, which South Carolinians called the Tariff of Abominations.

In 1829, after it became clear that President Jackson did not plan to reduce the tariff, the South Carolinians, led secretly by Vice President Calhoun, adopted the doctrine of nullification. According to this theory, the United States was a compact of sovereign states, and thus any state could use its sovereign powers to declare a federal law null and void inside its own territory. A law's constitutionality would be determined not by the U.S. Supreme Court but separately inside each state. Thus, a federal law might be upheld in some states and overturned in others.

JACKSON CHALLENGES CALHOUN   Jackson disliked the theory of nullification. He also knew the vice president's role in the scheme. In April 1830, Jackson attended a Democratic Party dinner, looked Calhoun square in the eye, and offered a toast: "Our Union: It must be preserved." Taking on Calhoun was risky, and to gain support from the Democratic Party's states' rights faction, a month later Jackson vetoed a bill to use federal money to build a road totally inside Kentucky. He said that the federal government should not pay for local roads. The Maysville Road Veto followed Jackson's constitutional principles, but it also blocked a project favored by Jackson's other enemy, Henry Clay. The inconsistent Jackson opposed most federal spending on roads and canals but approved money for improving rivers and harbors.

Jackson and Calhoun became personal enemies. Years before, in 1818, Jackson had provoked an international incident by pursuing the Seminole Indians into then-Spanish Florida. Shocked by Jackson's behavior, President James Monroe's cabinet narrowly decided not to court-martial the general. Jackson had long believed that, inside the cabinet, Secretary of War Calhoun had resisted Secretary of State John Quincy Adams's attacks, and Calhoun had hinted that Jackson's belief was correct. In 1830 Jackson learned that the roles of Calhoun and Adams had been the reverse, that Adams had defended Jackson against Calhoun's rage. Calhoun's actual position back then bothered Jackson much less than did the vice president's continuing deceit.

The Peggy O'Neale Eaton affair also rocked Jackson's administration in 1830. Secretary of War John Eaton, an old friend of Jackson, had shocked members of Washington's social elite by marrying a local barmaid. The wives of the other cabinet members, led by Floridé Calhoun, refused to call on Mrs. Eaton. Jackson, enraged at the insult to a woman, raised the issue at a cabinet meeting and received support only from Martin Van Buren, a widower. (The other cabinet officers may well have been afraid to cross their wives in a social matter.) In 1831 Jackson reorganized his cabinet and decided to make Van Buren his vice president in 1832 and his presumptive successor in 1836.

In 1831 an angry and defiant Calhoun supported nullification anew and, in a pamphlet entitled "Fort Hill Address," proposed a new constitutional arrangement with two sectional presidents, North and South, each with a separate veto. Although Congress reduced the tariff in 1832, the nullifiers gained strength in South Carolina and adopted resolutions nullifying the tariff laws of 1828 and 1832. Calhoun resigned as vice president and was elected to the Senate.

Jackson was furious. If the South Carolinians persisted in their crazy theories and actually resisted the collection of customs duties or other federal laws, then the president would personally lead an army to put down the rebellion. Ordering plans for both an invasion by land and a naval attack on Charleston, Jackson threatened to burn the city and hang Calhoun.

The president issued a tough proclamation declaring federal sovereignty. In 1833 he persuaded Congress to pass the Force Bill, which authorized the use of the military against South Carolina. Meanwhile, Jackson became amenable to reducing the tariff, and Congress adopted a new tariff, arranged by Henry Clay. South Carolina then "suspended" its nullification of the tariff, and the crisis ended.

JACKSON WRECKS THE BANKING SYSTEM AND THE ECONOMY

The second Bank of the United States had become a powerful institution. When the bank sought rechartering in 1832, Andrew Jackson vetoed the bill. Jackson's enemies sought to use the issue in the presidential election,

Many were enraged by Andrew Jackson's use of presidential power. His policies provoked a number of hostile cartoons, which gained wide circulation due to a decline in the cost of printing during the 1830s. (North Wind Picture Archives)

but Jackson won. From 1833 to 1836 Jackson waged an unrelenting war to destroy the bank. He succeeded but left the economy a shambles.

THE SECOND BANK CONTROLS THE ECONOMY   President James Madison, following Jefferson's constitutional view, had allowed the charter of the first Bank of the United States to expire in 1811. The War of 1812, however, had proved the need for some sort of national bank, and in 1816 the nearly bankrupt federal government had chartered the second Bank of the United States. Both the government and private investors owned its stock and had seats on its board.

Headquartered in Philadelphia, the bank had been ably run since 1823 by Nicholas Biddle. He opened branches throughout the country, made sound, nonpolitical loans, managed the money supply properly, and disciplined the nation's numerous local banks. These banks issued their own local paper money, and Biddle's bank fixed the exchange rate that determined their currency's value. By 1830, when the Second Bank had twenty-nine branches and one-third of the nation's deposits, it played such a major role in finance that it had become what economists call a central bank, like today's Federal Reserve System.

Not everyone liked these results. Many local bankers, especially in the South and West, were galled that Biddle could dictate the value of their currency. When he discounted their paper money with unfavorable exchange rates, local economic activity contracted, and if the money was discounted too much, their banks failed. Some people resented the Second Bank because it concentrated power in one place. Supporters of states' rights considered this philosophically wrong; others thought it unconstitutional. New Yorkers disliked the fact that the bank was headquartered in Philadelphia. Still others suspected that the bank showed favoritism by making loans to members of Congress.

RECHARTERING THE BANK, 1832   The Second Bank's charter was to expire in 1836, and as a practical matter, the bank needed rechartering several years in advance. After Jackson and others in his administration expressed hostility to the bank, Biddle decided in 1832 to ignore the administration and push a rechartering bill through Congress. Several politicians assured Biddle that the bank was so popular that Jackson would not dare veto a rechartering passed in a presidential election year.

Jackson, however, had come to hate Biddle's bank. Long suspicious of all banks and paper money and doubtful about the Second Bank's constitutionality, Jackson called the bank a "hydra-headed monster" that must be slain. "I will kill it," he swore as he promised aides that he would veto the recharter bill.

This 1832 veto, written by Jackson's aide Amos Kendall, was a masterpiece. It not only set forth Jackson's view that the bank was unconstitutional, but it also asserted that the president, even more than the Supreme Court, had a duty to block unconstitutional legislation. Prior to this time, presidents had used vetoes sparingly. Indeed, Jackson's six predecessors had vetoed a total of only nine bills in forty years, and most of those bills had been technically flawed. Jackson eventually killed twelve bills and established the right of the president to stop legislation on grounds of policy. The president's powers were greatly increased.

The bank became the main campaign issue in the presidential election of 1832. Henry Clay, Jackson's main opponent, believed that the public favored the Second Bank. Biddle, of course, was not neutral, but the more he maneuvered to help Clay, the more his actions confirmed the charge that the bank played political favorites. By campaigning for the bank,

Clay believed that he could defeat Jackson. Jackson, however, saw matters differently. Some Americans, especially the poor, hated all banks. Others, including those rich enough to own a local bank, hated the Second Bank. The veto made it possible for Jackson to get the support of people holding both views. Jackson won in a landslide.

KILLING THE BANK, 1833–1836   In 1833 Jackson decided to destroy the Second Bank by removing the federal government's deposits. Opposition inside the cabinet delayed this policy for a time, and the president had to fire two treasury secretaries before the policy could be carried out. A third secretary, Roger Taney, agreed to withdraw the deposits and place them in selected local banks. (He was later rewarded by being appointed chief justice of the U.S. Supreme Court.)

The removal of the deposits wrecked the banking system and the economy. In order to keep the Second Bank afloat, Biddle had to stop new loans and refused to renew old ones. As the economy contracted, businesses failed, and so did many local banks. By 1834 the country had fallen into recession. The twenty-three local banks chosen to receive the federal deposits had been picked for political reasons, not for sound banking practices. Opponents derisively called them the "pet banks." Even when sound, they were too small to manage the financial system. The Second Bank's central banking mechanism had been dismantled, and nothing was put in its place.

Over time, results worsened. In the short run, banks popped up like toadstools all over the country. Some were sound, but many were not. Without the Second Bank to regulate currency exchange rates, a bank could issue as much paper money as it pleased. The money supply grew rapidly, the economy boomed, and inflation soared. Eventually, of course, if too many people took paper money to the bank and demanded to be paid in gold or silver (together called *specie*), the bank failed. To avoid being asked for specie, many banks were located in remote areas. They were said to be among the wildcats, and they became known as "wildcat banks."

By 1836 even Jackson recognized that something was wrong. Convinced that paper money was the root of the evil, the president issued the Specie Circular. This proclamation required that all debts to the federal government be paid in gold or silver. Suddenly, postage, customs duties, and western land demanded specie. There was, of course, a tremendous shortage of specie, since so much paper money had been issued. As people clamored to get specie, the wildcat banks collapsed, and so did many of the pet banks. By 1837 the country was deep in depression.

JACKSON REMOVES EASTERN INDIANS
TO WESTERN RESERVATIONS

Thomas Jefferson's policy of seeking trade and friendship with Indian tribes had not always succeeded, and in the 1830s Andrew Jackson, with an eye to both peace and land, decided to relocate all Indians from the East to the West. Removal was expensive and devastating, leaving eighty-nine thousand Native Americans in dependency in Indian Territory (to-day's Oklahoma). A few tribes, including the Cherokee, tried to resist, but leaders such as John Ross understood the president's determination and in the end succumbed to his demands. To this day, there are few Indians in the East.

Although the Cherokee leader John Ross opposed Indian removal, he ulti-mately gave in and in 1838–1839 led his tribe on the "Trail of Tears" to Ok-lahoma, where he became chief. (National Portrait Gallery, Washington, D.C./ Art Resource, NY)

FEDERAL INDIAN POLICY BEFORE JACKSON   Thomas Jefferson had been the first president to establish an effective Indian policy. Federal agents offered tribal chiefs special shiny medals and other trinkets in ceremonies of friendship that stressed how the Great White Father in far-off Washington loved the Indians. Jefferson wanted friendly relations and particularly to prevent a British–Indian alliance on the frontier.

Jefferson also established government trading posts. Such posts not only provided the Indians with reliable places to market their valuable furs but also enabled American manufacturers to sell cloth and knives to the natives. These government trading posts failed. Staffed by self-serving political hacks, the posts' American trade goods were inferior to those the British stocked, and independent traders offered the Indians better deals. By the time Jackson became president, Indian policy needed revision.

JACKSON PLANS TO REMOVE INDIANS   Jackson, wishing to avoid further Indian–white wars, concluded that conflict could be avoided only by separation of the races. Believing that white contact threatened Indians with extinction, Jackson favored moving Native Americans away from white areas. Over time, he thought, some Indians might adopt white ways and survive if land was reserved for them. He planned to remove all Indians from east of the Mississippi River to federal reservations beyond the western frontier.

Other important political considerations contributed to the Indian Removal Act (1830). Jackson knew that opening vast new acreages in the East to white settlement would enhance his popularity. Land hunger was a major political force. At the same time, Jackson's Indian policy was designed to bring Georgia into an alliance with Jackson against Calhoun, South Carolina, and nullification. Georgia planters wanted a low tariff but were not prepared to support nullification, because they did not wish to lose federal support and thus face the Cherokee alone. By allying themselves with Jackson against nullification, Georgians could gain Jackson's support for Cherokee removal from Georgia.

Jackson adopted the idea of large-scale Indian reservations. Such areas could be self-sufficient. Both to avoid destructive white contact and to preserve racial harmony, the reservations should also be remote from areas densely settled by whites. The administration proposed to resettle numerous tribes on separate reservations in a buffer area along the United States–Mexico boundary called Indian Territory. Today it is Oklahoma.

Politicians disagreed about Indian Territory's future. Some believed that the Indians would vanish, and that whites would eventually settle there. Others thought that Native Americans would adopt white ways and create a separate Indian nation. Still others, like Jackson's friend Senator

Thomas Hart Benton of Missouri, hoped that an Indian state might be admitted to the Union. If there were an Indian state, a few people argued, then someday there might be black states settled by emancipated slaves.

CARRYING OUT REMOVAL   Jackson's agents used promises, bribes, and threats to persuade the leaders of Indian tribes living east of the Mississippi River to agree to relocate to reservations in Indian Territory. Sales of Indian lands in the East would pay for the move and provide a trust fund to help support the Indians in the early years in their new homes.

Although many tribal chiefs resisted these appeals, most eventually realized that Jackson intended to have them removed with or without their consent. Some Creek, Choctaw, Chickasaw, and Cherokee leaders agreed to removal. The first tribe to move were the Choctaw. A small tribe in Mississippi, they found resistance difficult, although a portion of the Choctaw retreated into a part of Mississippi where the soil was so poor that cotton planters did not want it. Most, however, moved west.

Jackson had boasted that all the Indians could be removed for $4 million, but it cost $5 million just to move the Choctaw. Although the Choctaw removal was hardly a model, conditions during the trip west were better than for some of the later tribes, who virtually starved en route. The Choctaw reached their new reservation disoriented by the strange setting and its unfamiliar trees, plants, and animals. Like most transplanted Indians, they fell into a permanent condition of dependency upon federal handouts and agents.

THE CHEROKEE RESIST REMOVAL   Jackson's greatest difficulty came from the Cherokee, who lived in northern Georgia and western North Carolina. In 1791 the United States government had signed a treaty with the Cherokee recognizing the tribe both as landowners and as a nation. The Cherokee claim to sovereignty came from sophisticated leaders. A number of white traders had married into the tribe, and their offspring had attained high positions while understanding white ways.

Despite this treaty, the state of Georgia began to sell Cherokee land in north Georgia to whites. Most of the land was bought by speculators rather than settlers, who risked being harassed by the Indians. Meanwhile, the Cherokee had rapidly adopted white ways. Many built log cabins and farmed in white fashion, and the tribal leader Sequoyah, with the help of New England missionaries, devised an alphabet and a written language. In 1820 the Cherokee adopted a republican constitution. The tribal legislature passed laws for the Cherokee Nation, erected a capitol building, and established schools. The leading families, like white planters, kept black slaves.

In 1828 Georgia voided the Cherokee laws, and after gold was discovered in north Georgia the following year, the rush of white prospectors into the area doomed Cherokee control. The Cherokee took their case to the U.S. Supreme Court, which ruled in *Cherokee Nation v. Georgia* (1831) that an Indian nation was not truly sovereign but a dependency of the federal government.

In 1830 Georgia ordered all whites living on the Cherokee lands to obtain a state license and swear allegiance to Georgia. Two northern missionaries refused, were arrested, and were eventually sentenced to four years in prison. In *Worcester v. Georgia* (1832) the Supreme Court overturned the convictions and ruled that Georgia's law was unconstitutional because the federal government had sole jurisdiction over Indians.

This ruling did not help the Cherokee, however, since Georgia simply ignored the ruling, and white Georgians poured ever faster onto Cherokee lands. In the end, the Cherokee were forced to move to the West, except for a small number who remained in a remote mountainous region of North Carolina.

In 1838 the federal government sent seven thousand army troops to escort the Cherokee to Indian Territory. The removal, plagued by fraud, poor planning, inept federal leadership, and rotten foodstuffs, was a disaster. Of the seventeen thousand Cherokee who moved, about one-quarter are said to have died on the way. The Cherokee recalled their removal as the Trail of Tears.

REMOVAL'S CONSEQUENCES   In 1832 Jackson's removal policy in the North led to the Sac and Fox Indians fighting the government in the Black Hawk War, which the Indians quickly lost. In the South, many Seminole resisted removal and fled into the Florida swamps. The army gave chase in the Seminole War, which lasted from 1835 to 1843. During that conflict the army captured the great Seminole guerrilla warrior Osceola under a white flag of truce. He died in prison in 1838, and the war continued. Finally, in 1843 the federal government gave up and allowed the remaining Seminole to stay in Florida.

Jackson's policy did change the distribution of Indian peoples. During the 1830s, 80 percent of the Indians living east of the Mississippi River were removed, and a decade later 89,000 Indians belonging to relocated tribes lived in Indian Territory, along with about 170,000 members of western tribes scattered throughout the West.

These changes produced profound consequences. In Indian Territory the original inhabitants did not welcome the newcomers. Incredibly, Jackson's policy had presumed Indian Territory to be unpopulated. Then, too, the relocation of numerous tribes into the concentrated space of Indian

Territory led Indians to begin thinking of themselves as Indians rather than as members of specific tribes. In the long run, this change would be important, because it would lead Indians to join together in more effective efforts to demand rights.

Finally, to this day, few American Indians live east of the Mississippi River. As a result, Indian issues are usually western rather than national. Jackson's policy was designed to eliminate Indian–white conflict as well as to obtain Indian land, but its principal effect may have been to make Native Americans less important in national politics.

JACKSON CASTS A SHADOW, 1836–1845

To perpetuate democratic values, Andrew Jackson personally picked Martin Van Buren as his successor. By 1836 a rival party, the Whigs, had formed around opposition to Jackson and support for a national bank. Although Van Buren won the White House in 1836, economic depression destroyed his presidency. In the 1840 election the Whigs defeated Van Buren with dazzling public relations. The Whigs had little to celebrate, though, because in 1841 their victorious candidate, President William Henry Harrison, died after thirty days in office and was succeeded by John Tyler, a states' rights Democrat who served until 1845.

THE ELECTION OF 1836 AND THE WHIG PARTY   In 1836 Jackson retired, and his handpicked successor, Martin Van Buren, easily won the Democratic Party nomination. Son of a tavernkeeper in upstate New York, Van Buren was one of the wiliest politicians to seek the White House. No one completely trusted the "Little Magician," as he was called, and southern planters strongly suspected that he secretly opposed slavery.

By the time of this election, Jackson's political enemies, under Henry Clay's leadership, had combined into the Whig Party. Always defensive, Whigs found it difficult to articulate a positive philosophy, except for support for a national bank, because they disagreed among themselves about almost everything else. An unstable political coalition, they primarily defined themselves as opponents of Jackson and the Democrats.

Although the Whigs, like the Democrats, had a party organization, newspapers, pamphlets, songs, and rallies, they never felt entirely comfortable appealing to the masses in democratic fashion. Despite this limitation, the Whigs became competitive with the Democrats. Almost every state had a two-party system. The Whigs attracted large numbers of well-educated lawyers, doctors, and businessmen as a party favorable to business and devoted to notions of just rewards for those who worked hard.

This party of opportunity attracted gifted leaders like Clay, Daniel Webster, and the young Abraham Lincoln.

A northern merchant elite, however, formed the inner core of the Whig Party. Never numerous and always maintaining somewhat strained relations with the wealthy planters who led the southern Whigs, these merchants could not control the party but did enjoy an influence beyond their numbers. The party also attracted evangelical reformers, who found Whigs more congenial than Democrats in pressing for laws to ban the mail on Sunday or to stop the sale of liquor. Pointing to the Democrats' appointment of uneducated, vulgar men to office under the spoils system, the Whigs claimed to be the party of respectability.

In 1836 the Whigs experimented with the strategy of running different candidates in different parts of the country. This strategy failed, and Van Buren won, but the Whig leaders noticed that William Henry Harrison had run a surprisingly strong race in the Midwest.

MARTIN VAN BUREN FACES DEPRESSION, **1837–1841**   Martin Van Buren's presidency was dominated by the depression that began in 1837. A financial panic, set off by Jackson's Specie Circular, led to a full-fledged economic disaster. Unemployment soared, reaching 25 percent in some cities during the winter in early 1838. People faced starvation. Although the worst was over within a year, the economy limped along until 1845. With the exception of the depression in the 1930s, it was the worst economic crisis in American history.

Lacking an understanding of economic processes, including business cycles, people looked for villains. Because Jackson had killed the Second Bank, few blamed the bank. Some people, correctly, attacked land speculators. Others denounced the increasing concentration of capital. These radicals praised labor unions, approved of the right to strike, and sought more government regulation of the economy. Still other people wanted the economy reorganized, with private businesses replaced by producer and consumer nonprofit cooperatives.

The restlessness even extended to the Supreme Court, where Chief Justice Roger Taney, who had been appointed by Jackson upon John Marshall's death in 1835, began to reshape the court's views. In the *Charles River Bridge Case* (1837), the court overturned a legislative grant of a toll bridge monopoly. In contrast with Marshall's ruling in the *Dartmouth College Case* (1819), Taney held that the sanctity of contract had to yield to competition and equal opportunity.

Practically the only accomplishment of Van Buren's presidency was the establishment of the Independent Treasury in 1840. Van Buren had found a way to manage finances without a national bank by having the government maintain its funds inside the Treasury Department.

THE ELECTION OF **1840**   The depression ruined Van Buren's presidency. By 1840, when Van Buren sought reelection, the opposition was well organized. Following in the footsteps of the Jacksonians, the Whigs nominated a War of 1812 war hero, William Henry Harrison. A native of Virginia, Harrison had been both territorial governor of Indiana and senator from Ohio. Like Jackson, he linked the South and the West.

In a brilliant campaign, the Whigs exploited Van Buren's unpopularity. Their newspapers repeated rumors that the president, amid the depression, had refitted the White House with expensive furniture and carpets. He was said to sup on silver plate with a golden spoon. Van Buren thought these slanders beneath the dignity of a reply. Democratic Party denials only led the Whigs to chant, "Van, Van is a used-up man."

When a Democratic Party editor declared that Harrison was a country hick who had been born in a log cabin and liked to drink hard cider—that is, mildly alcoholic apple juice—Whig papers declared Harrison an ordinary guy. (In reality Harrison came from a prominent family and lived in a sixteen-room house.) By claiming to be a cider drinker, Harrison appealed both to drinkers and to those who had turned against hard liquor. The Whigs then built miniature log cabins near courthouses all across the country. They distributed campaign tracts with samples of hard cider. Bonfires, barbecues, fireworks, and parades—which included women waving campaign fans and children wearing badges and buttons—marked the Whig extravaganza.

Shouting "Tippecanoe and Tyler, too!" on their way to the polls, the voters elected Harrison, the hero of the battle of Tippecanoe, and his running mate, the eccentric John Tyler of Virginia, in a landslide. Poor Van Buren never had a chance. He had been undone not only by the depression but by the first media- and public-relations oriented presidential campaign. Turnout reached an astonishing 90 percent of the eligible voters, the highest ever recorded.

HARRISON AND TYLER OPPOSE JACKSONISM, **1841–1845**   In 1841 Harrison was sworn in and dutifully accepted a cabinet arranged by the Whig Party leader, Henry Clay. But the president spoke too long at his inauguration, caught a cold, and died thirty days later.

John Tyler became president. The Whigs did not trust Tyler, a renegade states'-rights Democrat, and some of them suggested that a vice president who succeeded to the presidency became only an acting president who had to follow the advice of the cabinet. Tyler ignored this strange theory, fought with his cabinet, and on constitutional grounds vetoed two Whig bills to reestablish a national bank. The cabinet then resigned, and Tyler, read out of the Whig Party, governed with the support of southern Democrats, including John C. Calhoun as secretary of state.

CONCLUSION

Andrew Jackson never forgot his frontier roots. Drawing upon western experiences and values, he brought to national politics a keen belief in white democracy, an intense opposition to nullification, a woefully ignorant belief that banks were evil, and a determination to remove Indians from the path of white advance. His administration defined the major political issues of the era, especially banking, and in doing so created both Democratic and Whig Parties, and caused a depression as well. Jackson cast a shadow that lasted through the administrations of Martin Van Buren, William Henry Harrison, and John Tyler.

Recommended Readings

DOCUMENTS: Rebecca Burlend, *A True Picture of Emigration* (1848); Alexis de Tocqueville, *Democracy in America* (2 vols., 1835–1840); Christiana H. Tillson, *A Woman's Story of Pioneer Illinois* [1873] (1919).

READINGS: (FRONTIER) Joan E. Cashin, *A Family Venture* (1991); Andrew Cayton, *The Frontier Republic* (1986); William Cronon, *Nature's Metropolis* (1991); John M. Faragher, *Sugar Creek* (1986); Malcolm J. Rohrbough, *The Trans-Appalachian Frontier* (1978); (JACKSON) Robert V. Remini, *Andrew Jackson* (3 vols., 1977–1984); (POLITICS) John Ashworth, *Agrarians and Aristocrats* (1983); Daniel Feller, *The Jacksonian Promise* (1995); Ronald P. Formisano, *The Transformation of Political Culture* (1983); Paul Goodman, *Towards a Christian Republic* (1988); Daniel W. Howe, *The Political Culture of the American Whigs* (1979); Richard R. John, *Spreading the News* (1995); Lawrence F. Kohl, *The Politics of Individualism* (1989); Harry Watson, *Jacksonian Politics and Community Conflict* (1981) and *Liberty and Power* (1990); (NULLIFICATION) Richard E. Ellis, *The Union at Risk* (1987); John Niven, *John C. Calhoun and the Price of Union* (1988); (INDIANS) Gregory E. Dowd, *A Spirited Resistance* (1992); R. David Edmunds, *The Shawnee Prophet* (1983); Theda Perdue, *Cherokee Women* (1998); Michael P. Rogin, *Fathers and Children* (1975); Bernard W. Sheehan, *Seeds of Extinction* (1973); Richard White, *The Roots of Dependency* (1983); (VAN BUREN) John Niven, *Martin Van Buren* (1983).

11

The Problem of Slavery

OVERVIEW Slavery first came under attack during the American Revolution, which expressed principles of liberty and equality, and northerners adopted gradual emancipation. In the South, slave life revolved around large plantations and especially cotton. Supporting abolition but believing that free blacks could not live with whites, colonizationists advocated freeing the slaves and resettling them in Africa. After this idea failed, white southerners defended slavery vigorously. Meanwhile, northern evangelicals opposed slavery as a sin, while militant abolitionists demanded not only abolition but full civil rights for blacks. Northern public opinion gradually turned against the continuation of slavery in the South.

THE REVOLUTIONARY GENERATION ATTACKS SLAVERY

The revolutionary generation found slavery inconsistent with the ideals of liberty and equality. After the revolution, the federal government acted to keep slavery out of the Old Northwest and to end the African slave trade. In addition, the northern states abolished slavery, and some southern states encouraged voluntary emancipation. This program to end slavery failed when southern opposition to slavery declined as the cotton boom drove up the price of slaves.

THE REVOLUTIONARIES OPPOSE SLAVERY In 1776 Americans of African ancestry formed nearly one-fifth of the population in the new United States, and more than 90 percent of African Americans were slaves. Slavery existed in every state, from New England, where slaves were fewer than 3 percent of the population, through Virginia with 40 percent, to coastal South Carolina with a black majority in bondage.

The Revolutionary War eroded slavery in two ways. First, many states allowed slaves to enlist in the Continental army in return for freedom at the war's end. The British adopted a similar policy. In Virginia about 10 percent of the blacks gained freedom this way, and after the war that state had a sizeable free black population. South Carolina, despite pleas from the Continental Congress, refused to allow slaves to enlist.

More important, revolutionary ideology that emphasized freedom and equality threatened slavery. Many white Americans found it inconsistent to liberate themselves from British bondage while continuing to hold slaves. Thomas Jefferson understood the conflict, and an early draft of the Declaration of Independence condemned slavery, but slaveholders' objections led to the removal of this provision. Thus, the Founding Fathers opposed the idea of slavery, even as they grappled with how to abolish it.

At the time the principal method of emancipating slaves was for owners to free their servants through wills. George Washington, for example, used this technique and tried to encourage others to do the same. However, many slaveholders, like Thomas Jefferson, became so trapped in debt that they were unable to release their slaves.

THE FEDERAL GOVERNMENT TAKES MODEST STEPS, 1787–1808   Thomas Jefferson's Northwest Ordinance (1787), which provided the framework for organizing territorial governments in the region west of Pennsylvania and north of the Ohio River, specifically banned slavery from that area. Jefferson believed that keeping the institution from spreading to new territories was more practical than abolishing it where it already existed. He once observed that abolition would be easy in Pennsylvania, where there were few slaves, hard in Maryland, and still harder in Virginia, where slaveholders dominated the political system. If slavery could be kept out of the West, Jefferson believed, the national influence of slaveholders would wane, and eventually the institution might be ended everywhere.

In 1787 slavery was a major issue at the constitutional convention. The drafters showed their defensiveness by refusing to use the word *slave* in the document. At the same time, they compromised in giving southern planters greater political representation by counting three-fifths of the slaves in the census that was used to apportion Congress. Another compromise provision gave Congress the right to abolish the African slave trade in 1808. In fact, few new slaves entered the United States after 1787, every state except South Carolina banned the overseas trade, and Congress did abolish this trade in 1808.

THE NORTH ABOLISHES SLAVERY   Even before the end of the revolution, the campaign to abolish slavery had gained ground in the North. In Massachusetts, a state with few slaves and a public increasingly opposed to slavery, the state supreme court ruled that slavery violated the state's constitution, which had been adopted during the revolution.

In other northern states the power of slaveholders led to gradual emancipation. In Pennsylvania, for example, no existing slaves were freed, but children born of slave mothers after 1780 were to become free at the age of twenty-eight. New York had many slaves, as many as 20 percent of the population on parts of Long Island, and for years its wealthy, influential slaveholders blocked gradual emancipation. A plan similar to Pennsylvania's finally went into effect in 1799. The last northern state to adopt gradual emancipation, New Jersey, still had a few slaves as late as 1846, when human property was abolished outright.

The abolition of slavery in the North did not lead to equality for blacks. Outside New England, blacks generally could not vote; they lost voting rights in Rhode Island in 1822 and in Pennsylvania in 1837 with the tide of Jacksonian democracy that stressed white equality. Most northern states prohibited free blacks from moving into the state, maintained segregated jails, poorhouses, and hospitals, and excluded African-American children from public schools.

When a sympathetic white, Prudence Crandall, attempted to open a private school for black girls in Canterbury, Connecticut, in 1833, local residents destroyed the school and drove Miss Crandall away. Not long after, a Philadelphia mob burned a meeting hall used by abolitionists. Although free, most northern blacks could find work only as unskilled laborers or household domestics, for which they increasingly competed with Irish immigrants.

THE SOUTH TRIES VOLUNTARY EMANCIPATION   In the 1790s in Delaware, in Maryland, and to a lesser extent in parts of Virginia—all tobacco-growing areas in economic decline, with worn-out land and surplus labor—a campaign for voluntary emancipation enjoyed considerable success. About 90 percent of Delaware's blacks and about half of Maryland's were freed. This movement by slaveholders to renounce slavery was rooted partly in economics, but the revolutionary values that had led to abolition in the North also played a role. So did the legal system, which encouraged voluntary emancipation and controlled freed slaves under the age of twenty-one through apprenticeship. In addition, a Methodist revival had swept the area, especially Delaware, and at the time, Methodist leaders disapproved of slavery. Born-again Christians routinely freed their slaves, who often converted at the same time.

After 1800 voluntary emancipation in the South more or less ceased. Revolutionary ideology waned, and the legal system changed. Apprenticeship eroded as a way to control young blacks, and Maryland learned that slaveholders had freed older slaves incapable of supporting themselves, while retaining ownership of vigorous workers. Welfare costs grew; free blacks who drifted to Baltimore competed with poor whites for jobs, and this rivalry produced racial violence. Southern states responded with laws making it increasingly difficult to free slaves. As the religious revival continued, its leaders came from the higher social classes, in which slavery was accepted, and so religious opposition declined.

At the same time, the economic situation changed as the Deep South began to plant cotton, which depended upon slave labor. By 1830 three-fourths of all slaves raised cotton. From 1790 to 1860 cotton production soared nearly a hundredfold, but the slave population increased less than sixfold. Slaveowners in the upper South either moved with their chattels into the cotton belt or sold them to the new cotton states. From 1820 to 1860 as many as two million slaves may have been sold, many in the interstate trade, separating perhaps 300,000 husband-and-wife pairs.

The high demand for slaves to grow cotton caused the price of slaves to rise dramatically. A prime field hand worth $300 in 1790 brought $1,500 by 1860. This period saw little inflation, so the difference in price represents an enormous increase in worth. By 1860 the value of the South's slave property exceeded that of all the real property put together, including factories, stores, houses, barns, farm implements, and animals. This high and growing value of slave property made voluntary emancipation less and less attractive to slaveholders.

BLACK LIFE IN THE SOUTH

Most slaves lived on large plantations and worked as agricultural laborers producing tobacco, sugar, rice, and especially cotton. In such settings African culture survived, including language patterns, family ways, and music. The black church played a special role in bonding African Americans together. Slaves who worked on small farms or slaves and free blacks who practiced skilled crafts were more knowledgeable about white culture but faced discrimination that limited their success. By 1850 southern industrialists had begun to use slave labor in factories.

SLAVERY ON LARGE PLANTATIONS   Here is the paradox: A mere one-quarter of the South's white families owned slaves, and most slaveowners held but a few, so that only one-eighth of the slaveholders were planters (defined as

These slaves pose for a photograph in front of a wooden structure typical of slave cabins. (© Bettmann/CORBIS)

holding twenty or more slaves). This tiny elite, 3 percent of the white population, owned a majority of the slaves. Thus, living on a large plantation with twenty to five hundred slaves was typical for blacks but rare for whites.

In some areas, particularly along the South Carolina seacoast, large numbers of blacks lived on plantations almost untouched by whites. On such plantations the planter's family and overseer's family were the only whites, and during the malaria season the whites, who were highly susceptible to the disease, fled to Charleston, leaving the slaves to manage for themselves.

Plantations produced cash crops, including tobacco in Virginia, rice in coastal South Carolina, sugar cane in Louisiana, hemp for rope in Kentucky, and cotton throughout the Deep South. Although some planters assigned laborers daily tasks, others, especially cotton producers, worked slaves in gangs of six to ten laborers under the supervision of a white overseer or a black driver. They planted, tended, and harvested the crops. Men, women, and children worked together.

To ensure order, overseers carried whips into the fields and whipped slow or lazy workers on the spot. Hands worked daily except Sunday from sunup to sundown, pausing only for meals. Slave women also prepared food and mended clothes; older slave women watched slave infants. Planter-provided cabins had dirt floors and lacked glass windows.

Some planters allowed slaves to plant vegetable gardens for their own use, and many slaves fished and hunted to supplement the limited diet provided by the planter, usually just corn flour and salt pork. Although a slave could not legally own or use a rifle, this restriction was often ignored when it came to hunting. Slaves were prohibited from having alcohol, but many planters provided barrels of liquor for a week-long celebration and period of general drunkenness between Christmas and New Year's Day.

THE AFRICAN HERITAGE SURVIVES   Slave culture had strong African roots. In predominantly black areas like coastal South Carolina, such influences were striking. The Gullah dialect, still spoken in one area, shows grammatical patterns typical of African languages and includes many words of African origin. Preferences in food, clothing, and housing (such as round or eight-sided cabins) also showed African influences.

African patterns of marriage and child naming also survived. Slaves lived in monogamous family units, although divorce occurred frequently; planters rarely interfered with these customs. The marriage ceremony consisted of the couple jumping over a broom, followed by joyous dancing. The law did not recognize slave marriages. Many children received African names, which whites generally refused to recognize, or were named in the African fashion: A pretty sound or the first word that came into a mother's head after birth might be given to the child as a name.

As in Africa, black women carried heavy baskets by balancing them on their heads. The slaves wove these baskets by hand in patterns that originated in Africa. Blacks used herbs and roots as medicine, and when African plants could not be found, they borrowed from the Indians. Wealthy planters provided good medical care, rather like a prepaid medical plan. This was self-interest, for a slave who sickened and died cost the owner money.

One striking legacy concerned music and dance. The African-style drum and the banjo—an African word and apparently a modified African instrument—provided the beat and strongly rhythmic melody that became the basis of black music in America and of modern American rock. This music appeared in its most exuberant form at festive occasions and at Saturday night dances, when slaves moved their bodies to complex rhythmic patterns.   .

Song always accompanied work in the fields, providing both a work rhythm (another African idea) and pleasurable sounds. Some lyrics were painfully astute. The ex-slave Frederick Douglass recalled singing:

> We raise de wheat,
> Dey gib us de corn;
> We bake de bread,
> Dey gib us de crust;

We sif de meal,
Dey gib us de huss;
We peel de meat,
Dey gib us de skin;
And dat's de way
Dey take us in.

When blacks became Christians, they took their music into the church.

ADOPTING BLACK CHRISTIANITY Black Christianity outwardly resembled its white counterpart, but slave religion served different purposes. Like the religions of other oppressed peoples, such as Irish Catholicism under English rule in Ireland, black churches gave African Americans as much stability as possible under harrowing circumstances. Planters, fearful of plots, prohibited almost all organized black activities, but Christian tradition made it impossible to prevent slaves from worshipping.

Although planters tried to get slaves to attend white churches and listen to sermons instructing servants to obey masters, the slaves preferred their own preachers, usually free blacks. They created powerful new denominations, especially the African Methodist Episcopal Church, founded in 1816 by the Reverend Richard Allen of Philadelphia.

Black religious services often contained veiled attacks against slavery, emphasizing blacks as the Chosen People desiring to reach the Promised Land. Moses leading the Israelites out of bondage in Egypt was a powerful theme.

Delicate matters were presented in a code that the slaves understood; worshipers sometimes shouted "Amen!" to indicate comprehension while the white person required by law to be present at all slave gatherings missed the point. Black preachers frequently talked about shepherds, flocks, and sheep, because, as one explained, "We know who has the wool," referring to tightly curled hair.

Services emphasized group singing unaccompanied by instruments. When the leader sang out a line, the audience repeated it. This practice gave instruction and promoted group solidarity. Black religion also incorporated African beliefs, including voodoo, magic, and conjuring (that is, summoning spirits).

BLACKS WORK ON SMALL FARMS AND IN SKILLED CRAFTS Slaves who lived on small farms had a very different experience from those who lived on large plantations. Deprived of the presence of other blacks, those on small farms lost contact with their African roots. At the same time, working day by day together with a poor master in a field promoted assimilation. However, the relative poverty of many small-scale farmers often made for a harsh life.

Some slaves and free blacks practiced skilled crafts. Planters usually kept slave carpenters, blacksmiths, and shoemakers, the three most common rural trades. Skills were passed down from slave to slave on the plantation. Normally, all young black males became field hands, and a few received training as craftsmen only after reaching an age at which their work as field hands deteriorated.

In areas with many small-scale white farmers, free blacks often provided skilled work. Local customs varied. In Virginia, where many whites also worked as skilled craftsmen, racial competition produced friction. Blacks were grudgingly allowed to enter the rougher trades, such as blacksmithing, but only whites practiced "high-class" crafts, such as watchmaking. Out of concern for public safety, laws barred black printers. (A slave printer might print posters announcing a slave revolt.) No southern state allowed slaves to be taught to read, although some learned on their own. In South Carolina, however, where black artisans were common, local whites refused to do most skilled work. Except for a few Yankees and European immigrants, all craftsmen were black, either slave or free.

INDUSTRIALISTS TRY SLAVE LABOR   By 1850 southern industrialists, such as the owners of Richmond's Tredegar Iron Works, had used slave labor successfully. Although less skilled than a northern factory worker and therefore less productive, a slave was cheaper. A slave received no wages and cost only $70 a year to house, clothe, and feed, whereas a northern laborer had to be paid as much as $300 in wages, out of which the worker covered his own expenses. Nor did a slave dare strike. Indeed, at Tredegar large numbers of slaves had first been employed as strikebreakers.

Most Southern factory owners did not wish to own slaves; they wanted to invest capital in machinery, not workers. Besides, if a factory had to be closed during an economic slump, slaves still had to be fed. Industrialists preferred renting slaves by the year, but slaveowners resisted sending their servants into factories, where harsh working conditions and accidents threatened lives.

COLONIZATIONISTS URGE ABOLITION WITH REMOVAL

Colonizationists proposed abolition but only on the condition that the freed ex-slaves be removed from the United States. In 1822 the American Colonization Society founded Liberia in Africa as a colony for freed slaves, but it proved inhospitable, and slaves declined to go. As a result, by 1830 the colonization movement was dead. With no more ideas of what to do with freed slaves, abolitionist sentiment in the South died out, too.

FOUNDING THE AMERICAN COLONIZATION SOCIETY, 1817   After 1800 the idealism of the revolution waned, and it became clear that neither state-mandated abolition nor voluntary emancipation would end slavery. Many thoughtful people, including southern slaveholders, believed that emancipation had come to a halt because abolitionists had failed to provide for ex-slaves. Whites feared that large numbers of free blacks would become a culturally unassimilated element that would threaten society.

In 1817 abolitionists founded the American Colonization Society with U.S. President James Monroe as its president. Henry Clay was also a sponsor. The colonizationists argued that slaveholders should be encouraged to free their slaves, provided the ex-slaves resettle in Africa. The proposal resembled Jackson's policy of Indian removal.

In 1822 the society established a colony in a swampy area of West Africa and named it Liberia. Its capital was named Monrovia to honor the society's president. Liberia was to be a black, Christian republic. Indeed, the society persuaded evangelical Protestants to support the colony in order to Christianize Africa. The ex-slaves who migrated were to spread the Gospel throughout the continent.

A number of ex-slaves and free blacks did migrate to Liberia, but they encountered culture shock, deadly disease, and hostile natives, who regarded them as interlopers. Blacks and white missionaries died faster than the society could replace them. Liberia's problems led some blacks to return to the United States, and the pace of migration slackened. Slaves who were offered freedom on condition that they move to Liberia often declined such offers. By 1860 only fifteen thousand African Americans had migrated there.

COLONIZATION FAILS   Even had Liberia succeeded, the colonizationists would have failed. Money was too scarce to send more than a handful of people to Liberia, and the number of ships was limited. So even if blacks had wanted to migrate to Liberia, the plan could not have relocated the entire race. In fact, of course, African Americans, most of whose families had lived in the United States for several generations, did not want to migrate to Africa.

As late as 1827 there were more antislavery societies in the South than in the North, but by 1830 the idea of colonization had collapsed and so had the South's antislavery movement. The failure of colonization put slavery's opponents on the defensive in the South. For years, proponents of slavery, while conceding the contradiction between slavery and America's revolutionary values, had argued that preserving the institution was necessary for security. Law, order, and white supremacy, said these southerners, could be maintained only through slavery. The white South could not control large numbers of free blacks. Colonization's failure led white southerners to accept the proslavery position by default.

SOUTHERNERS ADOPT A POSITIVE VIEW OF SLAVERY

Slave insurrections frightened white southerners and convinced them that a hard line on slavery was the only way to preserve order. After 1832 slavery was no longer even a subject of debate in the South, as southerners turned militant in defending it. The North and South then quarreled, and the major national churches split over the issue. Southerners, united in their belief in slavery, began to see themselves as a distinct society.

SLAVE REVOLTS PRODUCE PANIC   In 1800 a Virginia blacksmith, Prosser's slave Gabriel, planned an uprising. Betrayed by fellow slaves, he and his followers were executed. "Gabriel's Revolt," and the success of the black leader Pierre Toussaint L'Ouverture's revolution against French rule in Haiti in 1804, alarmed white southerners about their own safety.

In 1822 Denmark Vesey, a free black in Charleston who had purchased his freedom and become a preacher after winning a lottery years earlier, planned a sophisticated slave insurrection. Word of the uprising leaked from the slaves, and in the panic that followed, South Carolina executed thirty-seven blacks, including Vesey, and sent others into slavery outside the United States. The Vesey plot led many southerners to conclude that free blacks, especially if educated, posed a grave danger, and laws discouraging emancipation grew stronger. Southern fears were confirmed in 1829, when David Walker, a free black born in North Carolina, published his *Appeal* in Boston. Walker urged abolition by slave insurrection if necessary.

Then in 1831 the slave Nat Turner, a preacher and mystic who had learned to read and write, led a rebellion in rural southeastern Virginia. Turner and his seventy or so followers murdered fifty-seven whites in a house-to-house rampage before being captured and executed. Almost two hundred blacks lost their lives amid the hysterical reaction.

These revolts led white southerners to conclude that slavery was essential for order, that free blacks would assist slaves in rebellion, and that whites could no longer safely question slavery in public lest the discussion lead blacks to challenge their status.

PROSLAVERY MILITANCY GROWS   The South's last serious public discussion about abolishing slavery took place in Virginia in 1831–1832. The legislature considered gradual emancipation, including compensation to slave-

holders. Strongly pushed by delegates from the nearly all-white, mountainous, western part of the state (today West Virginia) and vigorously opposed by those from the slaveholding eastern region, the proposal proved
controversial. In the end, the fear of bloodshed destroyed any chance for
abolition, in the aftermath of Nat Turner's uprising and the collapse of the
belief in colonization. The lower house voted 73 to 58 to uphold slavery.

After 1832 southern intellectuals led a proslavery crusade. Compar-
ing the South to ancient Greece and Rome, they noted with pride that
those democracies had embraced slavery; they touted the institution as
the basis of civilization. In 1837 John C. Calhoun declared slavery "a positive good." Jefferson Davis said the institution came from "Almighty
God." The writer George Fitzhugh contrasted the lives of poor northern
whites, often unemployed and all but allowed to starve, with the fate of
southern slaves, always cared for by their owners. Southern evangelical
ministers played a crucial role in mounting this defense of slavery. Because slavery could be found in the Bible, they said, it was morally right.
These cheerleaders for slavery staked out the high moral ground, and almost no one in the South dared to disagree.

THE NORTH AND SOUTH QUARREL   White southern militancy produced friction. Northerners were outraged when southerners persuaded the post
office to ban antislavery books and pamphlets from the mails. Nor did
Yankees approve of South Carolina's laws harassing northern free black
sailors who put into port in Charleston, where they faced being sold into
slavery.

Bitter sectional controversy arose over the *Amistad* case. In 1839 the
Amistad, a Spanish slave-trading schooner, illegally carried slaves from
Africa across the Atlantic Ocean. In the middle of the voyage, the slaves,
led by a captive named Cinque (pronounced "sin-cue"), seized the ship.
The American navy later found the ship and brought it to New London,
Connecticut, where the federal government agreed to return the *Amistad*
and its slave cargo to the ship's owners.

The leader of the slave captives, Cinque, then claimed that all the
Africans had been kidnapped and should be freed and returned to Africa.
Outraged abolitionists sent former president John Quincy Adams to urge
the Supreme Court to release the Africans. Equally outraged southerners
protested that releasing the captives would violate sacred property rights.
In 1841 the Court finally freed Cinque and the other Africans, who returned to Africa.

As northern and southern views diverged, national institutions
groaned under the strain. No organizations felt more pressure than the
nation's evangelical churches, which split along regional lines. In 1837

slavery caused one branch of the Presbyterian Church to break away, and in 1844 the Methodists divided geographically. A year later many southerners formed the Southern Baptist Convention. By the time of the Civil War, only Catholics and Episcopalians maintained national organizations. They did so by ignoring slavery and scorning abolition.

Although proslavery arguments did not play well outside the South, they did unite white southerners, who increasingly saw themselves as a society distinct from that of the North. The sense of the South as a separate place was based mostly on slavery. That sense was to have tremendous repercussions. More important, white southerners no longer openly discussed slavery except to proclaim its virtues. Opponents either kept quiet or were driven from the South.

RELIGIOUS ABOLITIONISTS CALL SLAVERY A SIN

Religious abolitionists came to see slavery as a sin, a moral position that left little room for compromise. The Grimké sisters and Theodore Weld promoted abolition, and after 1834 so did a generation of ministers trained at Lane Seminary and Oberlin College. Weld's abolitionist revivals failed to end slavery immediately, and he retired without realizing how much he had changed northern opinion.

SEEING SLAVERY AS A SIN   During the early 1800s and especially during the 1830s, northern white evangelical Christians came to regard slavery as sinful. Ignoring the existence of slavery in the Bible, reform-minded evangelicals believed that the institution degraded everyone who came into contact with it. A slave kept in a barbaric, inhuman condition found it difficult to undergo a Christian conversion experience or to adopt high moral standards.

At the same time, the slaveholder also risked losing his soul, for slavery made the owner arrogant. Lacking humility and Christian feeling, he was apt to indulge in brutality and sexual exploitation of his female slaves. Interracial sex, often involuntary, was common. "Every woman is ready to tell you who is the father of all the mulatto children in everybody's household," wrote the southern diarist Mary Chesnut, "but those in her own she seems to think drop from the clouds."

The concept of slavery as a sin had profound consequences. A moral issue, unlike a political issue, left little room for compromise. Religious abolitionists, unlike colonizationists, found no support among southern owners, as these abolitionists called slaveholding immoral. They deeply offended their opponents.

At the same time, the position of the religious abolitionists was difficult to attack. The only way to argue against a person who declared slavery a sin was to deny the whole moral argument. In other words, middle
ground disappeared. This religious condemnation of slavery gradually
led most northerners to support abolition. Otherwise, they would have
had to deny that slavery was immoral and logically accept the southern
view that slavery was moral.

Those who found the institution immoral demanded its immediate
abolition. Sin was an absolute concept, and the sinning had to stop instantly. As a practical matter, the movement's leaders recognized that
slavery could not be abolished overnight without chaos. However, they
loathed the gradual emancipation formulas by which the northern states
had abolished slavery after the American Revolution.

Seeking to broaden their support, religious abolitionists urged "immediate emancipation gradually accomplished." Willing to see slaves
freed over some unspecified period of time, they nevertheless argued that
the sin of slavery required the abolition process to begin immediately. To
do otherwise was to implicate the nation and the abolitionists themselves
in the continuation of this immoral institution.

THE GRIMKÉ SISTERS AND THEODORE WELD PROMOTE ABOLITION   The religious
abolitionists included the important Grimké sisters from Charleston,
South Carolina. Daughters of a wealthy lawyer, Angelina and Sarah
Grimké had been sent to Philadelphia for a Quaker education. While
there, they were converted to that religion and became abolitionists. All
but banned from their native city, they spent the 1830s traveling around
the North explaining the evils of slavery to audiences of mostly females.

The Grimké sisters were especially influenced by Theodore Weld, another religious abolitionist who had been converted to evangelical Christianity by Charles Grandison Finney during the revivals in western New
York's Burned-Over District. Angelina and Theodore married and later
lived in a commune in New Jersey.

As early as 1826, Weld traveled through the South ostensibly as a temperance lecturer but secretly as a recruiter for abolition. He found little
sympathy for abolition, although he did make one important convert,
James Gillespie Birney. This Alabama planter publicly denounced slavery
while traveling outside the South. His home state then declared Birney a
traitor and seized his slaves and real estate. Birney dared not return. He
became a public lecturer in the North and ran for president as an abolitionist in 1840 and 1844.

Throughout the 1830s the funding for Weld's travels came largely from
the American Antislavery Society, founded in 1833 and headquartered in

New York. By 1840 the society had 200,000 members in 2,000 local organizations throughout the North. The national society, composed of wealthy white businessmen and evangelical ministers, was dominated by two brothers, the New York merchants Arthur and Lewis Tappan. New Englanders by birth, the Tappans had made their fortunes selling cloth made from slave-grown cotton to southern planters. The Tappans felt guilty about these connections to human bondage. Eventually, they withdrew from southern trade, promoted the sale of cloth that traced none of its content to slave labor, and contributed more than one-quarter of the annual budget of the American Antislavery Society.

FROM LANE SEMINARY TO OBERLIN COLLEGE, **1833–1835**   In 1833 a number of abolitionists decided that the key western city of Cincinnati, just across the Ohio River from the slave state of Kentucky, could be converted to the idea that slavery was a sin. These religious abolitionists took over Cincinnati's Lane Seminary and invited the Reverend Lyman Beecher to head it. Beecher's daughter Harriet accompanied him to Cincinnati. She saw slavery with her own eyes in Kentucky and met and married one of the Lane students, Calvin Stowe. Years later she would use her observations to write *Uncle Tom's Cabin*.

The leading professor at Lane Seminary was the same Theodore Weld who had traveled the South secretly recruiting for abolition. A charismatic speaker whom some students proclaimed "a God," Weld turned the seminary upside down. While Beecher temporarily left to raise funds, Weld and the students, mostly practicing evangelical ministers in their mid-twenties, held an abolitionist revival. In February 1834, for eighteen nights in a row, Weld led fervent meetings about slavery. Awash in prayer and song, the attendees sometimes stayed up all night.

The fifty-four students included Birney, Stowe, an ex-slave named James Bradley, and Henry B. Stanton, the husband of the future women's rights leader Elizabeth Cady Stanton. All began as opponents of slavery, and they soon came to agree that slavery was a sin, that it must be abolished immediately, and that colonization was inadequate.

The Lane students expressed their views among the residents of Cincinnati, who became alarmed. Cincinnati had a large free black population, and a number of students, noticing for the first time that the city barred black children from its public schools, began to teach these children to read and write. Beecher returned, to find the business community, anxious not to offend its southern customers, in an uproar. Merchants demanded that Beecher stop the students' activities, but the students refused to listen to the president's pleas and withdrew from Lane Seminary, which ceased to exist. The mayor led a mob that drove the blacks out of the city and burned down their neighborhood.

The Tappans then made a large donation to Oberlin College in northeastern Ohio's Western Reserve, an area settled mostly by New Englanders. Although Beecher and Weld did not move to Oberlin, many of the former Lane Seminary students did, and Oberlin became the center of religious abolitionist activity in the West for the next generation. In 1835 Oberlin became one of the first American colleges to admit a black student; two years earlier it had been the first male college to admit a woman.

Oberlin's graduates, largely evangelical ministers, preached the message that slavery was a sin from pulpits throughout the upper North for more than twenty years, and their congregations gradually adopted these beliefs. Northern public opinion about slavery was transformed.

WELD CONVERTS THE NORTH TO ABOLITION   The impatient Weld left Lane Seminary to hold abolitionist meetings throughout the North. Called the "most mobbed man in America," Weld patterned his sessions after religious revivals. He usually picked a small town where he enjoyed the support of at least one local minister. This gave him a church to use and guaranteed that someone would keep the abolitionist spirit alive after Weld's departure.

The first night's meeting often brought jeers and rotten fruit, sometimes thrown by public officials and leading citizens, but Weld's evangelical style and the novelty of his message that slavery was a sin brought people back for a second night. Usually, there was less hostility the second night. By the third or fourth night, Weld could count on a majority of the audience pledging its opposition to slavery on moral and religious grounds. Weld then took his revival to another town.

Weld exhausted himself and came to realize that his cause would grow only slowly. He also recognized, painfully, based on his earlier travels in the South, that few white southerners had embraced abolition. Although the North seemed well on its way to rejecting slavery, the North had no slaves, so his work showed no promise of freeing any slaves. After the Panic of 1837, the Tappans faced financial difficulty and withdrew their support. Weld, understanding that slavery would not soon be abolished by religious fervor, was tormented by psychological depression and retired from public life.

Although the religious abolitionists failed to convince Americans that slavery was a sin that needed to be abolished immediately, they did much to change northern attitudes over the long run. Furthermore, the adoption of the moral argument that could neither be compromised away nor easily attacked in a society devoted to liberty and equality gave abolitionists the upper hand in the debate over slavery. After the 1830s, proponents of slavery were always on the defensive. Outwardly frustrated and defeated, the religious abolitionists actually did more to abolish slavery than they ever recognized.

MILITANT ABOLITIONISTS DENOUNCE SLAVERY

Militant abolitionists, unlike slavery's religious opponents, focused on how slavery ruined the slave economically, politically, and socially, as well as spiritually. This total degradation, they argued, demanded the institution's immediate destruction. Militants like the white editor William Lloyd Garrison so hated slavery that they could never bring themselves to compromise. Some, like the black Harriet Tubman, who helped operate the Underground Railroad, risked everything. Others, like Elijah Lovejoy, gave their lives. The eloquent former slave Frederick Douglass focused on the slave's plight. The intense desire to abolish slavery set the militants apart, making them impatient, impolitic, unpopular, and feared.

In 1831 William Lloyd Garrison began to publish *The Liberator*, an abolitionist newspaper with a small circulation and a big impact on the discussion of slavery in the daily press. (Library of Congress)

WILLIAM LLOYD GARRISON FOUNDS A NEWSPAPER, 1831   Like the religious abolitionists, many militants had once been colonizationists. In 1830 the printer William Lloyd Garrison lived in Baltimore, where he helped edit a colonizationist newspaper, the *Genius of Universal Emancipation.* The paper alarmed some Maryland slaveholders, who had Garrison arrested. He could not make bail and had time to think while languishing in jail. He correctly concluded that white southerners were not ripe for conversion to abolition, even in the form of colonization, and he decided to take a much more militant position against slavery. Then the Tappans provided the money to bail him out of jail.

Garrison moved to Boston, the center of American reform movements, and in 1831 began to publish *The Liberator,* a militant abolitionist organ. Promising to be "as harsh as truth, and as uncompromising as justice," he vowed, "I am in earnest—I will not equivocate—I will not excuse—I will not retreat a single inch—AND I WILL BE HEARD."

His first issue denounced both colonization and the religious abolitionists' concept of gradual emancipation. Garrison apologized to the slaves, whom he called his brothers, for his own former views. He called not only for the immediate end of slavery but for blacks to have full civil rights, including the right to vote, to serve on juries, and to own property.

Although Garrison had fewer than five hundred subscribers, predominantly free blacks in the North, his strident language brought immediate notice. In those days, before the Associated Press, newspapers regularly obtained news by exchanging copies. Circulated all over the country, Garrison's paper so angered proslavery editors in the South that they quoted it in hostile editorials, which the northern press then reprinted with their own comments. Within a few years Garrison had become notorious.

The man had no tact. Calling the Methodist Church, then the largest in the country, a "cage of unclean birds" may have been amusing to some, but burning a copy of the U.S. Constitution on the Boston Common infuriated people. Garrison held the document in contempt because it allowed slavery. He suggested throwing the South out of the Union. Even in reform-minded Boston these views angered people, and in 1835 a mob nearly lynched Garrison, who was saved only by the mayor's timely arrival.

MOBS ATTACK MILITANT EDITORS   Other militant abolitionist editors paid dearly for their unpopular views. In Alton, Illinois, a town near St. Louis and just across the Mississippi River from the slave state of Missouri, local mobs three times dumped Elijah Lovejoy's printing presses into the river. Alton merchants hated Lovejoy because he drove away business from Missouri. Facing financial ruin after losing his third press, the editor vowed to defend his newspaper office. In 1837 a mob destroyed the office and murdered Lovejoy.

In Lexington, Kentucky, Cassius Clay, a cousin of Henry Clay, converted to the antislavery cause. He, too, decided to publish a newspaper expressing these views. Warned against the folly of his enterprise, Clay swore he would kill anyone who interfered with his free speech. Although mobbed at his office, Clay survived, but not without paying a price. Deprived of sleep by the need for constant alertness, he finally realized that he could no longer live in Kentucky. He moved to Ohio and became a powerful antislavery lecturer and organizer.

BLACK ABOLITIONISTS ACT   Many free blacks in the North strongly supported abolition. It was largely they who organized the Underground Railroad, a network of abolitionists who helped smuggle runaway slaves from the South to safe areas in the North or in Canada. A slave who made contact with an agent would be sent north, passed from person to person, transported at night by wagon under a load of hay, and hidden in secret rooms of the houses that served as way stations.

Harriet Tubman, an escaped slave, made twenty daring return trips to the South to rescue as many as three hundred others, including her parents. A legend, she was given the nickname "Moses" and had a $40,000 price on her head.

Another important black abolitionist was Sojourner Truth. Born in 1797 as a slave in New York state with the name Isabella Baumfree, she learned mystical religious practices from her mother. Freed in 1827 by New York's emancipation law, she took the name Sojourner Truth in 1843, after conversing with God, she said; she traveled the country to preach a religious message of abolition and women's rights. "I have borne thirteen children, and seen most of 'em sold into slavery," she said, "and when I cried out with my mother's grief, none but Jesus heard me—and ain't I a woman?"

FREDERICK DOUGLASS TELLS HIS STORY   The leading black abolitionist was Frederick Douglass. Son of a white planter and a black slave mother, he grew up in the 1820s as a slave on a Maryland plantation until he was sent to Baltimore to be trained as a house servant. This bright youth's mistress helped him learn to read and write (which alarmed his master), and he mixed with and learned from Baltimore's free blacks in the streets. Sent to a shipyard to learn to be a shipcaulker, he was nearly killed in a fight when a white worker decided to teach this proud, cocky, intelligent black youth about white supremacy.

The most prominent black abolitionist was the runaway slave Frederick Douglass. His writing and speaking did much to convince northern audiences that slavery should be abolished. (National Portrait Gallery, Washington, D.C./Art Resource, N.Y.)

Concluding that Douglass had been ruined by literacy and contact with independent-minded free blacks, his owner sent him to a plantation to be broken. Douglass resisted, received frequent beatings, and fled to the North. In 1838 he obtained a free Negro's pass, bought seaman's clothes, and sailed from Baltimore to Philadelphia. Feeling unsafe there, he quickly moved to New England but due to prejudice found no work as a caulker.

One day Douglass attended an abolitionist meeting, told his story, and electrified the crowd. This articulate, self-educated man refuted the argument for slavery merely by existing. Sent on a speaking tour through-out the North, Douglass told his audiences, "I grew up to manhood in the presence of this hydra-headed monster—not as a master—not as an idle spectator—not as the guest of the slaveholder; but as a *slave.*" The most successful of the abolitionist lecturers, in 1847 Douglass founded a major antislavery newspaper, *North Star,* in Rochester, New York. His autobio-graphical *Narrative* (1845) became an American classic.

Douglass occupied a key position in the abolitionist movement. An astute student of southern culture both white and black, he believed that northerners could do little either to change white southern opinion or to reach the slaves. Therefore, like Theodore Weld, he concluded that more could be accomplished in the North by converting the masses to abolition.

Like other militants, he advocated full civil rights for all blacks everywhere. Indeed, he frequently pointed out that free blacks in the North like himself lacked many rights, including, in most states, the right to vote, and were generally treated as second-class citizens. He stressed the importance of education and job training in the race's advancement and, being rather pessimistic about rallying whites to assist, called for black self-help.

Despite his militancy, he maintained good relations with the reli-gious abolitionists, especially Harriet Beecher Stowe. In part this was due to his calmness, which contrasted vividly with Garrison's stri-dency, and in part to the fact that he shared the religious abolitionists' concerns about the practical consequences of immediate emancipation. Mostly, however, they admired him for overcoming the handicap of having been born a slave. Douglass's success demonstrated what emancipation might accomplish. Such a message suggested that slav-ery was not only cruel but also a hoax, a form of exploitation disguised by a racial myth.

CONCLUSION

The American Revolution started the movement to abolish slavery. State emancipation succeeded in the North, where slaves were few, but failed in the South, where fears of free blacks and rising profits led whites to de-fend slavery vigorously. Meanwhile, northern evangelicals saw slavery as a sin, even as militant abolitionists demanded its immediate end. By 1850 the issue divided Americans sectionally and, as we shall see, was ripe for the political arena.

Recommended Readings

DOCUMENTS: Frederick Douglass, *Narrative of the Life* (1845); Harriet A. Jacobs, *Incidents in the Life of a Slave Girl, Written by Herself* (1861); Frances A. Kemble, *Journal of a Residence on a Georgian Plantation in 1838–1839* (1864); Solomon Northrup, *Twelve Years a Slave* (1853).

READINGS: (GENERAL) Charles C. Bolton, *Poor Whites of the Antebellum South* (1994); David B. Davis, *The Problem of Slavery* (2 vols., 1966–1975); John H. Franklin, *From Slavery to Freedom* (8th ed., 2000); George M. Frederickson, *The Black Image in the White Mind* (1971); Eugene D. Genovese, *Roll, Jordan, Roll* (1974); Peter Kolchin, *Unfree Labor* (1987) and *American Slavery* (1993); Lawrence W. Levine, *Black Culture and Black Consciousness* (1977); James Oakes, *The Ruling Race* (1982) and *Slavery and Freedom* (1990); Kenneth M. Stampp, *The Peculiar Institution* (1956); (SLAVE LIFE) John W. Blassingame, *The Slave Community* (2nd ed., 1979); Orville V. Burton, *In My Father's House Are Many Mansions* (1985); Victoria E. Bynum, *Unruly Women* (1992); Stephanie Camp, *Closer to Freedom* (2004); Douglas R. Egerton, *Gabriel's Rebellion* (1993); Elizabeth Fox-Genovese, *Within the Plantation Household* (1988); Jacqueline Jones, *Labor of Love, Labor of Sorrow* (1985); Charles W. Joyner, *Down by the Riverside* (1984); Wilma King, *Stolen Childhood* (1995); Stephanie McCurry, *Masters of Small Worlds* (1995); Leslie Owens, *This Species of Property* (1976); Albert J. Raboteau, *Slave Religion* (1978); Brenda E. Stevenson, *Life in Black and White* (1996); Deborah G. White, *Ar'n't I a Woman?* (rev. ed., 1999); (RELIGIOUS ABOLITION) Robert Abzug, *Passionate Liberator, Theodore Dwight Weld* (1980); Lawrence J. Friedman, *Gregarious Saints* (1982); John R. McKivigan, *The War against Proslavery Religion* (1984); Leonard L. Richards, *Gentlemen of Property and Standing* (1970); James B. Stewart, *Holy Warriors* (1976); (MILITANT ABOLITION) Waldo E. Martin, *The Mind of Frederick Douglass* (1984); William S. McFeely, *Frederick Douglass* (1991); Nell I. Painter, *Sojourner Truth* (1996); Benjamin Quarles, *Black Abolitionists* (1969); John Thomas, *The Liberator, William Lloyd Garrison* (1963).

12

🦋

Americans at Midcentury: Unbounded Optimism

OVERVIEW   The late 1840s and early 1850s formed a kind of turning point in the development of the United States. The year 1845 marked the beginning of an economic boom that lasted a generation, during which large numbers of Irish and German immigrants poured into the country. Amid prosperity, the optimistic middle class adopted rigid values, but the more adventurous prepared to lay claim to the continent. The annexation of Texas produced the Mexican War, which led to the acquisition of New Mexico and California. The only sour note was in politics, where slavery became an agonizingly divisive issue that optimistic Americans thought they could settle with the ill-fated Compromise of 1850. No piece of legislation has better expressed both the flavor of a period and its limitations. Throughout the era, Americans believed it was their Manifest Destiny to possess the entire continent.

RAPID GROWTH RESHAPES THE COUNTRY

In 1845 the economy began a long boom. Prosperity brought demands for labor that led to increasing immigration, especially from Ireland and Germany. Although assimilation proved difficult, hostility to immigrants faded due to good economic conditions and the spirit of optimism.

THE ECONOMY TAKES OFF   The period between 1845 and 1873 saw such unprecedented economic growth all over the world that economists have called it the "Long Boom." Although punctuated by recessions, including the Panic of 1857, the downturns never lasted long, were seldom deep, and were followed by vigorous recoveries.

During this boom, the American gross domestic product (that is, the value of the nation's total economic output) exceeded Great Britain's for the first time. Industrial output grew rapidly in the United States, and world trade blossomed as railroads and steamships linked remote areas, bringing agricultural produce and minerals such as copper, iron, and tin into a global market.

Many people believed that continued economic growth required access to new natural resources and markets. Explorers sought new resources all over the world. Europeans raced to colonize Africa; Americans, filled with unbounded optimism, became determined to push the boundaries of the United States to the Pacific Ocean.

IMMIGRATION SURGES TO RECORD LEVELS   The growth of the American economy could not have taken place without a large increase in the labor force. Natural resources were plentiful, and so was capital, generated by the textile industry, by profits made through increased trade, and by British investments in the United States. But labor was scarce and expensive.

Immigrants, particularly from Ireland and Germany, poured into the United States in unprecedented numbers during the 1840s and 1850s. Driven from Ireland by famine and from Germany by political turmoil combined with a sense that greater opportunities existed in the United States, the immigrants arrived to face economic exploitation and prejudice, especially if they were Catholic, as many were. Nevertheless, they continued to come.

Of a total population of 31 million in 1860, about 13 percent were foreign born. Some 1.6 million had been born in Ireland, 1.3 million in Germany, and another 1.2 million elsewhere. Almost all settled in the North, where by 1860 the foreign born constituted close to one-quarter of the adult population.

In most northern cities, immigrants and their American-born children were a majority. The Irish settled along the East coast, the Germans in the Midwest, where they established, among other things, breweries. Anheuser-Busch, Pabst, Schlitz, and Miller (originally Müller) date from this period. English-style beer all but disappeared. Immigration made the United States a much more diverse society.

In the 1840s regularly scheduled ships brought large numbers of Irish immigrants from Liverpool to New York. Conditions on board were often bleak. (Ellis Island Museum, National Park Service)

Although most immigrants worked as laborers or as skilled artisans, they quickly decided that they, or at least their children, would rise into the middle class. Even though skilled labor was becoming less and less needed and valued, these aspirations were realistic. The economy, growing ever more complex as it expanded, generated far more new, specialized, middle-class jobs than the native born could fill. Learning English, working two jobs, going to night school, pooling funds with relatives, and living frugally to save money to open family businesses were ways for immigrants to join the middle class. At the very least, many embraced middle-class values and claimed respectability even with modest incomes.

URBAN WORKERS PROTEST   The arrival of large numbers of upwardly mobile immigrants did not set well with the native-born Protestant working class in America's largest cities. As job competition drove down wages, the native born responded by rioting and, in 1844, by organizing the American Republican Party. Protesting against both the merchant-dominated Whigs and the immigrant-oriented Democrats, the American Republicans elected a mayor and city council in New York and a congressman from a working-class district in Philadelphia. The congressman was Lewis Levin, a Methodist street preacher, temperance advocate, and son of a Jewish merchant. The virulently anti-immigrant Levin served three terms before his party disappeared from view, the victim of rising prosperity. Even nativism could not survive the unbounded optimism of the boom.

THE MIDDLE CLASS ADOPTS MODERN VALUES

By the 1840s the Market Revolution (chapter 8) had created for the first time a substantial urban middle class. Increasingly, this class's core values—thrift, respectability, family life, and separate gender roles—became dominant in the society as a whole. Men competed in the marketplace to earn money; women guarded morality and cultivated family life. Young people carefully trained for future roles. The middle class stressed self-improvement and organized groups to enhance virtue in the community.

DEFINING THE MIDDLE CLASS   In small towns and cities across the United States, doctors, lawyers, ministers, many merchants, some master mechanics, and specialized white-collar workers and their families increasingly saw themselves as belonging to a new, self-defined middle class. Lacking great wealth, without inherited money, and often without much education, members of these families nonetheless enjoyed above-average incomes, a rising standard of living, and homeownership.

At a time when a laborer earned a maximum of $300 a year and a typical skilled artisan $600, a middle-class man made $1,200 or more. Such a man could support a wife who did not work outside the home and several children in a comfortable household, often with a female live-in Irish servant to help with the chores. Perhaps 20 to 40 percent of urban Americans lived in this fashion, and even more people tried to imitate middle-class ways the best they could.

Rigid values and practices marked the middle class, which believed in "a place for every thing and every thing in its place." This desire for boundaries, perhaps understandable amid the chaos of a rapidly changing and often unbounded society, led to complex formulas that governed all aspects of life. For example, a widow was expected to wear black mourning clothes for one year after her husband's death. The development of a rigid code of conduct made it possible for new people to join the middle class, since conduct defined membership, while at the same time conformity helped define the class and maintain its cohesion.

GENDER ROLES AND FAMILY VALUES   One important middle-class principle was to separate men and women in all aspects of life. In 1850 men were seen as strivers and doers, by nature aggressive and acquisitive. Accordingly, they were supposed to employ themselves competitively in business or the professions. If they succeeded, they married, established homes, and enjoyed family life with children. Women were seen as dreamers, by nature passive and fragile, and thus fit only to maintain the home as a refuge from the world for husbands and as a place to nurture children. The duty of women, who were thought to understand morality better, was to regulate the passions of men. The duty of men, inclined toward worldly success, was to use their earnings to take care of women.

At an early age, middle-class children learned that authority must be respected, that rules must be obeyed, and that men and women performed different lifework. Raising children, a principal duty for middle-class mothers, involved teaching the young to distinguish between right and wrong and to understand the importance of moral principles as defined by evangelical Protestants. Capable of both good and evil, children had to be guided along the correct moral path, which would all but guarantee that they would acquire proper manners, social graces, and practical work skills.

Institutions reinforced family training. Both church-sponsored Sunday schools and public schools, which often included the Bible in the curriculum, repeated values taught at home and provided social contacts in a moral setting. Encouraged to show responsibility, pupils were given assignments that combined learning, discipline, and morals. The new high schools emphasized practical preparation for life and work by teaching boys penmanship, accounting, and geography, all skills valued in the job market. They also stressed order, propriety, and obedience to authority.

Many young men had to carve out a middle-class life for themselves. Sunday school tracts and teenage advice manuals praised upward mobility and urged youths to become "self-made" men. These books both stressed the importance of high morals and favored formal education, especially technical training that made a young man more employable. Honesty, honor, and (perhaps most important) self-restraint gave a youth the character to survive in a world filled with evils that snared the unwary.

Young women learned from sermons, magazine essays, and popular novels to model themselves on their happy, successful mothers or other female relatives. Useful information could be found in household management manuals such as Catharine Beecher's. A young woman was expected to learn to cook, sew, care for children, and manage household money and servants, but her most important skill was sizing up young men. She was expected to marry and to remain married to the same man. In many ways he would control her life, so it was important for her to resist passion, which might lead her to fall in love with a scoundrel, and to marry a moral, virtuous man capable of earning a living.

THE IMPORTANCE OF THE HOME IN TOWN AND CITY   In small towns and large cities, wives typically set a moral tone in the home for their husbands and children and for their reputations among visitors. Religious and moral newspapers, magazines, and books, including *Harper's New Family Bible,* were piled prominently on tables in the living room. Moral or patriotic lithographs, designed to educate as well as enliven, hung on the walls. These devices added an element of piety and rectitude to the new, elaborate decorative style, which featured luxurious wall-to-wall carpets, lavish wallpaper, heavy drapes, and carved wooden furniture, including red horsehair sofas.

Pianos graced many middle-class living rooms. Although buying a piano might cost a family all of its income beyond the price of necessities, families often made this sacrifice. A skirt carefully covered the piano's legs, which were supposed to be kept hidden. The legs were called "limbs." The word *leg* was considered obscene.

After meals, family members adjourned to the piano and sang while a daughter played. A woman's musical skills might attract the attention of an eligible young man. Religious hymns and the melodic songs of Stephen Foster were favorites. No wonder that, when the singer Jenny Lind, dubbed "the Swedish Nightingale," toured the United States in 1850, middle-class Americans rushed to buy tickets at $50 apiece.

For the first time, the middle class began to eat in dining rooms separate from living rooms and kitchens. Meals were at fixed times, and all members of the family except young children were expected to be present. Dining became complex and elaborate, with expensive tablecloths, napkins, china, and silver covering the table. A place setting of silver included many utensils, each designed for a specific purpose. For example, strawberries and raspberries required different spoons. Carried from the kitchen by a servant, the food was simple but heaped high on platters to indicate wealth.

THE MIDDLE CLASS SEEKS SELF-IMPROVING ENTERTAINMENT   Although members of the middle class worked hard, they also enjoyed leisure. They rejected liquor at taverns in favor of ice cream sodas or fruit-flavored drinks with crushed ice at the new soda fountains. They organized games such as baseball with its elaborate rules. Children played with mechanical toys, including savings banks designed to teach thrift. Family members sat for their portraits before the camera at the new daguerreotype photographic studios.

Especially favored was entertainment that provided, or claimed to provide, self-improvement. Thus, middle-class Americans keenly read daily newspapers. By the 1840s every major city had several penny papers, such as James Gordon Bennett's *New York Herald*. The energetic Bennett often scooped the competition, helped organize the Associated Press, and quickly embraced Samuel F. B. Morse's newly invented telegraph, which sent out word of James K. Polk's nomination by the Democratic convention in 1844. The whole country was wired rapidly.

Lectures at local lyceums promised increased knowledge as well as fun. So did P. T. Barnum's American Museum in New York. To attract middle-class audiences, Barnum stressed his establishment's educational mission. He exhibited curiosities from the natural world, but many were fake. Barnum called the theater in his museum an "auditorium" and its live shows "illustrated lectures" to appease evangelicals who found theatrical shows sinful.

Despite its absurdities and faults, the middle class had one striking virtue. Surrounded by an atmosphere of evangelical Christianity, the middle class optimistically believed in charity and in doing good in the world. Women, especially, thought that a moral home offered insufficient protection in a largely immoral world. Thus, middle-class women organized moral societies, church welfare groups, and reform organizations to bring virtue to their communities.

AMERICANS LAY CLAIM TO THE CONTINENT

In the 1840s the spirit of unbounded optimism led Americans to see the whole of North America as theirs. Settlers flocked west to Texas, New Mexico, California, and the Oregon country. The Texas colonists never doubted that Texas would someday join the Union. Early American settlers in New Mexico and California had the same dream. So did the pioneers who trudged along the Oregon Trail. Boosters claimed that America's expansion was God-given Manifest Destiny.

STEPHEN AUSTIN COLONIZES TEXAS   Americans had long looked toward the day when their nation would reach the Pacific Ocean. In 1821, the year Mexico won its independence from Spain, Moses Austin received a Mexican charter to establish a colony in Mexico's province of Texas, which had only three thousand Mexican residents. When Austin died, his son Stephen took over the project. By 1824 as many as two thousand Americans, some southerners with slaves, had settled in Austin's colony. In 1829 Mexico abolished slavery, but the Texans evaded the law by turning their slaves into servants indentured for life.

During the early 1830s the Mexican government became so alarmed at the large number of Americans pouring into Texas that it halted further land grants. Mexican officials harassed the Texans about slavery, about customs duties, and about their religion (Mexico required the Americans to promise to convert to Catholicism). In 1833, when Austin went to Mexico City to protest, he was jailed. In 1835 General Antonio López de Santa Anna declared himself dictator of Mexico, a move that alarmed the democratically

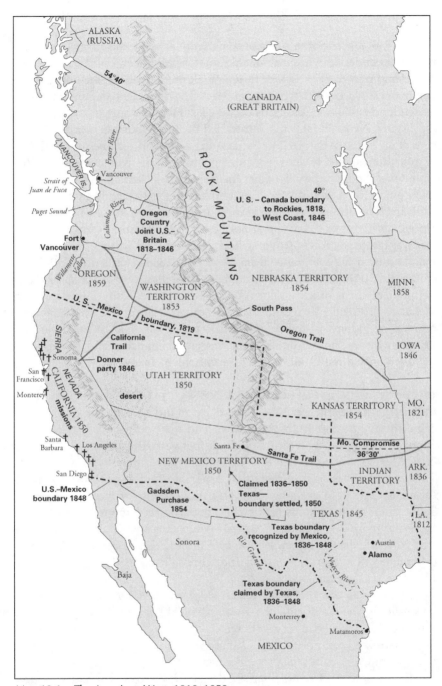

Map 12.1   The American West, 1818–1859

inclined Texans, and decided to march an army into Texas to punish the Americans.

In 1836, just as Santa Anna and his army arrived, the Texans declared their independence. A few days later, Santa Anna's forces took the fort called the Alamo in a bloody victory in which all the defenders, including frontiersman Davy Crockett, were slaughtered. The defenders' defiant refusal to surrender despite hopeless odds became a symbol of courage and honor to the Texans. A month later the Texans, led by Sam Houston, beat the Mexicans at the battle of San Jacinto. Santa Anna was captured and, under threat of execution, signed treaties recognizing Texas's independence and the Rio Grande as the boundary between the Republic of Texas and Mexico. The Mexican congress would later void these treaties as having been coerced.

Sam Houston asked President Andrew Jackson, an old friend from Houston's Tennessee days, to annex Texas to the United States, but Jackson wanted to avoid controversy and declined. The Texans continued to maintain their independence from Mexico. In 1836 Texas's population included thirty thousand white Americans, five thousand black slaves (the Republic of Texas quickly reintroduced slavery), and only four thousand Mexicans. By 1860 only 6 percent of Texas's population was Hispanic. The number of Indians in the population is unknown. The Texans killed or drove away the native inhabitants, largely Comanche, and to this day there are only three small Indian reservations in Texas.

TRADERS SETTLE IN NEW MEXICO AND CALIFORNIA   In 1821 the first American traders reached Santa Fe, New Mexico, by an Indian trail that quickly became the main road from the Midwest to the Southwest. Whereas the Spanish had jealously prohibited trade between the United States and New Mexico, Mexico's newly independent government did not object. This business was so profitable that American traders organized annual caravans, largely to exchange manufactured goods for mules and silver. Soon American merchants set up shop in Santa Fe, a town of about three thousand people, where they learned Spanish, became Catholic, and married New Mexican women. Within two decades an Anglo-Hispanic elite dominated New Mexico's politics and economics by exploiting the poorer Hispanic and Indian residents.

As early as the 1820s, American ships in the China trade began to barter along the California coast with the Californios, as the province's four thousand Mexican residents were called. The Americans exchanged both manufactured goods and Chinese tea and silk for fresh water and hides from California's vast *rancheros* (cattle ranches).

In the late 1700s the Spanish priest Junipero Serra had founded twenty-one Franciscan missions in California. Although these missions still held some power in the 1820s, a small number of Mexican land grantees increasingly dominated the region. Indians provided virtual slave labor both for the church missions and on the rancheros.

By the early 1840s a few hundred Americans, as well as some Europeans, had settled in California either as ranchers with Mexican grants or as hide merchants in the seaports. While sharing the Californios' contempt for the government in far-off Mexico City, the Americans had no desire for Californio rule, considering the locals backward, lazy, dishonest, impractical, and foolish. Many Americans awaited the day when California would drop like a ripe plum into American hands.

Talk of California's rich soil and mild climate reached the East, but moving to this fabled land was challenging. The only sea route, around the tip of South America, took travelers through dangerous storms, on cargo ships or on whaling ships ill equipped for passengers. The overland route meant crossing the desert and risking encounters with Indians.

Naively written guidebooks optimistically insisted that the "Yerba Buena River" flowed conveniently on a direct line from Colorado to San Francisco Bay. When knowledgeable explorers denied that there was such a river, they were accused of hiding the truth in order to make money by selling guide services to travelers. In 1846 a group of settlers led by George Donner migrated to California and, using a guidebook's faulty map, took a shortcut that left them trapped high in the Sierra Nevada all winter at Donner Pass. Some members of the Donner party froze to death, while others survived, including a number who turned to cannibalism.

THE OREGON TRAIL GOES TO GOD'S COUNTRY   In 1834 Jason Lee established a Methodist mission in Oregon's Willamette River valley. Due partly to his lavish praise of the area, American farmers began to settle there almost immediately. By 1836 these settlers already outnumbered the British in the valley, and in 1843 they were sufficiently numerous to organize a provisional democratic government.

In the early 1840s many more Americans migrated overland to the Oregon country than to California. The Oregon Trail had more reliable water for horses and cattle, and the Pacific Northwest was under joint British–American occupation rather than Mexican rule. In addition, the climate in the Willamette valley was nearly as mild as California's, but greater rainfall enabled Americans to grow familiar crops without irrigation.

Travel on the Oregon Trail, which usually took about six months from Missouri with horses pulling a covered wagon fifteen miles a day, was more arduous than dangerous. Indians approached the trail to make friendly trades, not to attack. Hundreds, later thousands, of settlers set out from Missouri each spring, usually selling their farms to raise the $600 that it cost a family of four to make the trip. By the mid-1840s the wagons were so thick on the trail that they stretched as far as the eye could see in both directions and were often a dozen abreast. The ruts from their wheels are still visible today.

BOOSTERS CLAIM MANIFEST DESTINY   As the economy gathered steam in the 1840s, so did promoters of national geographical expansion. Many young men, including Stephen A. Douglas and George N. Sanders, called themselves the Young America movement. Although motivated primarily by the desire to enrich themselves, advocates of expansion preferred to use moral arguments that expressed the spirit of the age.

As a "go–ahead" people, Americans considered themselves uniquely suited to acquire, develop, and exploit North America's rich natural resources. To do so was a God-given right, wrote the Democratic Party promoter John L. O'Sullivan, for the country had a Manifest Destiny to spread itself westward to the Pacific Ocean.

The phrase *Manifest Destiny* ostensibly marked the bold cry of confident Americans announcing to the world that they were God's chosen people destined for national greatness. In reality it masked many other tendencies, including self-aggrandizement, acquisitiveness, and exploitation of both people and resources. The assertion of American superiority implied the right of white Americans to enslave blacks or to take land from Indians, Mexicans, or anyone else.

In addition, Manifest Destiny suggested a coherent, logical policy of territorial expansion, when in truth Americans, especially those devoted to national glory, sought to expand anywhere and everywhere at any price. Such gluttony raised serious questions about the country's stability.

THE TEXAS QUESTION LEADS TO WAR WITH MEXICO

Political realists like Henry Clay and Martin Van Buren worried that the country's enthusiasm recognized no limits. But the election of 1844, which put the obscure James K. Polk in the White House, proved that Americans were not prepared to accept limits, at least as far as Texas was concerned. In 1846 Polk made peace with Britain over Oregon but fought Mexico over Texas's annexation, and in 1848 the Mexican War ended with the United States acquiring California and New Mexico. In 1846 David Wilmot's Proviso reintroduced the slavery issue into politics.

THE ELECTION OF **1844**   As the 1844 presidential election approached, the expected candidates were the leaders of the two parties, the Whig Henry Clay and the Democrat Martin Van Buren. Both were realists rather than unbounded optimists. Although Clay owned slaves, neither man liked slavery, and both believed that a sectional dispute over slavery could wreck their parties and cause a civil war. Therefore, they quietly agreed not to discuss slavery, and both issued public statements opposing the admission of the Republic of Texas into the Union as a new slave state. Among other problems, the annexation of Texas invited war with Mexico.

As expected, the Whigs nominated Clay. But southern Democrats, unhappy over their party leader Van Buren's Texas position, sabotaged his candidacy. Going into the national convention, Van Buren held pledges from a majority of delegates, including southerners whose votes had been obtained before he announced his Texas policy. These delegates killed Van Buren's candidacy by persuading the convention to adopt a rule requiring the nominee to get a two-thirds vote. This provision, retained until 1936, gave southerners a veto over the Democratic Party's presidential nomination.

As the southerners knew, Van Buren could not be nominated with the two-thirds rule, and in order to break the deadlock, the Democrats on the ninth ballot picked an obscure former speaker of the House of Representatives, James K. Polk of Tennessee. "Young Hickory," as he was called, enjoyed Andrew Jackson's friendship and support. Polk and the Democrats, unlike Clay and the Whigs, favored annexing Texas. This position guaranteed southern votes. To get support in the North, the Democrats promised to acquire all of the Pacific Northwest, then under joint British–American control, to the southern boundary of Alaska, using the slogan "54°40' or fight." The only other issue was the tariff, which Polk promised to revise. Southerners said Polk would reduce the tariff; northerners thought he would raise it. Polk did not elaborate.

The Whigs, perplexed by the Democrats' first "dark horse" candidate, chanted derisively, "Who is James K. Polk?" The better-known Clay, however, had made many enemies. His pledge against Texas annexation hurt him in the South, and when he tried to retract it, he lost credibility among northerners without gaining any southern support. Abolitionists, mostly Whigs, refused to vote for Clay and instead cast ballots for James Gillespie Birney, the Liberty Party's antislavery candidate. In an extremely close election that remained in doubt for six days, Polk won by narrowly taking New York state. In that crucial state Polk's margin of victory was less than the number of votes cast for Birney.

POLK INHERITS TEXAS AND MAKES PEACE WITH BRITAIN   On March 3, 1845, President John Tyler's last day in office, Texas joined the Union after protracted negotiations conducted by outgoing Secretary of State John C. Calhoun. Thus, Polk's presidency began with Texas as a state, but the issue still troubled his administration. Mexico had never recognized Texas's independence, and the new state's boundary was uncertain.

Texans cited a border that ran along the Rio Grande to its headwaters and then straight north to meet the United States in what became Wyoming. They claimed half of New Mexico, including Santa Fe. The Mexicans contended that the Texas boundary ran along the Nueces River to its headwaters inside central Texas and then north to meet the United States in what became Oklahoma. Polk faced a war with Mexico over this boundary dispute.

Before tackling that issue, Polk decided to use diplomacy to divide ownership of the Pacific Northwest. The British had suggested extending the United States–Canadian boundary at the 49th parallel from the Rocky Mountains west to the Columbia River and then down the river to the ocean. Recognizing that the New Englanders who had begun to settle in Oregon's Willamette valley had given Americans effective control of that area, the British sought to retain the Hudson's Bay Company's Fort Vancouver on the Columbia and the great natural harbors on Puget Sound.

The Americans countered by proposing to extend the 49th parallel boundary to the Pacific Ocean. Wanting peace, the British in 1846 accepted the American proposal with the provision that Vancouver Island remain entirely under their control. The United States agreed to this boundary. The island was less important to the British than the navigation rights through the Strait of Juan de Fuca to the Fraser River, which flowed just north of the 49th parallel. The Hudson's Bay Company relocated its headquarters there, to what is now Vancouver, British Columbia.

THE MEXICAN WAR BEGINS, 1846   Polk's diplomacy with Mexico failed, in part because Mexican honor barred the yielding of territory and in part because Polk wanted even more land than that claimed by the Texans. Westward migration, the idea of Manifest Destiny, and the concept of a transcontinental railroad focused American attention on Mexico's provinces of New Mexico (which then included what became Arizona, Colorado, Utah, and Nevada) and California, especially on the great natural harbors at San Francisco and San Diego. One or the other of those bays was bound to be the site of the transcontinental railhead. Polk wanted both and offered to buy the largely unpopulated southwestern desert. He knew that the local peoples, whether New Mexicans, Californios, or Indians, despised Mexico. The Mexicans, however, refused to sell.

In 1846 Polk stationed American troops led by General Zachary Taylor on the north bank of the Rio Grande ostensibly to protect Texas, although no American settlers lived anywhere near the border. The Mexican army took Polk's bait and attacked. The president announced, "Mexico has . . .

shed American blood upon the American soil." On May 13, 1846, Congress declared war.

Taylor quickly occupied Matamoros, on the south bank of the Rio Grande; Colonel Stephen Kearny took Santa Fe and then marched his army to California. Under secret orders from Polk, Captain John C. Frémont also entered California, and in June 1846, with support from Frémont, some American settlers at Sonoma declared the independent Bear Flag Republic. In July, Commodore John Sloat sailed into the harbor at Monterey and annexed California to the United States.

In August, Commodore Robert Stockton occupied Santa Barbara and Los Angeles and declared himself governor, which provoked the southern Californios to revolt against the Americans. Kearny helped quell the rebellion, and then he and Stockton quarreled over the right to govern California. Kearny won the battle for Polk's support and had Frémont, who had sided with Stockton, court-martialed.

Meanwhile, Taylor's army had captured the city of Monterrey in northern Mexico. Peace talks began but broke off, and in 1847 General Winfield Scott persuaded Polk to try a bold new strategy. When Scott ordered Taylor to hold his position and transfer part of his army to Scott, the suspicious Taylor concluded that he was about to become the victim of political intrigue. Disobeying orders, Taylor marched his troops to Buena Vista and routed a larger Mexican force. Reprimanded for his withdrawal from Monterrey, Taylor resigned and toured the United States as a hero.

Scott's daring plan was to capture the key port of Vera Cruz on the Gulf of Mexico and march directly to Mexico City. After a technically brilliant amphibious assault on Vera Cruz, Scott's army defeated the Mexicans at Cerro Gordo and at Mexico City, which fell on September 14, 1847. United States Marines stood guard over the Halls of Montezuma.

THE UNITED STATES BUYS CALIFORNIA AND NEW MEXICO, 1848   After the fall of Vera Cruz, Polk sent Nicholas P. Trist to Mexico on a secret peace mission. In early 1848 Trist, whose legal authority from Polk had expired, persuaded the Mexican government to sign a treaty. The treaty of Guadalupe Hildalgo recognized the Rio Grande as the Texas boundary and ceded New Mexico and California to the United States in return for $15 million and the assumption by the American government of American citizens' claims against Mexico. Although embarrassed by Trist's unauthorized negotiations, Polk sent the treaty to the Senate, which ratified it despite objections from those who wanted to annex all of Mexico.

Throughout the war, controversy had swirled around the possible acquisition of California and New Mexico. Public opinion no longer doubted, as it had in 1844, the wisdom or indeed the inevitability of

American ownership, but now the question Clay and Van Buren had feared was openly raised: Should slavery be permitted in the new territory? Northerners opposed slavery, believing that the institution should not be allowed to spread and that, because Mexico had abolished slavery, New Mexico and California should remain free. Southerners argued that, having enlisted, fought, and died disproportionately as volunteers in the Mexican War, they had the right to take slave property into newly won territories.

CONGRESS DEBATES DAVID WILMOT'S PROVISO, 1846–1847   After war began in 1846, Congress considered a military spending bill. In the House, David Wilmot, an antislavery Democrat from Pennsylvania, proposed an amendment. Wilmot's Proviso banned slavery in any territory acquired from Mexico as a result of the war. Added to the bill in the House, where antislavery northerners predominated, the amendment failed in the Senate, where free states and slave states had equal representation and where several northern senators had proslavery views. Finally, the House swallowed the Senate version.

In 1847 the Wilmot Proviso again passed in the House and failed in the Senate; it suffered the same fate a third time. By then it had become clear to everyone, especially after the treaty of Guadalupe Hidalgo gave New Mexico and California to the United States, that slavery in the new western territories would be the major political issue in the 1848 presidential election.

ADOPTING THE COMPROMISE OF 1850

As the election of 1848 approached, unbounded optimism gave way to panic over the threat to the Union posed by slavery. Campaigning without a program, Zachary Taylor won without a mandate. To solve the slavery issue, Clay proposed the grand Compromise of 1850, which aimed to appeal to northerners and southerners alike but ultimately angered both sides, although it did delay civil war for a decade.

THE ELECTION OF 1848   In 1848 Polk kept his pledge not to seek reelection, and the Democrats, under southern influence, nominated Lewis Cass of Michigan, the first "dough-face" candidate, that is, a northerner willing to support the South on slavery. The Whigs, badly split over slavery, could not agree on a platform, did not adopt one, and nominated Zachary Taylor for president. This Mexican War hero proved to be an ideal candidate. He had no political record, had never voted, and declined to discuss any issues. Northerners noted that his brother was an abolitionist in Ohio, while southerners observed that his wife had inherited hundreds of slaves in Louisiana.

Martin Van Buren, still bitter over the way he had been cheated out of the Democratic nomination in 1844, decided to teach the southerners a lesson. He accepted the nomination of the Free Soil Party, which promised not to touch slavery in the South but opposed its expansion into the West. His running mate was the antislavery Whig Charles Francis Adams, the son of John Quincy Adams. Thus, in the strange ways of politics, Jackson's hand-picked successor now allied himself with the son of Jackson's enemy.

On Election Day southerners gave Taylor a landslide victory, while northerners split their votes. Van Buren's strong showing in parts of the North that had been settled by New Englanders indicated intense opposition to the expansion of slavery, especially among those of Puritan descent touched by the Second Great Awakening (chapter 9).

Taylor's clever strategy for winning the election without taking any positions now backfired. As president, he was bound to disappoint some of his supporters with any action he took. The temporary military governments in New Mexico and California had to be replaced, and with people pouring into California after gold was discovered there in 1848, the issue had to be settled quickly.

In 1849 Taylor proposed admitting both New Mexico and California to the Union. He dodged the territorial slavery issue by saying that, as states, they could decide for themselves if they wanted slavery. This scheme drew no support. Both northerners and southerners felt cheated. New Mexico did not seem ready for statehood, and southerners knew that California would enter the Union as a free state. For the first time, the number of free and slave states would not be the same, and the slave states would lose their equal representation in the Senate.

CLAY PROPOSES A GRAND COMPROMISE, 1850   Ignoring the stubborn Taylor, Henry Clay, the Whig Party leader, began in 1850 to arrange a grand compromise. Wanting legislation that gave each section something concrete, Clay's Omnibus Bill contained six provisions:

- California would be admitted as a free state. This reflected public opinion in California, which had more than enough population to be admitted. It also pleased the North. The Senate, however, would not be unbalanced, because many Californians were former southerners, and it was understood that one California senator would represent them.

- New Mexico would be split into northern and southern territories respectively called Utah and New Mexico. Congress would not bar slavery from these territories, and the territorial legislatures could do as they pleased. Utah, with its large Mormon settlement, would probably keep slavery out, but New Mexico, if later settled by Texans, might adopt slavery. The dry climate, however, made it unsuitable for cotton, and slavery was unlikely to thrive there.

- Texas would cede much of its land, including its claim to half of New Mexico, and in return the United States would take over Texas's enormous debt, which was owed to private bondholders. Many Texas bonds were now owned by the Washington banker W. W. Corcoran. He offered the bonds at reduced rates to members of Congress during the discussion of Clay's compromise. Clay knew that the Texas bonds, which would rise sharply in value if his bill passed, would generate votes for the compromise from corrupt congressmen who had recently bought bonds.

- Although slavery would remain in the District of Columbia, the slave trade would end. No longer would antislavery northern congressmen have to watch slave auctions taking place across the street from their offices inside the Capitol. Slaveowners, however, would hardly be inconvenienced, since they could sell their slaves a few miles away in Virginia or Maryland.

- Congress would pledge not to interfere with the interstate slave trade. Slaveholders in some states, especially Virginia, had made enormous profits selling their slaves to cotton growers in other states, and they did not want federal legislation that would ban these sales and thereby reduce the value of their slaves.

- A new Fugitive Slave Law would provide for the speedy return of runaway slaves from the North to their owners in the South. In some parts of the North, where local officials were abolitionists, slaveholders had found it impossible to recover slaves. Now federal officials would be appointed to settle these cases without jury trials. Southerners looked upon this provision in Clay's compromise as the one concrete benefit they expected to receive. They were willing to give up a great deal to obtain an effective law because a runaway slave represented a major financial loss.

CONGRESS DEBATES AND ADOPTS THE COMPROMISE OF 1850   Clay's attempted compromise produced the greatest debate in Senate history as the old lions roared for the last time. Daniel Webster of Massachusetts, Clay's rival, endorsed Clay's Omnibus Bill, saying that he spoke "not as a Massachusetts man, nor as a northern man, but as an American" wishing to preserve the Union. But in doing so, Webster antagonized his constituents, who opposed slavery.

A dying John C. Calhoun of South Carolina denounced Clay's effort and demanded a constitutional amendment giving the South control over its own affairs. Calhoun died even before the debate had concluded, and both Clay and Webster died two years later.

Younger senators, the leaders of the next generation, stridently opposed the bill. Abolitionist Salmon P. Chase of Ohio urged Congress to keep slavery out of the territories, and William H. Seward of New York said a "higher law" than the Constitution led him to oppose slavery's spread. On the other side, Jefferson Davis of Mississippi demanded that southerners have the right to take slave property into *all* federal territories.

Clay could not find enough votes to pass his Omnibus Bill, in part due to Taylor's opposition. But on July 9, 1850, Taylor died suddenly and was succeeded by Millard Fillmore, who enthusiastically endorsed the compromise. An old and tired Clay went on vacation, and a young representative from Illinois, Stephen A. Douglas, then split Clay's bill into five separate pieces of legislation. With support from the new administration and with many members of Congress voting only for portions of the overall compromise, Douglas pushed through all five bills. Only a handful of members voted for the total package. Few northerners favored the Fugitive Slave Law, which had become the compromise's most controversial feature.

LIVING WITH THE COMPROMISE OF 1850   The Compromise of 1850 was the last and greatest contribution of Henry Clay and his generation to American governance. Lacking the Founding Fathers' devotion to abstract ideals, Clay's generation struggled to pass imperfect but workable laws while hoping that future events would somehow allow revolutionary principles to be carried out. Meanwhile, it was more important to keep the country together, even when people disagreed on the interpretation of fundamental principles, and even if it was necessary to buy votes from some members with profits from Texas bonds.

Although Clay, unlike the gloomy Calhoun, remained an optimist, even he felt forebodings about the future. He was not sure that leaders like Seward and Jefferson Davis, with their energetic devotion to high-minded principles, could continue to make the political system work, especially with an issue as troubling as slavery. Clay did not feel, as young northerners did, embarrassment at living in a self-proclaimed free society in which some people were enslaved.

Devoted in his own way to a national greatness based on his own American system composed of industry, commerce, and cities, Clay had once been "Young Harry of the West," but he had opposed the annexation of Texas and Polk's unbounded vision of a transcontinental republic. He understood better than Polk the power of centrifugal forces in an ever-expanding United States, and he feared that the country, if it grew too fast, would fly apart.

The great compromise, so carefully constructed, solved nothing. It papered over the real problems: growing gaps between the North and the South in population, in wealth, in economic development, and in moral principles. In the end both sides felt cheated. Northerners were reluctant to hand over runaway slaves and resented the Fugitive Slave Law that ordered them to do so, while the law's ineffectiveness irritated southerners. California's admission to the Union broke the tradition that the number of free and slave states must be the same, and after 1845 no new slave states were admitted.

Congress's policy to allow Utah and New Mexico to decide about slavery for themselves generated controversy in those territories, and it inadvertently opened the question of slavery in other western territories, where that issue had supposedly been settled. If the compromise had any virtue, it was the prevention of civil war in 1850. Its long-term consequence, however, was not to settle the slavery issue but to invite further controversy.

MANIFEST DESTINY AND FILIBUSTERS

In 1849 would-be miners swarmed into California in search of gold, but few found it. Nonetheless, Americans clung to the notion of Manifest Destiny, either their own or the country's. Some particularly ambitious optimists, such as William Walker, aimed to combine national and personal greatness by trying to take over other countries.

THE LURE OF THE CALIFORNIA GOLD RUSH   At the end of the Mexican War, in 1848, the United States acquired California. That same year gold was discovered, and by 1852 California's population had surged to 250,000, about six times the pre-Gold Rush level. Almost 90 percent of Californians were male. About half were Americans from the eastern United States, and the others were Europeans, Mexicans, Chileans, Chinese, or settled Indians.

Of 900,000 young white single men in America, one in ten rushed to California, mainly to seek gold. Few were lucky. The shrewder ones, like Leland Stanford, quickly realized that more money could be made selling supplies to miners or in agriculture. Levi Strauss, an Alsatian Jew, turned blue tent canvas into tight-fitting pants called jeans that both made his fortune and popularized a uniquely American style of dress.

During the 1850s the California Gold Rush attracted people from all over the world, especially from the eastern United States. But swinging a pickaxe did not necessarily produce gold, and many left California, broke. (Brown Brothers)

The price of services grew so high that it was cheaper to have clothes sent to Hawaii to be laundered than to have them washed in San Francisco. Then the Chinese opened laundries and restaurants in San Francisco and soon constituted the bulk of California's unskilled workforce. Almost all the Chinese were male, few married or had children in California, and many returned to China. Within a few years most of the American miners had returned to the East, some with profits, some broke. The dream of the nation's Manifest Destiny, however, lived on.

THE FILIBUSTERERS SEEK FAME, FORTUNE, AND LAND   No men exemplified Manifest Destiny better than the filibusterers. They were American adventurers who used private armies to overthrow foreign governments so they could seize power for themselves. In 1849 Henry Crabb tried to take Sonora in northern Mexico, while two years later Narciso Lopez invaded Cuba, then a Spanish colony. Both were captured and executed.

The most persistent filibusterer was William Walker. After failing to capture the Mexican provinces of Baja California and Sonora in 1853, this "gray-eyed man of destiny" set out in 1855 to conquer the Central American nation of Nicaragua. Intending to have the country annexed to the United States as a new slave state, Walker landed with fifty-eight men, seized the capital, and proclaimed a government. To gain legitimacy, he had himself "elected" governor, although no election was held. Walker made up the election returns, which he carefully printed in his newspaper. In 1857 he suffered a military defeat and was forced to flee. Three years later the British foiled Walker's self-appointed mission to Honduras, which ended with Walker's execution by a firing squad. Filibustering ceased.

CONCLUSION

At midcentury Americans lived in a delicate balance, partly in a static world of the Founding Fathers' republican principles and rural virtues—which included slavery—and partly in a dynamic world of markets, industry, cities, immigrants, railroads, and national territorial expansion to the Pacific Ocean. This new world, brought into being by the Market Revolution and awash in evangelical Protestantism and reform, was only beginning to develop its own sense of poise, of rootedness, of self-confidence about the shape of the American future.

At midcentury Americans looked both backward and forward, and they took cues alternatively from those aspects of the society that were age-old and those that were new. Unbounded optimism masked their essential insecurity. This ambiguity, however, was about to dissolve, and in the decade that followed, Americans, especially young northerners, became fully modern people.

Recommended Readings

DOCUMENTS: Catharine E. Beecher, *A Treatise on Domestic Economy* (1841); George G. Foster, *New York by Gas-Light* (1850); George T. Strong, *Diary* (4 vols., 1952).

READINGS: (SOCIETY) Stuart M. Blumin, *The Emergence of the Middle Class* (1989); Richard L. Bushman, *The Refinement of America* (1992); Clifford E. Clark, *The American Family Home* (1986); Kenneth Cmiel, *Democratic Eloquence* (1990); Patricia C. Cohen, *A*

Calculating People (1982); Hasia R. Diner, *Erin's Daughters in America* (1983); Karen Halttunen, *Confidence Men and Painted Women* (1982); John F. Kasson, *Rudeness and Civility* (1990); Kerby Miller, *Emigrants and Exiles* (1985); (WEST) Julie R. Jeffrey, *Converting the West* (1991) and *Frontier Women* (rev. ed., 1998); Patricia N. Limerick, *The Legacy of Conquest* (1987); Michael A. Morrison, *Slavery and the American West* (1997); Malcolm J. Rohrbough, *Days of Gold* (1997); David J. Weber, *The Mexican Frontier* (1982); Richard White, *It's Your Misfortune and None of My Own* (1991); (POLITICS) K. Jack Bauer, *The Mexican War* (1974); Frederick J. Blue, *The Free Soilers* (1973); Charles H. Brown, *Agents of Manifest Destiny* (1980); Albert H. Z. Carr, *The World and William Walker* (1963); Thomas R. Hietala, *Manifest Design* (rev. ed., 2002); Robert W. Johannsen, *To the Halls of the Montezumas* (1985); (BIOGRAPHY) Irving H. Bartlett, *Daniel Webster* (1978); K. Jack Bauer, *Zachary Taylor* (1985); Maurice G. Baxter, *One and Inseparable, Daniel Webster and the Union* (1984); Merrill D. Peterson, *The Great Triumvirate* (1987); Kathryn K. Sklar, *Catharine Beecher* (1973).

13

The Sectional Crisis, 1852–1861

OVERVIEW The 1850s started with optimism, a booming economy, and political compromise. The decade ended with raw feelings, a soured economy, and the storm clouds of approaching civil war. If only, agreed Americans in both North and South, the issue of slavery had never cursed politics. If only, lamented experienced leaders, the political system had not broken down along sectional lines, smashing the old national parties and bringing in their place militant leaders of new, ideologically charged, sectional parties. Other people saw the growing sectional crisis in politics as a symptom of a more fundamental problem, the growing divergence of North and South. Whatever its origins, the sectional crisis had a rhythm and momentum all its own.

THE TERRITORIAL SLAVERY ISSUE RETURNS, 1852–1854

Although the Democrats won a landslide victory in 1852 by upholding the Compromise of 1850, northern concern over slavery remained high, as evidenced by high sales of *Uncle Tom's Cabin*. The Pierce administration planned a transcontinental railroad; to make Chicago the eastern terminus, Senator Stephen A. Douglas of Illinois pushed the Kansas–Nebraska Act through Congress in 1854. This measure allowed each territory to vote on slavery, an idea Douglas called "popular sovereignty." The act unleashed a firestorm of controversy that splintered the existing parties and resulted in the formation of two new parties, the free-soil Republicans and the nativist Know-Nothings.

THE ELECTION OF 1852   In 1852 the Democrats nominated Franklin Pierce of New Hampshire for president on a platform upholding the Compromise of 1850. Pierce, a handsome, amiable senator and former minor general in the Mexican War, exuded charm but had little substance. Known best in Washington for having arrived at the theater several times belligerently drunk, Pierce was considered by northerners to be one of their own, although they might have pondered the ease with which he had received southern votes for the nomination.

The Whigs, attempting to repeat their success with Zachary Taylor, picked another Mexican War hero, General Winfield Scott. The Whigs, however, quarreled over a platform; Scott's northern supporters were unwilling to endorse the Compromise, and southerners were angered by Scott's cranky statements about slaveholders. The candidate lived up to his military nickname, "Old Fuss and Feathers," not exactly a term of endearment.

Pierce won in a landslide. The election wrecked the Whig Party and affirmed popular support both north and south for the Compromise. Despite this victory, the slavery issue remained alive. After 1850 northern states responded to the new Fugitive Slave Law by passing personal liberty laws that enabled local elected officials to try to save black residents from the federal law. Slave catchers operating in the North risked arrest for kidnapping, and abolitionists defied the Fugitive Slave Law to rescue runaways who had been caught. Celebrated incidents took place in New York, Boston, Syracuse, and Christiana, Pennsylvania. Publicity angered northerners, who hated the federal law, and southerners, who cursed northern defiance.

HARRIET BEECHER STOWE PUBLISHES *UNCLE TOM'S CABIN*, 1852   Meanwhile, Harriet Beecher Stowe, daughter of the prominent evangelical minister Lyman Beecher, published her great antislavery novel, *Uncle Tom's Cabin* (1852). By 1853 sales had topped a million copies. It became the best-selling book in the United States before 1880, made Stowe famous, and was turned into a popular drama that played before teary-eyed audiences throughout the North in the 1850s.

Stowe's chilling story combined realism and morality in exactly the mix that her middle-class and largely female audience wanted. Based on facts collected from visits to Kentucky during her own residence in Cincinnati and on material provided by her abolitionist friends, the white Theodore Weld and the black Frederick Douglass, the book succeeded because it insisted that slavery was a sin for Christians. The South banned the book.

PLANNING A TRANSCONTINENTAL RAILROAD   The undercurrent of growing antislavery sentiment escaped the Pierce administration, which pondered the best route for a transcontinental railroad. Surveyors scouted various routes, and when they reported that mountains blocked a potential railroad from New Orleans to Los Angeles via El Paso unless the line went through Tucson, a desert town inside Mexico, the administration moved quickly to acquire the area. The Gadsden Purchase, ratified by the Senate in 1854, added what became southern Arizona and New Mexico to the United States and established the present boundary with Mexico.

The administration debated possible western rail routes. Southerners favored an eastern terminus at New Orleans, but northerners wanted Chicago, and many proposed St. Louis as a compromise. No man was more interested in this rail project than the Young America enthusiast and Chicago real estate speculator Senator Stephen A. Douglas. "The Little Giant," who had recently moved from the House to the Senate, wanted a Chicago railhead, and he decided to use his position as chair of the Committee on Territories to make this happen. All he had to do was organize the land west of Missouri, hitherto popularly known as the Great American Desert, into a new territory and then give a railroad company huge land grants in that territory as the incentive to build the railroad.

STEPHEN A. DOUGLAS PROMOTES POPULAR SOVEREIGNTY, 1854   In 1854 Douglas found that southern senators would support his bill to organize the territory only if he agreed to two changes. The first change created two territories: Kansas, just west of Missouri, and Nebraska, north of Kansas, including what became the Dakotas. The reason for the two territories became clear with the second change, which repealed the provision of the Missouri Compromise of 1820 that no territory north or west of Missouri would ever have slavery. With this repeal, Kansas and Nebraska would be organized, like New Mexico and Utah, on the principle that the territorial residents should decide whether to adopt slavery.

Boasting of his devotion to democracy, Douglas called this concept "popular sovereignty." Many southerners believed that Missourians would settle Kansas and choose slavery. Douglas doubted that outcome, but, unlike Harriet Beecher Stowe and Frederick Douglass, he did not care much about slavery. He was prepared to accept Kansas as a slave state if that was what its residents wanted. To Douglas it was important to organize the area so that land grants could be given to build the transcontinental railroad.

This bill generated a firestorm of opposition throughout the North. In early 1854 mass meetings condemned the proposal. Democratic and Whig newspaper editors, long at each other's throats, joined together to denounce the measure, as did governors, legislators, senators, and congressmen.

One devastating attack came from the abolitionist Senator Salmon P. Chase of Ohio. In a pamphlet entitled "Appeal of the Independent Democrats," he shrewdly rallied those opposed to territorial slavery, whether Democrats or Whigs, by arguing that slaveholders had plotted to repeal the Missouri Compromise and seize Kansas. This theory of a Slave Power conspiracy had popular appeal.

CONGRESS PASSES THE KANSAS–NEBRASKA ACT, 1854   Despite this opposition, Douglas and the Pierce administration persuaded Congress to pass the Kansas–Nebraska Act. The executive branch used its patronage powers shamelessly, although the final vote in the House was close, 113 to 100. More curious was Pierce's failure to understand the depth of the anger that had been unleashed. A weak, vacillating man, he had become notorious as a president who always agreed with whatever his last caller wanted. Southern politicians played upon his fears, while everyone who saw Pierce took the precaution of demanding his promises in writing because he broke his word so often. He broke the written pledges, too. The *New York Herald*, which had supported his election, sarcastically ran a daily column called "Poor Pierce."

A few Democrats, recognizing the danger of the territorial slavery issue to the national nature of their party, tried in Polk-like fashion to shift the issue to expansion. In October 1854, three American ambassadors in Europe, James Buchanan, John Y. Mason, and Pierre Soulé, met at Ostend, Belgium, and proposed that the United States buy Cuba from Spain. If Spain refused to sell its colony, which had a large slave population, then the ambassadors suggested that Cuba might be acquired through force. The Ostend Manifesto backfired. Instead of diverting attention from slavery, it only led abolitionists to charge that proslavery Democrats were plotting a war against Spain for the purpose of adding to the Union new slave states carved from Cuba.

REPUBLICANS AND KNOW-NOTHINGS EMERGE, 1854   No law ever produced such a disaster for its supporters as did the Kansas–Nebraska Act. Although northern Democratic officeholders believed that the furor would die down, it did not. Instead, antislavery Whigs and Democrats created a new political coalition known in various places as the Anti-Nebraska movement, the People's Party, or the Republican Party. They called for repeal of both the Kansas–Nebraska Act and the Fugitive Slave Law as well as abolition of slavery in the District of Columbia.

By focusing on the territorial slavery issue, antiadministration politicians appealed both to racists opposed to the presence of any blacks in the West and to outright abolitionists. In the fall 1854 elections, northern

Democrats who remained loyal to Pierce took a pounding, and a majority in the new House opposed slavery in the territories.

The Republicans, as the opponents of Pierce and Douglas increasingly called themselves, would have done even better had it not been for the revival of anti-Catholic and anti-immigrant sentiment in the country's cities. Wherever large numbers of immigrants lived, especially Irish Catholics, the native born surged into another new party called the American Party. Demanding lower taxes, reduced immigration, and a twenty-one-year waiting period for citizenship, the American Party gave voters yet another way to protest against the administration.

The American Party was a semisecret organization that traced its roots to the 1849 founding of a secret society, the Order of the Star-Spangled Banner. The party's trappings included a special raised-arm, palm-up salute, a Masonic-style secret hand grip, and the pledge that members, when asked about the organization, would reply, "I know nothing." To an inquiring member, this code phrase revealed a fellow member.

Claiming that the country had been engulfed by a Catholic, immigrant conspiracy, the Know-Nothings, as they were popularly called, operated with a self-selected secret leadership of political amateurs that picked electoral candidates without supporters' consent. Instead of an open party nominating convention, the leaders privately selected the candidates and printed party ballots, which members received already folded and then dropped into ballot boxes without knowing for whom they had voted.

The Jacksonian political system fractured overnight. In the South the Whig Party collapsed, and many white southerners, enthusiastic supporters of Pierce's policy, became Democrats. In the North a few conservative Whigs, fearful of civil war, joined the Democrats, while most Whigs became antislavery Republicans or nativist Know-Nothings. A few Democrats remained loyal to Pierce, often for reasons of patronage (for example, local postmasters), but antislavery Democrats bolted to the Republicans, and some working-class Protestant Democrats in the cities backed the Know-Nothings. No one knew how or even whether a stable two-party system could be constructed from these various fragments.

VIOLENCE HELPS THE REPUBLICAN PARTY, 1854–1856

A fraudulent election and civil war in Kansas proved that popular sovereignty was impractical. To many northerners, Preston Brooks's beating of Charles Sumner with a cane on the floor of the Senate in 1856 only confirmed southern arrogance. Democrat James Buchanan won the presidency in 1856, but John C. Frémont ran surprisingly well as the candidate of the new Republican Party, while Millard Fillmore, the Know-Nothing, finished a poor third.

KANSAS BLEEDS, 1854–1856   Popular sovereignty provided a formula for settling the question of slavery in the territories, but how such a formula might work in practice had yet to be tested. Kansas was to show Douglas's theory in action, although not with the results he wanted. Both proslavery and antislavery forces recognized that control of the territorial legislature, which would decide the slavery question, depended ultimately upon the views of the majority of settlers.

The proslavery forces, already living close to the border in Missouri, got an early start in filing land claims and actually moving to Kansas. Few of these Kansans owned slaves, but they were of southern stock, had long lived in the slave state of Missouri, and felt an intense loyalty to the southern conception of white supremacy based on slavery. Antislavery northerners responded by organizing the New England Emigrant Aid Company, which founded the town of Lawrence, Kansas, and settled more than two thousand pioneers in the territory in two years.

This competition produced hard feelings on both sides. In 1854 and 1855, when Kansans held their first territorial elections, thousands of proslavery Missourians crossed the border and either cast ballots or prevented antislavery residents from voting. Ironically, even without this illegal intervention there was probably a proslavery majority in Kansas at the time.

Governor Andrew Reeder at first resisted this massive fraud, which the northern newspapers widely reported, but in the end, fearing for his life, he recognized the election returns. The proslavery legislature, contemptuous of the cowardly Reeder, met and passed statutes defending slavery and banning discussion of abolition.

Kansas settlers from the free states denounced the election, the legislature, and its laws, held their own election, and organized a convention at Topeka to draw up an antislavery constitution, which free-state voters later ratified. By early 1856 Kansas had two territorial governments. Pierce appointed the proslavery William Shannon as governor to replace Reeder, but the antislavery settlers then elected Reeder as their territorial delegate to Congress.

On May 21, 1856, "border ruffians" from Missouri joined proslavery Kansans in attacking the antislavery town of Lawrence. They burned the hotel where prominent abolitionists had slept, and destroyed the presses of Lawrence's two antislavery newspapers. The northern press exaggerated the incident, in which two lives were lost, calling it the "Sacking of

Lawrence." In retaliation, three nights later abolitionist John Brown organized a party that raided the homes of several proslavery settlers and executed five men in what became known as the Pottawatomie Massacre.

Full-scale guerrilla warfare broke out. Henry Ward Beecher, son of Lyman Beecher, was the charismatic minister of a large church in suburban Brooklyn, New York. He sent rifles to Kansas in crates marked "Bibles." Shannon resigned as governor, and Pierce appointed John Geary, who restored order with help from the army. Kansas still had no government. A paralyzed Congress fumed; the Republicans persuaded the House to adopt a plan to admit Kansas as a free state under the Topeka constitution, and the Democrats got the Senate to pass a bill calling for new elections. Neither side budged.

THE CANING OF SENATOR CHARLES SUMNER, 1856 Congressional debate grew heated, many politicians carried pistols, and the quiet, conciliatory voice of Henry Clay was missed. Senator Charles Sumner of Massachusetts, one of the new breed of staunch abolitionists, spoke passionately about "the crime against Kansas." Bitter and sarcastic, Sumner condemned Senator Andrew Butler of South Carolina. Butler's nephew, Representative Preston ("Bully") Brooks, thought Sumner had insulted Butler. Had Sumner been a southern gentleman, Brooks would have challenged him to a duel. Brooks, however, considered Sumner no gentleman and decided to teach the abolitionist a lesson.

Approaching Sumner's Senate desk with a heavy cane, Brooks began to beat the tall, massive Sumner savagely. With his legs pinned under the desk, the senator struggled free, breaking the bolts that held the desk to the floor, and then slumped into unconsciousness as senators pulled Brooks away.

The northern-dominated House, outraged by Brooks's conduct, tried but failed to get the two-thirds majority necessary to expel him. Brooks then resigned and returned to his South Carolina district, which unanimously reelected him. The ladies of Charleston and other southern cities presented Brooks with gold-headed canes. One was inscribed, "Hit him again."

While Brooks received accolades, Sumner nursed his wounds, both physical and psychological. Claiming poor health, he did not return to the Senate for two years but toured Europe instead, angrily brooding on free speech and the arrogance of southern slaveholders. For many Americans, Sumner's empty Senate desk spoke more eloquently of where matters stood than any speech.

In 1856 the chaos in Kansas and the caning of Sumner permeated the northern consciousness. Republicans denounced Douglas's plan of popu-

lar sovereignty as a scheme that allowed slaveholders to use fraud and violence to seize territory that they could not lawfully claim under either the
Missouri Compromise or a fair and impartial implementation of Douglas's own plan.

At the same time, Republicans believed that Brooks's attack on Sumner revealed the arrogance of the South's rulers. Not content with controlling the federal government and using manipulation, deceit, and violence to take Kansas, southerners could not stand fair and open debate.
Their society, thought Republicans, had been so corrupted by proslavery
forces, which Republicans now called the Slave Power, that it was incapable of either political integrity or decency.

THE ELECTION OF 1856   Presidential politics moved in strange new directions. In 1856 the Know-Nothings nominated Millard Fillmore, the former Whig president and supporter of the Compromise of 1850. The
Know-Nothings, however, faced internal divisions. The party included
both native-born Catholics who hated immigrants, and non-Catholic immigrants such as the German "Sag Nichts" (Say Nothings), who despised
Catholics. The party's failure to oppose the extension of slavery led some
northerners to declare themselves "Know-Somethings" and bolt to the
Republicans.

The Republicans faced mixed prospects. Whigs had moved en masse
into the Republican Party in some states, including New York, under the
party boss Thurlow Weed. In Ohio, Salmon P. Chase had created a powerful party by merging Whigs, Democrats, and abolitionists, but in Indiana and Pennsylvania, where the Know-Nothings were strong, the Republican Party remained weak.

Few Republican leaders expected the party to win the presidency in
1856; some preferred to lose, fearing a divided North incapable of handling southern secession. Others felt that the Republicans had to avoid the
Whigs' two mistakes: becoming identified with business interests and
showing hostility to immigrants. Portraying their party as sympathetic to
both workers and immigrants, Republican leaders believed that the Know-
Nothing Party would collapse and that anti-immigrant voters could then
be obtained without offending immigrants. Most Know-Nothings did
eventually join the Republican Party, which also attracted Protestant immigrants. To this day, the party has retained its ties to business and has
lacked enthusiasm for immigrants.

Pledging to keep slavery out of western territories but also promising not to seek abolition in the South, the Republicans nominated John
C. Frémont, western explorer, sometime soldier in the Mexican War,
and son-in-law of Thomas Hart Benton, Missouri's former Jacksonian

Table 13.1   The 1856 Presidential Election

Candidate	Party	Popular Vote	Electoral Vote	States Carried
Buchanan	Democrat	1.8 million	174	14 slave, 5 free states
Frémont	Republican	1.3 million	114	11 free states
Fillmore	Know-Nothing	.9 million	8	1 slave state

senator. Adopting the slogan "Free Soil, Free Labor, Free Men, Frémont," the Republicans also praised the dignity of labor.

The Democrats adopted a platform upholding both the Compromise of 1850 and the Kansas–Nebraska Act and, passing over candidates embroiled in the Kansas controversy, nominated James Buchanan, a Pennsylvanian who had been out of the country serving as ambassador to Great Britain. As the only national party, the Democrats promised to hold the country together. Southerners vowed that the election of a Republican would be just cause for secession. Buchanan's strategy was to sweep the South and carry a few northern states to win narrowly in the Electoral College. As election day approached, pro-Fillmore southerners, recognizing that their candidate had no chance in the North, switched to Buchanan.

Buchanan won by carrying the South, the small free states of California, Illinois, Indiana, and New Jersey, and his home state of Pennsylvania amid charges of massive vote fraud.

Although Buchanan enjoyed a large electoral majority, he received only 45 percent of the popular vote. The election was really two separate sectional races. In the South's Buchanan–Fillmore contest, "Old Buck" handily defeated Fillmore, who carried only Maryland. In the North's Buchanan–Frémont race, Buchanan barely won. He ran well only in traditionally Democratic areas where no New Englanders had settled. The Republicans exceeded their expectations, including a landslide in New York, and looked forward to 1860, when the gain of two or three northern states promised victory.

JAMES BUCHANAN'S PRESIDENCY, 1857–1861

In 1857 James Buchanan encouraged the Supreme Court to rule definitively on slavery. Far from proving definitive, the proslavery Dred Scott decision only enraged the North. When proslavery Kansans tried to get Kansas admitted as a slave state in 1857 under the Lecompton constitution, the president backed the effort despite evidence that most Kansans then opposed slavery. In 1858 angry northerners voted Republican. In 1859 the abolitionist John Brown tried to lead a slave insurrection beginning in Harper's Ferry, Virginia, which succeeded only in producing panic throughout the South. His execution disgusted the North. The four-way election of 1860, fought sectionally as two two-way races, led to Abraham Lincoln's victory in a bitterly divided country. Sectional conflict had reached its limit.

THE SUPREME COURT ISSUES THE DRED SCOTT DECISION, 1857   James Buchanan arrived in Washington in early 1857. Before his inauguration he tried to arrange behind the scenes what he hoped would be the final resolution of the slavery controversy. The Supreme Court had just heard a slavery case, and Buchanan urged the justices to use the occasion for a definitive declaration about slavery in the territories. An emphatic court decision, he reasoned, would end once and for all the sectional political feud by establishing what the Constitution required.

Five of the nine justices, including Chief Justice Roger Taney, held slaves; Buchanan must have known how that fact would affect the outcome

In 1857 Dred Scott, a Missouri slave who had formerly lived in the free Territory of Iowa for four years, sued for his freedom. He lost in the U.S. Supreme Court in a decision that angered northerners. (Library of Congress)

of the case. In 1834 the owner of Dred Scott, a Missouri slave, had taken him into federal territory north of Missouri that was free under the Missouri Compromise of 1820. After four years Scott returned with his owner to Missouri. Later the owner died, and in 1846 Scott sued his new owner for freedom in the Missouri courts on the grounds that he had gained his freedom by living in free federal territory. After the Missouri Supreme Court ruled against Scott in 1852, he appealed to the federal court in Missouri, which denied jurisdiction. In 1853 *Dred Scott v. Sandford* reached the U.S. Supreme Court.

In considering this case, the justices faced numerous choices. They could have declined to accept it, or they could have overruled the Missouri federal court and ordered a trial. Either course would have been normal. They might have ruled that Scott had waited too long to bring the case or that Scott should have brought the case while living in federal territory. In other words, many technicalities could have been used to rule against Scott. Or the Court could have declared that Scott had gained his freedom by being in free territory, without elaborating whether he had gained that freedom instantly upon entering the territory or only after residing there.

The Court, however, used this case to resolve several constitutional issues that had not been argued at trial. On the question of Scott's freedom, the Court ruled 6 to 3, with all five slaveholders in the majority, that Scott's residence in free territory had not made him free upon his return to Missouri, since he had brought suit as a resident of Missouri, which did not recognize his freedom.

By the same margin the Court found both the Missouri Compromise and the popular sovereignty provisions of the Compromise of 1850 unconstitutional, since both laws deprived persons from taking their slave property into federal territory, violating the Constitution's guarantee of property rights under due process of law. Congress, in other words, could not ban slavery from any territory. This political idea, often called free soil, was unconstitutional.

The Court added, by a 3-to-2 vote, that Scott had no standing to sue in federal court, because no black could be a citizen of the United States or of any state, since all states had recognized slavery at the time of independence. This part of the decision sought to impose white supremacy upon both the federal government and the states.

Far from settling the slavery controversy, the Dred Scott decision worsened the situation. Defenders of slavery now had the Court on their side, but they would find it impossible to exercise their theoretical right to take slaves into any federal territory. Northern opponents announced that they would defy the ruling. Noting that slaveholding justices had issued the majority decision, abolitionists refused to accept the ruling's legitimacy. Instead, northerners increasingly saw the Dred Scott decision as proof of the Republican charge that slaveholders controlled the federal government through a Slave Power conspiracy.

KANSAS'S PROSLAVERY LECOMPTON CONSTITUTION, 1857–1858   Trouble brewed again in Kansas. In 1857 the proslavery legislature, meeting at Lecompton, ordered a convention to draft a state constitution. The legislature declined to require the new document to be submitted to a popular vote. Governor John Geary resigned in protest, and Buchanan appointed Robert J. Walker as the new governor. Walker supervised fair elections that gave the free-state faction control of the new territorial legislature.

Recognizing that a proslavery constitution would be voted down by the territory's growing antislavery population, which now formed a large majority, the proslavery Lecompton constitutional convention proposed a state constitution that would not be submitted for ratification. However, the drafters knew that Congress would not admit a state without some kind of vote. So voters could choose to have the Lecompton constitution "with slavery" or "without slavery." If Kansans voted against slavery, slaves already in residence would remain enslaved.

Walker refused to participate in this scheme, and he went to Washington to consult with Buchanan. To Walker's surprise, the president, under the influence of a proslavery cabinet, declined to back him. Walker then resigned. Meanwhile, Senator Stephen A. Douglas announced his opposition to the Lecompton constitution. In Kansas the free-state faction boycotted the Lecompton election, and about four thousand proslavery voters adopted the constitution with slavery. In early 1858 the new territorial legislature, dominated by the free-staters, called a second popular election, boycotted this time by the slave-staters, in which free-staters cast more than ten thousand votes against the document.

Buchanan then asked Congress to admit Kansas as a state under the proslavery Lecompton constitution. An infuriated Douglas, appalled by the administration's interpretation of popular sovereignty, revolted against the administration, which responded by removing Douglas's supporters from federal office. The Senate accepted Kansas as a slave state, but the House balked.

Finally, Representative William English of Indiana proposed a compromise. Kansans would vote directly on the Lecompton constitution. If they approved it, Kansas would be admitted with extra federal land and money. If they rejected it, Kansas would remain a territory. The English bill passed the House, 112 to 103, and was adopted by the Senate.

Kansans, however, spurned what Republicans called a federal bribe and voted down the proslavery Lecompton constitution by more than five to one. Although Kansas remained a territory technically open to slavery under the Dred Scott decision, public opinion in Kansas kept slaves out.

THE ADMINISTRATION LOSES THE MIDTERM ELECTIONS, 1858   Buchanan's administration faced other difficulties. The Panic of 1857 plunged the country into a sudden, sharp recession that led to high unemployment and mass suffering, especially in the North's large cities during the winter of 1857–1858. Southerners, noting that cotton prices remained high and that their region went untouched, said that slavery provided economic stability and that unemployed northern white laborers, largely Irish immigrants, faced a reality harsher than any faced by enslaved blacks.

Until he became president, Abraham Lincoln was a tall, clean-shaven trial lawyer known for political ambition and success with juries. (North Wind Picture Archives)

Not everyone accepted this analysis. Hinton Rowan Helper's book, *The Impending Crisis* (1857), argued that slavery had in fact retarded the South's economic development. The author, a native of North Carolina, saw his book banned in the South and was forced into exile in California. Meanwhile, as often happened during hard times, religious revivals swept the northern cities, and the upsurge of evangelicalism did the Democrats no good, since evangelicals leaned toward the Republicans.

Northern exasperation and impatience grew, and Republican leaders spoke with a new bluntness as the 1858 congressional elections approached. In New York, Senator William Henry Seward, considered the party's front-runner for the next presidential election, called the sectional controversy an "irrepressible conflict."

In Illinois, Abraham Lincoln, the Republican candidate for the Senate, warned, "A house divided against itself cannot stand," adding, "I believe that this nation cannot exist permanently half slave and half free." Running against Douglas, Lincoln engaged his better-known rival in a series of seven debates.

At Freeport, in a part of Illinois settled by slavery-hating Yankees, Lincoln asked Douglas how popular sovereignty could be reconciled with the Dred Scott ruling. Douglas replied that, despite the Court's decision, slavery could not exist without local territorial laws and their enforcement. According to Douglas's new Freeport Doctrine, territorial settlers could actually determine whether slavery would exist or not.

On election day Lincoln won the popular vote but lost the Senate seat because Douglas's supporters held a narrow margin in the malapportioned legislature, which actually picked the senator. Douglas's fame, Illinois's Democratic tradition, and the Freeport Doctrine enabled Douglas to survive. He was one of only a few northern Democrats to win, and the administration lost control of the House to the Republicans. As the Democrats became weaker in the North, the center of gravity inside the Buchanan administration shifted slowly but subtly to its southern base.

JOHN BROWN RAIDS HARPERS FERRY, 1859   In 1859 John Brown, already notorious for his Kansas killings, conspired with a small group of abolitionists—"the secret six"—to launch a slave uprising. Brown led eighteen men, including two of his sons and five blacks, to Harpers Ferry, Virginia, and seized the federal arsenal. He planned to distribute the arms to Virginia's slaves and then march south with an ever-growing band of armed slaves to end slavery once and for all. Brown's scheme so terrified the slaves he tried to recruit that they fled, and the United States military, under command of Colonel Robert E. Lee, quickly captured Brown and his followers inside the arsenal.

Virginia tried and executed Brown and the others for treason in a public hanging witnessed by more than ten thousand howling, jeering southerners. This public spectacle and the fears of slave insurrection that it revealed appalled the northern newspaper reporters covering the event. Meanwhile, in far-off Boston the evangelical clergy, strongly opposed to slavery, ordered church bells tolled. The fervor of the indignation on both sides did not go unnoticed.

SOUTHERNERS GROW FEARFUL, **1860**   As 1860 opened, a wave of fear that approached hysteria swept across the South. Sheriffs stopped Yankee peddlers and searched them for abolitionist literature or papers indicating that they planned to lead a slave revolt. Schoolmasters from the North were invited to go home. A northern accent was enough for its possessor to be told to move on. Rumors of slave insurrections in remote places filled the southern press, but when no hard evidence could be produced to show that a particular revolt had occurred, the report was restated to indicate that heroic southerners had blocked an insurrection just in time.

When some editors pointed out that all was quiet, opponents argued that the absence of overt actions proved that secret undertakings were afoot. Meeting in this curdled atmosphere, southern state legislatures passed laws denouncing abolitionists, prohibiting any discussion of slavery, increasing slave patrols, and enhancing the militia.

THE ELECTION OF **1860**   The discredited Buchanan administration, political party decay, sectional differences, southern fear, and northern anger combined to produce a bizarre atmosphere in 1860. The sour mood reflected both political irritation and lingering economic problems. Americans were increasingly frustrated with the large and growing inequality in the distribution of wealth. Compared with other decades in American history, older people were unusually rich and younger people particularly poor. The 1850s had favored the wealthy and to a lesser extent the middle class. In the North the richest 30 percent owned 92 percent of real estate or other kinds of property. Although many Americans had experienced economic failure, they remained a "go-ahead" people who believed in opportunity and success. Then, as now, they tended to blame current problems on the incumbent in the White House.

The Democrats, the one remaining national party, held their convention in Charleston, South Carolina. High humidity and a gallery packed with raucous locals did not deter the party from adopting a platform upholding popular sovereignty. Southern delegates from eight states, led by William Yancey of Alabama, walked out over the convention's refusal to endorse the Dred Scott decision. Yancey knew that such an endorsement would cause the party to lose in the North, but he did not want the Democrats to win the election. Rather, he wanted a Republican victory that would lead to southern secession and his dream of a new slaveholders' confederacy.

Because party rules required a two-thirds majority for nomination, Douglas could not be nominated, in large part because of southern irritation over his Freeport Doctrine, and after fifty-seven ballots the delegates adjourned. A month later the Northern Democrats met in Baltimore and nominated Douglas. Although he knew that he would lose the election, he was determined not to allow the southerners to take over the party.

A few days later the Southern Democrats also met in Baltimore and, adopting a platform calling for slavery in all the territories, nominated John Breckinridge of Kentucky. The Southern Democrats knew that they could not win in the electoral college, but they calculated that they might succeed if the election had to be decided in the House.

Meanwhile, the Constitutional Union Party, composed of conservative southern Whigs and Know-Nothings, also met in Baltimore and nominated John Bell of Tennessee. They declined to adopt a specific platform beyond a pledge to uphold the Constitution.

The Republicans held their convention in Chicago. Seward was the leading candidate, but party leaders from Indiana and Pennsylvania warned that Seward's inflammatory, radical rhetoric made it impossible for him to carry their states. In addition, Seward had tried unsuccessfully to woo Irish votes and in the process had antagonized the Know-Nothings. Seeking a candidate with Seward's antislavery views but without his acid-tongued reputation, the party turned to the trial lawyer Abraham Lincoln. His views were nearly identical to Seward's, but he seemed less likely to irritate southerners, immigrants, or nativists.

Although the Republicans stressed free soil, they also pledged to accept slavery in the South, to seek a higher tariff pleasing to both manufacturers and their workers, to build a transcontinental railroad, to encourage immigration, and to enact a homestead law giving farmers free federal land in the West. Southerners disliked most of these proposals, but the Republicans saw no reason to humor the South, where they would get no votes since they were not even on the ballot.

Table 13.2   The 1860 Presidential Election

Candidate	Party	Popular Vote	Electoral Vote	States Carried
Lincoln	Republican	1.9 million	180	17 free states, split 1 free state
Douglas	N. Democrat	1.4 million	12	1 slave state, split 1 free state
Breckinridge	S. Democrat	.8 million	72	11 slave states
Bell	Constitutional Union	.6 million	39	3 slave states

The election had four candidates, but it was really a two-way contest in each region. Lincoln easily defeated Douglas in the North, where "Honest Abe" got 55 percent of the vote. He won at least 50 percent in every northern state except California, New Jersey, and Oregon. He carried all the states that Frémont had won and added Pennsylvania, Illinois, Indiana, California, and the new states of Oregon and Minnesota. Douglas and Lincoln split New Jersey.

Douglas's only victory came in the border slave state of Missouri. By sweeping the North, the nation's most populous region, Lincoln guaranteed a large electoral victory. Breckinridge carried the South, but Bell won Kentucky, Tennessee, and Virginia, states in the upper South where views about slavery were moderate.

Lincoln's electoral total was impressive, but his share of the popular vote was only 40 percent. Three out of five voters voted against Lincoln, giving him the lowest popular percentage of any Electoral College winner in American history.

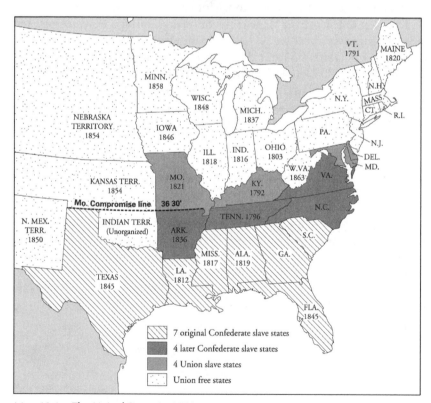

Map 13.1   The United States in 1861

Lincoln's political position was unenviable. Most Americans who voted for Lincoln's opponents considered that his views, far from representing a majority, were extreme. His strong support from the North had to be weighed against intense opposition, even loathing, in the South. The constitutionally prescribed structure of presidential elections favored candidates like Lincoln who had concentrated support in several key states over those like Douglas who had thinner support spread across many states, and it provided no mechanism, such as a runoff election, to allow voters to pick a moderate candidate.

SECESSION CRISIS, 1860–1861

In December 1860, Lincoln's election led South Carolina to carry out its threat to leave the Union, and in early 1861, as a lame duck Congress debated how to solve the crisis with compromise, six other cotton-producing states also seceded and formed the Confederacy. President-elect Lincoln could do little but watch and brood as President Buchanan vacillated between fatalism and toughness. Lincoln's inaugural address was the last hope for saving the Union as it had been. It was not enough.

SOUTH CAROLINA LEAVES THE UNION, 1860 Throughout the campaign southerners had warned that Lincoln's election would cause the South to leave the Union. Oddly, Republican leaders dismissed these pronouncements as election rhetoric. Only after Lincoln's election, as southerners living in the North began to buy arms and pack bags to return to their home states, did alarm grow.

Within weeks of Lincoln's election, on December 20, 1860, South Carolina's special state convention unanimously declared the state an independent nation free from the federal Union. The Carolinians spurred on the other southern states, where their agents carefully cultivated a general southern movement for secession to be followed by the organization of a new, slave-oriented southern confederacy. Such a union, the seceders believed, would combine with divided opinion in the North (as revealed by Douglas's vote in the recent election) either to force Lincoln to recognize the new nation without war or, even more deliciously, to lead Lincoln to resign so that the South might again claim its traditional leadership of the United States.

Congress met in a desperate attempt to save the Union. Wearing Henry Clay's mantle, Senator John Crittenden of Kentucky presented a compromise. He proposed a constitutional amendment pledging that Congress would never interfere with slavery in the South and that slavery would be allowed in western territories below 36°30', the old Missouri Compromise line. Crittenden found little support for his proposal among either northerners or southerners, who were beginning to leave town, and Republicans insisted that no legislation could be introduced without their prior approval. They did not wish to see the southerners manufacture a crisis to overturn the result of the presidential election.

THE COTTON STATES FORM THE CONFEDERACY, 1861   By February 1861, Mississippi, Florida, Alabama, Georgia, Louisiana, and Texas had joined South Carolina in secession. All were cotton-growing states heavily dependent upon slave labor. The seven states moved quickly to form the Confederate States of America. After adopting a constitution that resembled the United States Constitution but with a clause asserting states' rights and providing for a single six-year term for the president, they elected the Mississippi planter and former senator Jefferson Davis as provisional president. The new government's main business was seizing federal property, arming the South, and encouraging secessionists in the upper South.

LINCOLN BROODS AS BUCHANAN VACILLATES, 1861   Lincoln's term did not begin until March 4, and before that date the newly designated secretary of state, William Henry Seward, held negotiations with prominent southerners, particularly Virginians, on the Potomac River. Although Seward expressed a surprising willingness to accommodate the Virginians, whose presence in the Union gave the North many advantages, Lincoln and other Republican leaders feared appearing to give away principles under pressure and instructed Seward to break off the talks.

President-elect Lincoln sat quietly in his hometown of Springfield, Illinois. Although he believed strongly that secession was illegal, he avoided comment, because his position gave him no power, and he did not wish to be accused of meddling. Lincoln brought a slender reputation to the presidency. This tall, rawboned, moody man had less than a year's schooling. A former railsplitter and failed country storekeeper, he had served only one term in Congress. Yet Lincoln had become the West's premier trial lawyer; he had nearly defeated the popular Douglas for a Senate seat, and on an eastern tour in early 1860 he had deeply impressed an important audience in New York. This self-made man, a member of no church but a student of the Bible and Shakespeare, had substance. Even his numerous dirty stories made points.

Meanwhile, President James Buchanan pursued a strange policy. Determined to prevent civil war while still in office, the president allowed members of the administration to negotiate with southerners over federal military facilities in the South. After two southern cabinet members were caught transferring military supplies to the South, they were forced out.

The reorganized cabinet then followed a curious legal theory articulated by Buchanan's attorney general. According to Jeremiah Black, secession was illegal, but so was any attempt by the federal government to coerce states to remain in the Union. Whether intentional or not, this position played into the hands of politicians in the upper South, who asserted that their states would remain in the Union only so long as the federal government did not use force against the states that had left.

In February Lincoln traveled by train from Springfield to Washington. Taking a long route, he gave speeches along the way but had to sneak into Washington in the middle of the night due to the disclosure of an assassination plot in Baltimore. Both cities were infested with secession-minded southerners.

Lincoln agonized over his inaugural address, which he delivered March 4, 1861. He told Americans that he would not touch slavery in the South, that secession was illegal, and that the federal government would not fire the first shot. His policy, designed to keep states like Virginia and Kentucky in the Union, was to wait patiently until the South returned to reasoned calm and then to welcome the seceding states back into the Union.

CONCLUSION

The 1850s proved to be uniquely tumultuous for the United States. The apparently stable Jacksonian political structure collapsed. In its place came political chaos and chicanery in the form of the Know-Nothings, followed by the earnest morality of the sectionally based Republicans. Both northerners and southerners soured on the Union, with northerners determined to gain control of the federal government for the first time and many southerners gradually convincing themselves that they should go their own way rather than live under Yankee rule.

The nation choked on slavery, both its spread into the West and its very existence, as solutions for compromise failed. The Missouri Compromise had divided territory between the two sections, but by the 1840s northerners resisted any new slave territories because they opposed new slave states. Many who did so were racists who wanted a white-only West. Southerners worried that new free states would lead to an antislavery Senate, which, when combined with the populous North's ability to elect a president and a House, might produce a constitutional amendment banning slavery.

Douglas's idea of popular sovereignty was democratic, offered each side hope, and had the advantage of postponing the outcome until some future date when passions ran cooler. Kansas, however, proved the concept unworkable in practice. One might speculate how presidents more competent than Pierce or Buchanan would have handled the controversy. Yet the sense that the crisis was merely a matter of a blundering generation (a view some historians once held) ignores the overwhelming evidence that, no matter who was in charge, the political system could not stand the strain of the issue of slavery and its expansion. Of course, the emergence of such weak leaders as Pierce and Buchanan is itself a comment upon the political structure's difficulties. During the 1850s it seemed as if events, not presidents, were in charge.

Recommended Readings

DOCUMENTS: Hinton R. Helper, *The Impending Crisis* (1857); Robert M. Meyers, ed., *The Children of Pride* (1972); Harriet B. Stowe, *Uncle Tom's Cabin* (1852).

READINGS: (GENERAL) William J. Cooper, Jr., *Liberty and Slavery* (1983); William W. Freehling, *The Road to Disunion* (1990); William E. Gienapp, *The Origins of the Republican Party* (1987); Michael F. Holt, *The Political Crisis of the 1850s* (1978); David Potter, *The Impending Crisis* (1976); Richard H. Sewell, *A House Divided* (1988); (1856 ELECTION) Tyler Anbinder, *Nativism and Slavery* (1992); Jean H. Baker, *Ambivalent Americans* (1977) and *Affairs of Party* (1983); Eric Foner, *Free Soil, Free Labor, Free Men* (1970); John R. Mulkern, *The Know-Nothing Party in Massachusetts* (1990); (BUCHANAN'S PRESIDENCY) Stanley W. Campbell, *The Slave Catchers* (1970); David Donald, *Charles Sumner and the Coming of the Civil War* (1960); Don E. Fehrenbacher, *The Dred Scott Case* (1978); Stephen E. Maizlish, *The Triumph of Sectionalism* (1983); Kenneth M. Stampp, *America in 1857* (1990); Mark W. Summers, *The Plundering Generation* (1987); (1860 ELECTION) David H. Donald, *Lincoln* (1995); Mark E. Neely, Jr., *The Last Best Hope of Earth* (1993); Benjamin P. Thomas, *Abraham Lincoln* (1952); (SECESSION) Daniel W. Crofts, *Reluctant Confederates* (1989); Lacy K. Ford, *Origins of Southern Radicalism* (1988); Michael P. Johnson, *Toward a Patriarchal Republic* (1977); Christopher J. Olsen, *Political Culture and Secession in Mississippi* (2000); J. Mills Thornton III, *Politics and Power in a Slave Society* (1978).

14

Civil War, 1861–1865

OVERVIEW   As hope of peace faded, most Americans took comfort in the belief that the coming war would be short and almost bloodless. They were wrong. If the events of 1861 ended the hope of a short war, 1862 brought only frustration. The key year of 1863 marked a turning point in which Union victory began to seem inevitable, but only in 1865 did the Confederacy finally expire. Perhaps it was just as well that no one could see what was coming. If northerners had known the price of saving the Union, they might well have accepted secession; and if southerners had known how much failure would cost, they probably would never have seceded. The drama, however, unfolded one act at a time.

THE WAR BEGINS, 1861

South Carolina's attack on Fort Sumter led Virginia and three other southern states to join the Confederacy, but four border slave states remained in the Union, while patriotism grew in the North. Each side had some key advantages, with the balance favoring the North. Although both northerners and southerners looked for a quick victory, the Union troops' panicky retreat at Bull Run, as well as the Confederates' inability to take advantage of it, predicted a long war.

FORT SUMTER FALLS, 1861   In April 1861, just one month after Lincoln's inauguration, the self-proclaimed sovereign state of South Carolina demanded that the United States army withdraw from Fort Sumter in Charleston harbor. Under orders from President Abraham Lincoln, Major Robert Anderson refused. After learning that the president was sending food to Sumter, the Carolinians decided to attack. On the morning of April 12, Confederate General Pierre G. T. Beauregard's shore guns opened fire, and the following afternoon Anderson surrendered. The Civil War had begun.

Each side gambled by playing its Sumter card, and the result gave each side hope. The Carolinians believed that their action would force Lincoln to announce plans to make war against the seceding states and that his decision would destroy Union sentiment in the South. Wanting to bring the large and important state of Virginia into the Confederacy, the Carolinians tried to stir southern patriotic passions in Richmond. At the time of the attack, a Virginia convention debated leaving the Union, and secessionists met resistance. Virginia Unionists took the Buchanan position, that is, against both secession and federal coercion.

Over opposition from Secretary of State William Henry Seward and others in his cabinet, Lincoln refused to surrender Fort Sumter peacefully because he felt that northerners would find it cowardly. He did not wish to start a war, but if the Carolinians attacked, he planned to reply in kind.

Psychologically, Lincoln put the Carolinians on the defensive by portraying them as crazed aggressors. This portrayal, he hoped, would keep the upper South's eight remaining slave states in the Union. Residents there would surely be reluctant to join a confederacy dominated by the wild, warmongering Carolinians. At the same time, Lincoln believed that the firing on the American flag at Sumter would rally all northerners, even conservative Democrats, to the Union.

VARIED RESPONSES TO FORT SUMTER'S FALL, 1861   Fort Sumter's surrender forced Lincoln's hand. On April 15 he proclaimed a rebellion and asked the states to supply 75,000 volunteers for ninety days' duty to put down the insurrection. Although northern governors quickly rallied, this message received a frosty reception in the upper South. Thus, the Union cause gained popular support in the North but lost ground in the South. On April 17, citing Lincoln's proclamation as evidence of the administration's hostile intentions, the Virginia convention voted, 103 to 46, to secede.

The Confederates won a great prize. As the home of George Washington and Thomas Jefferson, Virginia had symbolic importance for southerners. More practically, the South needed Richmond's ironworks, and as an added benefit, Virginia's secession prompted Robert E. Lee, who had turned down Lincoln's offer to command the Federal troops, to join the Confederate army.

Virginia's addition to the Confederacy extended the new nation further north. This both protected the Deep South from immediate attack and caused the Federals much trouble by threatening the capital at Washington, D.C. In appreciation, the Confederates quickly moved their capital from Montgomery, Alabama, to Richmond, Virginia, which they recognized would be near the center of the coming war. Indeed, many Virginians had been reluctant to secede because they feared, correctly, that a war would be fought largely on their soil.

The secessionists, however, did not get all that they had expected. Although Arkansas, Tennessee, and North Carolina followed Virginia into the Confederacy, many Unionists remained in these states, especially in East Tennessee's mountains.

All the border slave states remained in the Union. Maryland's Unionist governor prevented the secessionist legislature from acting, and a majority of that state's residents, influenced by the large number of Federal troops called to defend Washington, supported the Union. Lincoln used drastic measures, including arrests and the suspension of habeas corpus, to secure Maryland.

The Delaware legislature unanimously rejected secession. Kentucky leaders declared their state neutral to prevent war in Kentucky. Missourians quarreled, but Unionists gained control, and the secessionist governor fled. Residents of mountainous western Virginia revolted against the Confederacy and created the new state of West Virginia, which the Union admitted in 1863.

In the North partisanship disappeared as Yankees rallied around Lincoln and the Union cause. Patriotism swept the land; flags waved everywhere. Senator Stephen A. Douglas denounced secession and vigorously supported war. In the Democratic stronghold of New York City, where Horace Greeley's *New York Tribune* and James Gordon Bennett's *New York Herald* had both clamored for northern concessions and peace during the secession crisis, mobs demanded that these newspapers' offices fly American flags. Greeley, suddenly converted into a war hawk, cheerfully complied. But when the proud, stubborn Bennett resisted, the crowd not only raised Old Glory but forced the publisher to apologize in public.

LOOKING FOR A QUICK VICTORY, 1861   By June, as attitudes hardened and neutrality became virtually impossible, one could calculate each side's advantages and disadvantages in the coming war. The North had 22 million people, an excellent railroad network, numerous factories, and diversified agriculture. Yankees dominated shipping, including overseas trade, and controlled the United States navy. The North did not face physical destruction, as no one believed that the war would be fought on northern soil.

The South had only 9 million people, including 3.5 million slaves, a poor rail grid, little manufacturing, a long coastline with no navy, and agriculture based largely on cotton exports. But the Confederacy did have a few advantages. Southern officers had long predominated in the United States army's combat divisions, so they had valuable experience. Moreover, a war fought in the South would mean that the South's supply lines would be short, that southerners would have excellent knowledge of local conditions, and that they could rally people against invasion.

Although the balance of advantages and disadvantages slightly favored the North, they could be interpreted so as to give the South hope. The North could win only by conquering the South, whereas the South could gain independence, as Americans had during the revolution, merely by holding on until a war-weary enemy gave up. Traditionally, military experts agreed, an offensive force needed a superiority of about three to one in order to win. The North could field more troops than the South, but it was questionable whether the Union's numerical superiority would be sufficient.

The South was physically large, much larger than the North, and the region's mountains, muddy roads, vine-tangled woods, swamps, and poor rail network hampered invaders as much as defenders. To send large armies into the South required an enormous system of support with supply lines running hundreds of miles through hostile territory.

In 1861 many people believed that the war would be decided quickly in a single big battle. Self-delusion aided this belief, since no one wanted a long, bloody war, and people chose to believe that their hopes would be fulfilled. But a few people did fear a long war. Horace Greeley, the reform-minded editor of the *New York Tribune*, spent hours at home on the parlor couch writhing and groaning from the certainty of massive bloodshed. William Tecumseh Sherman privately told government officials that the rebellion could not be put down with fewer than 500,000 soldiers. He predicted huge casualties. The government ignored him, and friends politely suggested he check himself into an insane asylum.

Arrogance also led both sides to the firm conviction of a short war. Yankees recited statistics to prove that the North's advantages made victory inevitable. Residents of New York City boasted that more whites lived inside their city than in all of South Carolina. Just how this fact would enable Lincoln's government to conquer South Carolina went unexplained.

White southerners believed that slavery had taught them how to command, which gave them a military edge. Disdainful of Yankee courage, they also thought that northern leaders would never be able to rally the North's alienated poor whites, especially immigrants, to invade the South.

With a smaller army, the Confederates necessarily chose a defensive military strategy, although at times they did contemplate seizing Washington, D.C. That threat forced the North to deploy troops to guard the capital. The North adopted General Winfield Scott's strategy, called the Anaconda Plan for the snake that encircles and crushes its victims.

First, the State Department cultivated Britain and France to ensure that they did not recognize the Confederacy. In diplomacy, the South's enthusiasm for slavery in a world opposed to slavery gave the North an edge. Second, the navy planned to blockade the South and cut off both its cotton exports and manufactured imports. This would disrupt the southern economy. Third, the army was to seize important southern cities and then move through the South destroying Confederate arsenals and forces. An early goal was to split the Confederacy by gaining control of the Mississippi River.

YANKEES FLEE BULL RUN, 1861   Northern newspapers and politicians demanded action, and so in July 1861 General Irvin McDowell's Federals marched south from Washington toward Richmond, only one hundred miles away. They did not get far. On July 21, at Bull Run, about twenty-five miles from the capital, McDowell's army of 30,000 men met and fought Beauregard's southern army. Spectators, including members of Congress, took the train from Washington to watch the battle with field glasses. Some even brought champagne to celebrate an anticipated northern victory.

At first the numerically superior Yankees fought well, although Confederate General Thomas J. Jackson refused to budge during a Union assault. Then General Joseph E. Johnston arrived with 9,000 fresh Confederates quickly brought over by rail from the Shenandoah Valley. These soldiers gave the war's first Rebel yell and caused the inexperienced Federal troops to retreat, with increasing panic, to Washington. The spectators fled, too. Amid the chaos, the Confederates might have marched into the capital without opposition. The Rebels, however, were too stunned by their triumph to act.

After Bull Run, called Manassas in the South, both sides recognized that the war would be neither short nor easy. Battles like Bull Run would yield neither southern independence nor Yankee victory. As the northern volunteers' ninety-day enlistments expired, Lincoln recognized the difficulties ahead. He reluctantly ordered new recruits to be enlisted for three years. The naval blockade of the South began to take hold, and by late 1861 the navy had captured part of the coastal Carolinas.

On the diplomatic front, the North made limited headway. The British did refuse to allow Confederates to use ports for privateering. To avoid war with Britain, however, the North had to release two Confederate agents, James Mason and John Slidell, who had been seized aboard a British vessel, the *Trent*, en route to Britain.

THE WAR GROWS LONG, 1862

Massive bloodshed and near misses marked 1862. In the West the war's first big battle took place at Shiloh, Tennessee. In the East General George B. McClellan nearly captured the Confederate capital, Richmond, before General Robert E. Lee drove him off. Lee moved into Maryland and was

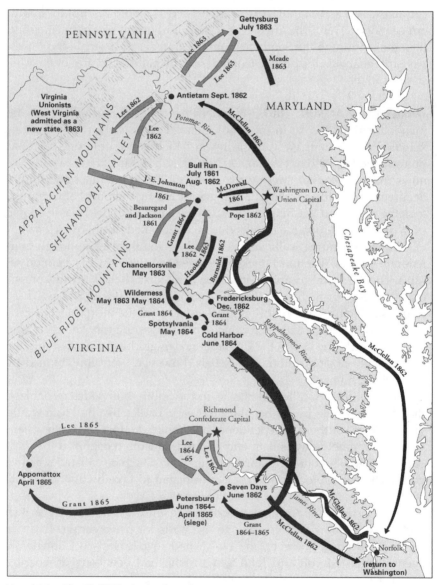

Map 14.1   The Civil War in the East, 1861–1865

defeated at Antietam on the bloodiest single day of the war, but he got away. Lincoln announced plans to free the slaves and enlist black soldiers in the Union army. In 1862 the Confederates adopted the draft; the Federals did the same in 1863.

THE 1862 CAMPAIGN BEGINS   At the beginning of 1862, during the lull brought on by winter weather, the North held the upper hand. No more states had left the Union, the border slave states had been secured, northern sentiment favored the war, the fighting had moved south, and the area controlled by the Confederacy was visibly shrinking.

In February Union General Ulysses S. Grant, in coordination with a river flotilla of gunboats, captured Fort Henry on the Tennessee River. After nearby Fort Donelson on the Cumberland River fell, the Confederates under General Albert Sidney Johnston evacuated Nashville, which Union

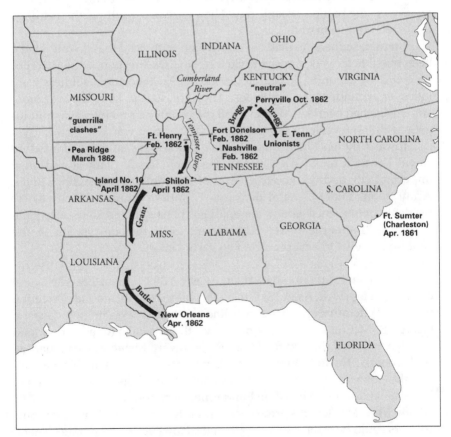

Map 14.2.   The Civil War in the West, 1861–1862

forces then occupied. In early March a Union victory at Pea Ridge in the Ozarks ended the Confederate military threat to Missouri, although guerrilla clashes there continued until the war's end.

JOHNSTON STRIKES GRANT AT SHILOH, 1862   Spring, that most glorious of seasons in the South, sent both sides roaming across the warm, lush landscape. Capturing the Mississippi River and its tributaries and thus dividing the Confederacy had been a major northern aim, and in April, following a three-week siege, the Confederates surrendered Island No. 10 in the Mississippi River above Memphis. While some of Grant's troops had been diverted toward this siege, that hard-drinking, cigar-smoking general had taken most of his understrength army further up the Tennessee River toward Alabama.

On April 6 Johnston's Confederates suddenly struck Grant's soldiers in their camp near the country church at Shiloh, Tennessee. A chaotic day of battle ended with Grant's forces exhausted and Johnston dead. During the night Union reinforcements arrived, and the Confederates gained no victory on the battle's second day. They retreated, with northern troops too bloodied for pursuit.

Grant described the field as "so covered with dead that it would have been possible to walk across the clearing, in any direction, without a foot touching the ground." At Shiloh, 13,000 of 63,000 northern soldiers were killed or wounded; the South lost 11,000 of 40,000. In two days, more Americans had been killed than in all the country's previous wars put together. Shiloh revealed the sickening reality of civil war.

Toward the end of the month, the Union navy under Commodore David Farragut took New Orleans, the Confederacy's largest and most important city and the key to control of the southern Mississippi River. Army troops under General Benjamin F. Butler occupied the city. Local residents complained about the soldiers' behavior and denounced the general as "Butler the Beast." Northerners hoped that, despite Shiloh, the capture of New Orleans predicted an early victory.

MCCLELLAN FLAILS AND FAILS AGAINST RICHMOND, 1862   In the East the Union cause went less well. As in 1861, the goal was to take Richmond. Declining to move Federal troops in a direct line south from Washington, General George B. McClellan led his army down the Potomac River, across land near Norfolk, and then up the James River toward Richmond's unguarded back door. At Norfolk, Virginia, the Union ironclad gunship *Monitor* battled the Confederate ironclad *Virginia* (earlier called the *Merrimac* when in Federal hands), and Norfolk fell under northern control.

By May, McClellan's army was within ten miles of Richmond; some soldiers could hear the city's church bells. However, Confederate General

Thomas J. Jackson, now nicknamed "Stonewall" for his stand at Bull Run, kept so many Union troops occupied by his lightning-like maneuvers in the Shenandoah Valley that a portion of McClellan's army had been sent to guard Washington. McClellan, doubting that he had enough men for a successful offensive, also learned that Richmond lacked defenses on its eastern side because that area was an impenetrable swamp.

At the end of the month, General Joseph E. Johnston's Confederates suddenly attacked. (Joe Johnston was not related to Albert Johnston, killed at Shiloh.) McClellan's troops barely avoided a disaster, and, even worse for the Union, Confederate President Jefferson Davis replaced a badly wounded Johnston as commander with the vastly more talented Robert E. Lee. In the Seven Days' Battles, begun on June 26, Lee tried to drive McClellan out of Virginia. Sending Jackson to attack McClellan's flank, Lee struck the Union center. Each day's skirmish ended with the Federals retreating, until they reached a base camp on the James River that was protected by gunboats. Although many Confederates died, Lee had driven McClellan from Richmond.

LEE ESCAPES FROM ANTIETAM, 1862   In July Lincoln put McClellan under General Henry W. Halleck's control. Determined to march overland to Richmond, Halleck ordered McClellan to withdraw his army from the Virginia peninsula and return to Washington to go south with General John Pope's army. The concentration of Union troops in Washington left Virginia open and gave Lee the freedom to maneuver. Lee was dangerous when not boxed in. After Jackson destroyed Pope's supply base in northern Virginia, Pope, believing that he faced only Jackson's small army and that Lee remained in Richmond, moved forward to attack.

Using a portion of Lee's troops, General James Longstreet's Confederates struck Pope's flank on August 29, caused a panic, and sent the Federal army across Bull Run to Washington. A Union defeat with heavy casualties, Second Bull Run (also called Second Manassas) cost Pope his command. Bowing to pressure, Lincoln restored command to the popular McClellan.

Carrying the war into the North for the first time, Lee crossed into Maryland, resupplied his army, and threatened Washington, while Jackson seized military supplies at Harper's Ferry. On September 17 McClellan caught Lee at Antietam, also called Sharpsburg. The bloodiest single day of the war, this Maryland battle produced more than 11,000 casualties on each side. One survivor wrote, "No tongue can tell, no mind conceive, no pen portray the horrible sights I witnessed this morning."

McClellan might have beaten the Confederates or chased them as they retreated into Virginia. Incredibly, however, he did not commit his reserves and instead settled for a battlefield draw. An exasperated Lincoln wrote McClellan, "If you don't want to use the army, I should like to borrow it for a while." Complaining that the general had "the slows," the president then replaced McClellan with General Ambrose E. Burnside.

LINCOLN FREES THE SLAVES, 1862–1863   Since June 1862 the northern cause had fared poorly, and northern opposition to the war was growing. At the same time, as casualty lists grew, Lincoln found it harder to argue that he wanted merely to restore the Union. Abolitionists in particular saw the war as a chance to rid the country of slavery once and for all. By this time almost all northerners blamed the war on that institution, and Yankees did not mind ending slavery—especially if it would help the war effort and hurt slaveholders, mostly Confederates, whose power within a restored Union was feared.

Table 14.1   Civil War Commanders*

In the East		
Union	Confederate	Battles or Places
Maj. Robert Anderson	*Gen. P. G. T. Beauregard*	Ft. Sumter, S.C., Apr. 1861
Gen. Irvin McDowell	*Beauregard, Gen. Thomas J. Jackson, Gen. Joseph E. Johnston*	Bull Run, Va., July 1861
Gen. George B. McClellan	Johnston, *Gen. Robert E. Lee,* Jackson	Seven Days, Va., June 1862
Gen. Henry W. Halleck, McClellan, Gen. John Pope	Lee, *Gen. James Longstreet*	Second Bull Run, Va., Aug. 1862
McClellan	Lee	Antietam, Md., Sept. 1862
Gen. Ambrose Burnside	*Lee*	Fredericksburg, Va., Dec. 1862
Gen. Joseph Hooker	*Lee,* Jackson	Chancellorsville, Va., May 1863
Gen. George G. Meade	Lee, Gen. Jeb Stuart, Longstreet, Gen. George E. Pickett	Gettysburg, Pa., July 1863
Gen. U. S. Grant	Lee	Wilderness, Va., May 1864
Grant	Lee	Spotsylvania, Va., May 1864
Grant	*Lee*	Cold Harbor, Va., June 1864
Grant	Lee	Petersburg, Va., June 1864–Apr. 1865
Grant	Lee	Appomattox, Va., Apr. 1865

*Names of victors are italicized.

Lincoln had been ambivalent. In 1861 he wrote Horace Greeley, "If I could save the Union without freeing *any* slaves, I would do it, and if I could save it by freeing *all* the slaves, I would do it, and if I could save it by freeing some and leaving others alone, I would also do that."

As public opinion shifted, Lincoln's policy changed. He considered issuing a proclamation abolishing slavery in the South by emergency wartime presidential decree. Frequently discussed in the cabinet, the proclamation had been withheld until after a Union victory. Because Lee had retreated after Antietam, Lincoln decided on September 23, 1862, to make a preliminary announcement.

At that moment, the president freed no slaves but warned that he would do so shortly if the war continued. On January 1, 1863, Lincoln issued the Emancipation Proclamation. This document did not actually free any slaves. It touched neither those in the loyal border slave states nor

Table 14.1   Civil War Commanders (*continued*)

In the West		
Union	*Confederate*	*Battles or Places*
Gen. U. S. Grant	Gen. Albert S. Johnston	Ft. Henry, Tn., Feb. 1862
Grant	A. S. Johnston	Ft. Donelson, Tn., Feb. 1862
		Pea Ridge, Ark., Mar. 1862
Grant	A. S. Johnston	Island No. 10, Apr. 1862
Grant	A. S. Johnston	Shiloh, Apr. 1862
Commodore David Farragut, Gen. Benjamin F. Butler		New Orleans, Apr. 1862
Gen. Don Carlos Buell	Gen. Braxton Bragg	Perryville, Ky., Oct. 1862
Grant		Vicksburg, Miss., July 1863
Gen. William Rosecrans	*Bragg*	Chickamauga, Ga., Sept. 1863
Gen. George H. Thomas	Bragg	Lookout Mountain, Tn., Nov. 1863
Thomas	Bragg	Missionary Ridge, Tn., Nov. 1863
Gen. William T. Sherman	J. E. Johnston	North Georgia, 1864
Sherman	Gen. John Bell Hood	Atlanta, Ga., Sept. 1864
Sherman	Hood	Savannah, Ga., Dec. 1864
	Hood	Franklin, Tn., Dec. 1864
	Hood	Nashville, Tn., Dec. 1864
Sherman		Columbia, S.C., Feb. 1865

those in portions of the Confederacy already under Union control. It promised freedom to any slave in areas then under Confederate control, but this promise would be meaningless unless Federal troops advanced.

Lincoln, however, understood that the North could no longer stomach slavery. Congress was already preparing to abolish the institution in the District of Columbia, and Lincoln urged the border slave states to adopt plans for compensated emancipation.

The war had thrown slavery into crisis. From the beginning northerners noticed that the Confederates used slave labor to build fortresses and other military facilities. In 1861, when Union troops invaded parts of the Confederacy, slaves frequently fled into the northern lines. A few commanders gave the blacks freedom; others respected property rights and returned slaves to their owners. Both policies caused political problems, and finally the army decided to treat the slaves as "contraband," like captured enemy guns or ammunition.

The contrabands, as the runaway slaves were called, would not be returned to the enemy. Nor would they be free. Rather, the army would hold them in camps until a later date. Meanwhile, they could dig ditches, build breastworks, and perform other useful labor for the Union cause.

More and more northerners questioned this limited use of black manpower. If the war was about slavery, why not arm the blacks and send them into battle to fight for their own freedom? Many Yankees, however, hesitated to adopt this policy. Some feared that the blacks would make poor soldiers. Others worried that using black soldiers would enrage white southerners and prolong the war. As casualty lists grew, many white northerners concluded that freeing the slaves and arming black soldiers were necessary to win the war.

BOTH SIDES DRAFT SOLDIERS In April 1862 the South adopted a military draft in order to raise larger armies. This draft law provoked resistance. It also contained occupational deferments, and the South suddenly sprouted many new schoolmasters and parsons. The greatest bitterness, however, was caused by a provision that allowed any planter who owned twenty or more slaves to claim an exemption. By war's end perhaps a million men, some more willingly than others, had donned Confederate gray.

In 1862 the North decided to recruit black soldiers in place of a draft. By war's end about 180,000 Union soldiers were black. Half were recruited from the Confederacy, but some were under northern sponsorship, as in the case of the famous Massachusetts 54th Regiment. As Frederick Douglass predicted, willingness to die for the Union gave African Americans a stronger claim to citizens' rights.

In 1863 the North enacted a draft that lacked the South's occupational deferments but did provide an exemption upon payment of $300. Poor men pooled money to protect themselves. The draft did not apply to the western states or territories, to which some men escaped. Willingly or not, more than 1.8 million men served in the Union army.

After Antietam, the war did not go well for the Union. In the West, Confederate General Braxton Bragg invaded Kentucky, and although stopped at Perryville in October 1862, he challenged northern control of that state. Bragg's army continued to threaten Tennessee; the Federals need to station troops there distracted the Union from its effort to take the Confederate river stronghold of Vicksburg, Mississippi.

In the East, Union General Burnside launched costly and stupid frontal assaults at Fredericksburg, Virginia in December. Watching the slaughter, Lee observed, "It is well that war is so terrible—we should grow too fond of it." Lincoln replaced Burnside with General Joseph Hooker. Hearing that "Fighting Joe" Hooker thought the country needed a dictator, presumably himself, Lincoln wrote him, "Only those generals who gain success can set up dictators." The president continued to look for a general who could outwit Lee. As the year ended, southerners still hoped for independence, and northerners wondered if victory would ever come.

THE KEY YEAR, 1863

Abroad, diplomacy prevented recognition of the Confederacy, but at home the Federals made no progress in defeating Lee in Virginia even as Grant captured Vicksburg and the Mississippi River. Lee entered Pennsylvania and fought General George G. Meade at Gettysburg. This battle, the largest ever fought in North America, marked a turning point in the war. Never again would Confederate troops threaten the North, and, as Lee knew, a purely defensive Confederate strategy made a northern victory likely. Lincoln's Gettysburg Address brilliantly expressed Union war aims. The home front witnessed labor restlessness, strained family life, alienated intellectuals, and sustained support for the war.

WAR RESUMES ON ALL FRONTS   Although the British did not recognize the Confederacy, they allowed the South to build naval raiding ships in Britain. Two raiders, the *Florida* and the *Alabama,* destroyed much northern shipping in the Atlantic Ocean, and when the American government learned that the Confederates were about to launch another newly built ship in Britain, the American ambassador, Charles Francis Adams, protested and persuaded the British government to block its sailing. British courts, however, eventually released the ship to its Confederate owners, thus straining Anglo-American relations once again.

Spring 1863 brought a resumption of the war in Virginia. On May 2, Hooker's 130,000 Federals advanced against Lee's 60,000 Confederates at Chancellorsville on the Rappahannock River halfway between Washington and Richmond. Lee sent Stonewall Jackson's army to attack Hooker's right through an area of tangled vines and briars called the Wilderness. Taken completely by surprise, Union troops retreated in confusion. Before Hooker could reorganize his right, Lee engaged Hooker's main and left forces as they tried to cross the river. Lee's artillery controlled the high ground; on May 5 Hooker withdrew to the river's north bank.

Although the battle saved Richmond, the Confederates paid dearly. More southerners than Yankees were killed, and among the dead was Stonewall Jackson, accidentally shot by his own men. Of Jackson, Lee said, "I have lost my right arm."

Meanwhile, Union General Ulysses S. Grant marched his troops past the Confederate stronghold at Vicksburg on the opposite, western side of the Mississippi River. His supply boats ran the river under Confederate guns in the middle of the night, picked up Grant's men, and ferried them to the Vicksburg side.

Then Grant began a siege that forced the 30,000 Confederates inside the city to the brink of starvation. Hopelessly penned in, eating dogs, cats, and rats, the Vicksburg defenders surrendered on July 4. Within a few days the last Confederate outpost on the Mississippi fell, leaving the river totally in Union hands. The Confederacy had been sliced in two. "The Father of Waters," said Lincoln, "flows unvexed to the sea."

Aware of the desperate situation in the West, Lee decided to be bold in the East. In June, Lee's troops, always in need of supplies, moved north through the Shenandoah Valley, crossed the Potomac, and advanced into southern Pennsylvania, a lush agricultural area previously untouched by the war. Jeb Stuart's cavalry rounded up livestock for Lee's army, but while Stuart was busy seizing provisions, Lee lost track of Hooker's Federal army, which had moved into Maryland to protect Washington.

Although Hooker wanted to attack Richmond, which was no longer defended, panic in Washington over Lee's possible moves against Washington, Baltimore, or Philadelphia made that idea impossible. "Lee's *army*, and not *Richmond*," an exasperated Lincoln wrote to Hooker, "is your true objective." Bickering within the military led Lincoln to replace Hooker with General George G. Meade.

Neither army knew the exact location of the enemy's main force. Then on June 30 a small portion of each army made a chance contact at Gettysburg, Pennsylvania, and set the stage for a great battle, the greatest ever fought in North America, with 150,000 combatants.

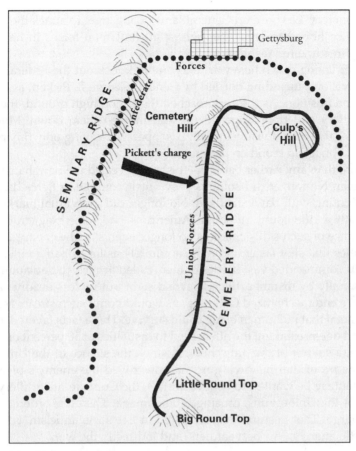

Map 14.3   Gettysburg

LEE FIGHTS MEADE AT GETTYSBURG, 1863   On July 1, 1863, the Confederates drove the Union troops out of Gettysburg into defensive positions atop Cemetery Hill and Culp's Hill. Across the way Lee's troops occupied Seminary Ridge, which was somewhat lower. Meade had 15,000 more soldiers, better artillery, and a better geographical position. Union forces repelled Confederate attacks and won the day. Lee, however, remained on the field.

By July 2 Lee's remaining forces had reached the site, and he attacked. Fresh Union troops also arrived, and the Confederates lost the crest of Seminary Ridge.

On July 3 Confederate assaults on Culp's Hill and Little Round Top failed. The latter position, which nearly fell, would have enabled Confederate artillery to rake the entire Union army. In a last, desperate attempt to gain victory, Lee ordered General James Longstreet to attack the Union center. Lee hoped to break through, split the Union forces in half, and march directly into Washington.

After laying down heavy artillery fire to knock out the Federal guns, three divisions, including one led by General George E. Pickett, assaulted the Union position. As they approached the Union high ground, the Federal artillery and troops opened fire and mowed them down. Much of Pickett's 5,000-man division literally disappeared, leaving only tiny pieces of cloth, bone, and blood on the ground.

More than any earlier battle, Gettysburg revealed the new, harsh reality of war. No longer did soldiers prove their courage in fierce hand-to-hand fighting with bayonets fixed. No longer did individual marksmanship with a rifle count, although Americans had long exaggerated the importance of such skills. Soldiers no longer even saw the enemy, as they fired rifles that shot faster and more accurately as far as half a mile. Now generals commanded vast hordes of men, called armies, to be slaughtered impersonally by distant artillery, beyond sight but no less deadly. Before the war's end mechanized Gatling guns would vomit such streams of hot, sharp metal that no human being could survive. These facts favored an entrenched defense; taking the offense led to casualties of 50 percent or more.

Lee, a soldier of the old school, mistook the silence of the Union artillery as proof that his own guns had destroyed the enemy's pieces. It was a fantasy he wanted to believe. In fact, the Confederate artillery had overshot the Union guns, causing little damage. Then Lee ordered Pickett's charge. That gesture, deeply rooted in Lee's romanticism, cost him the battle, many of his best soldiers, and indirectly the war.

THE AFTERMATH OF GETTYSBURG   On July 4 Lee retreated to the Potomac River, which was flooding. Meade followed but did not attack: The river subsided, and in the middle of the night Lee fled back to Virginia. At Gettysburg the more than 7,000 dead were still being buried. More than 40,000 men from the two armies had been wounded or were missing.

On November 19 a national cemetery was dedicated at Gettysburg. Lincoln spoke for five minutes. His Gettysburg Address, widely printed in the newspapers, expressed northern resolve to see the war to its conclusion. It also showed Lincoln's unusual devotion to "government of the people, by the people, for the people."

Most important, however, was the president's understanding of the sacrifices that had been made at Gettysburg. Neither sentimentalizing nor trivializing what had happened, Lincoln stated that the true meaning of these deaths would be defined by the subsequent devotion that Unionists showed for their cause.

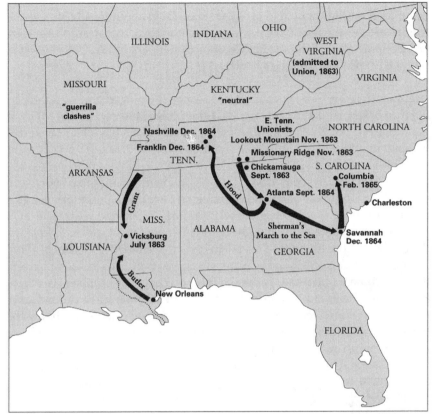

Map 14.4   The Civil War in the West, 1863–1865

Gettysburg marked a turning point. Never again did the Confederates have a large enough army to threaten the North. Lee was forced to adopt a more defensive strategy that both inhibited his own daring and predicted a war of attrition that the North would ultimately win. After Gettysburg, the South also lost its hope for diplomatic recognition by Britain or France, and the British government confiscated Confederate ships being built in British shipyards.

The battle of Gettysburg, however, did not end the war, and the North had to win on the ground. On September 19 at Chickamauga, Georgia, just outside Chattanooga, Tennessee, General Braxton Bragg's Confederates produced a panic in General William Rosecrans's Union ranks. Federal troops retreated to Chattanooga and were all but surrounded.

Grant, in command in the West, replaced the luckless Rosecrans with General George H. Thomas, whose stand at Chickamauga had prevented a rout. Thomas, now called the "Rock of Chickamauga," drove the Rebels from Lookout Mountain and on November 25, in an unusually successful frontal attack, off Missionary Ridge. Chattanooga was secure. As both armies settled in for the winter, Chattanooga looked like a Union dagger pointed at the Confederacy's heart.

THE WAR AT HOME   As the war dragged on, it changed the way people lived, worked, and thought. By 1863 the North had more than 900,000 men in arms; the South, half that many. Tremendous labor shortages developed in both regions, and wages soared. Apprentices left unpaid labor to be hired as journeymen, and skilled workers, threatening to strike, demanded and got large pay raises. Many previously unorganized northern workers set up unions, and the Republican Party, a coalition of business and labor hostile to slavery and cheap imports, cultivated workers.

Northern workers, however, became frustrated because wage increases did not keep up with rising prices. Their standard of living declined. With so many skilled workers in the army, economic productivity lagged, even though women joined the workforce in unprecedented numbers as seamstresses, teachers, and munitions workers. In the South, Richmond and other cities endured food shortages and bread riots. Speculators in both sections made fortunes illegally trading southern cotton for northern food.

Both North and South had trouble financing the war. Taxes and tariffs were raised and new ones imposed, including the first federal income tax in the North and a tax of 10 percent payable "in kind" on all agricultural production in the South. Revenues proved insufficient, however, and both sides resorted to selling bonds and to the Revolutionary War expedient of printing paper money. The Confederates issued $1 billion in paper money, which brought hyperinflation and eventually became a bad joke. The North's greenbacks greatly increased the money supply and caused prices to double by war's end, by which time the national debt had reached $2.8 billion.

AMERICANS EXPRESS THOUGHTS AND FEELINGS ABOUT THE WAR   Compassion grew with the casualty lists as both northern and southern women organized hospitals for the soldiers. They wrapped bandages, cooked meals, and nursed the wounded or sick. Told about the horrible suffering on the battlefields, the nurse Clara Barton and others took nursing directly to the front, where soldiers were most in need. All but ignored by the army and the federal bureaucracy, Barton received official recognition for her services only late in the war. In 1881 she founded the American Red Cross.

During the war northern intellectuals noticed that many soldiers in army camps died from disease. In fact, twice as many died in this way as in battle. Soldiers ignored regulations requiring them to dig and use latrines remote from water supplies. Unsanitary conditions, spoiled food, and lack of proper clothing in harsh weather led to many deaths.

A group of intellectuals, many of them pacifists and almost all abolitionists, set up the United States Sanitary Commission to inspect military camps. This body, led by the urban park planner Frederick Law Olmsted, collected health statistics and made practical recommendations that the Union army generally adopted.

Many Americans believed that civil war had been visited upon the nation as a just punishment for the sin of slavery. According to this view, which grew as the war raged on, both North and South had to pay a price for redemption. The South suffered for maintaining slavery, the North for not opposing slavery sufficiently in earlier years.

The songwriter Julia Ward Howe expressed this idea in her great war song, "The Battle Hymn of the Republic." According to Howe, Yankee soldiers battled at God's side, "trampling out the vintage where the grapes of wrath are stored," marching on with "His Truth." War, evangelical religion, and politics had become intertwined.

The South replied with "Dixie," a jaunty minstrel tune written by Dan Emmett, a Yankee, just before the war. The Confederacy's unofficial anthem, "Dixie" buoyed southern hopes even as it romantically and nostalgically portrayed a landscape dominated by cotton. This song stressed patriotism based on attachment to a locale. The Yankees, it suggested, had no right to invade the South. "I'll take my stand," went the lyrics, "to live and die for Dixie." This song's popularity led the South to be called Dixie.

In 1863 southerners took hope less from the battlefield than from signs of strain evident in the North. The Yankees might, after all, give up and go home. The first Union army draft had provoked serious riots, especially in New York City, where mobs of Irish immigrants spent four days in July attacking draft officials, demolishing abolitionists' homes, and lynching blacks. Lincoln was forced to send Federal troops to put down the disturbance.

Southerners incorrectly concluded that the ethnically diverse North would unravel. In fact, most northern immigrants strongly backed the war. Immigrants, mostly German and Irish, made up one-quarter of the Union army and composed such units as New York's famous "Fighting Irish" 69th Regiment.

THE CONFEDERACY CRUMBLES, 1864–1865

In 1864 Grant's slow movement toward Richmond and Sherman's capture of Atlanta provided visible proof of Union success. It came just in time to save Lincoln's otherwise doubtful bid for reelection. Sherman's march to Savannah and through South Carolina, a string of Confederate defeats, and Lee's evacuation of Richmond in April 1865 brought the war to a rapid close. Within days Lincoln was assassinated. Victory had not been cheap, and outwardly intense nationalism masked a dark undercurrent in the reunited country.

GRANT AND SHERMAN MOVE SOUTH, 1864   Noting Union success in the West, Lincoln at last called Grant to command Federal forces in the East. As the spring 1864 campaign opened, Grant's forces slogged on from Washington toward Richmond. Although the Union controlled the Shenandoah Valley and had plenty of troops along the James River southeast of Richmond, Grant's 100,000 Federals found it difficult to move against Lee's 60,000 Confederates.

In May, in the Wilderness and at Spotsylvania, Lee outmaneuvered the larger Union army and inflicted heavy casualties. Grant, unlike McClellan, calmly accepted these losses. Amid this grim war of attrition, Grant said, "I propose to fight it out along this line, if it takes all summer." On June 3 Grant's army failed in an assault at Cold Harbor. In one month Grant had suffered 60,000 casualties. Lee, however, had lost as many as 30,000 men. More Yankees would soon join Grant's force; Lee's casualties could not be replaced.

Changing his strategy, Grant moved his forces south of the James River and rushed to capture Petersburg, twenty-five miles south of Richmond. The Federals were unable to avoid tipping off the Confederates, and Lee reinforced Petersburg. In mid-June a Union attack failed, and Grant laid siege to Petersburg. The Confederates, however, were not trapped as they had been at Vicksburg. Southern forces controlled the railroad to Richmond, and one line there remained open to supplies from southwestern Virginia. In July the Union's attempt to blow up the Confederate forces at Petersburg with an underground mine produced what was called the war's single biggest explosion, but this experiment did not break the siege.

The Union enjoyed greater success in the West, where in May General William Tecumseh Sherman's 100,000-man army marched from Chattanooga through north Georgia toward Atlanta. Already eyeing Savannah and the Atlantic Ocean, Sherman intended to split the remaining Confederacy in two and destroy so much property that Georgia could no longer provision southern forces. After southern General Joseph E. Johnston's 60,000-man army failed to check Sherman's advance, President Jefferson Davis replaced Johnston with General John Bell Hood. The key city of Atlanta, an industrial and rail center, fell on September 2, 1864. The southern diarist Mary Chesnut wrote, "There is no hope."

THE ELECTION OF **1864**   Throughout the summer and fall, presidential politics engaged people both north and south. Confederates believed that high northern casualties might lead to Lincoln's defeat by a candidate willing to open peace negotiations with the South. Unionists looked desperately for military successes to plead for Lincoln's reelection. At times the president himself doubted that he could be reelected.

To improve his chances, Lincoln agreed to accept as his running mate Andrew Johnson of Tennessee. The only senator from a seceding state who had remained loyal to the United States and had stayed in Congress when other southerners resigned, Johnson was a conservative War Democrat. In putting him on the ticket, Republicans dropped their party name and adopted a prowar, bipartisan Union ticket.

The Democrats nominated McClellan on an antiwar platform. He accepted the nomination but rejected the platform. He dodged the issue because northern Democrats were divided. Nevertheless, Lincoln's defeat would have been such a repudiation of the war that the war could hardly have been continued. In some parts of the North, especially in sections of the Midwest where southerners had settled, opposition to the war was growing. Clement Vallandingham, a popular Democratic orator from Ohio, led the Copperheads, a faction of the Democrats who sought a peace treaty recognizing the Confederacy. Vallandingham endorsed McClellan.

Republican Party leaders took this threat seriously. Nineteen states gave Union soldiers the right to vote by absentee ballot. Lincoln got three-quarters of the soldier vote. As it turned out, Grant's determination at Richmond's door and Sherman's success in Georgia, along with McClellan's lack of political skills, tipped the balance in favor of Lincoln, who won reelection, though by a fairly narrow popular margin.

THE CONFEDERACY DISAPPEARS, **1864–1865**   While the presidential campaign proceeded, Hood's Confederates harassed Sherman's long supply line, and Sherman sent part of his army to protect Tennessee. Vowing to "make war so terrible . . . that generations would pass before they could appeal to it," Sherman marched through Georgia to the sea in a path sixty miles wide, foraging on the land and burning cotton, factories, warehouses, and bridges along the way. "The fields were trampled down," wrote one Georgia woman, "and the road was lined with carcasses of horses, hogs, and cattle that the invaders, unable either to consume or to carry away with them, had wantonly shot down to starve our people and prevent them from making their crops."

Sherman entered Savannah on December 22, 1864, and gave the city to Lincoln as a Christmas present. Meanwhile, Hood's Confederates were defeated at Franklin, Tennessee, and two weeks later at Nashville, when his army essentially disintegrated.

As the area controlled by the Confederacy shrank further, food short-ages developed, rail transport failed, and up to half the South's soldiers de-serted. Sherman marched and burned his way through South Carolina, which, as the initiator of secession, was singled out for harsh treatment. On February 17, 1865, the Federals burned the capital city of Columbia. Sher-man planned to proceed through the Carolinas and link up with Grant near Richmond.

Events then occurred with dizzying speed. On April 2, 1865, Lee abandoned Petersburg and Richmond, taking his army westward. Three days later Lincoln reasserted federal civilian authority by visiting Rich-mond. Blacks swarmed around him while Confederates remained in-doors. Then, on April 9, realizing the hopelessness of the military situa-tion, Lee surrendered his army to Grant at Appomattox Courthouse, eighty miles west of Richmond.

Lincoln and his cabinet discussed postwar policies, and on April 14 a war-weary president went to Ford's Theater, where the actor and Con-federate sympathizer John Wilkes Booth shot him. Lincoln died the next day. Booth's act was part of a conspiracy; Secretary of State William Henry Seward had also been attacked, although he survived. After a wild escape on a horse, Booth was trapped in a barn and, refusing to surrender, was killed by the army. Nine suspects were arrested, and four were hanged.

On April 18, Johnston surrendered to Sherman in North Carolina, and on May 26 a final surrender took place in New Orleans. Meanwhile, Jef-ferson Davis had been captured while fleeing through Georgia. A favorite Union song promised, "We will hang Jeff Davis from a sour apple tree," but he was not hanged.

CALCULATING THE FINAL BALANCE   The Civil War ended both the idea of both secession and slavery. Of the 2.8 million men who fought in the war, 620,000 (more than one-fifth) died. Perhaps more astonishing than the to-tal number of deaths, which was greater than in all other American wars combined, was the high rate of military service. In the frontier state of Iowa, for example, half of all white males of military age fought, creating forty-six separate regiments. The South—facing invasion, with a small white population, a long military tradition including the recent Mexican War, and an early draft—had both greater participation and a higher death rate. In that region, one-quarter of the white males of military age died in the war. Nationally the figure was close to one-sixth. This is a death rate similar to that suffered by Germany or France in World War I.

After the war Harriet Beecher Stowe wrote that, on every block in every town, at least one person had died. Not a family in the United States had escaped. Everyone had lost a father, a son, a husband, a brother, or at the least an uncle, a nephew, or a cousin. Many families, of course, had lost more than one member. Stowe herself was not untouched. One son, badly wounded, had been given morphine for the pain, became an addict, and destroyed himself. The death lists do not include those who died later from wartime injuries, amputated limbs, or psychological trauma.

Nor do casualty rates reveal the way the war seared the American soul. Before the war, since Andrew Jackson's time, Americans had seen their society as a perfect model for the world. The war, however, had revealed deep flaws in this particular model of democracy. After the war Americans outwardly expressed optimism, but deep, dark forebodings had entered the American psyche. Serious people found it difficult to reconcile the national calamity with prospects for a brighter tomorrow. Cynicism grew, and the nation behaved as though it had entered a permanent period of mourning.

Throughout the North, intense nationalism masked these anxieties. Yankees concluded that the nation could accomplish any difficult task, if only it put its mind to it. This "can-do" spirit reaffirmed that Americans were a special, "go-ahead" people. Noticing that vast armies commanded with discipline and backed by ingenious inventions and staggering industrial capacity had won the war, Americans concluded that the nation's future demanded large-scale organizations with power concentrated at the top. Individuals must sacrifice both themselves and their rights to the nation's greater needs. Giant corporations, like large armies, could achieve spectacular success. The purpose of government, then, was to foster and encourage such organizations.

Rejecting Jefferson's idea of minimal government, Americans now accepted that government, and particularly the federal government, must play a large role in national life. At the same time, as had Jefferson, Americans retained their innate suspicion of putting power into the hands of a single person. Thus, increasing federal power took the form of a weakened presidency, a stronger Congress, and a larger bureaucracy. Americans favored the popularly elected House of Representatives, which for the only time in history assumed prominence.

After the war the federal government built two buildings in Washington, D.C., that revealed these new attitudes. The Pension Building, which housed the army of bureaucrats hired to manage veterans' affairs, featured an exterior frieze portraying thousands of real Union soldiers. The large, lavishly decorated Library of Congress both glorified the nation and offered the knowledge found in books as the key to America's future.

A simpler, more innocent United States had vanished. Americans no longer saw expansion as a way to resolve or postpone resolution of political differences as they had during James K. Polk's presidency. They recognized that states' rights, a doctrine originally invented to protect the individual from centralized federal power, had so weakened the federal government during James Buchanan's presidency that southerners adopted the delusionary view that they could unilaterally break up the Union.

The Constitution's checks and balances had failed to prevent secession, and the war had been won by at times putting the national interest ahead of a strict construction of the Constitution. Legal mechanisms had validity only when credibly defended on the battlefield. A government existed only when people sacrificed and died for its existence. In the end, both secession and slavery ceased because Americans were willing to die in order to kill those ideas.

CONCLUSION

The Civil War decided the issues of secession and slavery, greatly diminishing states' rights and enhancing national power. Before the Civil War, many Americans said, "The United States are. . . ." After it, they said, "The United States is. . . ." The war's high price, however, did much to temper American idealism and optimism. Southerners found the war a bitter experience from which they did not fully recover, either psychologically or economically, for a hundred years. Northerners discovered common bonds that eased class, ethnic, and racial tensions. Industry and labor had both rallied to the Union, and immigrants' strong support for the war caused a sharp decline in nativist sentiments. Black participation in the war helped African Americans win new rights.

Politically, Republicans emerged as the nation's guardians, while Democrats remained tainted with treason for a generation. The Republicans, a crazy-quilt coalition held together by wartime solidarity, became the dominant political party for two generations. Even before the war's end, they had passed laws to build a transcontinental railroad from Omaha to Sacramento, to give free western land to settlers (the Homestead Act, 1862), and to use federal money to support colleges (the Morrill Act, 1862). These actions symbolized the growth of northern, federal, and business power as the nation remade itself. The old federation of states had died, and a new nation had been born.

Recommended Readings

DOCUMENTS: Mary Chesnut, *Mary Chesnut's Civil War* (1981); U. S. Grant, *Personal Memoirs* (2 vols., 1885); Thomas W. Higginson, *Army Life in a Black Regiment* (1870); Sam R. Watkins, *Co. Aytch* (1962).

READINGS: (GENERAL) Richard F. Bensel, *Yankee Leviathan* (1990); David W. Blight, *Race and Reunion* (2001); Gabor S. Boritt, ed., *Why the Confederacy Lost* (1992); Shelby Foote, *The Civil War* (3 vols., 1958–1974); James M. McPherson, *Battle Cry of Freedom* (1988); Mark E. Neely, Jr., *The Fate of Liberty* (1991); Phillip S. Paludan, *A People's Contest* (1988); George C. Rable, *The Confederate Republic* (1994); Emory M. Thomas, *The Confederate Nation* (1979); (WAR) Stephen V. Ash, *When the Yankees Came* (1995); Archer Jones, *Civil War Command and Strategy* (1992); Alvin M. Josephy, Jr., *The Civil War in the American West* (1991); Gerald F. Linderman, *Embattled Courage* (1987); John F. Marszalek, *Sherman* (1993); William S. McFeely, *Grant* (1981); Reid Mitchell, *Civil War Soldiers* (1988) and *The Vacant Chair* (1993); Charles Royster, *The Destructive War* (1991); Emory M. Thomas, *Robert E. Lee* (1995); Steven E. Woodworth, *Jefferson Davis and His Generals* (1990); (RACE) Herman Belz, *Emancipation and Equal Rights* (1978); Joseph T. Glatthaar, *Forged in Battle* (1990); V. Jacque Voegeli, *Free but Not Equal* (1967); (HOME FRONT) Iver C. Bernstein, *The New York City Draft Riots* (1990); Allan G. Bogue, *The Congressman's Civil War* (1989); Catherine Clinton and Nina Silber, eds., *Divided Houses* (1992); Adrian Cook, *The Armies of the Streets* (1974); Marilyn M. Culpepper, *Trials and Triumphs* (1991); Mary A. DeCredico, *Patriotism for Profit* (1990); Wayne K. Durrill, *War of Another Kind* (1990); Drew Faust, *Mothers of Invention* (1996); George M. Frederickson, *The Inner Civil War* (2nd ed., 1993); J. Matthew Gallman, *Mastering Wartime* (1990); Elizabeth D. Leonard, *Yankee Women* (1994); David Montgomery, *Beyond Equality* (1967); George C. Rable, *Civil Wars* (1989).

15

Reconstruction, 1863–1877

OVERVIEW Wartime chaos forced the adoption of Reconstruction policies even before the Civil War ended. In 1865–1866, President Andrew Johnson and the Radical Republican majority in Congress fought bitterly over policy. Congress won and in 1867–1868 imposed harsh Reconstruction policies on the South. Blacks gained political rights but lacked economic security, and southern whites responded with anger, intimidation, and violence. By the early 1870s Republican rule in the South began to fail, and the last Radical governments were sold out in the bargain over the presidential election of 1876.

WARTIME RECONSTRUCTION, 1863–1865

Reconstruction began in 1863 as a wartime experiment at Port Royal, South Carolina, when thousands of slaves came under Union army control. Late in that year President Abraham Lincoln proposed formal rules for readmitting the southern states to the Union, but Radicals in Congress found these rules too mild and in 1864 passed harsher requirements, which Lincoln pocket vetoed. At the end of the war, in 1865, thousands of ex-slaves embraced their new freedom, but without education, property, or consistent protection from mounting violence, their prospects were grim in the war-torn South.

EXPERIMENTING AT PORT ROYAL, 1863 Before the Civil War ended, Americans began to rebuild their war-ravaged country. As the war raged, President Abraham Lincoln, who understood the importance of symbols, ordered workers to finish the huge dome over the Capitol building. The Republicans also broke ground for a transcontinental railroad. With the exception cᶠ Senator Andrew Johnson, representatives and senators from the Confederate states had resigned, and the northern-dominated Congress easily designated a northerly route from Omaha to San Francisco. Northerners believed that this railroad would keep the West in the Union even if the South won independence.

The most strenuous efforts toward Reconstruction, however, involved parts of the South that the Union army had occupied. By 1862 Yankees controlled New Orleans, Louisiana's sugar plantations, and coastal South Carolina, where thousands of blacks, abandoned by their former masters, lived inside Union lines. Lincoln had to govern these areas, and he recognized that, if the North won the war, his policies would become models for postwar Reconstruction throughout the South.

Union commanders in coastal South Carolina tried a number of policies that became known as the Port Royal Experiment. Confederate landholders had fled. Black residents, who acted as if they were free even before the Emancipation Proclamation was announced, took over the plantations. They resisted planting rice or cotton, the normal cash crops, and refused to work in the usual gangs. Instead, they divided the land among themselves and, turning to family-based subsistence agriculture, primarily raised corn. Although blacks demanded ownership of the land they farmed, the army lacked the authority to grant it. The army could recognize only the right of black residents to use the land while the war continued. In some cases, white landowners did lose land for failure to pay property taxes, but most of these owners successfully reclaimed their property after the war.

The Port Royal Experiment captured the imagination of northern abolitionists. Experts from the U.S. Sanitary Commission traveled to Port Royal, offered technical advice about agriculture, and then brought in dozens of northern female schoolteachers, both black and white. These teachers, who included the black Charlotte Forten, found both children and adults eager to learn to read and write. The African-American community quickly chose its own black Christian preachers. The black church became the community's most important organization, performing social, economic, and political functions as well as religious ones. It continued to thrive after the end of Reconstruction.

Although residents prospered, supporters noted the lack of legal authority for the Port Royal Experiment. Technically, the blacks remained slaves, and absentee whites held legal title to the land. Many doubted that this new order in South Carolina would survive the end of the war. Few believed that such a change could be imposed across the entire South, due to massive white resistance and an inability to supply northern help on such a large scale. As feared, at the end of the war white landowners returned to Port Royal to demand that blacks either resume plantation-style agriculture or leave.

LINCOLN AND CONGRESS DEBATE RECONSTRUCTION, **1863–1864**   Louisiana, with a population about half white and half black and with a large number of free African Americans in New Orleans, proved more troublesome than coastal South Carolina to the occupying Union army. To free the army from controversy surrounding the occupation, Lincoln wanted to establish a new, pro-Union government as soon as possible.

In December 1863, he announced a plan for Reconstruction. Louisiana or any other Confederate state could rejoin the Union under simple terms. Residents who had participated in the rebellion could take a loyalty oath and then would be given amnesty. Lincoln would recognize a new state government after 10 percent of the number of men who had voted in the 1860 election had taken the oath, provided the state accepted slavery's end.

At first Lincoln did not propose political rights for blacks, but after some of Louisiana's numerous articulate free blacks protested during a visit to the White House, he privately asked the new state government to give literate African Americans the vote. However, the state's white Unionists, some of whom still defended slavery, declined. In 1864 Lincoln recognized governments in Arkansas and Louisiana under these terms, but Congress refused to seat their representatives.

Radical Republicans in Congress found Lincoln's plan too mild. They also resented the president's attempt to increase the power of the executive branch at their expense. In 1864 Congress passed its own plan for Reconstruction, the Wade-Davis Bill. This measure required a majority of the voters in each seceding state to take an oath pledging both past and future loyalty. Under this procedure some southern states were likely to remain out of the Union for a long time.

With the war ongoing, with the belief that former Whigs might lead new southern governments, and with the hope that mild terms might encourage Confederate states to capitulate, Lincoln determined that the harshness of the Congressional policy was unwise. He declined to sign the bill, which failed because it had been passed at the end of the session. (A bill becomes law without the president's signature if passed during a session, but an unsigned bill fails without the signature if Congress adjourns. This is called a pocket veto.) The Radicals attacked Lincoln, but he postponed further consideration of Reconstruction until after the 1864 election.

When the Civil War ended, African American soldiers in the Union Army were discharged with celebrations marking the end of slavery, like this one in Little Rock, Arkansas. (Library of Congress)

SLAVERY DIES, 1865   As the Confederacy collapsed in 1865, Union army officers and slaveholders throughout the region informed blacks that slavery was dead. Blacks hardly needed to be told. One said to his former master, a defeated Confederate soldier passing by, "Hello massa; bottom rail top dis time!"

Heralded as the Day of Jubilee, slavery's end brought joyous, even riotous, celebration. After the excitement of the moment waned, blacks often tested their newly won freedom by traveling—sometimes in search of lost relatives, but often just to prove to themselves that they had actually gained freedom. The ability to move unchallenged by slave patrols gave freedom vivid meaning.

Many African Americans, including previously loyal houseservants, deserted the plantations and farms where they had always lived to search for better opportunities or at least different whites with whom to deal. Freedmen, as the ex-slaves were called, shrewdly calculated that whites who remembered particular African Americans from slavery days would never treat them with respect. Better to trust a stranger.

The result was a kind of chaos. Searching for both opportunies and distance from white supervision, many blacks moved to southern towns and cities. Concentrated populations also discouraged the sporadic violence against blacks often found in rural areas. Used to slavery, slave patrols, and control over the black population, white city residents grew fearful.

Blacks also wandered through the countryside, seemingly uninterested in work. Confederate soldiers returned home and, finding their labor force gone, seethed when passing blacks declined their offers of work on the plantations. Blacks resented and resisted traditional modes of labor, and agriculture suffered. For example, production on Louisiana's sugar plantations dropped to 10 percent of its prewar level.

African Americans did not wish to work for whites on white-owned plantations. Rather, they wanted to acquire land for their own family farms. At the time, few blacks had either the capital or the valuable labor skills that would enable them to earn the capital to buy land. Indeed, the postwar South was a sorry place for anyone, white or black, to make money. Many years passed before the region regained its prewar number of farm animals and planted acres. As late as 1880 the per capita income in the South was only one-third of the national average.

Nor were blacks educated. In 1860 more than 90 percent could neither read nor write. Most southern states had prohibited teaching slaves to read. During Reconstruction blacks demanded that the South establish public schools. Eager for education, African Americans reluctantly accepted white insistence on segregated schools. Within a generation half of all blacks were literate.

JOHNSON AND CONGRESS QUARREL, 1865–1866

In 1865 President Andrew Johnson surprised the Radical Republicans in Congress by adopting conservative Reconstruction policies. The Constitution was amended to end slavery, but the southern states enacted Black Codes that all but reinstated slavery under another name. In 1866 Americans debated four distinct theories of Reconstruction, the harshest of which became congressional policy. Congress passed radical laws over Johnson's veto, as well as the Fourteenth Amendment to the Constitution. In 1866, northern voters backed the Radicals' program, and white southerners organized the Ku Klux Klan to intimidate blacks.

JOHNSON ADOPTS CONSERVATIVE RECONSTRUCTION POLICIES   After Lincoln's assassination, Andrew Johnson became president. An obscure former senator from Tennessee, he had been a lifelong Democrat. Born into poverty in North Carolina, he became an apprentice tailor and then ran away to the mountains of East Tennessee. There he married Eliza McCardle, who taught the ambitious but illiterate young man to read. A naturally good stump speaker with the common touch, Johnson successfully practiced law and politics.

In the prewar years he denounced slaveholding planters, even though he owned five slaves, and when Tennessee seceded, he became the only senator from a Confederate state who remained in office. He was a racist. "Damn the Negroes," he said during the war, "I am fighting these traitorous aristocrats, their masters." Hating both planters and slavery, this quarrelsome and eccentric man welcomed emancipation. He had been put on the Republican ticket in 1864 to help win Democratic votes. Most Republicans knew little about him except that he was a southern Unionist who had been drunk at his inauguration.

Johnson told Radical Republican leaders that he favored harsh measures against the South. Almost immediately, however, Johnson shocked the Radicals by adopting Lincoln's mild policies. The new president, with support from most of his cabinet, concluded that, to become a great president, he needed to heal the war's wounds by moving rapidly to restore power in the South to conservative whites.

Johnson believed, wrongly as it turned out, that the Confederacy's leaders had been discredited and lacked a constituency. Instead, he expected onetime Unionists to gain control, create stable governments, and generate the confidence that would produce postwar economic development. Though he was relieved by the way the war had destroyed slavery, he opposed extending any rights to blacks.

In mid-1865 Johnson issued a proclamation to recognize conservative, white-only governments in all eleven former Confederate states. He also granted amnesty to most Confederates who took an oath of allegiance. One important exception involved persons who held more than $20,000 worth of property. These wealthy planters had to apply to Johnson personally for a pardon. They did so and found the president generous. Johnson spent much of his time signing more than thirteen thousand pardons in two years.

Conservative state governments organized along these lines accepted the abolition of slavery by approving the Thirteenth Amendment to the Constitution, repudiated Confederate war debts, and made provisions for sending representatives to Congress. In December 1865, the Thirteenth Amendment was ratified.

THE SOUTH ENACTS BLACK CODES   These same state governments, often led by former Confederates, moved quickly to recreate the old order as closely as possible. They passed laws called Black Codes that regulated the conduct of blacks. Some states merely took old laws regulating slaves and changed the word *slave* to *freedman*. Under these laws blacks were treated as noncitizens without the rights to vote, serve on juries, or testify against whites. Furthermore, blacks had to sign annual labor contracts and could not change employment while under contract. In some states employers had the right to whip employees, who could be forced to work in gangs. In others blacks could not lease land independently. Blacks (but not whites) who lacked labor contracts or large sums of cash could be charged with vagrancy. The penalty for this crime was having the right to one's labor sold, with preference given to a former owner.

The Black Codes infuriated northern whites and southern blacks, including a good many Union army veterans. When Johnson accepted the southern white view that such laws were necessary to maintain order in the South, Radical Republicans in Congress became the president's bitter enemies. A new battle was about to be joined between the president and Congress over the direction of Reconstruction in the South.

CONGRESS BEGINS RADICAL RECONSTRUCTION, 1866   In Congress most Republicans, especially those from evangelical, moralistic New England, had become Radicals. Deeply offended by Johnson's behavior, they feared that the long, bloody war had changed little inside the South and that arrogant white southern planters would soon be running the federal government. In the North, Republicans faced a large and growing opposition from immigrant-oriented Democrats, and many Radicals worried that a coalition of white southerners and immigrant northerners might gain control of the national government. Indeed, southerners had dared to elect ex-Confederate officials to represent them in Congress. Georgia sent the former Confederate vice president, Alexander Stephens, to the Senate. The Radicals responded by refusing to seat representatives from any of the former Confederate states.

In early 1866 Congress passed a bill expanding the powers of the Freedmen's Bureau, which had been established a year earlier to distribute food and clothes to the former slaves in the South. The new bill placed nine hundred federal agents, most of them former Union soldiers, in those southern counties with large black populations to monitor race relations and negotiate disputes between whites and freedmen. Except for the post office, this was the first massive federal bureaucracy. Although the bureau could not stop white harassment, it did put such action under a watchful federal eye. Citing cost and states' rights, Johnson vetoed the bill. The angry Radicals quickly overrode the veto and showed that they had more than a two-thirds majority in Congress.

Congress then passed the Civil Rights Act. By granting citizenship to blacks and all other persons born in the United States, this law directly overturned the Black Codes and the 1857 Dred Scott ruling that denied citizenship to African Americans. The measure could also be interpreted to prohibit racial discrimination in public facilities, such as trains or restaurants. The bill, however, did not provide for voting rights. At this time most northern states had not granted the vote to blacks, and Radicals did not wish to irritate northern voters.

The Radicals passed this bill over Johnson's veto. The provisions concerning public accommodations were seldom enforced, and in 1883 the Supreme Court ruled the act unconstitutional.

PROPOSING THE FOURTEENTH AMENDMENT, 1866   Worried about a possible loss of power in the future, Radicals decided to use their overwhelming majority in Congress to guarantee black rights with the Fourteenth Amendment to the Constitution. The longest and vaguest of all amendments, this measure repealed the Dred Scott decision by granting citizenship to all persons born in the United States. Citizens were guaranteed "due process of law" and "equal protection of the laws." The federal government, in other words, would intervene if the southern states mistreated the freedmen. In the long term, the Supreme Court would apply these two clauses to all sorts of situations and greatly expand the power of the federal government.

To pressure the South to give blacks the vote, the amendment provided for reduced representation in Congress if the vote was denied. This provision was never enforced. The amendment also barred most former Confederates from federal office unless pardoned by *Congress,* and the southern states were prohibited from paying off Civil War debts.

To ensure the Fourteenth Amendment's adoption, Radicals indicated that representatives from each ex-Confederate state would be admitted to Congress only after that state had ratified the amendment. Congress was determined to take control of Reconstruction away from Johnson. Tennessee ratified and was readmitted, but the other ten ex-Confederate states rejected the amendment and waited for the fall 1866 congressional elections. The southerners, along with Johnson, believed that the Radicals had misjudged public opinion.

NORTHERN VOTERS BACK THE RADICALS, 1866   Taking his case for milder measures directly to the people, Johnson used the midterm congressional election of 1866 to make a campaign "swing around the circle" to the Northeast and across the Midwest and then south to St. Louis.

Although Johnson's trip went well at first, Radicals quickly organized an all-out attack. Radicals "waved the bloody shirt," a reference to wartime flags carried by the Union army in battle, by reminding northern voters how much the war had cost in treasure and lives and how the southern-born president now proposed yielding power to the former rebels.

By focusing on the war, by associating the Democrats with treason, and by linking the Republicans to the Union cause, the Radicals secured an overwhelming election victory. This success totally discredited Johnson's policies, and the already large Radical majorities in Congress actually increased.

CHAOS AND KU KLUX KLAN VIOLENCE ARISE IN THE SOUTH   Slavery had collapsed, but nothing had been put in its place. Blacks believed that the federal government would seize land owned by Confederate planters and give it to the freedmen, and some northerners encouraged this belief. "Forty acres and a mule!" cried some Radicals, including Thaddeus Stevens. African Americans quickly learned that this idea had little support. Northern property holders saw no advantage in endorsing a proposal that questioned the sanctity and permanence of private property. A government that confiscated land from planters today might take away someone else's property tomorrow.

Thomas Nast, America's greatest political cartoonist, portrayed the Democrats' White League as colluding with the Ku Klux Klan to oppress southern blacks during Reconstruction. (Library of Congress)

In addition, few northerners wanted to create a politically powerful, property-owning black society in the South, nor did most northerners want the planters to regain their prewar national political influence. The North's policy, then, was to keep the South poor, to maintain northern dominance of the country politically and economically, and to divide southern whites and blacks. Radicals accomplished this result by the paradoxical policy of giving blacks political rights while denying them the means to economic self-sufficiency.

Southern whites were self-confident, resourceful, educated, skilled, and well connected. They retained ownership of almost all the land, buildings, and tools but frequently lacked political rights. Insecure, illiterate, and ignorant blacks had political rights, granted through northern pressure, but lacked economic security. Blacks had no land, and whites had no labor. Both fell into dependency upon outside northern forces, especially Yankee-controlled railroad companies, which came to dominate the South's economy and politics.

Almost immediately, southern whites lashed out with violence. Infuriated by ex-slaves daring to assert their rights, frightened planters and ex-Confederate soldiers organized the Ku Klux Klan in 1866 in Pulaski, Tennessee, to force the freedmen to become docile, pliant tools. The Klan, which rapidly spread across the South, favored midnight visits to black homes, where they rousted blacks from bed, dragged them outside, and then took them into the woods to be beaten or killed. The Klan's whippings were designed, more than anything else, to remind freedmen of slavery.

The organization especially targeted African Americans perceived to be leaders in the campaign for rights, those who lacked proper humility in white eyes, and those known to be literate and therefore more capable of making trouble, such as writing complaining letters to federal officials. The Klan, even more than the Black Codes, led Radicals to seek federal intervention in the South.

At the same time, both races began to move toward a new relationship. Blacks insisted that they would not work as gang laborers on plantations. Instead, they rented land from planters and farmed in family units. Prewar slave housing, which had been built in dense blocks, gave way to freestanding family cabins in the middle of fields. Black tenant farmers adopted the white view that women should not work in the fields.

In desperate poverty, black tenants brought little except labor to this system and usually had to be financed by a planter or a merchant at a nearby general store. Many of these creditors were themselves in debt to railroad corporations. The planter or merchant usually got half the tenant's crop. Many tenants found that their living costs exceeded their earnings. Tenancy and the system of sharecropping quickly became ways of life in the rural South for poor whites as well as blacks.

RADICALS CONTINUE RECONSTRUCTION, 1867–1873

In 1867–1868 Radicals in Congress continued Reconstruction with stern new laws. Tiring of Johnson's opposition, they impeached the president but failed by one vote to convict him. Black votes in the South enabled the Radical Republican candidate, U. S. Grant, to win the 1868 presidential election narrowly. Blacks in the South gained some political power under Radical rule, but Radical power faded quickly. Conservative white southerners already were regaining control when Grant won a second term in 1872. The postwar years in the North brought immigration, factories, and the purchase of Alaska in 1867, but also labor strife and a depression that began in 1873.

CONGRESS PASSES STERN MEASURES, 1867–1868   In 1867 the Radicals moved to impose the kind of harsh military Reconstruction long advocated by Thaddeus Stevens. The Reconstruction Act, passed over Johnson's veto, established five military districts covering ten former Confederate states (Tennessee had been readmitted). Under this law and several supplementary measures, twenty thousand federal troops, including a number of black units, occupied the South. Military rule replaced the conservative state governments previously recognized by Johnson.

To be readmitted to the Union, the southern states had to adopt new state constitutions drafted by conventions elected by universal male suffrage. There was, however, a catch. Most ex-Confederates were barred from voting. This rule was consistent with the Fourteenth Amendment, which awaited ratification. Thus, in many southern states the freedmen's vote exceeded the white vote.

To guarantee fair elections, the United States army registered voters. In all ten southern states 703,000 blacks and 627,000 whites were registered. Blacks formed a majority of the registered voters in Alabama, Florida, Louisiana, Mississippi, and South Carolina. African Americans were more than half of the population in South Carolina and Mississippi. Congress also required that the new state governments guarantee blacks the right to vote and ratify the Fourteenth Amendment. The Radicals reserved to Congress all final decisions about what constituted compliance and when a state could regain its representation in Congress.

Throughout the South the Radicals used military rule, the Freedmen's Bureau, and the black vote organized through Union League Clubs to create a powerful Republican Party. In the upper South, including parts of Virginia and North Carolina, white Unionists formed an important Republican core to which were now added black voters from the former plantation districts.

This biracial Republican coalition proved inherently unstable. African Americans demanded protection for civil rights and massive increases in spending on public education, to be paid for with substantially higher property taxes on white landowners. On average, taxes rose to ten times the prewar level. Although poor white Republicans from the mountains disdained planters, they usually opposed black rights and resisted higher property taxes. Relatively quickly this unnatural Republican political alliance collapsed, and the planters regained their prewar political power.

In the Deep South the situation was different. These states had large black populations, and most whites had supported the Confederacy and could not vote. In South Carolina, Mississippi, and Louisiana the Republicans prevailed due to large black majorities among the electorate.

On the other hand, in these states most Republican Party leaders were white. Some were "scalawags," that is, southerners who had been Unionists or who now believed that personal advantage came from the Republicans. Others were "carpetbaggers," that is, northerners who had moved to the South, usually with initial hopes for economic gain, who had subsequently turned to politics.

In 1868 the Radicals in Congress approved the new state constitutions for seven states and readmitted them into the Union in time for the coming presidential election, in which they were expected to vote Republican.

Georgia's white Republicans, however, then proceeded to join with the few Democrats in the legislature to expel all twenty-eight black Republican members of the legislature. This action, which contradicted the pledges that Georgia had made to the Radicals concerning black rights, enraged the Radicals. They withdrew recognition, reinstated military rule, and demanded that the state reseat the black legislators and ratify the Fifteenth Amendment to the Constitution before being restored to the Union. Georgia was readmitted a second time in 1870.

CONGRESS IMPEACHES JOHNSON, 1868   Meanwhile, the Radicals had decided to impeach President Johnson and remove him from office. Thaddeus Stevens, leader of the Radicals in the House of Representatives, eagerly pushed the impeachment through the House. The Radicals charged Johnson with a number of violations, including the attempted removal of Secretary of War Edwin Stanton in defiance of a dubious prohibition passed by Congress, but in reality the issue was more political than legal.

Although the Radicals had a two-thirds majority in the Senate, seemingly enough votes to convict Johnson, public opinion began to question the proceedings. Business leaders disliked the impeachment because it made the government look unstable and upset the financial markets. In addition, the next person in line for the presidency was the president pro-tem of the Senate, Benjamin Wade of Ohio, a widely disliked, angry Radical. Johnson was acquitted, 35 to 19, one vote short of conviction. Seven Republicans joined the Democrats in opposing removal.

THE ELECTION OF 1868   For the 1868 presidential election the Republicans nominated General Ulysses S. Grant on a platform supporting Radical Reconstruction. The Democrats picked Horatio Seymour, a colorless New York governor. Public opinion had shifted away from the Radicals, and Grant won only a narrow victory. Due to an overwhelming vote among southern whites, Seymour won a majority among white voters, but Grant carried most of the electorally rich North. His margin was enhanced by Radical control in six southern states where there were many black voters. The Radical-dominated Congress barred three southern states suspected of Democratic tendencies from participation in the election.

The narrowness of this victory made the Radicals more determined to maintain control of the South. In 1869 Congress passed the Fifteenth Amendment to the Constitution, specifically guaranteeing the black vote. Congress brushed aside attempts by women's groups, led by Elizabeth Cady Stanton and supported by Senator Charles Sumner, to use the amendment to give women the vote too. Mississippi, Texas, and Virginia were finally readmitted to the Union in 1870, after they had banned ex-Confederate voters and ratified the Fifteenth Amendment.

BLACKS GAIN POWER BRIEFLY IN THE SOUTH   Mississippi became staunchly Radical and was the first and only state to elect two African Americans to the U.S. Senate, Hiram Revels and, later, Blanche K. Bruce. Of the fourteen blacks from the South who served in the House during Reconstruction, four were Union army veterans. The most flamboyant was Robert Smalls, a former South Carolina slave who, after the Emancipation Proclamation, had stolen a steamboat and sailed it through the Confederate navy to the federal fleet.

Although blacks provided about four-fifths of the Republican vote in the South, they accounted for less than one-fifth of the officeholders. Most blacks served in city and county offices or in state legislatures. South Carolina's legislature was the only one with a black majority. Black officials tended to be well educated and light-skinned. Many had been free before the war. Only a few held statewide office, and none was elected governor.

In 1872–1873, P. B. S. Pinchback, who had been elected lieutenant governor, served briefly as governor of Louisiana.

RECONSTRUCTION EBBS PRIOR TO THE ELECTION OF 1872   Radical Reconstruction, however, was already in decline. Georgia and Virginia slipped quickly under conservative control, and northerners resisted using federal troops to maintain Radical rule. At the same time, scandal had hurt the Grant administration. A number of officials had taken bribes, and in 1872 numerous prominent Republicans in Congress were revealed to have accepted stock from the Crédit Mobilier, a front for the Union Pacific Railroad, to which Congress had given huge land grants.

By 1872 many Republicans, including Horace Greeley, loathed both Radical Reconstruction and the era's sleazy, crooked politics. Organizing themselves as Liberal Republicans, they nominated Greeley for president. The Democrats endorsed Greeley, as did the German immigrant reformer and former Union general Carl Schurz, and two crusading journalists, E. L. Godkin of *The Nation* and Henry Adams. Grant, the regular Republican nominee, won by an increased majority, and a broken-hearted Greeley died suddenly. Grant, corruption, and Reconstruction lurched forward uneasily.

THE POSTWAR NORTH, 1867–1873   The immediate postwar years brought even more rapid change in the North than in the South. Fueled by the paper greenback currency issued during the war, the postwar northern economy boomed, along with considerable inflation, and industrialists converted factories from military to civilian production. Union army veterans returned home to resume farming, business, and handicrafts, but many soon made their way west along the newly built rail routes, including the transcontinental railroad to California, which opened in 1869. Largely stopped during the war, massive immigration from Europe resumed. Irish, Germans, and Britons were joined by Scandinavians, who settled on farms in the upper Midwest.

Dynamic growth even led to a renewed interest in territorial expansion. In 1867 Secretary of State Seward learned that the Russians, pressed for cash, wanted to sell Alaska. Partly to keep the territory out of the hands of the British, who controlled Canada, and partly in faith that a land as large as Alaska must contain valuable resources, Seward resolved to buy the frozen northland. The Russians demanded $7.2 million, generally considered an outrageous price, and the secretary had to cajole and bribe Congress to pay it. Popularly scorned as "Seward's Folly," the territory of Alaska more than paid for itself within a few years in timber and salmon alone.

Change was not always kind. Many workers had organized success-ful unions during the war, but returning soldiers and immigrants now en-larged the labor pool and made it possible for employers to break strikes. Workers also discovered that the Republican Party, which had rallied both business and labor to the antislavery cause, fell more and more under the control of business interests eager to pursue antilabor policies, including the outlawing of strikes. Labor newspapers that had started during the war collapsed, leaving only the probusiness partisan press.

By 1873, the year that brought the collapse of Jay Cooke's Philadel-phia bond firm and the beginnings of a depression, many northerners were bored by the Republicans, by Reconstruction, and by talk of north-ern wartime sacrifices.

CONSERVATIVES REGAIN POWER
IN THE SOUTH, 1868–1877

Conservative white southerners used both sophisticated political tactics and economic power to overthrow the Radicals and regain control of the political system. Violence and intimidation also played a role. In the dis-puted presidential election of 1876, a Republican–southern Democratic deal gave the Republicans the presidency and the Democrats the South. The last Reconstruction state governments were sold out.

WHITE REDEEMERS USE POLITICS AND ECONOMICS   White southerners, espe-cially ex-Confederates, had never accepted the legitimacy of Reconstruc-tion. Many resisted the end of slavery, and even those who accepted slav-ery's death found the freedmen's right to vote bizarre. Perhaps a few might have conceded the merit of universal suffrage as a theory, but al-lowing blacks to vote while depriving whites of the ballot enraged white southerners.

The enforcement of these rules by the military, by the Freedmen's Bu-reau, and by Radicals in Congress embittered white southerners. Deter-mined to restore what they considered to be the natural order of southern society—that is, white supremacy—they swore to use any and all means to achieve their goal.

Although most conservative white southerners were Democrats, some, like the opportunist Governor Joe E. Brown of Georgia, joined the Republi-cans. In addition to plotting the expulsion of black Republicans from the legislature, Brown sought to reduce black influence by moving the state capital from Milledgeville, in the heart of the black belt, to Atlanta, where railroad companies willingly paid legislators for votes. Brown, like many other white Republicans, emphasized economic development over civil rights. Southern Democrats soon realized that they, too, could make this same appeal to northern business interests.

Conservatives in South Carolina, where blacks had a legislative majority as late as 1876, felt they could regain control only by rallying virtually the entire white vote and winning a share of the large black vote. That state's Radical Republican regime self-destructed with weak leadership, internal bickering, and charges of corruption. The conservative Democrat Wade Hampton, an antebellum planter and ex-Confederate general, won election as governor in 1876. Hampton pledged to retain black voting rights and act honorably toward blacks. One wonders if he made the pledge with a wink.

Economics worked against black political power. Whites owned virtually everything and had a monopoly on the most valuable job skills. In 1876 only 5 percent of African Americans in the Deep South owned land. Economic intimidation, if not outright vote-buying, was used to produce a black electorate effectively controlled by whites. In those few areas where blacks had achieved a degree of landownership, such as parts of coastal South Carolina, economics tended to reinforce black political power, which remained potent for another generation. The last southern black congressman until modern times left office in 1901.

USING VIOLENCE TO INTIMIDATE BLACKS AND GAIN WHITE RULE   Conservative white southerners called themselves Redeemers because, they said, they were redeeming or saving the South from Radical Republican misrule. Most significant in the Redeemers' movement to reclaim the power of government for Democrats, however, was the use of intimidation and violence against blacks. Although southern whites learned that the high visibility of organizations such as the Ku Klux Klan generated unfavorable publicity in the North and threatened to bring a resumption of northern intervention, the Klan's mere existence intimidated blacks.

The Klan was not the only means to reclaim white rule. Other militant white supremacist political organizations, such as South Carolina's Red Shirts and Alabama's White League, countered the Republicans' Union League Clubs. Mississippi Democrats took the motto, "Carry the election peaceably if we can, forcibly if we must."

Most important were individual threats or acts of violence directed at politically active blacks and white Republicans. Campaigns of arson and assassination took place throughout the South. These were little publicized, since Democrats had no reason to advertise undemocratic methods, and Republicans knew that publicity only revealed their own weakness.

Blacks sometimes responded to the tension by deciding to move. Some talked about Africa, and a few actually went there, although most returned disillusioned. Others looked to homesteading on federal land in the West. A number, collectively known as the Exodusters, founded new black communities in Kansas. Others migrated to Texas or to western mining towns. Most blacks, however, remained in the South and increasingly under conservative white control.

By 1876 conservative white Democrats had, by one means or another, regained control of most southern states. When Democrats won state power, they routinely destroyed black power in predominantly African-American counties by requiring officials in those counties to be appointed by the governor rather than locally elected. In 1876 only South Carolina, Louisiana, and Florida remained under Republican rule, and Radical control in those states faced serious challenges, electoral and otherwise.

THE DISPUTED ELECTION OF 1876   Grant's second administration was dogged by more scandals, including the Whiskey Ring, where distillers bribed high officials to evade liquor taxes. Worse, the economy slipped into a depression following the Panic of 1873. In 1876 Democrats recog-

In 1877 it was announced that Rutherford B. Hayes had defeated Samuel J. Tilden for the presidency by a vote of 185 to 184 in the Electoral College. In a secret compromise, the Republicans won the White House, and Democrats got control of the southern states. Tilden became a great book collector and donated his collection to the New York Public Library. (Culver Pictures, Inc.)

nized that scandal and hard times gave them an excellent chance to win the presidential election.

The Republicans nominated Rutherford B. Hayes, an Ohio politician and the husband of a leading temperance reformer, and the Democrats picked Samuel J. Tilden, a wealthy Wall Street lawyer. Although Tilden won the popular vote, the Electoral College result was close and uncertain. Indeed, Republicans quickly realized that if South Carolina, Florida, and Louisiana were counted for Hayes, he could win, 185 to 184.

The actual vote in the three southern states will never be known. Black voters were intimidated into staying away from the polls, ballot boxes were stuffed or burned, and two sets of votes were collected in some communities. Incumbent Radical administrations in all three states declared both Hayes and new Republican state governments victorious. Democrats challenged those outcomes, organized their own vote counts, and announced victories for Tilden and themselves.

No one could say for sure who had won the southern "elections," but it was clear that southern white Democrats were prepared to seize power in the three states and could be stopped only by federal military authorities. Grant, Tilden, and Hayes opposed such a use of force, each for his own reason.

Controversy about the election continued into early 1877, as Congress deadlocked. Democrats controlled the House, Republicans the Senate. Finally, Congress arranged a grand compromise. Republicans got the presidency, Democrats control of the three southern states. Northern Republicans stood aside as the last Radical governments in the three southern states fell to conservative Democrats. Amid reassurances from Hayes that he would withdraw remaining federal troops from the South, Congress sent the presidential election to a special commission composed of five Democrats, five Republicans, and four specified Supreme Court justices. These four were to choose a fifth justice. David Davis, an independent expected to be tapped, suddenly resigned from the Court to take a Senate seat, and the justices were forced to pick from among the Court's remaining justices, all of whom were Republicans.

After a secret meeting between Republican and southern Democratic leaders at the Wormley House hotel in Washington in February 1877, the commission's eight Republicans and seven Democrats followed their leaders' orders and by a strict party vote awarded all the disputed electoral votes to Hayes, who won, 185 to 184. Tilden, fearing civil war, seemed relieved.

Reconstruction was over. Although slavery had ended, the right to vote and the other rights blacks had won and exercised during Reconstruction would be lost during the 1890s. Modest gains survived, including segregated schools and black colleges, such as Howard, Atlanta, and Fisk.

In part, white racism and the white southern desire for a political system based upon white supremacy were to blame. In part, the failure to provide the freedmen with land created economic dependency that made it difficult for African Americans to keep political rights. A measure of economic security, if not actual equality, is necessary to maintain democratic politics. In part, too, northern Republicans, having concluded that Reconstruction had brought their party few benefits, were prepared to sell out the southern Radical Republicans. In the new order, men of wealth from all sections had much in common.

CONCLUSION

Reconstruction cast a long shadow across the country and especially the South. Much more than the Civil War had, the era generated great bitterness among honor-driven southern whites, who looked upon northern-imposed black rights with seething anger. Maintaining white supremacy became a hallmark of southern politics for almost a hundred years. Blacks, too, grew bitter. Promised much by northern Radicals, they were handed modest amounts of power, only to be abandoned in the end for political convenience. Never again did blacks entirely trust Republicans. Reconstruction produced only losers and goes far toward explaining the tawdry politics of the generation that followed.

Recommended Readings

DOCUMENTS: Ira Berlin, et al., eds., *Freedom: A Documentary History of Emancipation* (5 vols., 1982–2001); W. E .B. DuBois, *The Souls of Black Folk* (1903); Whitelaw Reid, *After the War* (1866); Albion W. Tourgée, *A Fool's Errand* (1879).

READINGS: (GENERAL) David Donald, *Charles Sumner and the Rights of Man* (1970); Laura F. Edwards, *Gendered Strife and Confusion* (1997); Eric Foner, *Reconstruction* (1988); Leon F. Litwack, *Been in the Storm So Long* (1979); (WARTIME) Louis S. Gerteis, *From Contraband to Freedman* (1973); William C. Harris, *With Charity for All* (1997); James L. Roark, *Masters without Slaves* (1977); Willie L. Rose, *Rehearsal for Reconstruction* (1964); (BLACKS) Paul Cimbala, *Under the Guardianship of the Nation* (1997); Edmund L. Drago, *Black Politicians and Reconstruction in Georgia* (1983); Barbara J. Fields, *Slavery and Freedom on the Middle Ground* (1985); Jacqueline Jones, *Soldiers of Light and Love* (1980); Claude F. Oubré, *Forty Acres and a Mule* (1978); Nell I. Painter, *Exodusters* (1976); Julie Saville, *The Work of Reconstruction* (1994); Donald Spivey, *Schooling for the New Slavery* (1978); Clarence E. Walker, *A Rock in a Weary Land* (1982); (POLITICS) Richard H. Abbott, *The Republican Party and the South* (1986); Michael L. Benedict, *The Impeachment and Trial of Andrew Johnson* (1973); Dan T. Carter, *When the War Was Over*

(1985); Richard N. Current, *Those Terrible Carpetbaggers* (1988); Steven Hahn, *The Roots of Southern Populism* (1983); William C. Harris, *The Day of the Carpetbagger* (1979); Thomas Holt, *Black over White* (1977); Peggy Lamson, *The Glorious Failure* (1973); William E. Nelson, *The Fourteenth Amendment* (1988); Edward Royce, *The Origins of Southern Sharecropping* (1993); Jonathan M. Wiener, *Social Origins of the New South* (1978); (REDEEMERS) Michael Perman, *The Road to Redemption* (1984); George C. Rable, *But There Was No Peace* (1984); Terry L. Seip, *The South Returns to Congress* (1983); Allen W. Trelease, *White Terror* (1971).

Appendix I

The Declaration
of Independence

IN CONGRESS, JULY 4, 1776. *The unanimous Declaration of the thirteen United States of America.*

When in the Course of human Events, it becomes necessary for one People to dissolve the Political Bands which have connected them with another, and to assume among the Powers of the Earth, the separate and equal Station to which the Laws of Nature and of Nature's God entitle them, a decent Respect to the Opinions of Mankind requires that they should declare the causes which impel them to the Separation.

We hold these Truths to be self-evident, that all Men are created equal, that they are endowed by their Creator with certain unalienable Rights, that among these are Life, Liberty and the Pursuit of Happiness—That to secure these Rights, Governments are instituted among Men, deriving their just Powers from the Consent of the Governed, that whenever any Form of Government becomes destructive of these Ends, it is the Right of the People to alter or to abolish it, and to institute new Government, laying its Foundation on such Principles, and organizing its Powers in such Form, as to them shall seem most likely to effect their Safety and Happiness. Prudence, indeed, will dictate that Governments long established should not be changed for light and transient Causes; and accordingly all Experience hath shewn, that Mankind are more disposed to suffer, while Evils are sufferable, than to right themselves by abolishing the Forms to which they are accustomed. But when a long Train of Abuses and Usurpations, pursuing invariably the same Object, evinces a Design to reduce them under absolute Despotism, it is their Right, it is their Duty, to throw off such Government, and to provide new Guards for their future Security. Such has been the patient Sufferance of these Colonies; and such is now the Necessity which constrains them to alter their former Systems of Government. The History of the present King of Great Britain is a History of repeated Injuries and Usurpations, all having in direct Object the Establishment of an absolute Tyranny over these States. To prove this, let Facts be submitted to a candid World.

He has refused his Assent to Laws, the most wholesome and necessary for the public Good.

A-1

He has forbidden his Governors to pass Laws of immediate and pressing Importance, unless suspended in their Operation till his Assent should be obtained; and when so suspended, he has utterly neglected to attend to them.

He has refused to pass other Laws for the Accommodation of large Districts of People, unless those People would relinquish the Right of Representation in the Legislature, a Right inestimable to them, and formidable to Tyrants only.

He has called together Legislative Bodies at Places unusual, uncomfortable, and distant from the Depository of their public Records, for the sole Purpose of fatiguing them into Compliance with his Measures.

He has dissolved Representative Houses repeatedly, for opposing with manly Firmness his Invasions on the Rights of the People.

He has refused for a long Time, after such Dissolutions, to cause others to be elected; whereby the Legislative Powers, incapable of the Annihilation, have returned to the People at large for their exercise; the State remaining in the mean time exposed to all the Dangers of Invasion from without, and Convulsions within.

He has endeavoured to prevent the Population of these States; for that Purpose obstructing the Laws for Naturalization of Foreigners; refusing to pass others to encourage their Migrations hither, and raising the Conditions of new Appropriations of Lands.

He has obstructed the Administration of Justice, by refusing his Assent to Laws for establishing Judiciary Powers.

He has made Judges dependent on his Will alone, for the Tenure of their Offices, and the Amount and Payment of their Salaries.

He has erected a Multitude of new Offices, and sent hither Swarms of Officers to harrass our People, and eat out their Substance.

He has kept among us, in Times of Peace, Standing Armies, without the consent of our Legislatures.

He has affected to render the Military independent of and superior to the Civil Power.

He has combined with others to subject us to a Jurisdiction foreign to our Constitution, and unacknowledged by our Laws; giving his Assent to their Acts of pretended Legislation:

For quartering large Bodies of Armed Troops among us;

For protecting them, by a mock Trial, from Punishment for any Murders which they should commit on the Inhabitants of these States:

For cutting off our Trade with all Parts of the World:

For imposing Taxes on us without our Consent:

For depriving us, in many Cases, of the Benefits of Trial by Jury:

For transporting us beyond Seas to be tried for pretended Offences:

For abolishing the free System of English Laws in a neighbouring Province, establishing therein an arbitrary Government, and enlarging its Boundaries, so as to render it at once an Example and fit Instrument for introducing the same absolute Rules into these Colonies:

For taking away our Charters, abolishing our most valuable Laws, and altering fundamentally the Forms of our Governments:

For suspending our own Legislatures, and declaring themselves invested with Power to legislate for us in all Cases whatsoever.

He has abdicated Government here, by declaring us out of his Protection and waging War against us.

He has plundered our Seas, ravaged our Coasts, burnt our Towns, and destroyed the Lives of our People.

He is, at this Time, transporting large Armies of foreign Mercenaries to compleat the Works of Death, Desolation, and Tyranny, already begun with circumstances of Cruelty and

Perfidy, scarcely paralleled in the most barbarous Ages, and totally unworthy the Head of a civilized Nation.

He has constrained our fellow Citizens taken Captive on the high Seas to bear Arms against their Country, to become the Executioners of their Friends and Brethren, or to fall themselves by their Hands.

He has excited domestic Insurrections amongst us, and has endeavoured to bring on the Inhabitants of our Frontiers, the merciless Indian Savages, whose known Rule of Warfare, is an undistinguished Destruction, of all Ages, Sexes and Conditions.

In every stage of these Oppressions we have Petitioned for Redress in the most humble Terms: Our repeated Petitions have been answered only by repeated Injury. A Prince, whose Character is thus marked by every act which may define a Tyrant, is unfit to be the Ruler of a free People.

Nor have we been wanting in Attentions to our British Brethren. We have warned them from Time to Time of Attempts by their Legislature to extend an unwarrantable Jurisdiction over us. We have reminded them of the Circumstances of our Emigration and Settlement here. We have appealed to their native Justice and Magnanimity, and we have conjured them by the Ties of our common Kindred to disavow these Usurpations, which, would inevitably interrupt our Connections and Correspondence. They too have been deaf to the Voice of Justice and of Consanguinity. We must, therefore, acquiesce in the Necessity, which denounces our Separation, and hold them, as we hold the rest of Mankind, Enemies in War, in Peace, Friends.

We, therefore, the Representatives of the UNITED STATES OF AMERICA, in GENERAL CONGRESS, Assembled, appealing to the Supreme Judge of the World for the Rectitude of our Intentions, do, in the Name, and by Authority of the good People of these Colonies, solemnly Publish and Declare, That these United Colonies are, and of Right ought to be, FREE AND INDEPENDENT STATES; that they are absolved from all Allegiance to the British Crown, and that all political Connection between them and the State of Great Britain, is and ought to be totally dissolved; and that as FREE AND INDEPENDENT STATES, they have full Power to levy War, conclude Peace, contract Alliances, establish Commerce, and to do all other Acts and Things which INDEPENDENT STATES may of right do. And for the support of this Declaration, with a firm Reliance on the Protection of divine Providence, we mutually pledge to each other our Lives, our Fortunes, and our sacred Honor.

John Hancock
(MASSACHUSETTS)

NEW HAMPSHIRE
Josiah Bartlett
William Whipple
Matthew Thornton

MASSACHUSETTS
Samuel Adams
John Adams
Robert Treat Paine
Elbridge Gerry

NORTH CAROLINA
William Hooper
Joseph Hewes
John Penn

MARYLAND
Samuel Chase
William Paca
Thomas Stone
Charles Carroll of Carrollton

PENNSYLVANIA
Robert Morris
Benjamin Rush
Benjamin Franklin
John Morton
George Clymer
James Smith
George Taylor
James Wilson
George Ross

DELAWARE
Caesar Rodney
George Read
Thomas McKean

NEW YORK
William Floyd
Philip Livingston
Frank Lewis
Lewis Morris

NEW JERSEY
Richard Stockton
John Witherspoon
Francis Hopkinson
John Hart
Abraham Clark

SOUTH CAROLINA
Edward Rutledge
Thomas Heyward, Jr.
Thomas Lynch, Jr.
Arthur Middleton

RHODE ISLAND
AND PROVIDENCE
Stephen Hopkins
William Ellery

CONNECTICUT
Roger Sherman
Samuel Huntington
William Williams
Oliver Wolcott

VIRGINIA
George Wythe
Richard Henry Lee
Thomas Jefferson
Benjamin Harrison
Thomas Nelson, Jr.
Francis Lightfoot Lee
Carter Braxton

GEORGIA
Button Gwinnett
Lyman Hall
George Walton

Appendix II

The Constitution of the United States of America

Adopted September 17, 1787
Effective March 4, 1789

WE THE PEOPLE OF THE UNITED STATES, in order to form a more perfect union, establish justice, insure domestic tranquility, provide for the common defense, promote the general welfare, and secure the blessings of liberty to ourselves and our posterity, do ordain and establish this Constitution for the United States of America.

ARTICLE I

Section 1. All legislative powers herein granted shall be vested in a Congress of the United States, which shall consist of a Senate and House of Representatives.

Section 2. 1. The House of Representatives shall be composed of members chosen every second year by the people of the several states, and the electors in each state shall have the qualifications requisite for electors of the most numerous branch of the state legislature.

2. No person shall be a representative who shall not have attained to the age of twenty-five years, and been seven years a citizen of the United States, and who shall not, when elected, be an inhabitant of that state in which he shall be chosen.

3. Representatives and direct taxes shall be apportioned among the several states which may be included within this union, according to their respective numbers, [*which shall be determined by adding to the whole number of free persons, including those bound to service for a term of years, and excluding Indians not taxed, three-fifths of all other persons.*]* The actual enumeration shall be made within three years after the first meeting of the Congress of the United States, and within every subsequent term of ten years, in such manner as they shall by law direct. The number of representatives shall not exceed one for every thirty thousand, but each state shall have at least one representative; *and until such enumeration shall be made, the state of New Hampshire shall be entitled to choose three, Massachusetts eight, Rhode Island and Providence Plantations one, Connecticut five, New York six, New Jersey four, Pennsylvania eight, Delaware one, Maryland six, Virginia ten, North Carolina five, South Carolina five, and Georgia three.*

---

*Changed by section 2 of the Fourteenth Amendment.

4. When vacancies happen in the representation from any state, the executive authority thereof shall issue writs of election to fill such vacancies.

5. The House of Representatives shall choose their speaker and other officers; and shall have the sole power of impeachment.

Section 3. 1. The Senate of the United States shall be composed of two senators from each state, [*chosen by the legislature thereof*]* for six years; and each senator shall have one vote.

2. Immediately after they shall be assembled in consequence of the first election, they shall be divided as equally as may be into three classes. The seats of the senators of the first class shall be vacated at the expiration of the second year, of the second class at the expiration of the fourth year, and of the third class at the expiration of the sixth year, so that one third may be chosen every second year; [*and if vacancies happen by resignation, or otherwise, during the recess of the legislature of any state, the executive thereof may make temporary appointments until the next meeting of the legislature, which shall then fill such vacancies.*]**

3. No person shall be a senator who shall not have attained to the age of thirty years, and been nine years a citizen of the United States, and who shall not, when elected, be an inhabitant of that state for which he shall be chosen.

4. The vice president of the United States shall be president of the Senate, but shall have no vote, unless they be equally divided.

5. The Senate shall choose their other officers, and also a president pro tempore, in the absence of the vice-president, or when he shall exercise the office of the president of the United States.

6. The Senate shall have the sole power to try all impeachments. When sitting for that purpose, they shall be on oath or affirmation. When the president of the United States is tried, the chief justice shall preside: and no person shall be convicted without the concurrence of two thirds of the members present.

7. Judgment in cases of impeachment shall not extend further than to removal from office, and disqualification to hold and enjoy any office of honor, trust or profit under the United States: but the party convicted shall nevertheless be liable and subject to indictment, trial, judgment and punishment, according to law.

Section 4. 1. The times, places, and manner of holding elections for senators and representatives, shall be prescribed in each state by the legislature thereof; but the Congress may at any time by law make or alter such regulations, except as to the place of choosing senators.

2. The Congress shall assemble at least once in every year, and such meeting shall be [*on the first Monday in December*],*** unless they shall by law appoint a different day.

Section 5. 1. Each House shall be the judge of the elections, returns and qualifications of its own members, and a majority of each shall constitute a quorum to do business; but a smaller number may adjourn from day to day, and may be authorized to compel the attendance of absent members, in such manner, and under such penalties as each House may provide.

2. Each House may determine the rules of its proceedings, punish its members for disorderly behavior, and, with the concurrence of two thirds, expel a member.

3. Each House shall keep a journal of its proceedings, and from time to time publish the same, excepting such parts as may in their judgment require secrecy; and the yeas and nays of the members of either House on any question shall, at the desire of one fifth of those present, be entered on the journal.

---

*Changed by the Seventeenth Amendment.
**Changed by section 2 of the Twentieth Amendment.
***Changed by the Sixteenth amendment.

4. Neither House, during the session of Congress, shall, without the consent of the other, adjourn for more than three days, nor to any other place than that in which the two Houses shall be sitting.

Section 6. 1. The senators and representatives shall receive a compensation for their services, to be ascertained by law, and paid out of the treasury of the United States. They shall in all cases, except treason, felony, and breach of the peace, be privileged from arrest during their attendance at the session of their respective Houses, and in going to and returning from the same; and for any speech or debate in either House, they shall not be questioned in any other place.

2. No senator or representative shall, during the time for which he was elected, be appointed to any civil office under the authority of the United States, which shall have been created, or the emoluments whereof shall have been increased during such time; and no person holding any office under the United States shall be a member of either House during his continuance in office.

Section 7. 1. All bills for raising revenue shall originate in the House of Representatives; but the Senate may propose or concur with amendments as on other bills.

2. Every bill which shall have passed the House of Representatives and the Senate, shall, before it becomes a law, be presented to the president of the United States; if he approve he shall sign it, but if not he shall return it, with his objections to that House in which it shall have originated, who shall enter the objections at large on their journal, and proceed to reconsider it. If after such reconsideration two thirds of that House shall agree to pass the bill, it shall be sent, together with the objections, to the other House, by which it shall likewise be reconsidered, and if approved by two thirds of that House, it shall become a law. But in all such cases the votes of both Houses shall be determined by yeas and nays, and the names of the persons voting for and against the bill shall be entered on the journal of each House respectively. If any bill shall not be returned by the president within ten days (Sundays excepted) after it shall have been presented to him, the same shall be a law, in like manner as if he had signed it, unless the Congress by their adjournment prevent its return, in which case it shall not be a law.

3. Every order, resolution, or vote to which the concurrence of the Senate and the House of Representatives may be necessary (except on a question of adjournment) shall be presented to the president of the United States; and before the same shall take effect, shall be approved by him, or being disapproved by him, shall be repassed by two thirds of the Senate and House of Representatives, according to the rules and limitations prescribed in the case of a bill.

Section 8. The Congress shall have power:

1. To lay and collect taxes, duties, imposts, and excises, to pay the debts and provide for the common defense and general welfare of the United States; but all duties, imposts, and excises shall be uniform throughout the United States;

2. To borrow money on the credit of the United States;

3. To regulate commerce with foreign nations, and among the several States, and with the Indian tribes;

4. To establish a uniform rule of naturalization, and uniform laws on the subject of bankruptcies throughout the United States;

5. To coin money, regulate the value thereof, and of foreign coin, and fix the standard of weights and measures;

6. To provide for the punishment of counterfeiting the securities and current coin of the United States;

7. To establish post offices and post roads;

8. To promote the progress of science and useful arts, by securing for limited times to authors and inventors the exclusive right to their respective writings and discoveries;

9. To constitute tribunals inferior to the Supreme Court;

10. To define and punish piracies and felonies committed on the high seas, and offenses against the law of nations;

11. To declare war, grant letters of marque and reprisal, and make rules concerning captures on land and water;

12. To raise and support armies, but no appropriation of money to that use shall be for a longer term than two years;

13. To provide and maintain a navy;

14. To make rules for the government and regulation of the land and naval forces;

15. To provide for calling forth the militia to execute the laws of the Union, suppress insurrections and repel invasions;

16. To provide for organizing, arming, and disciplining the militia, and for governing such part of them as may be employed in the service of the United States, reserving to the States respectively, the appointment of the officers, and the authority of training the militia according to the discipline prescribed by Congress;

17. To exercise exclusive legislation in all cases whatsoever, over such district (not exceeding ten miles square) as may, by cession of particular states, and the acceptance of Congress, become the seat of the government of the United States, and to exercise like authority over all places purchased by the consent of the legislature of the state in which the same shall be, for the erection of forts, magazines, arsenals, dockyards, and other needful buildings; and

18. To make all laws which shall be necessary and proper for carrying into execution the foregoing powers, and all other powers vested by this Constitution in the government of the United States, or in any department or officer thereof.

Section 9. 1. The migration or importation of such persons as any of the states now existing shall think proper to admit, shall not be prohibited by the Congress prior to the year one thousand eight hundred and eight, but a tax or duty may be imposed on such importation, not exceeding ten dollars for each person.

2. The privilege of the writ of haheas corpus shall not be suspended, unless when in cases of rebellion or invasion the public safety may require it.

3. No bill of attainder or ex post facto law shall be passed.

4. [*No capitation, or other direct, tax shall be laid, unless in proportion to the census or enumeration hereinbefore directed to be taken.*]*

5. No tax or duty shall be laid on articles exported from any State.

6. No preference shall be given by any regulation of commerce or revenue to the ports of one state over those of another: nor shall vessels bound to, or from, one state be obliged to enter, clear, or pay duties in another.

7. No money shall be drawn from the treasury, but in consequence of appropriations made by law; and a regular statement and account of the receipts and expenditures of all public money shall be published from time to time.

8. No title of nobility shall be granted by the United States: and no person holding any office of profit or trust under them, shall, without the consent of the Congress, accept of any present, emolument, office, or title, of any kind whatever, from any king, prince, or foreign state.

Section 10. 1. No state shall enter into any treaty, alliance, or confederation; grant letters of marque and reprisal; coin money; emit bills of credit; make anything but gold and silver coin a tender in payment of debts; pass any bill of attainder, ex post facto law, or law impairing the obligation of contracts, or grant any title of nobility.

2. No state shall, without the consent of the Congress, lay any imposts or duties on imports or exports, except what may be absolutely necessary for executing its inspection laws;

---

*Changed by the Sixteenth Amendment.

and the net produce of all duties and imposts laid by any state on imports or exports, shall be for the use of the treasury of the United States; and all such laws shall be subject to the revision and control of the Congress.

3. No state shall, without the consent of Congress, lay any duty of tonnage, keep troops, or ships of war in time of peace, enter into any agreement or compact with another state, or with a foreign power, or engage in war, unless actually invaded, or in such imminent danger as will not admit of delay.

ARTICLE II

Section 1. 1. The executive power shall be vested in a president of the United States of America. He shall hold his office during the term of four years, and, together with the vice president, chosen for the same term, be elected as follows:

2. Each state shall appoint, in such manner as the legislature thereof may direct, a number of electors, equal to the whole number of senators and representatives to which the state may be entitled in the Congress: but no senator or representative, or person holding an office of trust or profit under the United States, shall be appointed an elector.

3. [*The electors shall meet in their respective states, and vote by ballot for two persons, of whom one at least shall not be an inhabitant of the same state with themselves. And they shall make a list of all the persons voted for, and of the number of votes for each; which list they shall sign and certify, and transmit sealed to the seat of the government of the United States, directed to the president of the Senate. The president of the Senate shall, in the presence of the Senate and House of Representatives, open all the certificates, and the votes shall then be counted. The person having the greatest number of votes shall be the president, if such number be a majority of the whole number of electors appointed; and if there be more than one who have such majority, and have an equal number of votes, then the House of Representatives shall immediately choose by ballot one of them for president; and if no person have a majority, then from the five highest on the list the said House shall in like manner choose the president. But in choosing the president, the votes shall be taken by states, the representation from each state having one vote; a quorum for this purpose shall consist of a member or members from two thirds of the states, and a majority of all the states shall be necessary to a choice. In every case, after the choice of the president, the person having the greatest number of votes of the electors shall be the vice president. But if there should remain two or more who have equal votes, the Senate shall choose from them by ballot the vice president.*]*

3. The Congress may determine the time of choosing the electors, and the day on which they shall give their votes; which day shall be the same throughout the United States.

4. No person except a natural born citizen, or a citizen of the United States, at the time of the adoption of this Constitution, shall be eligible to the office of president; neither shall any person be eligible to that office who shall not have attained to the age of thirty-five years, and been fourteen years a resident within the United States.

5. [*In case of the removal of the president from office, or of his death, resignation, or inability to discharge the powers and duties of the said office, the same shall devolve on the vice president, and the Congress may by law provide for the case of removal, death, resignation, or inability, both of the president and vice president, declaring what officer shall then act as president, and such officer shall act accordingly, until the disability be removed, or a president shall be elected.*]**

6. The president shall, at stated times, receive for his services a compensation, which shall neither be increased nor diminished during the period for which he shall have been

---

*Changed by the Twelfth Amendment.
**Changed by the Twenty-fifth Amendment.

elected, and he shall not receive within that period any other emolument from the United States, or any of them.

7. Before he enter on the execution of his office, he shall take the following oath or affirmation:—"I do solemnly swear (or affirm) that I will faithfully execute the office of president of the United States, and will to the best of my ability, preserve, protect and defend the Constitution of the United States."

Section 2. 1. The president shall be commander in chief of the army and navy of the United States, and of the militia of the several states, when called into the actual service of the United States; he may require the opinion, in writing, of the principal officer in each of the executive departments, upon any subject relating to the duties of their respective offices, and he shall have power to grant reprieves and pardons for offenses against the United States, except in cases of impeachment.

2. He shall have power, by and with the advice and consent of the Senate, to make treaties, provided two thirds of the senators present concur; and he shall nominate, and by and with the advice and consent of the Senate, shall appoint ambassadors, other public ministers and consuls, judges of the Supreme Court, and all other officers of the United States, whose appointments are not herein otherwise provided for, and which shall be established by law: but the Congress may by law vest the appointment of such inferior officers, as they think proper, in the president alone, in the courts of law, or in the heads of departments.

3. The president shall have power to fill up all vacancies that may happen during the recess of the Senate, by granting commissions which shall expire at the end of their next session.

Section 3. He shall from time to time give to the Congress information of the state of the Union, and recommend to their consideration such measures as he shall judge necessary and expedient; he may, on extraordinary occasions, convene both Houses, or either of them, and in case of disagreement between them with respect to the time of adjournment, he may adjourn them to such time as he shall think proper; he shall receive ambassadors and other public ministers; he shall take care that the laws be faithfully executed, and shall commission all the officers of the United States.

Section 4. The president, vice president, and all civil officers of the United States, shall be removed from office on impeachment for, and conviction of, treason, bribery, or other high crimes and misdemeanors.

ARTICLE III

Section 1. The judicial power of the United States shall be vested in one Supreme Court, and in such inferior courts as the Congress may from time to time ordain and establish. The judges, both of the Supreme and inferior courts, shall hold their offices during good behavior, and shall, at stated times, receive for their services, a compensation, which shall not be diminished during their continuance in office.

Section 2. 1. The judicial power shall extend to all cases, in law and equity, arising under this Constitution, the laws of the United States, and treaties made, or which shall be made, under their authority;—to all cases affecting ambassadors, other public ministers and consuls;—to all cases of admiralty and maritime jurisdiction;—to controversies to which the United States shall be a party;—to controversies between two or more states; [*between a state and citizens of another state;*—]* between citizens of different states;—between citizens of the same state claiming lands under grants of different states, and between a state, or the citizens thereof, and foreign states, citizens, or subjects.

---

*Changed by the Eleventh Amendment.

2. In all cases affecting ambassadors, other public ministers and consuls, and those in which a state shall be party, the Supreme Court shall have original jurisdiction. In all the other cases before mentioned, the Supreme Court shall have appellate jurisdiction, both as to law and to fact, with such exceptions, and under such regulations as the Congress shall make.

3. The trial of all crimes, except in cases of impeachment, shall be by jury; and such trial shall be held in the state where the said crimes shall have been committed; but when not committed within any state, the trial shall be at such place or places as the Congress may by law have directed.

Section 3. 1. Treason against the United States shall consist only in levying war against them, or in adhering to their enemies, giving them aid and comfort. No person shall be convicted of treason unless on the testimony of two witnesses to the same overt act, or on confession in open court.

2. The Congress shall have power to declare the punishment of treason, but no attainder of treason shall work corruption of blood, or forfeiture except during the life of the person attainted.

ARTICLE IV

Section 1. Full faith and credit shall be given in each state to the public acts, records, and judicial proceedings of every other state. And the Congress may by general laws prescribe the manner in which such acts, records and proceedings shall be proved, and the effect thereof.

Section 2. 1. The citizens of each state shall be entitled to all privileges and immunities of citizens in the several states.*

2. A person charged in any state with treason, felony, or other crime, who shall flee from justice, and be found in another state, shall on demand of the executive authority of the state from which he fled, be delivered up, to be removed to the state having jurisdiction of the crime.

3. [*No person held to service or labor in one state under the laws thereof, escaping into another, shall in consequence of any law or regulation therein, be discharged from such service or labor, but shall be delivered up on claim of the party to whom such service or labor may be due.*]**

Section 3. 1. New states may be admitted by the Congress into this Union; but no new state shall be formed or erected within the jurisdiction of any other state, nor any state be formed by the junction of two or more states, or parts of states, without the consent of the legislatures of the states concerned as well as of the Congress.

2. The Congress shall have power to dispose of and make all needful rules and regulations respecting the territory or other property belonging to the United States; and nothing in this Constitution shall be so construed as to prejudice any claims of the United States, or of any particular state.

Section 4. The United States shall guarantee to every state in this Union a republican form of government, and shall protect each of them against invasion; and on application of the legislature, or of the executive (when the legislature cannot be convened) against domestic violence.

ARTICLE V

The Congress, whenever two thirds of both Houses shall deem it necessary, shall propose amendments to this Constitution, or, on the application of the legislatures of two

---

*See the Fourteenth Amendment, section 1.
**Changed by the Thirteenth Amendment.

thirds of the several states, shall call a convention for proposing amendments, which in either case, shall be valid to all intents and purposes, as part of this Constitution when ratified by the legislatures of three fourths of the several states, or by conventions in three fourths thereof, as the one or the other mode of ratification may be proposed by the Congress: Provided that no amendment which may be made prior to the year one thousand eight hundred and eight shall in any manner affect the first and fourth clauses in the ninth section of the first article; and that no state, without its consent, shall be deprived of its equal suffrage in the Senate.

ARTICLE VI

1. All debts contracted and engagements entered into, before the adoption of this Constitution, shall be as valid against the United States under this Constitution, as under the Confederation.*

2. This Constitution, and the laws of the United States which shall be made in pursuance thereof; and all treaties made, or which shall be made, under the authority of the United States, shall be the supreme law of the land; and the Judges in every state shall be bound thereby, anything in the Constitution or laws of any state to the contrary notwithstanding.

3. The senators and representatives before mentioned, and the members of the several state legislatures, and all executive and judicial officers, both of the United States and of the several states, shall be bound by oath or affirmation to support this Constitution; but no religious test shall ever be required as a qualification to any office or public trust under the United States.

ARTICLE VII

The ratification of the conventions of nine states shall be sufficient for the establishment of this Constitution between the states so ratifying the same.

Done in Convention by the unanimous consent of the States present the seventeenth day of September in the year of our Lord one thousand seven hundred and eighty-seven, and of the independence of the United States of America the twelfth. In witness whereof we have hereunto subscribed our names.

George Washington
President and deputy from
VIRGINIA

Attest: *William Jackson*, Secretary

---

*See the Fourteenth Amendment, section 4.

DELAWARE
Geo. Read
Gunning Bedford, jun
John Dickinson
Richard Bassett
Jaco: Broom

MARYLAND
James McHenry
Dan: of St Thos Jenifer
Danl Carroll

VIRGINIA
John Blair
James Madison Jr.

NORTH CAROLINA
Wm Blount
Richd Dobbs Spaight
Hu Williamson

SOUTH CAROLINA
J. Rutledge
Charles Cotesworth Pinckney
Charles Pinckney
Pierce Butler

GEORGIA
William Few
Abr Baldwin

NEW HAMSPHIRE
John Langdon
Nicholas Gilman

MASSACHUSETTS
Nathaniel Gorham
Rufus King

CONNECTICUT
Wm Saml Johnson
Roger Sherman

NEW YORK
Alexander Hamilton

NEW JERSEY
Wil. Livingston
David Brearley
Wm Paterson
Jona: Dayton

PENNSYLVANIA
B Franklin
Thomas Mifflin
Robt. Morris
Geo. Clymer
Thos. FitzSimons
Jared Ingersoll
James Wilson
Gouv Morris

AMENDMENTS

First Ten Amendments proposed by Congress September 25, 1789.
Ratified by three-fourths of the States December 15, 1791.

AMENDMENT I

Congress shall make no law respecting an establishment of religion, or prohibiting the free exercise thereof; or abridging the freedom of speech, or of the press; or the right of the people peaceably to assemble, and to petition the government for a redress of grievances.

AMENDMENT II

A well regulated militia, being necessary to the security of a free state, the right of the people to keep and bear arms, shall not be infringed.

AMENDMENT III

No soldier shall, in time of peace, be quartered in any house, without the consent of the owner, nor in time of war, but in a manner to be prescribed by law.

AMENDMENT IV

The right of the people to be secure in their persons, houses, papers, and effects, against unreasonable searches and seizures, shall not be violated, and no warrants shall issue, but upon probable cause, supported by oath or affirmation, and particularly describing the place to be searched, and the persons or things to be seized.

AMENDMENT V

No person shall be held to answer for a capital, or otherwise infamous crime, unless on a presentment or indictment of a grand jury, except in cases arising in the land or naval forces, or in the militia, when in actual service in time of war or public danger; nor shall any person be subject for the same offense to be twice put in jeopardy of life or limb; nor shall be compelled in any criminal case to be a witness against himself, nor be deprived of life, liberty, or property, without due process of law, nor shall private property be taken for public use without just compensation.

AMENDMENT VI

In all criminal prosecutions, the accused shall enjoy the right to a speedy and public trial, by an impartial jury of the state and district wherein the crime shall have been committed, which district shall have been previously ascertained by law, and to be informed of the nature and cause of the accusation; to be confronted with the witnesses against him; to have compulsory process for obtaining witnesses in his favor, and to have the assistance of counsel for his defense.

AMENDMENT VII

In suits at common law, where the value in controversy shall exceed twenty dollars, the right of trail by jury shall be preserved, and no fact tried by a jury shall be otherwise reexamined in any court of the United States, than according to the rules of the common law.

AMENDMENT VIII

Excessive bail shall not be required, nor excessive fines imposed, nor cruel and unusual punishments inflicted.

AMENDMENT IX

The enumeration in the Constitution of certain rights shall not be construed to deny or disparage others retained by the people.

AMENDMENT X

The powers not delegated to the United States by the Constitution, nor prohibited by it to the states, are reserved to the states respectively, or to the people.

AMENDMENT XI

Proposed by Congress March 5, 1794. Ratified January 8, 1798.

The judicial power of the United States shall not be construed to extend to any suit in law or equity, commenced or prosecuted against one of the United States by citizens of another state, or by citizens or subjects of any foreign state.

ARTICLE XII

Proposed by Congress December 12, 1803. Ratified September 25, 1804.

The electors shall meet in their respective states, and vote by ballot for president and vice president, one of whom, at least, shall not be an inhabitant of the same state with themselves; they shall name in their ballots the person voted for as president, and in distinct ballots, the person voted for as vice president, and they shall make distinct lists of all persons voted for as president and of all persons voted for as vice president, and of the number of votes for each, which lists they shall sign and certify, and transmit sealed to the seat of the government of the United States, directed to the president of the Senate;—The president of the Senate shall, in presence of the Senate and House of Representatives, open all the certificates and the votes shall then be counted;—The person having the greatest number of votes for president, shall be the president, if such number be a majority of the whole number of electors appointed; and if no person have such majority, then from the persons having the highest numbers not exceeding three on the list of those voted for as president, the House of Representatives shall choose immediately, by ballot, the president. But in choosing the president, the votes shall be taken by states, the representation from each state having one vote; a quorum for this purpose shall consist of a member or members from two-thirds of the states, and a majority of all the states shall be necessary to a choice. [*And if the House of Representatives shall not choose a president whenever the right of choice shall devolve upon them, before the fourth day of March next following, then the vice president shall act as president, as in the case of the death or other constitutional disability of the president.*]* The person having the greatest number of votes as vice president shall be the vice president, if such number be a majority of the whole number of electors appointed, and if no person have a majority, then from the two highest numbers on the list, the Senate shall choose the vice president; a quorum for the purpose shall consist of two-thirds of the whole number of Senators, and a majority of the whole number shall be necessary to a choice. But no person constitutionally ineligible to the office of president shall be eligible to that of vice president of the United States.

AMENDMENT XIII
Proposed by Congress February 1, 1865. Ratified December 18, 1865.

Section 1. Neither slavery nor involuntary servitude, except as punishment for crime whereof the party shall have been duly convicted, shall exist within the United States, or any place subject to their jurisdiction.

Section 2. Congress shall have power to enforce this article by appropriate legislation.

AMENDMENT XIV
Proposed by Congress June 16, 1866. Ratified July 23, 1868.

Section 1. All persons born or naturalized in the United States, and subject to the jurisdiction thereof, are citizens of the United States and of the state wherein they reside. No state shall make or enforce any law which shall abridge the privileges or immunities of citizens of the United States; nor shall any state deprive any person of life, liberty, or property, without due process of law; nor deny to any person within its jurisdiction the equal protection of the laws.

Section 2. Representatives shall be apportioned among the several States according to their respective numbers, counting the whole number of persons in each state, excluding Indians not taxed. But when the right to vote at any election for the choice of electors for president and vice president of the United States, representatives in Congress, the executive and judicial officers of a state, or the members of the legislature thereof, is denied to any of the male inhabitants of such state, being twenty-one years of age, and citizens of the United States, or in any way abridged, except for participation in rebellion, or other crime, the basis of representation therein shall be reduced in the proportion which the number of such male citizens shall bear to the whole number of male citizens twenty-one years of age in such state.

Section 3. No person shall be a senator or representative in Congress, or elector of president and vice president, or hold any office, civil or military, under the United States, or under any state, who, having previously taken an oath, as a member of Congress, or as an officer of the United States, or as a member of any state legislature, or as an executive or

---

*Superseded by section 3 of the Twentieth Amendment.

judicial officer of any state, to support the Constitution of the United States, shall have engaged in insurrection or rebellion against the same, or given aid or comfort to the enemies thereof. But Congress may by a vote of two-thirds of each House, remove such disability.

Section 4. The validity of the public debt of the United States, authorized by law, including debts incurred for payment of pensions and bounties for services in suppressing insurrection or rebellion, shall not be questioned. But neither the United States nor any state shall assume or pay any debt or obligation incurred in aid of insurrection or rebellion against the United States, or any claim for the loss or emancipation of any slave; but all such debts, obligations, and claims shall be held illegal and void.

Section 5. The Congress shall have power to enforce, by appropriate legislation, the provisions of this article.

AMENDMENT XV

Proposed by Congress February 27, 1869. Ratified March 30, 1870.

Section 1. The right of citizens of the United States to vote shall not be denied or abridged by the United States or by any state on account of race, color, or previous condition of servitude.

Section 2. The Congress shall have power to enforce this article by appropriate legislation.

AMENDMENT XVI

Proposed by Congress July 12, 1909. Ratified February 25, 1913.

The Congress shall have power to lay and collect taxes on incomes, from whatever source derived, without apportionment among the several states, and without regard to any census or enumeration.

AMENDMENT XVII

Proposed by Congress May 16, 1912. Ratified May 31, 1913.

The Senate of the United States shall be composed of two senators from each state, elected by the people thereof, for six years; and each senator shall have one vote. The electors in each state shall have the qualifications requisite for electors of the most numerous branch of the state legislature.

When vacancies happen in the representation of any state in the Senate, the executive authority of such state shall issue writs of election to fill such vacancies: Provided, That the legislature of any state may empower the executive thereof to make temporary appointments until the people fill the vacancies by election as the legislature may direct.

This amendment shall not be so construed as to affect the election or term of any senator chosen before it becomes valid as part of the Constitution.

AMENDMENT XVIII

Proposed by Congress December 17, 1917. Ratified January 29, 1919.

Section 1. [*After one year from the ratification of this article, the manufacture, sale, or transportation of intoxicating liquors within, the importation thereof into, or the exportation thereof from the United States and all territory subject to the jurisdiction thereof for beverage purposes is hereby prohibited.*]

Section 2. [*The Congress and the several states shall have concurrent power to enforce this article by appropriate legislation.*]

Section 3. [*This article shall be inoperative unless it shall have been ratified as an amendment to the Constitution by the legislatures of the several states, as provided in the Constitution, within seven years from the date of the submission hereof to the states by Congress.*]*

AMENDMENT XIX

Proposed by Congress June 5, 1919. Ratified August 26, 1920.

The right of citizens of the United States to vote shall not be denied or abridged by the United States or by any state on account of sex.

The Congress shall have power to enforce the provisions of this article by appropriate legislation.

AMENDMENT XX

Proposed by Congress March 3, 1932. Ratified January 23, 1933.

Section 1. The terms of the president and vice president shall end at noon on the 20th day of January, and the terms of Senators and Representatives at noon on the 3d day of January, of the years in which such terms would have ended if this article had not been ratified; and the terms of their successors shall then begin.

Section 2. The Congress shall assemble at least once in every year, and such meeting shall begin at noon on the 3d day of January, unless they shall by law appoint a different day.

Section 3. If, at the time fixed for the beginning of the term of the president, the president-elect shall have died, the vice president-elect shall become president. If a president shall not have been chosen before the time fixed for the beginning of his term, or if the president-elect shall have failed to qualify, then the vice president-elect shall act as president until a president shall have qualified; and the Congress may by law provide for the case wherein neither a president-elect nor a vice president-elect shall have qualified, declaring who shall then act as president, or the manner in which one who is to act shall be selected, and such person shall act accordingly until a president or vice president shall have qualified.

Section 4. The Congress may by law provide for the case of the death of any of the persons from whom the House of Representatives may choose a president whenever the right of choice shall have devolved upon them, and for the case of the death of any of the persons from whom the Senate may choose a vice president whenever the right of choice shall have devolved upon them.

Section 5. Sections 1 and 2 shall take effect on the 15th day of October following the ratification of this article.

Section 6. This article shall be inoperative unless it shall have been ratified as an amendment to the Constitution by the legislatures of three-fourths of the several states within seven years from the date of its submission.

AMENDMENT XXI

Proposed by Congress February 20, 1933. Ratified December 5, 1933.

Section 1. The Eighteenth Article of amendment to the Constitution of the United States is hereby repealed.

Section 2. The transportation or importation into any state, territory, or possession of the United States for delivery or use therein of intoxicating liquors in violation of the laws thereof, is hereby prohibited.

---

*Repealed by the Twenty-first Amendment.

Section 3. This article shall be inoperative unless it shall have been ratified as an amendment to the Constitution by conventions in the several states, as provided in the Constitution, within seven years from the date of the submission thereof to the states by the Congress.

AMENDMENT XXII

Proposed by Congress March 24, 1947. Ratified February 26, 1951.

Section 1. No person shall be elected to the office of the president more than twice, and no person who has held the office of president, or acted as president, for more than two years of a term to which some other person was elected president shall be elected to the office of the president more than once. But this article shall not apply to any person holding the office of president when this article was proposed by the Congress, and shall not prevent any person who may be holding the office of president, or acting as president, during the term within which this article becomes operative from holding the office of president or acting as president during the remainder of such term.

Section 2. This article shall be inoperative unless it shall have been ratified as an amendment to the Constitution by the legislatures of three-fourths of the several states within seven years from the date of its submission to the states by the Congress.

AMENDMENT XXIII

Proposed by Congress June 16, 1960. Ratified March 29, 1961.

Section 1. The district constituting the seat of government of the United States shall appoint in such manner as the Congress may direct:

A number of electors of president and vice president equal to the whole number of Senators and Representatives in Congress to which the district would be entitled if it were a state, but in no event more than the least populous state; they shall be in addition to those appointed by the states, but they shall be considered, for the purposes of election of president and vice president, to be electors appointed by a state; and they shall meet in the district and perform such duties as provided by the twelfth article of amendment.

Section 2. The Congress shall have the power to enforce this article by appropriate legislation.

AMENDMENT XXIV

Proposed by Congress August 27, 1962. Ratified January 23, 1964.

Section 1. The right of citizens of the United States to vote in any primary or other election for president or vice president, for electors for president or vice president, or for Senator or Representative in Congress, shall not be denied or abridged by the United States or any state by failure to pay any poll tax or other tax.

Section 2. The Congress shall have the power to enforce this article by appropriate legislation.

AMENDMENT XXV

Proposed by Congress July 6, 1965. Ratified Febuary 10, 1967.

Section 1. In case of the removal of the president from office or of his death or resignation, the vice president shall become president.

Section 2. Whenever there is a vacancy in the office of the vice president, the president shall nominate a vice president who shall take office upon confirmation by a majority vote of both Houses of Congress.

Section 3. Whenever the president transmits to the president pro tempore of the Senate and the Speaker of the House of Representatives his written declaration that he is unable to discharge the powers and duties of his office, and until he transmits to them a written declaration to the contrary, such powers and duties shall be discharged by the vice president as acting president.

Section 4. Whenever the vice president and a majority of either the principal officers of the executive departments or of such other body as Congress may by law provide, transmit to the president pro tempore of the Senate and the Speaker of the House of Representatives their written declaration that the president is unable to discharge the powers and duties of his office, the vice president shall immediately assume the powers and duties of the office as acting president.

Thereafter, when the president transmits to the president pro tempore of the Senate and the Speaker of the House of Representatives his written declaration that no inability exists, he shall resume the powers and duties of his office unless the vice president and a majority of either the principal officers of the executive department or of such other body as Congress may by law provide, transmit within four days to the president pro tempore of the Senate and the Speaker of the House of Representatives their written declaration that the president is unable to discharge the powers and duties of his office. Thereupon Congress shall decide the issue, assembling within forty-eight hours for that purpose if not in session. If the Congress, within twenty-one days after receipt of the latter written declaration, or, if Congress is not in session, within twenty-one days after Congress is required to assemble, determines by two-thirds vote of both Houses that the president is unable to discharge the powers and duties of his office, the vice president shall continue to discharge the same as acting president; otherwise, the president shall resume the powers and duties of his office.

AMENDMENT XXVI

Proposed by Congress March 23, 1971. Ratified June 30, 1971.

Section 1. The right of citizens of the United States, who are eighteen years of age or older, to vote shall not be denied or abridged by the United States or by any state on account of age.

Section 2. The Congress shall have power to enforce this article by appropriate legislation.

AMENDMENT XXVII

Proposed by Congress September 25, 1789. Ratified May 8, 1992.

No law, varying the compensation for the services of the Senators and Representatives, shall take effect, until an election of Representatives shall have intervened.

Appendix III

U.S. Population Characteristics

U.S. Population Characteristics for Selected Years (in Thousands)

	1790	1840	1890	1940	2000
White	3,172	14,196	55,101	118,215	211,461
Black	757	2,874	7,489	12,866	34,658
(slave)	(698)	(2,487)			
Asian	NA	NA	NA	204	10,243
Amerindian	NA	NA	NA	334	2,476
Other Minorities*	—	—	358	589	22,584
(Hispanic)**	—	—	NA	NA	(35,306)
Urban***	202	1,845	22,106	74,424	NA
Women	NA	8,381	30,711	65,608	143,368
Median Age	NA	17.8	22.0	29.0	35.3
Total	3,929	17,069	62,980	132,165	281,422

*Definitions varied in different census years; in 2000 includes persons who were of more than one race.
**Hispanics may be of any race.
***Defined as living in a place with 2,500 inhabitants.

Appendix IV

Population for Selected Large Cities

Population for Selected Large Cities for Selected Years (in Thousands)	1800	1850	1900	1950*	2000*
New York	60	696	3,437	12,912	21,200
Los Angeles	—	2	102	4,152	16,374
Chicago	—	30	1,699	5,586	9,158
San Francisco	—	35	343	2,136	7,039
Philadelphia	70	409	1,294	3,671	6,188
Boston	25	137	561	2,411	5,819
Detroit	—	21	286	3,016	5,456
**Dallas	—	—	43	744	5,222
**Washington	3	40	279	1,464	4,923
**Houston	—	2	45	807	4,670
**St. Louis	NA	78	575	1,755	2,604
**Baltimore	27	169	509	1,405	2,553
Cincinnati	1	115	326	1,023	1,979
**New Orleans	NA	116	287	712	1,338

*Metropolitan area population.
**City with slavery before the Civil War.

Appendix V

Presidential Elections

Year	Candidates	Party	Electoral Vote	Popular Vote (in Thousands)
1788	**George Washington**	Federalist	69	—
1792	**George Washington**	Federalist	132	—
1796	**John Adams**	Federalist	71	—
	Thomas Jefferson	Democrat	68	—
1800	**Thomas Jefferson**	Democrat	73*	—
	Aaron Burr	Democrat	73	—
	John Adams	Federalist	65	—
	Charles Pinckney	Federalist	64	—
	John Jay	Federalist	1	—
1804	**Thomas Jefferson**	Democrat	162	—
	Charles Pinckney	Federalist	14	—
1808	**James Madison**	Democrat	122	—
	Charles Pinckney	Federalist	47	—
	George Clinton	Democrat	6	—
1812	**James Madison**	Democrat	128	—
	DeWitt Clinton	Federalist	89	—
1816	**James Monroe**	Democrat	183	—
	Rufus King	Federalist	34	—
1820	**James Monroe**	Democrat	231	—
	John Quincy Adams	Democrat	1	—
1824	**John Quincy Adams**	Democrat	84**	114
	Andrew Jackson	Democrat	99	153
	William H. Crawford	Democrat	41	47
	Henry Clay	Democrat	37	47
1828	**Andrew Jackson**	Democrat	178	647
	John Quincy Adams	Natl. Repub.	83	508

Year	Candidates	Party	Electoral Vote	Popular Vote (in Thousands)
1832	**Andrew Jackson**	Democrat	219	702
	Henry Clay	Natl. Repub.	49	484
	William Wirt	Antimason	7	101
	John Floyd	Democrat	11	
1836	**Martin Van Buren**	Democrat	170	764
	William H. Harrison	Whig	73	
	Hugh L. White	Whig	26	738
	Daniel Webster	Whig	14	
	Willie P. Mangum	Whig	11	
1840	**William H. Harrison**	Whig	234	1,275
	Martin Van Buren	Democrat	60	1,129
1841	**John Tyler***	Ind. Democrat	—	—
1844	**James K. Polk**	Democrat	170	1,339
	Henry Clay	Whig	105	1,300
	James G. Birney	Liberty	—	62
1848	**Zachary Taylor**	Whig	163	1,361
	Lewis Cass	Democrat	127	1,223
	Martin Van Buren	Free Soil	—	292
1850	**Millard Fillmore***	Whig	—	—
1852	**Franklin Pierce**	Democrat	254	1,608
	Winfield Scott	Whig	42	1,387
	John P. Hale	Free Soil	—	155
1856	**James Buchanan**	Democrat	174	1,836
	John Frémont	Republican	114	1,342
	Millard Fillmore	American	8	873
1860	**Abraham Lincoln**	Republican	180	1,866
	Stephen A. Douglas	N. Democrat	12	1,380
	John Breckinridge	S. Democrat	72	848
	John Bell	Const. Union	39	591
1864	**Abraham Lincoln**	Republican	212	2,218
	George McClellan	Democrat	21	1,813
1865	**Andrew Johnson***	Union Democrat	—	—
1868	**U. S. Grant**	Republican	214	3,014
	Horatio Seymour	Democrat	80	2,709
1872	**U. S. Grant**	Republican	286	3,598
	Horace Greeley	Democrat	66	2,835
1876	**Rutherford B. Hayes**	Republican	185	4,034
	Samuel J. Tilden	Democrat	184	4,289
1880	**James A. Garfield**	Republican	214	4,454
	Winfield Hancock	Democrat	155	4,445
1881	Chester A. Arthur***	Republican	—	—
1884	**Grover Cleveland**	Democrat	219	4,875
	James Blaine	Republican	182	4,852

Year	Candidates	Party	Electoral Vote	Popular Vote (in Thousands)
1888	**Benjamin Harrison**	Republican	233	5,440
	Grover Cleveland	Democrat	168	5,540
1892	**Grover Cleveland**	Democrat	277	5,557
	Benjamin Harrison	Republican	145	5,176
	James B. Weaver	Populist	22	1,041
1896	**William McKinley**	Republican	271	7,112
	William J. Bryan	Democrat	176	6,509
1900	**William McKinley**	Republican	292	7,220
	William J. Bryan	Democrat	155	6,358
1901	**Theodore Roosevelt***	Republican	—	—
1904	**Theodore Roosevelt**	Republican	336	7,629
	Alton Parker	Democrat	140	5,084
1908	**William H. Taft**	Republican	321	7,679
	William J. Bryan	Democrat	162	6,409
1912	**Woodrow Wilson**	Democrat	435	6,293
	Theodore Roosevelt	Progressive	88	4,119
	William H. Taft	Republican	8	3,486
	Eugene V. Debs	Socialist	—	900
1916	**Woodrow Wilson**	Democrat	277	9,130
	Charles E. Hughes	Republican	254	8,538
1920	**Warren G. Harding**	Republican	404	16,153
	James M. Cox	Democrat	127	9,133
1923	**Calvin Coolidge***	Republican	—	—
1924	**Calvin Coolidge**	Republican	382	15,720
	John W. Davis	Democrat	136	8,387
	Robert La Follette	Progressive	13	4,833
1928	**Herbert Hoover**	Republican	444	21,437
	Alfred E. Smith	Democrat	87	15,007
1932	**Franklin Roosevelt**	Democrat	472	22,830
	Herbert Hoover	Republican	59	15,761
1936	**Franklin Roosevelt**	Democrat	523	27,757
	Alfred Landon	Republican	8	16,680
1940	**Franklin Roosevelt**	Democrat	449	27,313
	Wendell Willkie	Republican	82	22,348
1944	**Franklin Roosevelt**	Democrat	432	25,613
	Thomas E. Dewey	Republican	99	22,018
1945	**Harry Truman***	Democrat	—	—
1948	**Harry Truman**	Democrat	303	24,179
	Thomas E. Dewey	Republican	189	21,991
	Strom Thurmond	States Rights	39	1,176
	Henry Wallace	Progressive	—	1,157
1952	**Dwight Eisenhower**	Republican	442	33,936
	Adlai Stevenson	Democrat	89	27,315
1956	**Dwight Eisenhower**	Republican	457	35,590
	Adlai Stevenson	Democrat	73****	26,023

Year	Candidates	Party	Electoral Vote	Popular Vote (in Thousands)
1960	**John F. Kennedy**	Democrat	303	34,227
	Richard Nixon	Republican	219	34,108
	Richard Byrd	Independent	15	286
1963	**Lyndon B. Johnson*****	Democrat	—	—
1964	**Lyndon B. Johnson**	Democrat	486	43,130
	Barry Goldwater	Republican	52	27,178
1968	**Richard Nixon**	Republican	301	31,785
	Hubert Humphrey	Democrat	191	31,275
	George Wallace	American Ind.	46	9,906
1972	**Richard Nixon**	Republican	520	47,170
	George McGovern	Democrat	17	29,170
1974	**Gerald Ford*****	Republican	—	—
1976	**Jimmy Carter**	Democrat	297	40,831
	Gerald Ford	Republican	40****	39,148
1980	**Ronald Reagan**	Republican	489	43,904
	Jimmy Carter	Democrat	49	35,484
	John Anderson	Independent	—	5,720
1984	**Ronald Reagan**	Republican	525	54,455
	Walter Mondale	Democrat	13	37,527
1988	**George H. W. Bush**	Republican	426	48,881
	Michael Dukakis	Democrat	112	41,805
1992	**William J. Clinton**	Democrat	370	44,908
	George H. W. Bush	Republican	168	39,102
	Ross Perot	Independent	—	19,217
1996	**William J. Clinton**	Democrat	379	47,401
	Robert Dole	Republican	159	39,197
	Ross Perot	Reform	—	8,085
2000	**George W. Bush**	Republican	271	50,459
	Albert Gore	Democrat	266****	51,004
	Ralph Nader	Green	—	2,834

Winners in bold.
*Jefferson and Burr tied in electoral votes, and the House of Representatives elected Jefferson.
**No candidate had an electoral majority, and the House of Representatives elected Adams.
***Vice presidents who succeeded to the presidency.
****In these elections one elector strayed from a pledged vote.

Appendix VI

Chronology

B.C.	38,000	Ice Age land bridge migration from Asia
	6000	Central Americans raise corn and beans
A.D.	300–900	Mayan civilization
	700–1600	Southeastern mound builders
ca.	1000–1010	Vikings in Vinland
	1300–1500	Aztec civilization
	1492	Columbus sails to America
	1534–1542	Cartier in Canada
	1539–1542	DeSoto in Southeast
	1585–1590	Roanoke colony
	1607	Virginia founded
	1618	Virginia headright system
	1619	First slaves in Virginia
		Virginia House of Burgesses
	1620	Pilgrims go to Plymouth
	1624	Dutch found New Netherland
	1629	Dutch patroon plan
	1630–1642	Puritan migration to Massachusetts
	1632	Maryland chartered to Lord Baltimore
	1636	Roger Williams flees to Rhode Island
		Thomas Hooker founds Connecticut
	1638	Massachusetts banishes Anne Hutchinson
	1649	Maryland Toleration Act
	1651–1696	English Navigation Acts
	1663	Carolina chartered to eight lord proprietors
	1664	English capture New Netherland (renamed New York)
		New Jersey split from New York
	1675–1676	Bacon's Rebellion in Virginia
		King Philip's War in New England
	1676	New Jersey split into East and West Jersey (reunited in 1702)
	1682	William Penn founds Pennsylvania

1686–1689	Dominion of New England
1689	Leisler's Rebellion in New York
1692	Salem Village witchcraft trials
1704	Delaware split from Pennsylvania
1729	North Carolina split from South Carolina
1732	Gen. James Oglethorpe founds Georgia
1733	John Peter Zenger wins libel trial
1741–1742	Jonathan Edwards leads Great Awakening
1754–1763	French and Indian War
1764	Sugar Act
1765	Stamp Act
1767	Townshend Acts
	Tryon's Palace built
1771	North Carolina Regulators
1773	Tea Act
1774	Coercive Acts
	Shakers arrive
1775	Battles of Lexington, Concord, and Bunker Hill
1776	Declaration of Independence
1777	Battle of Saratoga
1780–1846	North abolishes slavery
1781	Cornwallis surrenders at Yorktown
1781–1789	Articles of Confederation
1783	Peace treaty grants independence
1785	Land ordinance
1786	Shay's Rebellion in Massachusetts
1787	Northwest Ordinance
	Constitutional Convention (ratified 1788)

1789–1797	George Washington's presidency
1789	Bill of Rights
1790s	Second Great Awakening begins
1790	Assumption of war debts
	Slater's spinning mill founded
1791	Bank of the United States chartered
1793	Citizen Genêt
	Whitney's cotton gin invented
1794	Whiskey Rebellion in Pennsylvania
1795	Treaties with Britain, Indians, and Spain
1796	Washington's Farewell Address

1797–1801	John Adams's presidency
1797	XYZ Affair
1798	Alien and Sedition Acts
	Kentucky and Virginia Resolutions
1798–1800	Quasi-War with France

1801–1809	Thomas Jefferson's presidency
1803	*Marbury v. Madison*
	Louisiana Purchase

1804–1806	Lewis and Clark expedition
1807	Fulton's steamboat invented
1808	Embargo of foreign trade
	Congress abolishes slave trade
1809–1817	James Madison's presidency
1810	Macon's Bill No. 2
1811	Bank of the United States expires
1812–1815	War of 1812
1813	Waltham weaving mill founded
1816	Second Bank of the United States chartered
	African Methodist Episcopal Church founded
1817–1825	James Monroe's presidency
1817	American Colonization Society founded
1819	*Dartmouth College Case*
	McCulloch v. Maryland
1820s	Americans settle Texas
1820	Missouri Compromise
1822	Liberia founded
1823	Monroe Doctrine
	Lowell weaving mills founded
1825–1829	John Quincy Adams's presidency
1825	Erie Canal opens
1828	Tariff of Abominations
1829–1837	Andrew Jackson's presidency
1829–1832	Nullification
1830–1840	Indian removal
1830	Peggy O'Neal Eaton affair
	First railroads open in Baltimore and Charleston, S.C.
	Church of Jesus Christ of Latter-day Saints founded
1831	*Cherokee Nation v. Georgia*
	Nat Turner's Rebellion
	Garrison's *The Liberator* begins
1832	Second Bank of the United States recharter veto
	Worchester v. Georgia
1833	American Antislavery Society founded
1836	Specie Circular
	Texas independence
1837–1841	Martin Van Buren's presidency
1837–1845	Depression
1837	*Charles River Bridge Case*
1838	Frederick Douglass escapes from slavery
1839–1841	*Amistad Case*
1840–1860	Record Irish and German immigration
1840	Independent Treasury

1841	William Henry Harrison's presidency
	Brook Farm founded
1841–1845	John Tyler's presidency
1844	Millerites
	Morse's telegraph invented
1845	Texas annexed
	Thoreau retreats to Walden Pond
1845–1849	James K. Polk's presidency
1846	U.S.–Canada boundary settled
1846–1848	Mexican War
1846–1847	Wilmot Proviso
1848	California and New Mexico acquired
	Seneca Falls Declaration of Female Independence
	Oneida Community founded
1849–1850	Zachary Taylor's presidency
1849–1852	California Gold Rush
1849–1860	Filibusterers
1850–1853	Millard Fillmore's presidency
1850	Compromise of 1850
1851	Maine Prohibition begins
1852	Harriet Beecher Stowe's *Uncle Tom's Cabin* published
1853–1857	Franklin Pierce's presidency
1854	Gadsden Purchase
	Kansas-Nebraska Act
	Ostend Manifesto
1854–1856	Bleeding Kansas
1856	Charles Sumner caned
1857–1861	James Buchanan's presidency
1857	*Dred Scott v. Sandford*
1857–1858	Kansas's Lecompton Constitution
1859	John Brown's Harper's Ferry raid
1860	South Carolina secedes
1861	Confederate States of America founded
1861–1865	Abraham Lincoln's presidency
1861	Fort Sumter falls
	Upper South secedes
	Battle of Bull Run
1862	Battles of Shiloh, Antietam
1862–1863	Drafting of soldiers
1863	Emancipation Proclamation
	Battles of Vicksburg, Gettysburg
	Port Royal experiment
1864	Battles of Petersburg, Atlanta

1864	Wade-Davis Bill veto
1865	Lee surrenders
	Lincoln assassinated

1865–1869	Andrew Johnson's presidency
1865	Thirteenth Amendment
	Black Codes
1865–1866	Freedmen's Bureau
1866	Civil Rights Act
	Fourteenth Amendment
	Ku Klux Klan founded
1867	Reconstruction Act
	Alaska bought
1868	Johnson impeached (but not convicted)

1869–1877	Ulysses S. Grant's presidency
1869	Fifteenth Amendment
1872	Crédit Mobilier scandal
1873	Depression
1876–1877	Disputed election
1877	Last Reconstruction government falls

1877–1881	Rutherford Hayes's presidency
1877	National railway strike
	Thomas Edison invents phonograph
1879	Bland-Allison Act requires silver purchase
	Terence Powderly elected head of Knights of Labor
	Edison invents electric light
	F. W. Woolworth opens five-and-ten-cents store

1881	James Garfield's presidency
	Garfield shot by disturbed office-seeker and dies

1881–1885	Chester Arthur's presidency
1882	Chinese Exclusion Act
1883	Pendleton Act passed

1885–1889	Grover Cleveland's first presidency
1886	Haymarket riot and bombing
	Geronimo surrenders
	American Federation of Labor (AFL) founded
1887	Interstate Commerce Commission created

1889–1893	Benjamin Harrison's presidency
1890	Battle of Wounded Knee
	Sherman Antitrust Act passed
	Sherman Silver Purchase Act passed
1892	Populists organize
	Homestead strike

1893–1897	Grover Cleveland's second presidency
1893	Financial panic begins depression
1894	Coxey's Army
	Pullman strike
1895	United States intervenes in Venezuela boundary issue
1896	*Plessy v. Ferguson* establishes "separate but equal" doctrine
1897–1901	William McKinley's presidency
1898	Spanish-American War
1899	Hay's "Open Door" policy
	Philippine guerrilla war begins
1900	Boxer Rebellion in China
1901	McKinley shot by anarchist
1901–1909	Theodore Roosevelt's presidency
1901–1917	Progressive years
1901	U.S. Steel formed
1903	Panama declares independence; signs Canal Treaty
	Wright Brothers' first flight
1906	Pure Food and Drug Act and Meat Inspection Act passed
1907	Financial panic
1908	Henry Ford introduces Model T
1909–1913	William Taft's presidency
1909	Payne-Aldrich Tariff passed
1910	Pinchot controversy
1911	Triangle Shirtwaist Factory fire
1912	Progressive Party (Bull Moose) formed
1913–1921	Woodrow Wilson's presidency
1913	Sixteenth Amendment (income tax) and Seventeenth Amendment (direct election of senators) ratified
	Federal Reserve System founded
1914	First World War begins in Europe; Wilson declares neutrality
	Clayton Antitrust Act
	Federal Trade Commission created
	"Ludlow Massacre" in Colorado
1916	Wilson sends General John Pershing to Mexico
1917	Bolsheviks take power in Russia
1917–1918	United States fights in World War I
1918	Wilson's Fourteen Points
	Sedition Act
	War Industries Board created
1919	Race riots
1920	Red Scare
	Defeat of Versailles Treaty by Senate
	Eighteenth Amendment (Prohibition) and Nineteenth Amendment (woman suffrage) go into effect

1921–1923	Warren G. Harding's presidency
1921	Immigration restriction through national quotas
	Limitation of Armaments Conference in Washington
	Ku Klux Klan begins revival
1923	Teapot Dome scandal
	Harding dies

1923–1929	Calvin Coolidge's presidency
1924	National Origins Immigration Act
	Nellie Taylor Ross elected governor of Wyoming, first woman governor
1925	Scopes trial
1926	National Broadcasting Corporation, first radio network, formed
1927	Charles A. Lindbergh's solo Atlantic flight
	First "talkie" motion picture, *The Jazz Singer*
1928	Kellogg-Briand Pact outlaws war

1929–1933	Herbert Hoover's presidency
1929–1941	Great Depression
1930	Smoot-Hawley Tariff raises protective barriers
1931	Japan invades Manchuria; Stimson Doctrine issued
1932	Bonus Army
	Reconstruction Finance Corporation founded

1933–1945	Franklin Roosevelt's presidency
1933	Frances Perkins, U.S. Secretary of Labor; first woman in cabinet
	"100 Days" special session, March 9–June 16
	Twenty-first Amendment (repealing prohibition) ratified
	Emergency Banking Act halts banking crisis
	National Industrial Recovery Act (NRA) provides wage-price codes
	Agricultural Adjustment Act (AAA) provides farm supports
	Glass-Steagall Act establishes Federal Deposit Insurance Corporation (FDIC)
1934	Father Charles Coughlin starts National Union for Social Justice
	Francis Townsend proposes old-age pensions
1935	Works Progress Administration (WPA) established
	Supreme Court strikes down NRA
	Wagner Act sets up National Labor Relations Board (NLRB)
	Social Security Act passed
	Huey Long assassinated
	Congress of Industrial Organizations (CIO) founded
1936	Supreme Court strikes down AAA
1937	Roosevelt proposes packing Supreme Court
	CIO expelled from AFL
	Japan invades China
1938	Munich Conference

1939	Germany and Soviet Union sign pact
	Germany invades Poland; World War II begins
	Neutrality Act
1940	Germany captures Belgium, Holland, and France
	Roosevelt wins third term
1941	Lend-Lease Act
	Germany invades Soviet Union
	Japan attacks U.S. naval forces at Pearl Harbor; United States enters the war
1942	United States evacuates Japanese from West Coast
	Battle of Midway; North African invasion
1943	Race riot in Detroit
	Allied invasion of Italy
1944	GI Bill enacted
	Allied invasion of France (D-Day)
1945	Yalta Conference
	Roosevelt dies

1945–1953	Harry Truman's presidency
1945	Germany surrenders
	Atomic bombs dropped on Hiroshima and Nagasaki; Japan surrenders
1946	Military demobilization
1947	Taft-Hartley Act
	Truman Doctrine announced
	Marshall Plan launches economic recovery in Europe
1948–1949	Berlin airlift
1948	Truman integrates armed forces
1949	North Atlantic Treaty Organization (NATO) established
1950	Alger Hiss convicted of perjury
	United States sends troops to Korea
1951	Julius and Ethel Rosenberg sentenced to death
	MacArthur removed from Korean command
	Twenty-second Amendment (presidential term limits) ratified
1952	H-bomb developed

1953–1961	Dwight Eisenhower's presidency
1953	Korean War ends
1954	*Brown v. Board of Education of Topeka* decision ordering integration of schools
	Senate censures Senator Joseph McCarthy
1955–1956	Montgomery, Alabama, bus boycott
1956	Interstate highway system begins
	Suez crisis
1957	First civil rights law since Reconstruction passed
	National Guardsmen sent to Little Rock, Arkansas
	Soviet Union launches *Sputnik*
1960	Black students stage sit-in in Greensboro
	First birth control pill introduced in United States

1961–1963	John Kennedy's presidency
1961	Peace Corps established
	Bay of Pigs invasion of Cuba fails
	Freedom rides in South begin
1962	Cuban missile crisis
1963	Nuclear Test Ban Treaty ratified
	Betty Friedan's *The Feminine Mystique* published
	Kennedy assassinated

1963–1969	Lyndon Johnson's presidency
1964	Gulf of Tonkin Resolution authorizes war in Vietnam
	Civil Rights Act passed
1965	Race riot in Watts
	Great Society begins, including Medicare, federal aid to education, and urban renewal
	U.S. combat troops sent to Vietnam
	Voting Rights Act passed
1967	Thurgood Marshall becomes first black appointed to Supreme Court
	Black riots in Newark, New Jersey, and Detroit, Michigan
1968	Tet offensive in Vietnam
	Johnson withdraws from presidential race
	Martin Luther King, Jr., assassinated
	Robert Kennedy assassinated

1969–1974	Richard Nixon's presidency
1969	Nuclear Nonproliferation Treaty signed
1970	Environmental Protection Agency founded
	U.S. troops invade Cambodia; student strikes
1971	United States goes off international gold standard
	Twenty-sixth Amendment lowers voting age to eighteen
	Pentagon Papers reveal U.S. involvement in Vietnam
1972	Nixon travels to China
	United States enters into Strategic Arms Limitation Treaty with the Soviet Union
	Equal Rights Amendment sent to states for ratification
1973	U.S. role in Vietnam War ends
	Senate begins Watergate break-in hearings
	Supreme Court upholds abortion in *Roe v. Wade*
	Arab oil boycott creates stagflation in U.S. economy
1974	Nixon resigns from the presidency

1974–1977	Gerald Ford's presidency
1974	Ford pardons Nixon
	Economic recession
1975	South Vietnam and Cambodia fall to communists
1976	United States celebrates bicentennial of independence

1977–1980	Jimmy Carter's presidency
1977	Energy Department created

1978	Panama Canal turned over to Panama
1979	Chrysler Corporation federal bailout
1979–1981	Iranian hostage crisis
1980	Soviet invasion of Afghanistan

1981–1989	Ronald Reagan's presidency
1981	Iranian hostages released
	Tax cut
	Federal air traffic controllers' strike broken
	Sandra Day O'Connor first woman appointed to Supreme Court
1982	Equal Rights Amendment defeated
	Economic recession
	U.S. marines sent to Lebanon
1983	United States invades Grenada
1984	CIA acknowledges mining of Nicaraguan harbors
	Reagan visits China
1985	Reagan and Soviet leader Mikhail Gorbachev meet
1986	William Rehnquist appointed as chief justice and Antonin Scalia appointed as associate justice of the Supreme Court
	Tax Reform Act enacted
1987	First trillion-dollar budget
	Iran-Contra hearings
	Arms limitation treaty with the Soviet Union
1988	Amnesty offered to 1.4 million illegal immigrants

1989–1993	George Bush's presidency
1989	Savings and loan bailout
	Supreme Court allows state laws restraining abortion
	United States invades Panama
1990	Physical and Mental Disabilities Act passed
	Iraq invades Kuwait; United States sends troops to Saudi Arabia
	Clean Air Act passed
	Taxes increased
1991	United States and allies defeat Iraq in Gulf War
	Economic recession
	Clarence Thomas appointed to Supreme Court

1993–2001	William Clinton's presidency
1993	Branch Davidian complex assaulted at Waco
1994	North American Free Trade Association Agreement (NAFTA) ratified
	Whitewater investigation
	Republicans gain control of Congress for first time since 1954
1995	Oklahoma City bombing
	Khobar Towers, Saudi Arabia, bombing
1996	Welfare Reform Act passed
	Defense of Marriage Act passed
1998	U.S. embassies in Nairobi and Dar es Salaam bombed
	U.S. attacks Serbia after Serbia invades Kosovo

1998–1999	Monica Lewinsky affair; Clinton impeachment fails
2000	Disputed Bush–Gore presidential election

2001–	George W. Bush's presidency
2001	Al Qaeda attacks World Trade Center and Pentagon
	Department of Homeland Security established
2002	U.S. topples Taliban in Afghanistan; bin Laden sought
2003	U.S. invades Iraq; Saddam caught
	Massachusetts court rules for same-sex marriage

Glossary

abolition/abolitionist the policy of the government to end slavery; abolitionists were people who urged government action to end slavery

adventurist a term often used in foreign policy to connote a hazardous or dangerous undertaking or policy

Allies those nations that fought against the **Axis powers** (Germany, Italy, Japan) during World War II

amnesty an act of government pardoning a large number of individuals

Anaconda a copper-mining city in southwestern Montana; site of the world's largest copper **smelter**

Anglophobia hatred of England or English customs, people, manners, or institutions; used by certain American politicians to inflame voters, especially Irish voters

annex/annexation the process by which a government takes in a new territory

antebellum literally, "before the war," usually before the Civil War

anti-Semitism intolerance of Jews or Jewish culture

antitrust federal and state statutes that limit the ability of businesses and unions to exercise monopolistic control or restrain trade, such as the Sherman Antitrust Act of 1890 (see also **trust**)

apartheid a policy of **segregation** and political and economic discrimination against non-European groups in the Republic of South Africa

appeasement/appease to bring peace by making concessions; a policy of appeasement was pursued by Neville Chamberlain, prime minister of Great Britain (1937–1940) in negotiating with the Nazis

apprenticeship a system for training youths for careers in skilled crafts

appropriations funds set aside by a legislature to pay for something authorized by law

aristocracy a hereditary ruling class; commonly found in Europe

Articles of Confederation the document that in the 1780s created the government of the United States before the U.S. Constitution; like Canada today, the United States under the Articles was a weak alliance of loosely associated states

artillery very heavy guns used for long-range firing in war

artisans skilled workers such as butchers, bakers, and candlestick makers

assimilation the process by which one group of people gradually becomes like another group of people by adopting the other group's language, religion, and culture

asylum a refuge, retreat, or shelter

Axis powers a **coalition** that developed from the Rome-Berlin Axis of 1936 and eventually included Germany, Italy, Japan, and others; opposed by the **Allies** in World War II

belligerent a person or nation engaged in warfare or fighting

Bible Belt those portions of the rural South and Midwest dominated from the early 1800s to the present by **evangelical Protestant** Christians

Big Three Franklin Roosevelt (United States), Winston Churchill (Great Britain), and Josef Stalin (Soviet Union)

bill draft of a proposed law not yet passed by Congress or signed by the president

bimetallic standard the concurrent use of both gold and silver as the standard of currency and value; advocated by the Populist Party in 1896

black nationalism the belief that African Americans should form their own nation or society separate from white society

bohemian a person, usually of artistic or literary tastes, who lives in an unconventional manner; a term that became popular among intellectuals at the turn of the twentieth century

boll weevils a long-used term for southern Democrats in Congress, including those who supported Ronald Reagan during his presidency

Bolsheviks a political faction of **communists** who gained control of Russia in 1917 following the overthrow of the czar

bond in finance, an interest-bearing certificate of debt, usually issued by a government, municipality, or corporation; the federal government issues bonds to finance its debt

bootlegging/bootlegger the sale and distribution of illegal alcohol during **Prohibition** in the 1920s

breastworks hastily built low barriers from behind which gunners fire

burgess a legislator, specifically a member of Virginia's House of Burgesses during colonial times

busing a method of transporting students from one school district to another to ensure racial balance

Calvinism the religion of John Calvin and his followers, including Presbyterians, **Puritans,** and **Pilgrims,** which stressed that only certain people could be saved and go to heaven (compare with **universal salvation**)

capital wealth (money and property); an accumulated source of wealth used to produce more wealth; also, used to define **capitalists** collectively as distinguished from labor

capitalists/capitalism people who invest money in business enterprises in the hope of making profits; an economic system in which all or most of the means of production and distribution are privately owned and operated for profit

capitalization the total capital funds of a corporation, represented by stocks, bonds, undivided profit, and surplus

carpetbaggers northerners who moved south to assist Radical Republicans during Reconstruction (compare with **scalawags**)

cash and carry a system imposed by the Neutrality Act (1937) in which goods were to be paid in cash

charter an important government document; under English law, charters were more important than laws or court rulings; they could be granted either by the king or by **Parliament**; persons often gained great power through the land or privileges granted in a charter; colonies such as Virginia and Massachusetts were started under the authority of charters

checks and balances the principle in the U.S. Constitution, derived from colonial and English experience, that power should be divided rather than concentrated; the U.S. Constitution divides power among three branches of government: legislative, executive, and judicial

Church of England the official **Protestant** church in England founded when Henry VIII broke with the Catholic church; in America, it became the Episcopal church after the American Revolution

coalition an alliance of interests or groups; the New Deal coalition brought together urban ethnic groups with southern whites and blacks

coattails a political expression meaning to help win an election for a follower or supporter; a congressional candidate will sometimes win election on the coattails of a strong presidential candidate from the same party

coinage the act to make coins; free coinage meant unlimited use of certain metal, often used in the silver controversy in 1872–1900

cold warrior a person who supported the cold war against the Soviet Union

cold war war by other than military means; the hostile but nonlethal relations between the United States and the Soviet Union, 1945–1989

collective a body of people brought together in a common enterprise; the Soviet Union formed agricultural collectives under Stalin; in the 1970s, New Left students formed revolutionary collectives to challenge **capitalist** society

collectivism a general term often suggesting **socialism** or **communism**, as opposed to individualism

colonizationists/colonization people who favored abolishing slavery and resettling the ex-slaves from the United States to Africa; this movement was strongest from 1817 to 1830 (not to be confused with colonialism)

combine an agricultural machine that reaps, threshes, and cleans grain while harvesting it; invented and manufactured by Cyrus McCormick

communes groups in which members live together on an equal basis, sharing work and leisure; there were many communes in the 1800s; the most successful had religious roots

communion a Christian ceremony commemorating Christ's resurrection through the partaking of wine and bread; Christians often disagree on the ceremony's conduct and meaning

communist/communism a member of the Communist Party; or one who supports communism, a theory and social system conceived by German philosopher Karl Marx (see also **Bolsheviks, socialism, Marxism**)

compensated emancipation a system by which the government freed **slaves** by paying slaveholders for the value of their slaves

congregational churches churches governed by their congregations rather than by bishops or other outside groups; in New England both **Puritans** and **Pilgrims** governed their churches this way, and they became known by this name

conscientious objector a person who is opposed to war on religious or moral grounds

contraband in warfare, any items valuable to an enemy that might therefore be seized; during the Civil War, the North for a time considered **slaves** to be contraband

conversion experience for some Christians, the process by which a person becomes a Christian; Puritans believed that a person had to undergo a rebirth of the spirit that could be described convincingly to others; later **evangelicals** found a statement of having had such an experience sufficient

cotton gin Eli Whitney's 1793 invention, no bigger than a breadbox, for easily separating cotton fibers from the seeds

covert not openly shown, as in "covert CIA operations"

cubism a movement in modern art about 1907–1925, concerned with abstract and geometric interpretation of form

customs duties see **tariff**

daguerreotype an early photographic process that did not use negatives; the pictures were remarkably clear and detailed, but the cost was high and no copies could be made

dark horse an obscure presidential candidate picked by a political party as a compromise to break a deadlock; James Polk and Warren Harding are examples of dark horses who won

deferment the act of delaying or postponing, especially used with the draft, such as a student deferment, which allowed students to postpone entering the draft during the Vietnam War

deficit the amount by which expenditures exceed revenues

defoliant a chemical spray or dust applied to plants to make leaves fall off prematurely

depression a period marked by slackening business activity, widespread unemployment, falling prices, and falling wages (compare with **recession**)

desegregate to end segregation, which is often practiced in schools, businesses, and public places against racial minorities (primarily African-American)

détente a relaxation of strained relations between two nations (pronounced *day-TAHNT*)

discount rate the interest rate paid by a commercial bank when it borrows from the Federal Reserve System

disfranchisement removal of a person's right to vote; many southern states disfranchised African Americans in the late 1800s

divisions military units usually composed of three **regiments;** in the American Civil War, about five thousand soldiers

dole that which is distributed through charity in the form of a small gift of food or money; often used for those receiving public aid during the Great Depression in the 1930s

domino effect the theory that if a critically situated country falls to **communism,** its neighbors will soon follow; a rationale for American involvement in the Vietnam War

dove an advocate of peace; a term often used for those opposed to the war in Vietnam (compare with **hawk**)

draft compulsory military service; the practice of drafting people into military service is called *conscription*

due process the constitutional requirement that "no person shall be deprived of life, liberty, or property without due process of law," a right guaranteed by the Fifth, Sixth, and Fourteenth Amendments to the U.S. Constitution

duties see **tariff**

egalitarian favoring absolute equality

Electoral College the U.S. Constitution's method for electing presidents; the members of the Electoral College, called *electors*, elect the president; the states determine how the members of the Electoral College are picked (see also **electoral vote**)

electoral vote the votes cast for president and vice president by the **Electoral College** as established in Article II, Section 1, and the Twelfth and Twenty-third Amendments of the U.S. Constitution

elitism rule by an elite or dominant group

emancipate/emancipation the voluntary freeing of a slave by a slaveholder

Emancipation Proclamation the executive order by President Abraham Lincoln in 1863 that freed the slaves inside the Confederacy on the grounds that slavery aided the Confederate military cause

embargo a federal law barring merchant ships from leaving or entering port and thus totally ending all foreign trade; imposed by Thomas Jefferson in 1807, the embargo prevented war with Britain but ruined the American economy (compare with **blockade**)

eminent domain the right of the government to take private property forcibly but with compensation, for public purposes such as to build a road or railroad

enfranchise to give the right to vote

Enlightenment a movement occurring in the 1700s based on the idea that reason and logic determined all; highly favorable to science and suspicious of religion (see also **romanticism**)

envoy a diplomatic representative

evangelical a **Protestant** Christian who stresses the authority of the Bible, exhortation to faith, and usually the availability of universal salvation

expansionism the act of expanding the state

expressionist a movement in the arts, originating about 1914, that had as its object the free expression of the artist's inner experience

factionalism the practice of dividing an organization or other body into contentious or self-seeking groups

fascism a political philosophy that advocates governance by a dictator to maintain a totalitarian, regimented society; fascism appeared in Italy and Germany in the 1920s and 1930s (pronounced *FASH-izm*)

Federal Reserve System the central bank of the United States created by the Federal Reserve Act (1913)

feudalism the political, economic, and social system emphasizing graded classes by which Europe was organized in the Middle Ages, circa 1000–1500

filibuster the use of a delaying tactic to prevent action in a legislative assembly, especially the U.S. Senate; the taking of foreign territory in a private war in the 1850s

filibusterers leaders of private armies who tried to seize territory in the 1850s for the purpose of adding it to the United States (not to be confused with **filibuster**)

flapper an informal name given to women in the 1920s who tried to appear sophisticated in dress and behavior

flotilla a fleet of boats or ships

foreclosure to take away the right to redeem a mortgage when regular payments have not been made on a home, farm, or other property

49th parallel in the West, the boundary between the United States and Canada, which runs along this straight line of latitude

franchise the right to vote

free coinage the issuing of currency based on a silver or bimetallic standard

free love a celebration of sex and a rejection of traditional restrictions, including marriage; advocated by Frances Wright in New York in the 1830s

free silver the free and unlimited coinage of silver, particularly at a fixed ratio to gold

free soil the policy of keeping **slavery** out of the western territories without interfering with slavery in the South; Van Buren's position in 1848; the Republican Party position in 1856 and 1860

free trade the right to buy or sell anything to anyone across national borders without regulation or taxes; free trade exists among states within the United States (see also **tariff**)

freedmen the name given to the former **slaves** during Reconstruction

frieze a three-dimensional sculpture placed in a band around the top of a building

fundamentalism a movement organized in the early twentieth century to defend orthodox **Protestant** Christianity against the challenges of theological liberalism, evolution, and liberal interpretations of the Bible

Gatling guns machine guns invented and first used in the Civil War

Gentlemen's Agreement an agreement reached with Japan in 1908 by which the Japanese government promised to issue no more passports to peasants or workers coming directly to the continental United States

gentry in England, the landowning farmers who enjoyed some wealth, some prestige, and some political power; in Virginia and the South, the owners of **plantations**

GI Bill Servicemen's Readjustment Act (1944) under which $13 billion was spent for veterans on education, medical treatment, unemployment insurance, and loans for homes and businesses

gold standard a monetary system in which gold is used as the standard of value for the money of a country; inflationists in the 1800s wanted a bimetallic standard of gold and silver; the United States remained on a domestic gold standard until 1933

GOP Grand Old Party, the Republican Party

Grange laws state laws passed in the 1870s with the support of farmers, represented by the **Grange**, that strove to regulate railway rates and storage fees charged by railroads and by operators of warehouses and grain elevators; these laws were overturned when the Supreme Court decreed in the *Wabash* case (1886) that individual states had no power to regulate interstate commerce

Grange formally called the Order of Patrons of Husbandry, an association of U.S farmers founded in 1867 to promote agricultural interests

Great Awakening a series of religious **revivals** that swept the colonies in the 1740s

greenbacks United States paper money, first issued during the Civil War, so called because the back side was printed in green ink (compare with **specie** and **hard money**)

gross domestic product the value of all the nation's goods and services in a given year

guerrilla/guerrilla war a combatant who fights secretly and with terrorism; a type of warfare carried on behind enemy lines through surprise raids, sabotage, and disruptive attacks; used in the Philippines against American troops following the Spanish-American War and later during the Vietnam War (1965–1973)

habeas corpus a court order requiring authorities to free a person held in custody

Halls of Montezuma Mexico City, captured by the U.S. marines in the Mexican War in 1847

hard money money issued in gold coins; the opposite of paper (or **soft**) money (see also **specie**)

hawk a person who supports a military action or war, as opposed to a **dove**

headright system the method in some colonies by which a person could gain free land in return for bringing laborers from England to America

hierarchy persons arranged by rank or status, often for political purposes; a king, for example, would be at the top of the hierarchy

holding company a company that invests in the stocks of one or more other corporations, which it may thus control

holocaust a thorough destruction, often used to describe Hitler's destruction of Jews in World War II or the result of using nuclear weapons

Holy Spirit God's presence in the third person of the Trinity; also called the Holy Ghost

homestead/homesteading a tract of land occupied under the Homestead Act (1862) that provided a person with 160 acres of free public land in return for settling and farming it

Huguenots French Protestant Christians who left France to avoid persecution after 1685

impeach/impeachment the U.S. Constitution's method for removing the president, vice president, or judges from office before their terms have expired; used against Federalist judges in 1801, against Andrew Johnson in 1868, against Richard Nixon in 1974, and against Bill Clinton in 1998–1999; charges are brought by the House, and conviction requires a two-thirds vote in the Senate; Johnson and Clinton were not convicted; Nixon resigned

imperialism the creation or extension of an empire comprising many nations and areas; advocated in the late 1800s by certain social thinkers and policy makers

import duties see **tariff**

impound the withholding by the executive branch of funds authorized and appropriated by law

impressment the British policy, especially in the early 1800s, of stopping American ships at sea and seizing sailors by claiming that they were British subjects whether they were or not; a main method used to staff the British navy; impressment led to poor relations between Britain and the United States and helped cause the War of 1812

indemnity that which is given as compensation for a loss or for damage

indentured servants persons whose passage from England to America was paid in return for signing a written contract (called an *indenture*) agreeing to serve as laborers for a term of years, usually seven; a large number of whites used this method to migrate to the South and to the Middle Colonies in the 1700s; used in Texas in the 1830s as a disguised form of slavery

inflation the rise in prices resulting from an increase in circulating currency and a mounting demand for available commodities and services

initiative a procedure that allows citizens, as opposed to legislators, to propose the enactment of state and local laws; promoted by progressive reformers in the early twentieth century

internationalism the belief that mutual understanding and cooperation among nations will advance the common welfare

isolationism the policy of curtailing a nation's international relations; isolationism was dominant in U.S. foreign policy during much of the 1800s and the two decades between the world wars

Jesuit a member of the Catholic religious order called the Society of Jesus; Jesuits were very active in missions and education throughout the world after 1600

Jim Crow a name given to racial **segregation;** the name comes from a popular dance tune in the 1830s performed by a black-faced white actor

jingoism an aggressive, highly nationalistic foreign policy

journeymen skilled workers who had completed apprenticeships but lacked the means to go into business for themselves *journeyed* around working for other craftsmen; they used part of their wages to set up their own businesses

junta a Latin American legislative council, or a political body gathered together for some secret purpose; exiled Cuban rebels opposed to Spanish rule (pronounced *HOON-tah*)

kaiser title of German emperors, 1871–1918

kamikaze a suicidal Japanese tactic of ramming with a piloted airplane or boat carrying explosives in World War II; from Japanese *kami* (god) and *kaze* (wind) (pronounced *kahm-i-KAHZ-ee*)

kleptocracy government by theft

Kremlin the governing center of Russia

Ku Klux Klan a white supremacist group established in the South following the Civil War and revived in the early twentieth century

laissez-faire literally, "to let do"; a hands-off style of governance that emphasizes economic freedom; the concept is associated with Adam Smith and his book *The Wealth of Nations* (1776) (pronounced *lay-say FAIR*)

lame duck an officeholder who has not been reelected and who waits for his or her successor to assume office

land grants land given to a person, usually by government, often for political reasons

legal tender items defined by law as money, which must be accepted in payment of debts; governments have frequently made paper money legal tender; such paper money could be produced by the government in large quantities cheaply

lend-lease terms of the Lend Lease Act (1941) which furnished goods to Allied powers

lien a legal right to claim or dispose of property in payment for a debt (pronounced *lean*)

lobbyist a person, group, or organization that seeks to influence legislation or administrative action

lode a deposit of ore located in rock; also called a *vein*

lyceum a series of well-organized public lectures stressing self-improvement, held each year in most northern towns and cities in the 1840s and 1850s (pronounced *lie-SEE-um*)

machine an informal political organization, often centered on a single politician, that controls the formal process of government through corruption, **patronage,** and service to its constituents

magnate an important or influential person, often in business, e.g., John Pierpont Morgan

Manifest Destiny the belief that Americans had a God-given right to own all of North America and perhaps South America too; common from 1844 to 1861

manors large tracts of land owned by wealthy, politically powerful New Yorkers during the colonial period; most manors were along the Hudson River

martial law law administered by military force, invoked by a government in an emergency

Marxist a follower of German philosopher Karl Marx; a **communist** or socialist

masonic pertaining to Freemasons, whose lodges stress charity and sociability

McCarthyism extreme and irresponsible anticommunism; the use of unproven association with any individual, organization, or policy that the accuser perceives as un-American (see also **communism, Marxism**)

mechanic a skilled manual worker; an artisan

mercantilism an economic theory and practice popular from 1500 to 1800 that used government regulation and **monopolies** to control business, and especially to maintain colonies as part of a global system; the British empire is one example

midterm election a congressional election held midway between presidential elections

militia ordinary citizens called to temporary duty as soldiers, especially from the colonial period to about 1850; the equivalent of the National Guard

mobilization to prepare for war by organizing industry, personnel, and national resources

monopoly the exclusive control of a commodity, service, or means of production in a particular market that allows the fixing of prices and the elimination of competition (see also **trust**)

moratorium a waiting period set by an authority

mores folkways considered conducive to the welfare of society (pronounced *MOHR-ayz*)

mugwump a Republican who bolted the party when James G. Blaine was nominated as the presidential candidate in 1884; a term used for any political independent

munitions guns, bullets, and other necessary war materiel

nationalism strong, sometimes chauvinistic, devotion to one's own nation (see also **jingoism;** not to be confused with **nationalization**)

nationalization to transfer ownership of land, resources, or industries to the federal government; advocated by various parties such as the Populists and the Socialist Party (not to be confused with **nationalism**)

nativism/nativist a belief in the superiority of Americans born in the United States and a rejection of the foreign born

natural law the idea prevalent in the 1700s that nature operates according to rules laid down by God; discovering the rules was a major undertaking

naval blockade use of warships to close off trade to or from a seaport or coastline (see also **embargo**)

Nazi a member or supporter of Adolf Hitler's National Socialist German Workers' Party

New World North and South America; the term used by Europeans after Columbus's voyage in 1492

nullification the idea, promoted by John C. Calhoun, that a state could act to overrule a federal law inside its own borders; thus, laws would be declared unconstitutional by the states rather than by the Supreme Court; opponents pointed to the chaos caused by different states acting differently

Open Door policy the policy or practice of giving to all nations the same commercial privileges in a region or area open to trade; the United States advocated an Open Door policy toward China in the late 1800s

out work in certain industrial processes, especially shoemaking, the practice of sending some work out of the main shop or factory, often to be performed in the home by women or children at low wages

papal edict a Catholic pope's proclamation, which has great authority among Catholics both spiritually and politically

parity a level for farm prices that gives to the farmer the same purchasing power averaged during each year of a chosen period; also used during the cold war to refer to the rough equivalence of missiles between the United States and the Soviet Union

Parliament the legislative body that governs England

party ticket a political term used to pair presidential and vice-presidential candidates

patronage the system by which political winners fill all government jobs with their supporters (see also **spoils system**)

patroons wealthy, powerful landowners in Dutch New Netherland who received much land in the 1600s in return for bringing settlers to the colony

pay dirt soil containing enough metal, especially gold, to be profitable to a mine

peace protocol the preliminary draft of an official peace treaty

Pentagon headquarters of the Defense Department; the U.S. military establishment

pig iron crude iron as it comes from the blast furnaces

Pilgrim one of a group of **Protestant** Christians who found the **Church of England** so corrupt that a new church must be formed; they migrated to Holland, then to Plymouth, Massachusetts (compare with **Puritan**)

pink a derogatory term often associated with a position or person accused of being sympathetic to a socialist or **communist** (red) position

Pinkerton a name given to employees of the Pinkerton Detective Agency, who were often used to infiltrate labor organizations and break strikes in the late 1800s

plantations large-scale farm units in the South usually devoted to one crop for sale in the world market and worked with **slave** or, less commonly, **indentured servant** labor; plantations began in the 1600s and lasted until the end of slavery in 1865

pluralism cultural diversity in a society stratified along racial lines; also, any political system in which there are multiple centers of legitimate power and authority

plurality the greatest number of votes cast for a candidate, but not more than half of the votes cast

pocket veto an indirect **veto** in which the president declines to sign a **bill** after Congress has adjourned; after adjournment, a bill passed by Congress does not become law without the president's signature

polarized broken up into opposing groups

political machine an informal organization, often centered on a single politician, that controls the formal process of government through corruption, **patronage**, and service to its constituents

polity an organized society, such as a state; governing structures of a political community

pool the combined investment of a group of persons or corporations, and the sharing of responsibility for a joint enterprise; employed by John D. Rockefeller in the oil industry in the late 1800s

populism a political movement that grew out of a farmers' protest movement in the 1890s

pork barrel favoritism by a government in the distribution of benefits or resources; legislation that favors the district of a particular legislator, often through public works

preemptive strike a military attack aimed to prevent aggressive military action by an opponent or enemy

primary election a state or local election held before a general election to nominate a political party's candidates for office

privateer/privateering a private ship commissioned by a government in time of war to act as a warship against an enemy country's merchant ships

profiteer/profiteering a person who obtains excessive profits during times of shortages, frequently during wartime

progressivism a designation applied to reform in the decades between 1890 and 1920, a period of rapid urbanization and industrialization

Prohibition law forbidding the manufacture, transportation, or sale of alcoholic beverages; adopted by some cities and counties in the 1840s and by some states beginning with Maine in 1851; enacted nationally in the Eighteenth Amendment (1919), repealed with the Twenty-first Amendment (1933) (compare with **temperance movement**)

proprietary colony a colony owned by one person, called a proprietor, such as Lord Baltimore's Maryland or William Penn's Pennsylvania; a few proprietary colonies, such as North and South Carolina, had multiple owners

protectionist one who favors high **tariffs** to protect a domestic market from foreign trade competition

protectorate a country or region under the protection or political domination of another

Protestant a Christian belonging to any number of groups that rejected the Catholic Church

Puritan a **Protestant** Christian who wished to purify the **Church of England** but did not wish to form a separate church; some stayed in England, others went to Massachusetts (compare with **Pilgrim**)

quagmire literally, soft mucky ground which, once stepped in, is difficult to get out of; a difficult or dangerous situation; the war in Vietnam was often described as a quagmire

Quaker a member of a militantly pacifist Protestant group, more formally called the Society of Friends, that settled Pennsylvania in 1682

rapprochement establishment or state of peaceful relations (pronounced *ra-prosh-MAHN*)

ratify/ratification approval by a legislature of a treaty, a constitutional amendment, or a new constitution

rationing during times of scarcity and war, the allotment of fixed allowances or portions of food, fuel, or goods

reactionary one who favors political and social reaction and is hostile to radicalism or rapid political change

receivership a legal term in which a business enterprise is placed in the hands of a court-appointed administrator

recession a period of reduced economic activity, less serious than a **depression** (compare with a **depression**)

Redcoats British soldiers in the American Revolution; this nickname came from the color of the soldiers' uniforms

reds a name given to **communists**; the Red Scare in 1919 expressed anxiety among the public and politicians concerning communist influence in America (see also **pink**)

referendum a procedure for submitting proposed laws or state constitutional amendments to voters for their direct approval or rejection; favored by **Progressive** reformers at the turn of the twentieth century (compare with **initiative**)

regiments military units of one thousand to two thousand soldiers; the most common Civil War units (see also **divisions**)

reparations compensation paid by defeated countries for acts of war; following World War I, the Allied Powers, especially France and Great Britain, insisted that Germany pay war reparations

republic a democratic, constitutional form of government, such as that established by the U.S. Constitution; not to be confused with the Republican Party

reservations land set apart by the government for a particular use; for example, Indian reservations

revival a large, popular gathering for religious purposes, especially among **Protestants**; revivals have been common in America at periodic intervals since the 1740s

romanticism/romantic movement in the early 1800s, the rejection of the rational **Enlightenment** in favor of seeing emotion and the need for its expression as the central element in life; many romantics were poets and artists (see also **transcendentalism**)

run (on a bank) a panic in which all of the bank's customers try to withdraw all of their deposits at the same time, thereby causing the bank to fail; bank runs often occurred during a **depression** or a panic

salt pork pork stored and preserved without refrigeration by packing it in barrels filled with salt

salvation the Christian idea that people could be saved spiritually and go to heaven (see also **Calvinism** and **universal salvation**)

sanctions coercive measures, usually economic and usually adopted by several nations at the same time, to force a nation to stop violating international law

Sandinista a member of a revolutionary group that came to power in Nicaragua in the late 1970s; named after Cesar Augusto Sandino, a Nicaraguan rebel who resisted U.S. marines sent into the country in the 1920s

scalawags white southerners who supported Radical Republican rule during Reconstruction (compare with **carpetbaggers**)

secession formal declaration by a state that it is no longer part of the United States

securities any evidence of debt or ownership, especially stocks and bonds

segregate/segregation to separate by race, often imposed by law (see also **apartheid**)

separatism the belief that white and black races should be separated physically, culturally, and socially (see also **apartheid** and **segregation**)

settlement house a welfare institution established in a congested part of a city, having a resident staff to conduct educational and recreational activities for the community

sharecropper/sharecropping a **tenant farmer**, usually heavily in debt to a local merchant or bank, who rented land and paid the rent by splitting the money from the sale of the crop with the landowner; common in the South after the Civil War

Sino Chinese (pronounced *SIGH-no*)

sit-in a demonstration of protest, as by African Americans in the southern United States in the 1960s, in which participants entered and remained seated in a public place

skid row a district of a city inhabited by vagrants and derelicts (slang); originally, a road used to skid logs to a mill in Seattle

Slave Power Republican Party phrase in the 1850s to describe slaveholders' political influence

slave/slavery a person totally owned and controlled by another person under the law; slavery became an important institution in colonial America, especially in the South

smelter a furnace used to reduce ores to obtain a metal

Social Security the popular name for the Old Age, Survivors, and Disability Insurance system established by the Social Security Act (1935)

socialism a system of government in which the government owns many of the means of production and trade and in which many welfare needs are provided directly by the government; an early advocate was Eugene Debs, leader of the Socialist Party (see also **communism**, **Marxism**, and **Bolsheviks**)

soft money paper money, as opposed to hard money and coins (see also **specie** and **greenbacks**)

sortie one mission or attack by a single plane

sovereignty complete independence and self-government

specie gold or silver money, as opposed to paper money (see also **hard money** and **soft money**)

speculators/speculation persons who engage in risky business, often with borrowed money, in the hope of large profits; Americans have often speculated with land

spiritualism a movement founded in the 1840s whose followers believed the living could communicate with the dead, especially through séances with crystal balls

spoils system the widespread practice of awarding government jobs to political supporters without consideration of their qualifications for the jobs (see **patronage**)

squatters frontier farmers who used land they did not own without anyone's permission; they moved frequently

Stalinist a follower of the Soviet dictator Josef Stalin, chief of state in the Soviet Union, 1924–1953

states' rights a political view that power more properly belongs to the states than to the federal government; most often found in the South

steerage a section in a passenger ship for passengers paying the lowest fare and given inferior accommodations

strict construction an interpretation of the U.S. Constitution that stresses the limited powers of government rather than broad provisions; Thomas Jefferson first argued this view in the 1790s

subsistence farmers farmers who produced food and clothing for their own use and only rarely sold their produce in the market

suffrage the right to vote; by the 1830s most states had universal white male suffrage; the Fifteenth Amendment (1870) held that suffrage shall not be denied "on account of race"; the Nineteenth Amendment (1920) extended the right to vote to women in all states

supply-side economics the belief that lower tax rates encourage capital to flow into the economy; an economic theory adopted by President Reagan and his advisers

tariff taxes placed on goods brought into the United States; in the late 1800s Republicans favored high tariffs, and Democrats favored low tariffs or no tariffs (**free trade**)

tax base the value on which taxes are levied, including individual income, real property, corporate income, and wealth

tax shelter an investment in which any profits are fully or partially tax free

teetotaler one who abstains totally from alcoholic beverages

temperance movement in the 1790s, a movement urging people to use alcohol only in moderation; by the 1830s, a movement asking people to give up all alcohol voluntarily; strongly connected to **evangelical** religion; many female reformers were involved in this movement; especially well-known was the Woman's Christian Temperance Union (WCTU) (compare with **Prohibition**)

tenant farmers farmers who lacked the means to buy land and therefore rented it; already common in colonial America, the practice grew in the late 1800s, especially in the South (see also **sharecropper**)

tenement an urban apartment building that is poorly constructed and maintained, typically overcrowded, and often part of a slum

theocracy government controlled by a church or church leaders

ticket a political term referring to the presidential and vice-presidential candidates of a particular party for a particular election; for example, the Bush–Cheney ticket of the Republican Party for the 2000 presidential election

titled nobility the highest rank in British society, except for the royal family; examples are dukes and lords

Tories in the 1700s in England, the conservative political faction emphasizing the king and hierarchy; in 1776, Americans who opposed the American Revolution and sided with the British

transcendentalism associated with Ralph Waldo Emerson in the 1840s and 1850s, the belief that doing good deeds, **romanticism**, and contemplating nature enabled people to transcend ordinary life and get close to God intuitively

transcontinental railroad railroad begun during the Civil War under acts of 1862 and 1864, completed in 1869 by the Union Pacific Railroad and Central Pacific Railroad, and linking Omaha, Nebraska, and Sacramento, California

Trotskyist a follower of the radical **communist** Leon Trotsky, an exiled rival of Soviet dictator Josef Stalin

trust a group of companies that work together to maintain an effective monopoly that inhibits competition, such as the Standard Oil Trust developed by John D. Rockefeller in the late 1800s to control the oil industry

U-boat a German submarine or *Unterseeboot* (undersea boat); a popular term during World War I and World War II

unilateral undertaken by a single nation, party, or society without reference to other nations, parties, or societies

universal salvation the belief of some Christians that everybody can be saved as a Christian and go to heaven (compare with **Calvinism**)

vagrancy shiftless or idle wandering

veto the U.S. Constitution's method by which a president may stop a **bill** passed by Congress from becoming law; the House and the Senate, each by a two-thirds vote, can overturn a veto

war hawks in 1812, supporters of war against Britain on the grounds that Britain had snubbed American rights

weir a fence or obstruction placed in a stream to catch fish; this technology was known and used by American Indians before white contact (pronounced *weer*)

wet a political term used to designate a person opposed to **Prohibition**, especially in the 1920s; Al Smith ran for president in 1928 as a "wet" opposed to Prohibition

Whig in the 1700s in England, the liberal and political faction emphasizing rural interests and liberty; in 1776, a supporter of the American Revolution; in the 1830s to 1840s, an American political party led by Henry Clay and favorable to a national bank

Wilmot Proviso in 1846, Wilmot's amendment to a **bill** that sought to keep slavery out of any Mexican territory acquired by the United States in the Mexican War

Wobbly a slang term for a member of the Industrial Workers of the World (IWW), a radical labor group, circa 1900

write-off a tax deduction

Yankee in a narrow sense, a resident of New England; in the broad sense, any American; during the Civil War, any northerner

yellow press a type of journalism that features cheap, sensational news to attract readers, from the use of yellow ink in a cartoon strip, "The Yellow Kid" in the *New York Journal* (1896)

yeoman a farmer who owned and operated a small farm

Zionism originally a movement to resettle Jews in Palestine; support for the state of Israel

Index

About the Authors

W. J. Rorabaugh is professor of history at the University of Washington, Seattle. In addition to this book, he is author of *The Alcoholic Republic: An American Tradition* (1979), *The Craft Apprentice: From Franklin to the Machine Age* (1986), and *Berkeley at War: The 1960s* (1989).

Donald T. Critchlow is professor of history and chair of the Department of History at Saint Louis University. He is the founding editor of the *Journal of Policy History*, the author of *The Brookings Institution, 1916–1952: Expertise and the Public Interest in a Democratic Society* (1985), and the editor of four books on history and public policy in the United States.

Paula Baker is an associate professor of history at Ohio State University. She is the author of *The Moral Frameworks of Public Life* (1991), and edited volumes on recent American history and the history of campaign finance in the United States.